THE MASARYK CASE

1817

THE

Claire Sterling

MASARYK

HARPER & ROW, PUBLISHERS
New York
Evanston
and London

CASE

The excerpts quoted in Chapter 12 are taken from *Jan Masaryk: A Personal Memoir* by R. H. Bruce Lockhart (Dropmore Press, 1951). Used by permission of the author.

The excerpts quoted in Chapter 13 are from *The Good Soldier Schweik* by Jaroslav Hašek, translated by Paul Selver. Copyright 1930 by Doubleday & Company, Inc. Used by permission of the publisher.

Chapter 19 first appeared in the January, 1969, issue of *Harper's Magazine* in somewhat different form.

FIRST EDITION

LIBRARY OF CONGRESS CATALOG CARD NUMBER: 70-83623

To Stanley,

who never told me everything he knew

ACKNOWLEDGMENTS

I am indebted to the Czechoslovak people for the privilege of having witnessed their rare courage at first hand.

I am particularly grateful to Madame Smutný for her generosity.

I couldn't have written this book without my husband's help, and my children's forbearance.

Illustrations

(FOLLOWING PAGE 110)

Jan Masaryk, his mother Charlotte Garrigue, and his sister Alice, 1916

Jan Masaryk; his niece Anička; his father, Tomáš Masaryk; and his sisters, Alice and Olga, 1935

Jan Masaryk as a young man

Jan and Tomáš Masaryk, 1933

Jan and Alice Masaryk

Masaryk at a public demonstration, 1947

Masaryk with puppet democrat Zdeněk Fierlinger and Stalin's emissary Valerian Zorin

Members of Czechoslovak Parliament who fled to England in 1948 to plan government-in-exile

Masaryk at his last public ceremony, Old Town Square, Prague, March 7, 1948

Masaryk at President Beneš's summer house the last day of his life

Photostat and translation of a draft of speech written by Masaryk the night of his death

Czernin Palace, Masaryk's residence and headquarters of the Ministry of Foreign Affairs

Masaryk's bedroom and adjoining sitting room

Masaryk's bathroom window, from which he allegedly jumped

Ledge outside Masaryk's bathroom window

View from Masaryk's bathroom window down to the courtyard below

Members of the Czechoslovak Parliament beside Masaryk's empty chair the morning of Masaryk's death

Members of the Communist regime at Masaryk's funeral

Masaryk's body in casket

Troops and dignitaries escorting Masaryk's bier in funeral procession

Czechoslovakian people mourning Masaryk's death

Masses of bereaved Czechs at Old Town Square, Prague

Pavel Straka, clerk allegedly on duty at Czernin Palace the night of Masaryk's death

Dr. Jaromír Teplý, who was called to examine Masaryk's body, with his wife after their wedding in 1929

Masaryk's private secretaries: Jiří Špaček; Antonín Šum; Lumír Soukoup

Russian invasion after Czechoslovak liberal reforms, 1968, town of Liberec

Jiří Kotlar, State Prosecutor in charge of reinvestigation into the Masaryk mystery

Characters

KAREL BACÍLEK, Minister of State Security during the 1952 purges

EDUARD BENEŠ, President of Czechoslovakia; died of natural causes in September, 1948

HANA BENEŠ, widow of the late president; living in Czechoslovakia

LAVRENTI BERIA, Stalin's Interior Minister; rumored in 1968 to be Jan Masaryk's murderer

FRANTIŠEK BORKOVEC, brother of Zdeněk; executed in 1948

ZDENĚK BORKOVEC, head of the Prague CID, in charge of investigating Masaryk's death until security police took over; living in Prague

JAROSLAV BOUDA, former security officer who investigated Schramm's death and was dismissed shortly afterward; living in Bohemia

O. HENRY BRANDON, diplomatic correspondent for the London *Sunday Times* and personal friend of Beneš and Masaryk; writer of the *Saturday Evening Post* article in 1948 which claimed that Masaryk had planned to escape

DR. JOSEF BŘESTANSKÝ, Vice President of the Supreme Court, found hanging from a tree, April 1, 1968

PROFESSOR FRANCIS CAMPS, director of the Forensic Medicine Institute, London Hospital; consultant to the British Home Office

ALEXEJ ČEPIČKA, Gottwald's son-in-law, alleged to have originated an unsuccessful earlier plot to assassinate Masaryk in September, 1947; replaced Drtina as Minister of Justice

M. ČERNOUŠEK, a member of Choc's group; sentenced to twenty years in jail, escaped, then was reimprisoned; fate unknown

MAJOR CHLUMSKÝ, alias for Vítězslav Kadlcák, victim of assassination attempt near Prague on February 19, 1969, while carrying information he said proved Masaryk's murder; present whereabouts unknown

MILOSLAV CHOC, officially alleged assassin of Schramm, executed for Schramm's death

VLADIMÍR CLEMENTIS, Deputy Foreign Minister; at Czernin Palace March 10, 1948; executed in Slánský trials, 1952

MARCIA DAVENPORT, an American writer and Masaryk's close friend since 1942; Masaryk sent her to London two days before his death; now lives in the United States

DOHNÁLEK, Masaryk's chauffeur

JINDŘICH DOLEŽAL, cell mate of Vávra-Stařík

PROKOP DRTINA, Czechoslovak Justice Minister, jumped from a window before Masaryk's death but survived; imprisoned for twelve years; now living in Prague

EVA DUŠKOVÁ, Choc's fiancée; living on outskirts of Prague

JOHN ENNALS, Secretary of the British United Nations Association; close friend of Masaryk's

FIALA, member of Choc's mission; sentenced to life imprisonment but later liberated

ZDENĚK FIERLINGER, Czechoslovak chairman of the Social Democratic Party

JAROSLAV FILIPOVSKÝ, police guard in office wing of Czernin Palace the night of Masaryk's death; living in Prague

RŮŽENA FIŠEROVÁ, Major Schramm's secretary and a Communist militant; still living

BEDŘICH GEMINDER, Comintern agent, head of the Czechoslovak Communist Central Committee's International Section, member of the Commission on State Security, coadministrator of purge after 1948 coup; executed in Slánský trials, 1952

PROFESSOR GERIN, Director of the Forensic Medicine Institute, Rome

JOSEF GORNER, national CID chief, retired in 1951; still living

KLEMENT GOTTWALD, head of Czechoslovak Communist Party since 1929, Communist Premier of Czechoslovakia; now dead

PROFESSOR FRANTIŠEK HÁJEK, performed autopsy on Masaryk's body, Director of Forensic Medicine Institute of Charles University; now dead

GENERAL HASAL, Minister of Transport under Beneš; present at Beneš's country home with Masaryk the day of Masaryk's death

VILIBALD HOFMAN, Czechoslovak security police inspector, sent to investigate Masaryk's death

DR. JAN HORA, chief of state security, dismissed from job two months after Masaryk's death

JARIN HOSEK, Czechoslovak operative in the Soviet Centrum, Major Pokorný's liaison with the Centrum; said by Karel to have killed Schramm; lives near Prague

B.J., taxi driver for security police the night of Masaryk's death, imprisoned one year after Masaryk's death for two years, apparently as warning against disclosing his account of the night; living in Czechoslovakia

EMMANUEL JINDŘÍČEK, head porter, on guard in residence wing of Czernin Palace the night of Masaryk's death; now dead

PROFESSOR KAREL KACL, Tomíček's successor as head of Chemical Medicine Institute, said Hájek signed autopsy under duress; living in Prague

VÍTĚZSLAV KADLCÁK, real name of Major Chlumský

JOSEF KADLEC, police superintendent who saw Masaryk's body and asserted that evidence suggested murder; died soon afterward under police interrogation

VLASTIMIL KAPLAN, an STB investigator into Schramm's death

KAREL, Czechoslovak Communist security police officer, interviewed secretly in Prague in 1968 by author

OTTO KATZ, real name of André Simon; Czechoslovak agent for NKVD, allegedly at Czernin Palace March 10, 1948; hanged in Slánský trials, 1952

DR. PAVEL KAVAN, Counselor of the Czech Embassy in London; visited Masaryk on the night of his death; died after release from prison in 1960

DR. JOSEF KAZIL, chief of Prague Municipal Health Service; close friend of Dr. Teplý's; living in Prague

JOSEF KLAPKA, SNB sergeant major, on duty at Czernin Palace office

wing the night of Masaryk's death; fired from service three
months after Masaryk's death; living in Prague

DR. OSKAR KLINGER, Masaryk's personal physician and friend;
escaped to London and then to New York in 1948

P. KONEČNÝ, engineer and Prague Secretary of Beneš's National
Socialist Party; murdered by Pich-Tůma in 1948

JOSEF KORBEL, Ambassador to Yugoslavia under Beneš

DR. JIŘÍ KOTLAR, Director of Prosecutor General's Criminal Investigation Department, named to head the 1968–69 reinvestigation of Masaryk's death

B.L., a high-ranking democratic leader, escaped to West in April,
1948; sentenced to death in his absence; still living

HERBERTA MASARYK LAND, Jan Masaryk's niece, living in Prague

FRANCES CRANE LEATHERBEE, Jan Masaryk's wife; left him in 1932;
living in United States

VÁCLAV LIMAN, porter at Czernin Palace

SIR ROBERT BRUCE LOCKHART, first met Masaryk as member of the
British Legation in Prague; became one of Masaryk's few inti-
mate friends; Masaryk sent a message to him just before
Masaryk died

ALICE MASARYK, Jan Masaryk's sister

ANNA MASARYK, Jan Masaryk's niece; living in Prague

JAN MASARYK, Czechoslovak Foreign Minister and popular national
leader, son of Tomáš G. Masaryk, founder of the republic; died
violently the night of March 9, 1948

JAN MERXBAUER, Czernin Palace stoker, brother-in-law of Jan
Pomezný

VÁCLAV NOSEK, Interior Minister

ANTONÍN NOVOTNÝ, Premier of Czechoslovakia, replaced in January
Revolution, 1968, by Alexander Dubček

FRANTIŠEK NOVOTNÝ, Communist security officer in STB, ordered
killed by Pich-Tůma in June, 1948

AMBASSADOR JOZEF OLSZEWSKI, new Polish Ambassador who was
present at Sezimovo Usti with Masaryk March 9, 1948

JÁN PAPÁNEK, Czechoslovak representative to the United Nations
and a friend of Masaryk's; lives in Scarsdale, New York

JOSEF PAVEL, Interior Minister after January Revolution, 1968, member of Commission on State Security

CAPTAIN M. PICH-TŮMA, operative for Soviet Centrum, Czech security police officer; tried in 1968 by Dubček regime for past crimes but trial was adjourned at Russian insistence in December, 1968

JIŘÍ POČEPICKÝ, Chief of Prague Criminal Investigation Department; found hanging from a tree April 27, 1968

MAJOR BEDŘICH POKORNÝ, operative of the Soviet Centrum, director of secret police in the Interior Ministry; prime investigator into Masaryk's death; found hanging from a tree March 31, 1968

JAN POMEZNÝ, Czernin Palace stoker who said he discovered Masaryk's body

BOHUMIL PŘÍHODA, butler in the Masaryk family since 1920; now lives in Czechoslovakia

VÁCLAV PROVAZNÍK, member of Choc's anti-Communist underground

GENERAL BEDŘICH REICIN, operative of the Soviet Centrum, director of the Army's Second Department for Counter-Espionage; executed in Slánský trials, 1952

OLGA REVILLIOD, Jan Masaryk's sister, living in Geneva

ZDENĚK ŘÍPA, trusted aide of Major Pokorný's, involved in Konečný's killing; at Czernin Palace March 10, 1948

HUBERT RIPKA, former Czechoslovak Foreign Trade Minister under Beneš

SLAVOJ SADEK, Choc's alleged accomplice, executed for murder of Schramm

SIR ORME SARGENT, British Foreign Officer; Masaryk gave a message to him through Marcia Davenport about his escape

OLGA SCHEINPFLUGOVÁ, widow of playwright Karel Čapek and close friend of Masaryk's; died of heart attack April, 1968

MAJOR AUGUSTIN SCHRAMM, alleged NKVD agent, liaison between Soviet Centrum and Czechoslovak Army Counter-Intelligence; rumored to be Masaryk's assassin; assassinated May 27, 1948, in Prague

VÁCLAV SEDM, allegedly a guard at Czernin Palace who was off his post the night of Masaryk's death; reportedly killed in a car accident, June, 1948, and cremated without an autopsy

GENERAL JAN ŠEJNA, head of Defense Ministry's Party Committee; intimate of Novotný's; fled to United States in 1967

ANDRÉ SIMON, alias of Otto Katz; Czechoslovak Information Service head, said by some experts to have been of Soviet Centrum in Moscow

VLADIMÍR SIS, an editor of Catholic Party paper *Lidová Demokracie*, intimate friend of the police doctor Jaromír Teplý; arrested the day Dr. Teplý died; died in prison

DR. SKALICKÝ, chief of protocol for Foreign Affairs; at Beneš's home on March 9, 1948

RUDOLF SLÁNSKÝ, Communist Party Secretary-General, executed 1952

SLAVIK, Czech Ambassador to Washington; resigned March 2, 1948

JOSEF SMRKOVSKÝ, Workers' Militia leader in 1948, National Assembly Chairman in 1968

JAROMÍR SMUTNÝ, Chancellor under President Beneš, escaped to London; now dead

MADAME SMUTNÝ, widow of Jaromír Smutný, living in London

DR. JOSEF SOMMER, chief physician of Ruzyne state security prison; murdered, April 26, 1968

LUMÍR SOUKOUP, Masaryk's third secretary and an ordained minister; now in Glasgow

JIŘÍ ŠPAČEK, Masaryk's first secretary, served since 1945; living in Prague

RICHARD SPURNÝ, Nosek's private secretary; director of the Institute for Compatriots Living Abroad, Prague

MADAME STANĚK, widow of Václav Staněk, Czernin Palace guard

VÁCLAV STANĚK, police guard in residence wing of Czernin Palace, officially on duty but absent from porter's lodge at time of Masaryk's death; now dead

PAVEL STRAKA, clerk in Czech Foreign Ministry, allegedly on duty at Czernin Palace the night of Masaryk's death; sentenced to twelve years in prison for "high treason"

JAROSLAV STRÁNSKÝ, Education Minister under Beneš

C. L. SULZBERGER, *New York Times* columnist

ANTONÍN ŠUM, Masaryk's second secretary, served since September, 1947; spent thirteen years in jail after 1948; appointed head of Boy Scouts in fall, 1968

KAREL ŠVÁB, head of Communist Party's Commission on State Security

IVAN SVITÁK, author of *Student* article based on *Der Spiegel* article by Benno Weigl

LUDVÍK SVOBODA, Defense Minister under Beneš, President of Czechoslovakia in 1968

DR. JAROMÍR TEPLÝ, police physician called to examine Masaryk's body; died suddenly later, allegedly a suicide

MADAME TEPLÝ, widow of Dr. Teplý; committed suicide one year after Dr. Teplý's death

DR. FRANTIŠEK TESAŘ, assistant to Dr. Hájek at autopsy; became Director of Forensic Medicine Institute, Charles University, after Hájek's death; living in Prague

PROFESSOR TOMÍČEK, conducted chemical analysis for the Masaryk autopsy; head of Institute of Chemical Medicine; now dead

TOPINKA VÁCLAV, household purser at Czernin Palace; living in Prague

VÁVRA-STAŘÍK, leader of anti-Communist underground Regensburg camp, Choc's superior; hanged

JINDŘICH VESELÝ, Deputy Interior Minister; Moscow-trained head of Gottwald's secret services, among those directing secret police operations in Czernin Palace; survived attempted assassination, 1949; committed suicide by jumping out of window, 1950

VILÉM VYŠÍN, Masaryk's bodyguard, officially on payroll of Czech security police but fired a year after Masaryk's death; living in Prague

BENNO WEIGL, alias Michael Rand, Czech émigré after release from ten years in prison; alleged agent of Western intelligence, author whose article in *Der Spiegel* in 1965 built a case for murder; now in London

PETER ZENKL, leader of Czechoslovak National Socialist Party

VALERIAN ZORIN, Stalin's Deputy Foreign Minister, supervised the Communist *Putsch* of February, 1948

Prologue

Jan Masaryk, Foreign Minister of what had just become the Communist government of Czechoslovakia, fell from a window of Czernin Palace in Prague in the early hours of March 10, 1948. He was mourned for himself and what died with him: liberty in his country and civilized communion between the world's Communist and capitalist societies. Both were going before he went, but people weren't used to such things then and couldn't quite take them in until the shock of his death.

They knew nothing about his death except for the stark fact of it.

He was found at sunrise, spread-eagled in the palace courtyard, barefoot and half-naked, dirty, his face contorted in fright. He appeared to have fallen on his feet; grotesque stumps of bone were thrust outward at the heels and strewn over the cobblestones. Some tidy, inconsequent soul had scooped the splintered bones into a neat little mound. Nobody was sure how long he'd been lying there.

Jumping out of a window was a slovenly way to die: he had thought so himself. It was something servant girls did, he'd remarked only a couple of days before. Had he been going over his own plans then, discarding this one for another? Would he have cared much, when and if he decided to end his life, whether his corpse would be discovered suitably dressed, limbs decorously composed, features serene? Would he have cared more than a servant girl might, this most fastidious and elegant of men, bearing his country's most illustrious name?

Twenty years went by before his countrymen dared to ask such questions aloud, and dozens died, disappeared, or were held in solitary confinement because they knew, or thought they knew, the answers. However he died, he had to be forgotten. He wasn't yet in his grave before a vastly intricate machinery was already in motion to wipe out every trace.

Then, from January 5 to August 21, 1968, the Czechoslovaks tried to establish a democratic Communist order. One of the first things they did in those seven months was to reopen the Masaryk case. Solving the mystery of Jan Masaryk's death became a national obsession, contributing in good part to the Soviet military decision that put an end to their democratic experiment. Within a few months of the Red Army's arrival, witnesses who had spoken out about how and why Masaryk died were not only silenced again but facing prosecution and imprisonment for having said things they could not prove. Much of what they said could not in fact be proved. Most witnesses could offer nothing more than oblique and fragmentary evidence, and an exceptionally large number turned out to be calculating or compulsive liars. Yet somewhere in that huge, bewildering, unfinished mosaic of testimony they left behind was a faint but discernible line of truth.

Nearly all of them thought he was murdered. But that in itself wasn't why so many remembered him twenty years later and took such risks for his sake. Even their loving affection for him wasn't enough to explain it. In grieving for Jan Masaryk, they were grieving for their lost liberty, dignity, pride, national sovereignty. Seen in that light, their refusal to forget him ought to have been instructive. Apparently the Russians underestimated the pigheadedness of Czech nationalism, forgetting what the Hapsburgs went through before them. The Czechs' obstinate insistence on a national identity might seem laughable: their country was impossibly small and in exactly the wrong place. And still, lying at just the point in Europe where they were bound to be overrun by history's conquering armies, they were the living—and exasperating—proof that nationalism is an indestructible force, for better or worse.

The Hapsburgs took three hundred years to concede this point, whereas the Russians have been trying to run Czechoslovakia for barely more than twenty. With luck, and the ten Red Army divisions stationed in the country since August, 1968, they could conceivably hold out for as long again—perhaps longer. But the latent power of Czechoslovak nationalism is reflected in the behavior of the entire nation with regard to the twenty-year-old mystery of just one man's death.

He wasn't just any man, of course: he was Tomáš Garrigue Masaryk's son. In his country, you could scarcely get closer to God than that. Czechoslovakia might never have existed as a modern state if it were not for Tomáš Masaryk, founder of the Golden Republic between the two world wars and nearest of twentieth-century Europe's statesmen to Plato's ideal philosopher-king. An ascetic intellectual with a genius for diplomacy and a will of steel, he had talked the skeptical Allied powers into giving fourteen million Czechs and Slovaks their independence in 1918, three centuries after they had lost it in the Battle of the White Mountain. The democratic republic he headed from then until his death, in 1937, was an island of sanity in a disorderly continent. Nowhere in Europe was there a nation so free, enlightened, prosperous. The Czechoslovaks idolized him, and loved his son.

Jan was not cast in his father's large mold. He was no born hero, thinker, or leader of men. But he was an enchanting human being, warmly generous, compassionate, sentient, loyal, ribald, witty, full of faults, mischievously mocking of those who pretended to have none.

It was only after his father was gone that the Czechoslovaks came to know Jan as he was, or had grown to be. They had seen him as an engaging but not very serious youth who could charm a bird out of a tree, hold any drawing room entranced, deflate the most pompous windbag in any continental chancellory. He was in his late fifties before they saw what else was in him. By then he was far from home, in England, the Foreign Minister of Eduard Beneš's wartime government-in-exile. The Munich Agreement had been signed, Hitler's Nazi storm troopers had overrun Prague, the nation was their helpless captive. Happily, Tomáš Masaryk had not lived to see his Golden Republic in ashes. Of all those who tried to keep a spark alive, Jan did the most.

Week after week, during the six terrible years of world war and German occupation, he spoke to his countrymen over the air with a homely eloquence. To tune in on "London Calling," the BBC signal for his weekly talk, was to risk arrest, torture, possibly the firing squad. Millions tuned in regularly. He never lied to keep their courage up. "We had a bad bombardment here last Friday," he would say, going on to report the casualties and physical damage. "The British reacted as we expected: 'We can take it, but we shall never forget it.' . . . The German murderers should remember this. Truth is bound to win in the end, and one of these days their Axis will stop turning. It is a very difficult task for civilized people to perform, but it is sacred and very, very necessary. Good night." The Nazis detested him for those talks of his: "Palestine Jew Jan," they called him. The Czechoslovaks embraced him, when he came back after the war, as a beloved brother.

"You're free!" were his first words for them. "You need many things, and we'll do what we can to find food for you. But I'm not worried about you. If you've stood what you've stood, you can bear this for a few months. . . . Don't ask me to say any more. I'd start to cry. I'm glad to be home."

They didn't know then, but he did, that they were unlikely

to be free much longer. "You here, at last—I'm the happiest woman in the world!" his niece Anna had cried. "Wait a month or two," he had answered in a despairing voice she hardly recognized, "and you'll see." By prior agreement among the Allies, liberation had come from the east. General Patton's advance from the west was halted at Pilsen, sixty miles from Prague, on Russian insistence; two thousand Czechoslovaks died in the Prague uprising during the next two days before the Red Army, a hundred and twenty miles away, reached the capital. From then on it belonged to the Russians. Czechoslovakia had fallen on Moscow's side of a line drawn down the center of Europe by Stalin, Churchill, and Roosevelt. If the people had regained their freedom, as Jan always said they would, they were about to lose it again. In effect, he realized, they had lost it already.

He did not tell them so, nor would many have believed him if he had. Details of the Big Three's decisions at Teheran and Yalta were still a secret, to be guarded for almost a decade. Soviet Russia was seemingly absorbed in the heartbreaking work of reconstruction. Stalin had so far given little evidence of the predatory design that, within another three years, was to incorporate three-quarters of a billion people forcibly into his Communist empire. Czechoslovakia would be the last to go; and the Czechoslovaks, confident of Stalin's benevolent friendship, would not finally grasp the fact of their doom until their dear Honza, Jan Masaryk, fell from a third-story window of Czernin Palace.

He had lived there since the war, but it wasn't home. In one wing were the offices of the Foreign Ministry, which he headed. In another was his private apartment, where he slept, ate, wrote, brooded, and swore, and fled whenever he could. Masaryk had loathed the job toward the last not only for its wearisome formalities—protocol was an abomination for him—but because he had the gift, or curse, of prescience. Nearly everything to come was already reflected in his mind. Others returning with him from London might believe that Czechoslovakia was the one country on earth where Communists and democrats could share power equably, forming a bridge between East and West. Horses walk over bridges, he once told King George, who delighted in the comment, and often litter them with droppings.

Even in the first months, the pretense of power equably shared had a burlesque quality. President Beneš could sit in Hradcany Castle, seat of the ancient Bohemian kings, with all the imposing authority of a constitutional Head of State; and Klement Gottwald, the Communist leader who would move into the Castle before long, could accord him all the elaborate deference his position required. But Gottwald already had his men, Communist party members or puppets, in the Prime Minister's chair and Ministries of Education, Industry, Agriculture, Social Welfare, Defense, Information, and the Interior. The schools, the mass media, the army, the police were in the hands of practiced revolutionaries taught by Lenin to use "any ruse, dodge, trick, cunning, unlawful method, concealment, veiling of truth" to achieve their aims. The arrangements were made in Moscow before the war was over, by Stalin, with Beneš's consent.

Later, when the whole tragicomedy was finished and Beneš was dead, a high Communist functionary taunted the President for his innocence. "Eduard Beneš was a typical bourgeois democrat of the French-English school," he wrote, "whose insistence on all the appurtenances of Western democracy was fatal for him, and with him, the bourgeoisie. For it is a historical fact that, in this case, all the postulates of formal bourgeois democracy were on the communists' side." The author of this accurate observation was Jindřich Veselý, Moscow-trained head of Gottwald's secret services, who was among those directing security-police operations in Czernin Palace when Jan Masaryk's body was found. His own fall from innocence must have been less enjoyable than he had anticipated. He cut his wrists eventually and, that failing, jumped out of a window.

Jan, though, was anything but an innocent. He knew, and the Communists knew he knew. Both played their parts with a certain style. Gottwald, an unregenerate vulgarian and a drunk, was unfailingly jovial with his Foreign Minister. His Foreign Minister, who couldn't stand the sight of him, was unfailingly amiable in turn. They understood each other very well.

Gottwald had taken pains to make the position clear at their first encounter. They first met in Moscow in March, 1945. Gottwald had been there throughout the war. Jan had come from London with Beneš and other members of his government-in-exile for the fateful negotiations which were to bring the democratic leaders back to Prague in the wake of the advancing Red Army, only to sweep them into oblivion. Stalin had put himself out to captivate Beneš on that occasion, singing Georgian folksongs for him, telling stories, even dancing, and the President was dazzled. "My greatest mistake," he wrote in his dying days, "was that I refused to believe to the very last that even Stalin lied to me cynically." Gottwald, on the other hand, went straight to the point with Masaryk. Postwar Czechoslovakia, he said in a two-hour confidential talk, was not going to have a parliamentary democracy in the quaint prewar sense, or a bridge-building foreign policy either. From now on, it must "adjust without reservation" to a policy of complete cooperation with the Soviet Union. He was not quite sure if Masaryk, with his well-known Western bias, fully understood this new situation. Masaryk said he did. And he did. Gottwald never had to spell things out so crudely for him again.

He went through it for nearly three years. He was miserable most of the time and altogether wretched after the summer of 1947, when his last shred of professional dignity was stripped away. The United States had just offered the Marshall Plan to Europe, a road to economic recovery for all countries, East and West, exhausted by the war. The Russians had agreed tentatively to attend a Paris conference on the subject. The Poles, Rumanians, and Yugoslavs were going, too. Masaryk proposed acceptance to the Czechoslovak cabinet, which agreed unanimously, whereupon Stalin sent for him. He went off almost airily, expecting to talk of other matters—a Soviet loan among them. "Russia," he told a Western reporter who asked why he was going, "is like a big, fat cow with its head grazing in Prague and its udders in Moscow. I'm hoping to turn the cow around." But Stalin had other plans in mind. He informed Masaryk that the Kremlin had concluded that the Marshall Plan was "solely a device to isolate Soviet Russia." All the other Slavic states had therefore backed out, he went on, and the Soviet government "has been surprised to note that you are acting differently." Persistence in such behavior would be interpreted by the Soviet Union as an unfriendly act. There was no mistaking the menace behind his words. Masaryk was obliged to call Prague twice that afternoon, urging the cabinet to back out, too, before morning. He was sick with rage and humiliation. "I went to Moscow as the Foreign Minister of a sovereign state," he said on returning, "and I came back a stooge of Stalin. *Finis Bohemiae.*"

He was not back more than two months when they tried to kill him. The bombs came in wooden boxes marked "Perfume," one for him, one for the leader of President Beneš's National Socialist Party, Peter Zenkl, one for the courageous Minister of Justice, Prokop Drtina. Clumsily contrived, the bombs were readily detected. The Communists at once accused the democrats of concocting the plot for propaganda purposes. Drtina, though blocked at every turn by Gottwald's Interior Minister, managed to trace the maker of the boxes, then the maker of the bombs, then the sender, finally the instigator. The evidence, backed by confessions, was too clear for denial. But the plotters, saved by a Communist *Putsch*, were never brought to trial. All were Communist functionaries, from the Olomouc region. The instigator, Alexej Čepička, was Gottwald's son-in-law.

People who were there say that Gottwald's voice broke with joy when, five months after those perfume boxes were sent, he announced to a delirious crowd in Wenceslas Square that Alexej Čepička would be his new Minister of Justice. That was on February 25, 1948, the day of the Communist *Putsch*. Prokop

Drtina, replaced by his would-be assassin, jumped from a third-story window the following night. "You will remember my words," Gottwald had warned him when he persisted in investigating the perfume-box plot. "You will meet with a bad end."

Drtina didn't die. He spent the next five years, three months, and eighteen days in prison awaiting trial, and seven years more to complete his prison sentence for "false accusations of attempted assassination." He is alive today, and I have met him. Of all the motives for his abortive suicide, he told me, the strongest was Jan Masaryk's behavior in the tragic weeks before the *Putsch*. It had taken away his last illusion, he said. He still cannot understand it.

Drtina was the friend Jan was thinking about when he spoke of the way servant girls choose to die. He had immensely admired the brave democrat who fought on, without giving quarter, against impossible odds. The news of Drtina's desperate gesture shook him badly. He could have no illusions himself, about the kind of end in store for him. Gottwald might need him, for his valued name, in this delicate moment when the Communists had grasped but not yet consolidated their power. Sooner or later, however, there would be no room for him in their People's Republic. Either he must escape into exile, take his life, or wait for the Communists to take it. They were unlikely to be so clumsy the next time.

The choice was unbearably hard. He belonged intimately to his country, and so could not easily hump and run. He was, too, in love with his countrymen after half a lifetime of wandering abroad, and anxious as a protective lover to shield them as far as he could. Above all, he had made a vow at his father's deathbed, more holy than any he might make to a supernatural power he had no passionate faith in, to remain at the side of his father's chosen political heir, President Beneš.

It would be commonplace to say that Jan was deeply attached to his father. He revered him, with an untempered humility rare in the Masaryk family. The Masaryks were proud—not snobbish, certainly not haughty, far above trivial considerations of money or class, but simply aware of being a breed apart. Jan, the exception, used to say that his only distinction was his clever choice of a parent. For him, Tomáš Masaryk's word was not only law, but wise and just law. He could not have questioned the wisdom of naming Eduard Beneš as the Founder and Liberator's successor, or doubted for a moment where his duty lay while Beneš lived.

They were on curious terms. With Hana Beneš, the President's wife, he was informal and relaxed. He called her Hanci, as she called him Jendo, spoke to her with the intimate "thou," gossiped, told jokes, would casually break an appointment for lunch. With her husband, whom he had known since 1919, he was reserved, even deferential. He always addressed Beneš as "Mr. President," shied away from offering warnings or advice, seldom argued, never quarreled. Though more aware than most of the President's declining strength and growing irresolution, he never failed, either, to consult Beneš before making important decisions, and bow to his judgment. He paid for it.

On the last morning of his life, he had an hour's private talk with Beneš at the latter's country house in Sezimovo Usti. The President was utterly spent, ravaged by two brain hemorrhages and shock. Twelve days before, he had delivered Czechoslovakia to the Communists unconditionally and irrevocably by signing the new list of cabinet ministers presented to him by a now peremptory Gottwald. He had sworn that he would never sign but had been too weak to hold out. The Communist takeover had been handled with clockwork precision and stunning brutality. Thousands were already under arrest and tens of thousands thrown bodily out of their offices. The democratic parties were destroyed, their headquarters wrecked, documents seized, members harassed by police, leaders imprisoned or fleeing the country. Beneš and Masaryk were alone, trapped in a suddenly terrifying world. The one was still President in name, the other still Foreign Minister—the only democrats identified with a

Communist regime whose harsh rule would endure unrelieved for two decades.

What did they say to each other that morning? Neither left notes of the conversation, and there was no chance to look into it further. The case was closed six hours after Masaryk's body was found. An official communiqué was issued around noon on March 10. Jan Masaryk committed suicide in a fit of sudden insanity, it said, brought on by Western telegrams criticizing his "manly and patriotic attitude during the government crisis." An investigation was under way, the communiqué added. If so, the findings were never made public. *Rudé Právo,* the Communist daily, carried moving reports of the funeral on March 13 and the orations of grief-stricken Communist leaders. That was all, the last word on the subject from 1948 to 1968.

Nevertheless there are people alive who can still throw light on Masaryk's last meeting with the President, an important link in the chain of circumstances leading to his death. I have talked with them, and with others who know, or claim to know, whether, why, or how Jan Masaryk killed himself, or was murdered.

I doubt that any told me the whole truth, even the part they thought they knew. Their testimony is encrusted with the imperfections of memory, by years of confinement and torture, by broken careers and lives, by political ambition, vanity, or old age, by a fear they could not dismiss even when their freedom was restored, in the Prague spring of 1968. They were never sure the freedom would last, and before I left them they had lost it once more: Czechoslovakia was occupied by half a million Russian and other Warsaw Pact troops, sent to put down a revolution for human rights without precedent in Communist history.

Yet they talked to me, and not just to me. The revolution had no sooner begun than the Masaryks, father and son, were triumphantly summoned back from the dead. Thousands of Czechoslovaks made Sunday pilgrimages to the quiet cemetery in Lany where they were buried. Exhibitions were dedicated to them and streets renamed for them. Their portraits were in every Prague shopwindow, framed in flowers. "Truth prevails," the Founder and Liberator's motto, was written under the portraits, scrawled on the capital's walls, blazoned on banners carried through the streets by jubilant students who had tacked on the jaunty phrase "But It Takes a Lot of Doing!" Overnight the press became free. For a moment, those who had thought they must be buried with their secrets could speak out. They spoke about a thousand crimes of the fallen Stalinist regime, tingling with the pleasure of it, and the relief. But it was Jan Masaryk's death they spoke of most, the stone lying on the nation's heart for twenty years.

Chapter 1

In Prague's Old Town Square, a Renaissance glory of ocher and pink, is the statue of an older national hero than Tomáš Masaryk, the fifteenth-century Protestant martyr Jan Hus. Beneath are the words he went to the stake for: "Seek the truth, Listen to the truth, Teach the truth, Love the truth, Abide by the truth, and Defend the truth unto death." Miles away, across the ancient Charles Bridge spanning the Vltava River, up the Loretanska hill past Mala Strana's jumbled rooftops and the aching beauty of Hradcany Castle, lies the massive stone pile of Czernin Palace, where Jan Masaryk, more lovable than strong, no saint, not born to be a martyr, tried in his modest way to defend the truth, unto death.

In September, 1968, the last chance seemed gone to solve the mystery of how he died. Black flags hung from the windows looking down on Jan Hus, Mala Strana's medieval walls bore the raw scars of passing Soviet tanks, and Red Army troops patrolled the gates of Czernin Palace. Prague was an occupied city. It was in September that I came to finish the search I'd begun in the spring, for the living and dead, servants and secretaries, sisters, nieces, and women friends, cabinet ministers and foreign diplomats, the President and his Chancellor, the Communists who engineered the *Putsch* and their Russian patrons, the secret police, professional killers, intelligence agents for

East and West—Jan Masaryk's links to the world tilting under him on the night of March 9, 1948.

Once there, I hardly knew why I'd come. "Give it up," was the advice of my fellow reporters at the Alcron Hotel, and they seemed to be right. Who cared whether Jan Masaryk jumped or was pushed so long ago—now, a week after the Red Army's invasion, when the Czechoslovaks were mourning their lost freedom for the third time in thirty years? Would any of them still want to talk about it, or dare to? How should I even go about finding people in this forbidding place? Soviet tanks were clogging the main squares, surrounding ministries and government offices, backed up into outlying suburbs. On Wenceslas Square, a young Czech honor guard kept vigil at the statue of the Good King, where Soviet machine guns had shot down several youths. Otherwise the streets were empty, the silence broken only by occasional gunfire after nightfall. Almost everybody I knew had disappeared within hours of the invasion, slipping across the border, hiding out in country cottages, moving from house to house to dodge agents of the Russian KGB. My interpreter and driver had both fled to Vienna. Without them I was lost in a once familiar city, stripped overnight of signposts, street names, house numbers—an entire capital gone underground. I was afraid to use the telephone; an English-speaking voice overheard might compromise those I called and the friend who had lent me his flat, tossing me the keys at the Austrian frontier as he drove out while I rode in with a somber busload of returning Czechoslovak vacationers. I was even afraid, for his sake, to be seen going in and out of those rooms abandoned in such nervous haste, beds unmade, dirty dishes in the sink, a gnawed dog biscuit on the kitchen floor. In seventeen years as a foreign correspondent, I had never felt so much an intruder. What was I doing there among those luckless people, lonelier in their trouble than any I'd known?

I was looking for a small truth, an intoxicating pursuit for a reporter, our presumed objective always, for which we never have time. Commuting from country to country, strained on occasion to recall which one we're in, we're usually the first to unfasten our seat belts and bolt for the gangway, barely a jump ahead of our deadlines. It isn't a bad life, we often say, running into each other in Tel Aviv, or Bangui, or Bucharest. But there are moments, racing to catch a plane for the next assignment, when we'd give a lot to turn back and browse among the curiosities of politics and history. For once, in Prague, I did. Not in years had I come across a story as fascinating as Jan Masaryk's, a mystery unsolved and unforgotten a generation later, a human drama and national tragedy, a chilling omen of the times we've lived in since the night Masaryk died—the night when Stalin brought the Iron Curtain down, ending a romantic interlude in East-West relations, opening the Cold War.

There was something else. All of us covering Czechoslovakia were caught up by the magnificent spirit of its people. We were always outsiders, well-meaning, frequently useful, occasionally taken into their confidence, but only as spectators incapable of sharing their experience. They were alone in their fight and knew it, never thinking for a moment that salvation might come from the West: this was a Communist affair, not ours. Yet we could not help feeling guilty when the Western powers carefully looked away as the Red Army moved in, seven months after the January revolution began—and uneasy, as we watched the Czechs slowly going under. The last time that happened to them, the Cold War began in Europe, and the time before that marked the beginning of the Second World War. Diplomats might tell us, but history would not seem to suggest, that this was merely a parochial Communist affair. The fate of this small country had been too often and unhappily linked to ours. If we couldn't help the Czechs, we might do ourselves a service by trying to understand them.

Truth was really what they were after in the revolution. They had put up with a house of lies longer than most, tolerating a Stalinist regime for years after styles changed in Moscow. But when that house fell in at last, it rattled the foundations of Soviet Russia's empire.

For a while, we Western reporters were half-convinced it was all a mirage. It looked real from where we were sitting, viewing the national scene from Prague, and seeing Prague through the eyes of its exultant intellectuals. Nevertheless, a nagging thought kept recurring. Where, outside this charmed circle of writers, journalists, students, professors, movie directors, and poets, were all the other Czechs? In the Great Beyond where most workers and peasants lived, nothing stirred.

A Communist Party which has owned a country body and soul for twenty years is unlikely to thrust freedom upon undemanding and perhaps ungrateful workers and peasants, merely because a few intellectual hotheads say it should. That was what we thought we were seeing. A free press, radio, and television; the right to criticize, organize, assemble, worship, travel; authentic elections with a choice of independent parties and candidates; autonomous management of factories; full rehabilitation, with compensation, for former political prisoners; an independent judiciary; liquidation of the security police—all this was promised in the Communists' Action Program soon after Alexander Dubček's regime replaced the Stalinist Antonín Novotný's in January. The Czechoslovak working class was suspicious; neighboring Communist states were distressed; the Russians were faced with the worst case of heresy to come up in their realm since their own Bolshevik Revolution in 1917. But nobody in Prague seemed to worry in the least.

From the end of February, when censorship was lifted, to late August, when the Red Army reimposed it, Czechoslovak journalists were the freest, and surely the happiest, in the world. No official effort was made to restrain them, and the last thing they thought about was self-restraint. They talked their heads off about everything under the sun. One by one, the frauds perpetrated by a degenerate Communist regime were spread out on display, like grinning harpies on a Hieronymus Bosch canvas. There they were: the myth of the kind policeman and the even-handed judge, the bountiful state employer and farseeing state planner, the divine muse of socialist poets and the culture buffs in the censorship office, the patriots and freedom fighters in the Party Presidium, the Party Secretary devoted singlemindedly to his country's welfare, the selfless Stalin, Czechoslovakia's benevolent protector.

The journalists weren't alone. No Socialist Republic in Stalin's postwar empire had suffered as cruel a purge as this one, with a hundred and sixty-six Communists sentenced to death, a hundred thousand Czechoslovaks imprisoned, and another hundred thousand driven from their jobs, homes, villages, often without ever learning why. Most Czechoslovak intellectuals had spent years in jail; so had nine top Communists in the new Dubček regime. Invited and at times commanded to speak up— Josef Smrkovský, Chairman of the National Assembly, was grilled by students at a marathon session lasting eighteen hours —they did.

The revelations went back to the closing months of the Second World War. Smrkovský himself destroyed a dogma religously preserved in Communist history books since 1945: that Czechoslovakia was liberated by a solicitous Red Army, hurrying to the rescue during the Prague uprising when imperialist Western armies deliberately withheld their help. It was already established, by 1968, that General Eisenhower had offered to send in Patton's troops directly after the uprising broke out on May 5, only to be turned down by the Soviet High Command. Smrkovský, who was Vice President of the underground Czechoslovak National Council, which led the uprising, was in an excellent position to add further details. He had already confessed to part of the truth. "On May 7, 1945," he wrote in May, 1965, "three American tanks reached Prague. . . . I negotiated with the Americans in the presence of a dozen members of the Czechoslovak National Council. . . . They brought us a message from General Patton, saying his armored units were ready to enter Prague on May 8 at 4:00 A.M. to crush the German forces, providing our Council made the request. Certain Council members cried joyously: 'Hurrah! Let's go to see Patton!' But we [Communists] realized that if we let American troops enter

Prague they would be our liberators. The result would be an important political shift in the bourgeoisie's favor. We therefore felt duty-bound to turn the offer down." In April, 1968, Smrkovský confessed to an interesting omission in his 1965 confession. The Czechoslovak National Council, which was by no means Communist-dominated, did not turn General Patton's offer down—in fact, it accepted the offer. Smrkovský personally disregarded his Council's decision and thus, by default, let the offer drop. When the Red Army entered Prague instead of General Patton's, on May 9, 1945, the commanding Soviet officer put the suitable finishing touch to this story. "Our armies have come here to liberate the valiant people of Prague, so close to the Soviet people," he said. "We do not want to impose any form of government, knowing that the Czechoslovaks are all good patriots who will know how to govern themselves."

Apparently, the Russians weren't quite sure of this in February, 1948, when Stalin sent in his Deputy Foreign Minister, Valerian Zorin, to supervise the Czechoslovak Communist *Putsch.* That too came out now, along with several other fascinating items on the *Putsch,* and on Jan Masaryk's death two weeks later. In the month of April, 1968, alone, two hundred and eighty-four articles were published on the Masaryk case. Nearly all implied, or said outright, that Masaryk was murdered by Stalin's satanic Interior Minister, Lavrenti Beria.

That was just the beginning. Relatives of Rudolf Slánský and Vladimír Clementis, respectively the Communist Party's Secretary-General and Foreign Minister until 1951, described the nightmare trials and execution of these two and nine others, in 1952, for espionage, economic sabotage, Titoism, bourgeois revisionism, and Zionist conspiracy—all these charges wholly invented, as the Communist Party admitted eleven years later. Slánský's brother Richard told the press of his own arrest the night after Rudolf's, along with the arrest of his wife, Rudolf's wife, Rudolf's sixteen-year-old son and two-year-old daughter, their brother-in-law, *his* wife, and *their* four-year-old daughter, another brother-in-law, *his* wife, and *their* three-year-old daughter. Nothing happened to his parents and two other brothers, he explained, because, being Jews, they had been murdered by the Gestapo. Declared completely innocent twelve years after his own arrest, Richard Slánský spent seven years in Ruzyne prison and the Leopoldov penitentiary for hardened criminals. During his interrogation, he said, he was questioned in shifts, forced to stand, not allowed to sleep, half-starved, and kept insufficiently clothed in an icy, unlit cell. "In those first months I lost forty pounds. My investigators almost daily pressed a sharpened pencil against my forehead to see 'how much fat is still left.' "

Other inmates of Ruzyne, Leopoldov, and Pankrac prisons testified to having been beaten regularly by sadistic guards and seeing fellow prisoners die after repeated kicks in the groin. Interior Minister Josef Pavel, in jail seven years, recalled how an empty pail was put over his head, with interrogators beating against it until he nearly went mad. Slovak leader Gustav Husák, later chosen by the Russians to replace Alexander Dubček as party leader, told of "brutal and violent interrogations" during his six-year imprisonment, and party instructions to his presiding judge to "keep this pig Husák in hand." The prominent Slovak economist Eugen Loebl said he was obliged to stand on his feet for eighteen hours of questioning daily—his Russian questioners using truth drugs to break him down—and waked at ten-minute intervals in the six hours remaining for sleep. Karel Bacílek, Minister of State Security during the purges, confessed that he knew exactly what was going on. He "did not have the courage to swim against the tide," he said, because "twenty-six Soviet advisers were active in all departments of my Ministry," and Stalin had sent Anastas Mikoyan to Prague, with falsified documents, to "stage-manage" the Slánský trials.

It is questionable that anything said or done in Prague between January 5 and August 21, 1968, did more to inflame the

Kremlin than these revelations of its guilty past. The Soviet press reacted with the fury of an outraged parent when a naughty child is caught reading forbidden letters in the attic. But the naughty children were too absorbed in their game to take notice. Little by little, their disclosures were catching the attention of the working class. Though few sensed it then, the Czechoslovak workers were in fact on their way to becoming the revolution's true heroes, defending its principles and new leaders by the following autumn with a ferocity that sent the Russians reeling.

In those early months, however, the biggest worry for progressive Communists around Alexander Dubček was not so much the Kremlin as the Czechoslovaks whose thinking it had conditioned over the years: the Novotný hard-liners and the mass of workers they had degraded morally and politically. Whatever the number of factory resolutions supporting Dubček, workers were plainly not rejoicing to a man over the explosion of democratic passion in the capital. The suspicions were not overt, but they were there. "We know about you so-called progressives," an anonymous worker wrote to the Party's trade-union daily, *Práce*, "that you're parasites of our nation, indifferent to its destinies; and in your dark souls you want the present regime to disappear. When our patience is exhausted, we'll send you to hell."

Puzzled by so strong an attachment to a regime offering such meager rewards—wretched wages, shoddy clothes, a shabby one- or two-room apartment, a bicycle with luck—I asked a Charles University professor why. He wanted first to know how much I earned myself and, when I told him, shrugged. "That's five times more than our Prime Minister gets," he said. "It's one small reason, and there are many, and bigger, why somebody like you could never understand Czechoslovakia." In this country, he explained, nobody could aspire to such prodigious sums and very few, the professor included, to anything but a fraction more than the workers themselves. Furthermore, four out of five workers earned the same standard wage whatever they did or didn't do. The Czechoslovak Communists had, in fact, created an equalitarian system without parallel in history, in or out of the Communist orbit. The effects were deadening and debasing. Starved for consumer goods, workers saw no point in working harder to get them, finding it easier to pilfer instead. Thievery was an accepted occupation, the ordinary citizen's way to acquire a television set and cheat the state. Hard work, on the other hand, was an unpardonable violation of the fraternal code. With nobody to envy and nowhere to go at the top of the ladder, workers made a virtue of the main vice encouraged by the system: to put in a poor day's work for a poor day's pay. In this curious sense, they could rightly feel pampered. The government was obliged by the constitution to give them a job, foremen looked the other way when they filched spare parts, and local Party functionaries would rather leave them in peace than risk their wrath. The policy had clearly paid off for Novotný's regime in the past. It had also contributed greatly to the impoverishment of a once-thriving industrial nation.

This, more than anything, was why Communist leaders finally decided that Novotný must go. The Czechoslovaks could not survive economically much longer by clinging to primitive socialist habits copied from Moscow twenty years earlier, when the Russian economy was half a century behind their own. At the time they were wrenched from the heart of Europe by the 1948 coup, their industries were technically abreast of the West's, their foreign trade was soundly in balance, and their workers were highly skilled, decently dressed, and comfortably housed. Faced about smartly toward the Communist East, they lost it all.

By 1968, nearly two-thirds of Czechoslovakia's industrial plant was obsolete and the rest—heavy industry developed at the killing pace that Bolshevik doctrine (and Soviet requirements) demanded—was producing far above Western costs. Productivity was barely a third of the United States' and well behind Western Europe's. Czechoslovakia was at the bottom of the European list, with Portugal and Spain, for the number of housing units built in proportion to hours worked. A nation of fourteen million people was turning out a million and a half types of manufactured goods and three-quarters of the world's entire range of heavy engineering equipment, much of it inferior in quality. Huge stockpiles rusted in warehouses; rejects of defective merchandise ran to $200 million a year; two-thirds of the merchandise in retail stores was, by official estimate, unfit to be on the market. Large trade surpluses were piling up with the East—Russia alone owing the Czechoslovaks $350 million—as was a heavy deficit with the hard-currency West. Young couples waited ten years for an apartment, and living standards, though certainly higher than the Russians', were a dreary joke compared even to little Austria's next door.

All this was brought about in the name of the Czechoslovak working class, another lie that fell apart under inspection. "The greatest deception of our rulers, who simply assumed the position of the overthrown class, was that they presented their license as the will of the workers," wrote Ludvík Vaculík, the Writers' Union spokesman whose Manifesto of Two Thousand Words was answered eventually by five hundred thousand Warsaw Pact troops. "If we believed this deception, we would have to blame the workers for the decline of our economy, incorrect investments, loss of trade, shortage of living quarters, crimes against innocent people, and the censorship that kept us from writing about it. But we know that the workers, in practice, decided nothing."

Pushed to the background by political events in that memorable Prague spring, the economy was the key to them. It was not for love of liberty that the Party's Central Committee decided to get rid of the man presiding over his country's economic disintegration for fifteen years. The disintegration was uppermost in these Communists' minds. When love of liberty did emerge and carried them away, nobody was more surprised than they were.

Everybody was surprised, including the students and writers who helped to finish Novotný off between them. For two or three years, members of the Writers' Union had been probing at the Party's frontiers, advancing, retreating, advancing again. Four times in 1967, before the Central Committee suppressed it altogether in a fit of Zhdanovite rage, the Union's weekly, *Literární Noviny*, was forced to accept a different editor. Each simply took up where the last had left off. The climax came at a Writers' Congress in June, 1967, when the bravest of Czechoslovak writers—Ludvík Vaculík, Antonín Liehm, Jan Procházka, Ivan Klíma—finally broke out of bounds.

"Czechoslovakia," said Klíma, "is the one country in the socialist camp possessing century-old traditions of parliamentary liberties. This is an ineffaceable and undebatable reality. If some of us have the impression that several fundamental rights, written into the [Austro-Hungarian] Constitution of 1867, are no longer recognized today, we must feel a certain sense of anomaly. It is against this anomaly that we rise in protest. . . ."

"In the last twenty years," wrote Vaculík, "none of humanity's problems has been resolved in our country—starting with elementary needs such as lodging, schools, and economic prosperity, going on to the most beautiful of life's requirements, which no nondemocratic system can satisfy, for example the sense of having one's full value in society, the subordination of political decisions to ethical criteria, confidence among all men, the education of all the people. I fear that our Republic has lost its good reputation, that we have given no original ideas to humanity, that we ourselves have found no fresh inspiration to avoid being asphyxiated by the results of industrial production, that we are following without reacting along the American course of dehumanized civilization, that we are repeating the errors of East and West . . . and I suggest that what we note today was known and felt in our progressive Czechoslovak culture as far back as the thirties."

The final resolution of the Writers' Congress, written by Liehm, was openly defiant: "In the days between the two wars, our state, though rocked by the conflicts of capitalism, enjoyed a high degree of democratic freedom. . . . The revolution attempted to bridge the diversity of work and culture bequeathed by the old society. In this process there were necessarily failures: from genuine emotion it was but a short step to pseudo art, from popularization it was not far to vulgarization. But what should have been only the shortcomings of a youthful experiment, while democratic methods prevailed, were frozen into virtues. Writers who lived through that period have a moral obligation never to permit a repetition of those tragic mistakes."

These were *Communist* writers, intellectuals who had supported the Communist Party with all their hearts in 1948: the most dangerous kind. Three months after their Congress, the Central Committee expelled Liehm and his most outspoken colleagues from the Party, sequestered the Union's funds, and took over *Literární Noviny*. It was the penultimate spasm of a dying Stalinist order.

The final spasm came on October 31 when about fifteen hundred students in Prague's Strahov dormitory, fed up with perpetual breakdowns in their electricity and heating systems, marched through Mala Strana bearing candles, shouting, "We want light." Had Novotný's police not made the error all the world's policemen seem to make, he might have hung on a bit longer. But they did make it, breaking up the parade with clubs, invading the dorms and savaging the students there, hauling scores off to prison. A relatively passive student body was thoroughly aroused and a wave of shock spread through the nation. Though the lights came on in Strahov soon afterward, along with a formal apology to the students (!) from Novotný, the damage was done.

Yet neither students nor writers dreamed of the marvels to come. Most Czechoslovaks took it for granted that, after dumping Novotný, the Party would merely go on to mild reforms—less mild than some, perhaps, but not too far out of line with the changes gently rocking the international Communist community. Instead, Party leaders made a momentous and still baffling decision: they freed the press.

Unnerved by the consequences, some Presidium members would have given a lot to retract their decision soon after making it. But within a week came General Jan Šejna's spectacular flight to the United States. Head of the Defense Ministry's Party Committee and an intimate of Novotný, General Šejna had fled the country—with a diplomatic passport procured by a Russian Warsaw Pact general, later arrested in Moscow—after disclosures that shook the country to its soul. The army's new political chief, writing in the army weekly *Obrana Lidu,* had revealed a military plot to save Novotný during the January Party Plenum, with the armed Workers' Militia mobilized and tanks ready to roll on Prague. Sickened, as the nation was, at the realization of what they had so narrowly escaped, the Party's new leaders saw the free press for the first time not as a political luxury but an indispensable weapon in their own defense. From then on there was no turning back.

But they didn't know where they were going. What they needed most was a pause for reflection, Antonín Liehm told me, so that a nation incapable of self-communication for two decades—three, counting the Nazi occupation—could come to know itself. "We're asking for the moon these days," he said, "without any idea whether that's the planet our people prefer."

I realized how right he was after a long spring afternoon spent with leaders of the emerging student movement. Intense, implacable in their judgments, talking at times with a virtuoso brilliance, they spoke of the "so-called January revolution" as at once a miracle and a fraud. The intellectual climate might have improved at the top, they said, but not in their ranks, "where the substitute for political discussion is a kind of infantile ranting." They were, after all, a generation raised under the "prehistoric" Novotný regime, and trapped by it. "For years," said one, "Novotný has played with us, giving a little, taking it away, and we ourselves have been moving from nowhere to nowhere, not to get someplace—we aren't that innocent —but just to keep our moral backbone. Right now, Dubček seems to be going somewhere because he has gunpowder at his backside. But can he do anything worthwhile without giving us political parties, and if he tried, would the Russians let him? We're not that innocent either."

"We have only a negative unity: we're revolted by the past," said another. "But what are we *for?* Do we want socialism in any form? Capitalism in whatever form? A mixed economy taking the worst from both? A consumer society of witless shoppers, buying their moral values at the supermarket? Would we prefer to leave the Communist orbit, fight it out with the Russians, trust our future to the West? Look at Hungary in 1956. Can we invent a new, more bearable Communism? Nobody else has. We don't know what we want. We only want to be able to want."

The new Communist hierarchy was hardly in better shape. Rushed off their feet in those first hectic months, moderate leaders had joined with radicals in a hasty marriage, to repent at leisure. Were they actually prepared to give up their old Marxist ways? Reanimate the economy with Western investment capital, dump centralized planning, introduce the profit motive and free-market prices, shift their foreign trade back toward the West? Encourage authentic trade unions, with the right to strike? Give the press unlimited license to attack and expose everything and everyone, themselves included? Above all, permit an organized political opposition which, not inconceivably, could put the Communist Party out of business? It was all very well for the radicals to renounce the "dogma of the Party's immaculate conception" and insist that the Communists must henceforth "earn" their ruling position by winning popular support, as the Action Program provided, instead of "imposing" it by constitutional fiat. But what if the Party should fail to earn its keep?

Not many were prepared to go that far. At most, they were

ready to allow or even encourage "countervailing forces" within the party-controlled National Front, but assuredly not a full-fledged, still less "antisocialist" opposition party. While the encouraging of "countervailing forces" might leave ample room for political lobbies—the new KAN clubs of "committed non-party members," for instance—the radicals considered it a sell-out. They refused to believe that the discredited Socialist and Catholic Popular Parties, bent with servitude in the National Front, could ever raise their heads effectively again. The whole array of Communist promises would be worthless, they argued, unless the Party was forced to behave itself through fear of a legitimate, independent opposition.

It was perhaps the decisive point in Moscow's calculations. Nothing is more sacred in Marxist canon law than the supremacy of the Communist Party. Somewhere along the line, when and if the Dubček regime carried out its Action Program, must come the grand confrontation between the "progressive" progressives and "Communist" Communists in the Party, between those who were prepared to stake the Party's supremacy in the gamble for democracy and those who were not. On this and everything else, a Central Committee of a hundred and ten was sharply divided. The progressives (both kinds) numbered thirty-five altogether, against forty conservative Novotnýites. In the middle were thirty-five irresolute centrists led by Dubček himself, pushed and pulled between one faction fearing that the Action Program would not be carried out and another fearing that it would.

They were expecting to settle their quarrels at a national party congress in September—an interesting item in the Kremlin's timetable—or at least get a clearer idea of how to proceed. Even then, the revolution would barely have gotten started. The Czechoslovaks' single solid achievement so far was a free press, in itself precarious. "Truth hasn't triumphed yet," said Vaculík in his Two Thousand Words. "The Party has merely paid a first installment on its debt. . . . It took several months before many of us believed we could speak out. But we did speak out, exposing ourselves so much that we simply must realize our intention of humanizing this regime. Otherwise the vengeance would be cruel. . . ."

The revolution was already seven months old when he wrote this. None of the democratic institutions proposed in the Action Program was yet written into law, or could be, until a new constitution was drafted in two or three years. From here to there was a long voyage through uncharted land, never explored by any Communist regime from Moscow to Havana and Peking. Nobody knew how far Czechoslovakia's new leaders were ready to go in search of what they called Communism with a human face. Nobody is likely to find out, now.

The Czechs have a legend about a mountain in southern Bohemia called Blanik, where the Good King Wenceslas is said to live with his troops, ready to come out when necessary and strike the invader down. At the foot of the mountain is a small lake whose magical powers were recorded by a Bohemian poet in the Middle Ages. The waters of Blanik would dry up when catastrophe was coming, he wrote: and early in August, 1968, they did.

When calamity struck some weeks later, the Czechoslovaks were too stunned to understand it. Day after day they put anguished questions to Red Army soldiers, in tears, the soldiers often crying, too. Why are you here? Why should our allies send thousands of troops to invade us, from thousands of miles away —Warsaw, East Berlin, Budapest, Sophia, Moscow? What harm have we done to the Poles, Hungarians, Russians? Aren't we Communists like all the others, like the Russians themselves?

But they weren't like the Russian Communists, or any others, anywhere. Geography and history, and Tomáš Masaryk most of all, had seen to that.

Historians will doubtless be arguing for years over the motives behind the Warsaw Pact invasion. My Czechoslovak friends had worked up an imposing list by the following January, when I came back to see them: political, theological, psychological, imperial, military. In one way or another, though, most could be traced to the quiet cemetery in Lany where, buried with the Masaryk family bones, was a way of life that the Czechoslovaks alone had experienced before entering a Communist society. They could still remember and compare it to what had come since. Their disillusion was all the greater because they had expected so much more than their neighbors in Poland, or Hungary, or Rumania, where the Red Army simply imposed a Communist regime without ceremony on the decaying remains of a feudal or Fascist state. Gottwald didn't need the Red Army, withdrawn from Czechoslovakia six months after the war. He had plenty of willing troops at home.

The Golden Republic was full of Communists who, under its meticulously democratic President, had the same rights as everybody else. Their party bloomed in that winy air, wilting only after Gottwald came to power. Well over a third of the electorate, 38 percent, voted for him in the last free elections, in 1946. Many assumed that Communism would really mean Masarykism with an extra social dimension. Only in the final months before the coup did a good number come to realize how gravely mistaken they were: too late.

That, no doubt, was why Gottwald staged his *Putsch* in February, 1948, well after the rest of Eastern Europe had fallen, and three months before an election which could no longer give him the majority he had counted on. A confidential Party poll showed a steep drop in electoral support, to somewhere around 28 percent. The sole state which might have brought Communism to power by popular mandate was drifting beyond Stalin's grasp; and Gottwald was Stalin's man, chosen unerringly by the Georgian ruler nineteen years earlier. Where his precedessor in the party leadership had shown a lamentable taste for parliamentary methods, Gottwald was dependable. In 1927, when he was accused in the democratic Czechoslovak Parliament of taking orders from Stalin, he replied: "I go to Moscow to learn—you know what? To learn from the Russian Bolsheviks how to twist your necks."

He was an apt pupil, but it wasn't enough. Whatever Gottwald did, and Novotný after him, the past could not be erased. The Kremlin had good reason to fear the Prague insurrection in 1968. Only the Czechoslovaks, in a Communist world embracing three-quarters of a billion people, knew what it was like to live under democratic rule, the best the West had to offer. They alone moved on to a Communist order with a substantial measure of popular consent, an advanced industrial economy, a sophisticated Western culture, superbly civilized traditions. They alone had carried Communist theory to its outermost equalitarian limits. Nobody else was so thoroughly familiar with the relative merits of Soviet-style Communism and Western democracy. They knew too much.

Chapter 2

DEAR COMRADE GENERAL PROSECUTOR:
We are informed by the press that from now on people who were incorrectly imprisoned and persecuted in Stalin's time will be rehabilitated. Some are no longer alive, and a state prosecutor will thus have to be charged with their defense. This is especially important in cases where reconstruction of true historical events will be necessary. In the name of an independent judiciary and our new democratic procedures, I ask you to begin an immediate investigation to determine whether the Minister of Foreign Affairs in Gottwald's government was murdered twenty years ago, as the first victim on the road to totalitarian dictatorship. . . .

So began an open letter in the weekly *Student* on April 3, 1968, cracking the twenty-year silence. The revolution was then exactly two months old. It was a moment, unique in Communist annals, when Party and people were in perfect communion, happily ignorant of where they were heading, too soon for caution, too late for retreat. On April 5, the Dubček regime ordered a formal inquiry into Masaryk's death.

Jiří Kotlar, director of the Prosecutor-General's criminal investigation department, was named to conduct it. Dr. Kotlar wasn't at all the kind of man you'd expect to find in an office at

Pankrac prison. Comfortable, unhurried, serene in his acceptance of a prematurely receding hairline and any other of life's unaccountable vagaries, his mild blue eyes beamed understanding and invited confidence. Witnesses lined up at his door, warming at once to the friendly young man in baggy trousers who was never too busy to hear them out. The new Interior Minister, Josef Pavel, turned over two bulging cases of material from the archives. Letters of advice and encouragement rained down on him from every corner of the republic, not one showing the smallest interest in the suicide theory. He was grateful for these many signs of support and would do his best, he said, adding wistfully that he would like the public to be as dispassionate as he was trying to be.

Regrettably indifferent to his plea, the public persisted in cluttering up a stale and tangled trail with fresh clues often leading nowhere. The Interior Ministry's archives had passed through several hands, none too clean, since 1948. Many important witnesses had died meanwhile, naturally or otherwise, and at least four whose testimony might have been invaluable died unnaturally just around the time Dr. Kotlar's investigation began. They were: Dr. Josef Břestanský, Vice President of the Supreme Court, found hanging from a tree on the outskirts of Prague on April 1; Dr. Josef Sommer, chief physician of the Ruzyne state security prison, found with a bullet in his head on April 26; Lieutenant Colonel Jiří Počepický, chief of the Prague Criminal Investigation Department, found hanging from a tree in a forest near Marianske Lazne on April 27; Major Bedřich Pokorný, director of Gottwald's counterespionage service in 1948 and a prime investigator into Masaryk's death, also found hanging from a tree, in a Moravian forest near Brno, on April 9.

The first three were reported to have committed suicide and may have done so. But Major Pokorný was certainly murdered. Whether or not his throat was cut before the noose was slipped around it, as a high security officer told me, the authorities plainly did not believe he tied the noose himself: the Institute of Forensic Medicine in Brno, where the autopsy was performed, refused to certify the cause of death. The pointed announcement to this effect, carried by the official news agency Ceteka, was made by a former security officer who, in 1948, was in charge of the secret-service guard at Czernin Palace.

Any number of people might have been anxious to get rid of all four, for reasons unrelated to the Masaryk case. They were all deeply involved in activities, during the early fifties, that fallen Stalinist leaders greatly preferred to leave unmentioned after January, 1968. But Major Pokorný stood out even among these. Few Czechoslovaks had a finer knowledge of security matters under the old regime than this fanatic Stalinist, whose name runs like a black thread through accounts of the years between 1945 and 1948. I came across it again and again, always in a sinister context, as I tried to reconstruct the events preceding and surrounding Masaryk's death.

I was sorry to have missed the knowledgeable Major Pokorný, as I started out on the hunt that spring. How many others would turn up missing as I went along? Were there enough people alive to prove anything one way or another? Who, in an endless procession of witnesses, was telling the truth and who gained what by lying? Where, among all those printed words— a million in April, as many again in May—was the hard evidence of suicide or murder?

The first sensational evidence of murder, presented by *Student* on April 3, was reportedly taken in part from the secret files of the Czechoslovak Interior Ministry. The main points were these:

1. Dr. František Borkovec, Vice President of State Security in the Interior Ministry, who came to Czernin Palace an hour after Masaryk's body was discovered, found the Minister's bedroom in a state of disorder, broken glass in the bathroom, pillows in the bathtub, and a window open there.

2. Jaromír Teplý, a police physician, found excrement on

the body, a physiological symptom of extreme terror unknown in suicide cases.

3. Masaryk's butler, Bohumil Příhoda, was surprised by the unusual disorder in the apartment, and especially by the open bathroom window, always closed because it was too high.

4. Another police physician, Vilibald Hofman, stated that the bedroom window was only two feet from the floor, whereas the bathroom window was twice as high. He also found fourteen cigarette stubs of different brands in the bedroom.

5. Masaryk's personal physician, Dr. Oskar Klinger, was not permitted to see the body.

6. The autopsy report signed by Professor E. Hájek was a forgery. Professor Hájek later told close friends that he did not sign it, and had been kept a good three yards from the body.

7. On the day of Masaryk's funeral, police banned publication of a photograph officially released earlier, showing a little nosegay behind his right ear in the coffin.

8. Gottwald's Interior Minister prohibited police investigation immediately after the funeral. Dr. Borkovec, however, continued to investigate on his own, and found suspicious connections between a certain Major Franz Schramm and a Václav Sedm, possibly bearing on Masaryk's death.

9. Major Franz Schramm, liaison officer between the Czechoslovak secret police and the Russian NKVD, was the organizer of Masaryk's murder, and was himself murdered in the summer of 1948, probably by Western counterespionage agents.

10. Václav Sedm, a guard at Czernin Palace, was killed in a car accident in June, 1948, and cremated without an autopsy. On the night of March 9, he left his post at the palace claiming he had a toothache. Soon after, he became administrator of a big jewelry shop. When he was later accused of illegal blackmarketing in gold, the investigation was quashed by Major Schramm.

11. Police Superintendent Josef Kadlec, who suggested exhumation of Masaryk's body and asserted that a spot behind

the right ear was caused by the prick of a needle, died soon afterward under police interrogation.

12. Dr. František Borkovec, the ranking security officer who pried too deeply into Masaryk's death and the NKVD's role in it, was executed at the end of 1948.

For all anybody knew in Prague, there might not have been a word of truth in this story. The information was taken from a three-year-old article in an anti-Communist Western magazine, *Der Spiegel,* signed by an unknown journalist calling himself Michael Rand—obviously a phony byline—who turned out to be a Czechoslovak émigré of dubious connections and uncertain financial prospects. Furthermore, Dr. Ivan Sviták, the man who republished this material in *Student,* making no effort to verify it, could hardly be said to have disinterested motives. A professor of aesthetics at Charles University, Dr. Sviták had the right credentials, and excellent prospects, for a spectacular political career in the new Czechoslovakia. He was expelled from the Academy of Sciences as an "unbearable element" in the fifties, spent years in prison under Novotný, and, as a "victim of Stalinist persecution," had just been rehabilitated at the end of March. With his open letter in *Student,* he shot into national prominence. By May, he had founded the KAN clubs and become the recognized leader of the country's emerging non-Communist forces.

All the same, there was enough truth in the *Student* article to send the Czechoslovaks haring off in search of more. By mid-April it was established that there *had in fact* been a Major Schramm (not Franz, but Augustin), probably connected with the NKVD, *who was* murdered under mysterious circumstances in May, 1948. His Hungarian-born wife, now the London correspondent for a Hungarian Communist daily, was recalled to Budapest twenty-four hours after the Masaryk case was reopened. There was a Dr. Oskar Klinger, Masaryk's personal physician, now living in the United States, who did tell Western reporters long ago that he was not permitted to see Masaryk's body. There were friends of Professor Hájek's, himself dead, who claimed he did not sign the autopsy report, or signed it under duress. There were still copies of a photograph—republished in April—showing Masaryk in his coffin with a nosegay behind his right ear. Masaryk's former butler, Příhoda, was alive and agreed that he'd found unusual disorder in the Minister's apartment. Dr. Borkovec (not František, but Zdeněk), the ranking police officer said to have investigated the deaths of both Masaryk and Schramm, showed up before the television cameras—not executed after all—and confirmed the disorder. Dr. Jaromír Teplý, the police doctor who first examined Masaryk's body, turned out to have died soon after Masaryk did, also under mysterious circumstances: at Police Headquarters, allegedly by his own hand, with an injection of gasoline. His wife committed suicide also.

That wasn't all. Two days after the formal state inquiry began, Pavel Straka, a former clerk in the Czechoslovak Foreign Ministry, came out with a striking story. Assigned to night duty on March 9, 1948, Straka was alone in the office wing of the Czernin Palace, working in Room 7, connected to all the Ministry telephones. Around eleven in the evening, he heard several cars driving from Pohorelec Square through Loreta Square, usually silent at that hour, and into the palace grounds. Curious, he tried to telephone the porter's lodge for information, but the lines were cut. Then he thought of going down to inquire, only to find that he'd been locked in. Sometime around three or four in the morning, he heard cars leaving the palace, tried his door, which was now unlocked, and rushed downstairs. He found the porter, Liman, pale with fright and speechless. The porter pointed to the courtyard, where Straka found Masaryk's body.

"He lay on his left side, three or four yards from the wall, his knees slightly bent, left hand under his body, right hand stretched out," reported Straka. "When I touched him, the hand was cold, and I could not feel the pulse. . . . I turned the head so that I could see the face and be sure it was Jan Masaryk's. I don't know how long I sat there with his body. I only know that I began to shiver with cold, and stood up to go. Looking up, I saw that all the windows facing the courtyard were closed. . . . It was clear to me that this was neither accidental death nor suicide."

Terrified himself, Straka went back to Room 7 and sweated it out until he could go off duty, writing in the office register before leaving: "There was no telephone call and no extraordinary announcement." Back home, he telephoned at once to Olga Scheinpflugová, widow of the playwright Karel Čapek and a famous actress in her own right. The Čapeks had been friends of the Masaryk family for years; she herself was said to be more than a close friend of the Foreign Minister's, and she was also well acquainted with Straka, an ardent amateur actor. "I have terrible news for you," he told her. "The Minister is dead: I saw him with my own eyes, in the courtyard. You'll soon hear about it on the radio—but don't believe it was suicide!"

A few days later Straka called on Madame Scheinpflugová and told her more about the cars in the palace grounds, the cut telephone lines, the locked office door, the closed windows. Shortly thereafter he was arrested and sentenced to twelve years for "high treason." On leaving prison in 1960, he communicated with nobody in Prague, went back to his birthplace in Slovakia, and got a job in a brewery. He did not tell another soul about his experience until April 7, 1968.

On that date, Straka could not have known about the position of Masaryk's body simply from reading the papers. The first eyewitness to confirm these details was Borkovec, the police inspector, whose interview did not appear in the press until two weeks after Straka's did. Furthermore, Straka's story—as told to Madame Scheinpflugová, at any rate—was corroborated by the actress herself, before she died of a heart attack some weeks following publication of the Straka interview. What's more, several details in his story were confirmed by another witness

whose interview appeared in a Prague newspaper *on the same
day* that Straka's came out in Bratislava, the Slovak capital, several hundred miles away.

Unwilling to disclose his name (though he gave it to the editors, with his address), B.J. was a taxi driver who had worked
for the Security Police in 1948 and was on night duty at the
Bartolomejska Headquarters on March 9. Sometime around
four in the morning, he drove three security officers to Czernin
Palace, where the porter led them to Masaryk's body in the
courtyard. The body was not directly under the window, he
said, but "at least three yards from the wall" and approximately
half a yard from the side of the window. There was very little
blood, though the heels of the feet were badly damaged (other
details confirmed later by Dr. Borkovec). Instructed to stay by
the body, B.J. picked up the splinters of bone and put them
near the wall: he didn't know why.

They all waited "quite a while" until the official investigators
arrived: Dr. Borkovec and the police doctor, Teplý. He remembered Dr. Teplý's saying that Masaryk had died three or four
hours earlier—contrary to the official announcement putting the
time of death at 6:30 A.M. Then a stretcher was brought, and
Teplý gave orders for the body to be carried upstairs. "I clearly
remember that the room was in a state of extreme disorder," he
went on. "We were told to guard the Minister's study and, after
a while, an unknown person came, demanding to be let in. I
refused. But then the Interior Minister, Nosek, gave me a hint
to let the man in, and I couldn't prevent it. He remained in the
study about half an hour, and came out with a briefcase he
didn't have before. A few minutes later, I was sent back to
Headquarters."

B.J. was arrested in May, 1949, and spent two years in prison,
without being charged or tried. On his release, he was told he'd
been "punished as a warning." "In the next eighteen years, I
confided what I knew to only three people, high security officers, so that this testimony could be preserved if anything happened to me. I know I'm only alive because I was an insignifi-

cant driver. I did not have the courage to speak sooner and I must confess I'm afraid even now. I speak out today because all this lay in me like a heavy stone."

Four days after publication of this testimony, a still more dramatic witness appeared, or his name did, in banner headlines: "WHERE'S CHLUMSKÝ?" Where, indeed? The only clue to the whereabouts of this shadowy figure was an anonymous letter so alluring that all Prague joined the hunt. Major Chlumský, according to the letter—which was sent to several newspapers and State Prosecutor Kotlar as well—was a Czechoslovak intelligence agent and former partisan leader, with a glittering record in the last world war. As a member of the 10th Army Group in Holesov, he had been one of the most reliable links between the underground resistance and the Beneš government-in-exile in London. Seriously wounded in 1945, he was treated at a hospital in the Olomouc region, where he unearthed evidence that Alexej Čepička—the Communist leader who tried to assassinate Jan Masaryk in 1947—was betraying non-Communist partisan fighters to the Gestapo. After his discharge from the hospital, Major Chlumský went to Prague, where he was received by President Beneš and Foreign Minister Masaryk, just back from London. Thereafter, he acted as their secret contact with a Western intelligence service. It was in this capacity that he tried to save Masaryk's life on the night of March 9.

Returning from the President's country seat at Sezimovo Usti that afternoon, Masaryk reportedly stopped at the house of his Deputy Foreign Minister, Vladimír Clementis. There he was approached by a tall man in a leather coat, who had just pulled up in a black Tatra.

"Sir, Chlumský has entrusted me to tell you not to return to Czernin Palace. I am supposed to take you to safety, in England," the man said.

"I was in England long enough," replied Masaryk. "My place is here, and I shall either win or fall. Please tell that to Chlumský."

On leaving the Clementis home some time later, Masaryk was

accosted by the same man: "Sir, Chlumský is well informed about the situation, and has instructed me to tell you that it is really necessary for your safety to go abroad immediately. Let me take you to the airport. Don't go to Czernin Palace, I beg you."

"I am still the Foreign Minister," answered Masaryk, getting into his car, "and I'm going back to the palace. My place is here. Come and see me tomorrow."

"Tomorrow will be too late," the man called after him.

That night, beginning at 11:15, Masaryk received several threatening telephone calls, said the letter. Then the Ministry's telephone lines were cut; two men in rough workmen's clothes entered the palace; the light in Masaryk's apartment was switched off, to come on again later and remain burning until dawn.

With a popular dragnet out for him, Major Chlumský walked into a Prague newspaper office in person ten days later. He denied being a Western intelligence agent, or having himself been the man who warned Masaryk to flee the country on March 9. Nevertheless, he brought with him a rich file of documents confirming the contents of the anonymous letter. A great many more were smuggled abroad in 1948, he said: protocols of testimony, photographs, dossiers of people using pseudonyms and disguises, a detailed chronology of Masaryk's last days. Among the documents, he said, was a dossier on the police doctor Jaromír Teplý and a secret testament he allegedly had smuggled abroad, another on Major Schramm and his links to the NKVD, a third on Masaryk's murder by agents of the NKVD and the Czechoslovak STB (security police). All this material, added Major Chlumský, would be turned over to State Prosecutor Kotlar for study.

A month went by, each day bringing a tantalizing item, on the front pages, over the radio, on television. The Czechoslovaks were ravished to be told what they'd privately believed all along. But then, from distant Scotland, came the voice of an exile who knew that Jan Masaryk committed suicide, and said so with such authority that they fell back in momentary confusion.

Dr. Lumír Soukoup was an ordained preacher; and his most persuasive proof was Tomáš Garrigue Masaryk's Bible, which was found, he claimed, on Jan's bedside table, lying open to the following underlined passage:

The fruit of the Spirit is love, joy, peace, quietness, gentleness, goodness, fidelity, meekness, temperance. . . .
And those that are Christ's have crucified their own flesh. . . .

This, asserted Dr. Soukoup, was the message Masaryk decided to leave for his countrymen before making the supreme sacrifice. As the Foreign Minister's private secretary, he ought to know.

He first met Masaryk in Edinburgh during the Second World War and worked for him in various capacities. As he put it in an article in *The Scotsman* on May 13, 1968, he was Masaryk's private secretary "in both senses of these two words. I doubt whether there were any of his political or diplomatic secrets that I did not know. . . ."

In that article, Soukoup narrated the events of Saturday, March 6, Sunday, March 7, and Monday, March 8, the last time he saw Masaryk alive (he later prepared Masaryk's body for the state funeral) .

On that Saturday, Soukoup reported that he was "shocked" when Masaryk failed to greet him after the parade in Old Town Square. They went to Masaryk's apartment, where he touched the bronze cast of his father's hand, saying, " 'The shamming is over.' " When Soukoup asked if he might go with him to the cemetery at Lany the next day, Masaryk agreed.

Soukoup thought later that the speeches at the parade distorting his father's name had so distressed Masaryk that it drove him to a final decision "to demonstrate the worthlessness of a life deprived of values such as decency, respect, and freedom."

He spoke to Soukoup in this vein several times during the two weeks before his death, and also to others, so Soukoup wrote. "In vain we tried to dissuade him."

Soukoup told a dramatic story of their journey on Sunday to Lany, where Masaryk knelt briefly at his father's graveside. On the return to Prague, the two rode in silence until Masaryk finally spoke, saying, " 'God and father will forgive me. They will understand.' " Soukoup said that "a very great and remarkable change" came over his face.

"On Saturday he returned with horror in his eyes. His whole face was distorted. On Sunday serenity returned. . . ." Monday, March 8, was little different from a "normal" working day, Soukoup said. There was one difference. The new Parliament was scheduled to open on Wednesday, March 10. As part of the public relations staging, a film was to be made of the members of the new government. Soukoup, handing in his own final report, passed on a request telephoned from Gottwald's office asking Masaryk to come a half-hour early on Wednesday to participate in the film. As Soukoup reported it, Masaryk was silent for a few seconds, and then "firmly" said, " 'I SHALL NOT BE THERE.' And then came slowly that smile which reflected an inner peace and regained equilibrium. He gave me his hand and turned away. I was driven home where I collapsed."

Soukoup never saw Masaryk alive again.

Whether or not Masaryk left a message behind remained a mystery. Soukoup referred to a vague reference from Masaryk several days before about leaving " 'perhaps something written down' " but did not elaborate. He said nothing was found after Masaryk's death but the Bible, which was opened to a page Masaryk had tried to find a day or two earlier, at that time unmarked, according to Soukoup. The night before his death, Soukoup said, Masaryk remained alone, "facing the might of the opposing forces, with their materialistic philosophy and greed for power, seemingly victorious." Soukoup believes that Masaryk saw St. Paul's Epistle to the Galatians, "discovered the inadequacy of all his eloquent words and phrases," then read chapter 5, drawing a circle around verses 22 and 24. "And he underlined each word. . . . Then, carefully laying it open on his bedside table, he walked to the adjoining room, opened the window, and . . ."

Thus ended Dr. Soukoup's article in the *Scotsman* and his case. The contents were dampening, the prose hardly less so, the author almost unknown to his compatriots, having fled to Scotland in July, 1948, and stayed there. Nevertheless, Dr. Soukoup had unquestionably known Masaryk well, and possessed a quantity of material on the Foreign Minister's dealings with the Russians over the years. He could not be ignored, and was not. Reporters traveled up from Fleet Street to see him; a Czechoslovak television crew went all the way to Glasgow to film him; so did State Prosecutor Kotlar, coming back with an eight-hour tape-recorded interview. Eventually, I went too. By then, however, it was not so much to learn what he had to say as why he was saying it.

It was clear from the beginning that a strong argument could be made for Masaryk's suicide. But it didn't take long to discover that Dr. Soukoup—who happened to have been down with a fever during the week Masaryk died—was telling some whoppers. I had only to drop in on Jan's pet nieces, Herberta and Anna, to discover at least two. The rally in Old Town Square which so enraged Masaryk did not take place on Saturday, March 6, as Soukoup had written, but on Sunday, when Soukoup was not in his office and thus could not have been present to notice Masaryk's reaction upon returning. When Masaryk went to Lany on the afternoon of that same Sunday, his niece Herberta went with him. He sent his car for her, she told me, and they drove to the cemetery together, along with Jan's sister Alice. Dr. Soukoup was nowhere in sight. Jan spent five minutes at his parents' grave. He showed no disturbing signs of melancholy, decidedly did not kneel to touch the ground, and, on returning to Prague, assuredly did not say a word about God and his father forgiving him. Had he been guilty of such revolting bathos, both ladies agreed, he could not be the uncle they had adored since infancy.

But Soukoup wasn't the only one to tell tall stories. An astonishing amount of the testimony appearing in those early weeks consisted of half-truths, evasions, delusions, fancies, and deliberate falsehoods. I was awash in them from the day I rang my first doorbell.

Chapter 3

The man answering my ring was one of the only two alive who were summoned officially to Czernin Palace when Masaryk's body was found. Dr. Zdeněk Borkovec wasn't expecting me, and I waited some time on the drab landing, tan wallpaper curling over the mottled molding, a dejected fifteen-watt bulb overhead. It was hard to tell in the gloom whether he was pleased or reluctant to let me in. Both, I decided, after we'd talked a while.

The living room was cramped and cheerless—iron day bed, bookcase, sagging armchair, a square table covered in plastic—and Dr. Borkovec seemed to take up most of the space. He wasn't heavy but there was a generous sweep to him: bulky frame, strong jaw, beak of a nose, direct blue eyes startlingly light and clear under a close cap of white hair. Any movie director would have snapped him up for the role of a veteran Scotland Yard detective. Yet a hesitant note, a flicker of caution, jarred with the rest. A criminologist of international standing, for half a lifetime, he had spent most of the other half learning to keep his mouth shut: four years in prison, sixteen more as a truck driver. He was obviously longing to talk about the case, but he was not uttering a syllable he might be sorry for.

"I really have very little tell you, except that I'm not dead, of course," he began, pulling chairs up to the table, bringing coffee. "You've probably heard that it was my brother František who was executed in 1948, and he wasn't in police work. Neither was I, after the spring of 1948, and I wasn't on the Masaryk case long enough to learn much. What can I do for you?"

He could probably do more than anyone to help me get my bearings, I told him. I already knew, after working my way through a mass of conflicting testimony, that none of the evidence coming out in the press could be taken for granted. Dr. Borkovec was a highly trained investigator, among the first to reach the scene on the morning of March 10 and reportedly among the few, living or dead, who may have gotten close to the truth. Would he set me straight, first of all, about his role in the case?

He assured me at once that *Student's* story about him was fiction almost from beginning to end. He was not working for the security police when Masaryk died but was Chief of Criminal Investigation for the regular Prague police. As such, he was taken off the case almost as soon as he got on it—in fact, within an hour of his arrival at Czernin Palace. He did not continue to investigate on his own, and was hardly in a position to look into the murder of the shadowy Major Schramm, supposedly responsible for Masaryk's death, still less to track down Schramm's alleged accomplice, the palace guard with a convenient toothache. Major Schramm was murdered at the end of May, 1948, as Dr. Borkovec recalled. He himself was dismissed from the Police Department at least two weeks earlier. Nobody ever told him why. Perhaps he saw something he shouldn't have seen at the palace, I suggested. Possibly, he answered, but he barely had time to look around.

He was called to the palace a little before seven, sending the car back at once for the police doctor, Jaromír Teplý. The Minister's body was lying on its back slightly twisted to one side, about three yards from the courtyard wall and a few feet to the left of his bathroom window. The head lay toward the wall, the face was uninjured, the heels splintered. There was scarcely any blood. He did not examine the body carefully; that was Teplý's job.

"But Teplý told you what he found?"

"No, he didn't. I was off the case by eight o'clock. It wasn't my business any more."

"You did get to see the apartment, though, before you left?"

"We both did. I went upstairs with Teplý fifteen minutes later. There was some disorder up there, but too many officials were milling around the place for me to examine it properly." The bed was unmade, he went on, and the ashtray on the night table was full of cigarette butts; there was a copy of Hašek's *Good Soldier Schweik* beside it. He didn't notice a Bible. In the bathroom, he saw the window open, a smear of excrement on the window sill, crushed glass on the floor, and a pillow in the tub. He had no chance to see or do much more before somebody from the Interior Ministry gave him "a tactful hint to disappear," saying the security police would take over.

"That was irregular?"

"Very irregular."

"And suspicious?"

He smiled. "I said irregular."

Would he call the excrement, broken glass, and pillow in the bathroom suspicious?

"I'd call them worth looking into." His smile this time was apologetic, but the flicker remained in those clear blue eyes. "Naturally I would have sent that stuff in the bathroom to the police laboratory, and ordered a reconstruction of the body's fall besides. I have no idea if the Security Police did that. Probably not; they didn't have the right equipment."

I asked who was there, milling around that morning. The names read like the roster of a Communist board meeting:

Klement Gottwald, Premier
Vladimír Clementis, Deputy Foreign Minister

Václav Nosek, Interior Minister
Jindřich Veselý, Deputy Interior Minister
Jan Hora, Chief of State Security
Josef Gorner, National Director of the CID

Dr. Borkovec was the only non-Communist present. Could this have been the reason he was told to leave? Might the others have tampered with the evidence before he came, or after he went? He wouldn't speculate on things like that. In any event, they closed the case in six hours, with an official verdict of suicide. Would he have done this, if he were in charge, after what he had seen?

"I probably wouldn't close a chicken-stealing case in six hours." The extraordinary eyes warmed from ice blue to the color of a pale sea. "Certainly I would have looked into it further, as a matter of course. But I was *not* in charge, and I couldn't say, from the little I saw, whether or not the verdict was wrong. No professional would make up his mind about suicide or murder without knowing a lot more than I did, or do. I've never seen the results of the laboratory tests, if there were any, or the testimony collected that morning, or the contents of the autopsy report, or Dr. Teplý's findings. The State Prosecutor's office has all that material now. You should be talking to Kotlar, not me. More coffee?"

I was expecting polite dismissal, Dr. Borkovec having apparently said as much as he intended to say. But it was evident, when he had pottered around the kitchen and come back with the tray, that he was tempted to go on. Was there anything in particular to make him think of reconstructing the body's fall, I asked, uncertain where to probe. It was standard procedure, often the quickest way to determine murder or suicide, he replied. Nobody could be sure, just from looking at the position of the body, whether Masaryk jumped or was pushed; and there was no point guessing about it, as so many people were doing nowadays. His former superior in the CID, Dr. Gorner, had come up with the notion, for instance, that Masaryk sat on the window sill facing inward, and threw himself out in a backward somersault. Dr. Gorner, being younger, had less experience than he, Dr. Borkovec, had had in such situations, and so might indulge in such theories—not that the backward somersault idea was any sillier than several others. The question could easily be settled by experimenting with a simulated body of Masaryk's height and weight, dropping the precise distance from the window to the courtyard. He presumed that State Prosecutor Kotlar would get around to doing this eventually. Obviously the experiment would have to take other things into account—for instance, the internal injuries and external marks on the body. Here again, secret documents in the archives were essential. The autopsy report would not be enough; one would also have to see what Dr. Teplý had to say. . . .

He had approached the subject of Dr. Teplý several times and always skittered away. Now, I tried to hold him to it. There were rumors that Teplý had died—might even have been killed —because he knew, or suspected, that Masaryk was murdered. Dr. Borkovec himself seemed to imply possible discrepancies between Teplý's findings and the official suicide verdict. He was present when Teplý examined the corpse, knew the police doctor well, had worked closely with him. Did Teplý never mention the case to Dr. Borkovec after the morning of March 10? Was it true that excrement was found on the body as well as the window sill, raising doubts in Teplý's mind about suicide? Was there anything else about the appearance or position of the corpse to justify such doubts? Did Teplý die by his own hand?

Dr. Borkovec gave me a long blue look. He had no firsthand knowledge about Teplý's death, he answered. It might "perhaps" have been suicide, but that didn't really matter. What mattered was *why* Teplý died, not how. "I don't know what he saw—or said he saw, in his report to the security police. I can only tell you this: whatever he wrote or didn't write was probably the reason he died. If you want to get to the bottom of Masaryk's death, I'd advise you to look into Dr. Teplý's."

He stood up, the interview over. "Come back if you like, and let me know how you're doing."

Gladly, I thought, ducking through a fine drizzle to the car, wondering how much he was holding back. I had no great hopes of finding out from other eyewitnesses. Apart from the dead Teplý, the only others I knew of who must have seen what Dr. Borkovec saw that morning were those six Communist functionaries he mentioned. There could scarcely be much help from that quarter.

The list was in fact among the most intriguing items I'd picked up from Dr. Borkovec. All the names were familiar to me, clicking into place as I thought back over the country's troubled history from 1945 to 1948. At the head of the list was Klement Gottwald, guiding the Czechoslovak Communist Party since 1929, devotedly carrying out Stalin's instructions, preparing since the outbreak of the Second World War, with elaborate attention to detail, for the takeover in February, 1948. The preparations required two kinds of activists. Some worked among the masses, dispensing political prescriptions and patronage; others operated offstage, technicians responsible for the smooth transition to power and its maintenance thereafter. Only one of the six present at Czernin Palace in the early hours of March 10 belonged in the first category: Vladimír Clementis, Jan Masaryk's Deputy in the Foreign Minstry, a popular and sympathetic figure above the common run of sectarian party hacks, liked and respected by many non-Communists, including Masaryk. Among the others present at the palace were some of the best technicians in the business.

Although Václav Nosek was titular head of the Interior Ministry at the time, he was outranked in the party hierarchy by his Deputy, Jindřich Veselý (author of those deadly accurate lines on President Beneš) . A Stalinist of impeccable faith and morals, Veselý belonged to a restricted ruling caste presiding over the murky underworld of the secret-police and espionage services, answerable for his actions directly to the Czechoslovak Party

Presidium and the Kremlin. Within days of the February coup, he was chosen by the Presidium, after consultation with Stalin's emissary Valerian Zorin, as one of the five top Communists—Interior Minister Nosek not among them—responsible for state security.

Doubtless it was Veselý, therefore, who took charge at Czernin Palace that morning; and if there was indeed something to be covered up, he had plenty of helping hands. Jan Hora, Director of State Security, was a trusted lieutenant officially under his command. So was Josef Gorner, national director of the Criminal Investigation Department for the regular police. Interior Minister Nosek was a competent and loyal collaborator. All three not only had unblemished party records but also had helped personally to suppress or falsify evidence of the Communist plot to assassinate Jan Masaryk barely half a year before he died.

Among the dozens of books I had read on the background of the 1948 *Putsch* were several describing in detail the perfume-box plot in September, 1947. Hubert Ripka, Minister of Foreign Trade in those days and a leading member of Eduard Beneš's National Socialist Party, reported it this way:

"The day after the bombs were sent (September 11), Rudolf Slansky, the Communist Party's Secretary-General, declared at a public meeting that the National Socialists had organized the attack themselves. Faced with this revolting calumny, we demanded a thorough investigation without delay. During the first two days, the police limited themselves to providing a stenographic record of the questioning of persons to whom the packets were delivered [National Socialist Chairman Peter Zenkl, Justice Minister Prokop Drtina, Masaryk himself]. The Interior Minister, Nosek, then announced that he had set up a special investigating commission headed by *Hora* and *Gorner,* both Communists known for their fanaticism. The commission bustled about to give the impression that it was doing its utmost to discover the authors of the crime. Thus special films were exhibited in all cinemas showing the most minute details of the three boxes of explosives, and promising substantial rewards to anyone putting the authorities on the trail of the culprits.

"A little later the Interior Minister announced that boxes identical to those used in the crime were manufactured in Prague by one Stanislav Pilař, who had sold them to a retail store. Pilař identified the boxes as being of his manufacture. Finally the police reported having found, in a small pond on the banks of the Vltava, several packages of explosives of German origin, identical to those used in the attempt.

"These were the only two facts revealed by the investigation. Every time we put questions on this matter to the Interior Minister at cabinet meetings, he answered that in spite of unremitting search, no clue had been discovered leading to the identification of the guilty persons. But we on our side were working to throw light on the affair. . . ."

Gradually, the democrats unraveled this story, as reported by Hubert Ripka and Josef Korbel, former Czechoslovak representative to the United Nations:

The alleged box manufacturer, Pilař, was a militant Communist; he often went fishing near the spot where the explosives were discovered. This spot was a depression several yards deep and filled with dirty water, an unlikely place to search unless the police knew where to look. It soon turned out that Pilař hadn't made the boxes anyway. They were made by a carpenter in Krčmáň, near Olomouc, called Jan Kopka, who admitted to knowing their intended use. Also a Communist, Kopka confessed to the regional police in Brno, the Moravian capital, and was sent to Prague for questioning. There he was interrogated by Dr. Gorner, the CID chief, who interrupted his confession—and precise identification of the boxes—to say he was lying, since the police already knew who made the boxes. Gorner then personally dictated the minutes of the testimony, told the astonished Kopka to sign, and ordered his release. Later, Gorner telephoned to the secret police in Olomouc—his call was tapped

—giving detailed instructions for destroying all traces of the plot.

The democrats were not yet beaten. They brought charges before the District Court of Olomouc, permitting Drtina's Ministry of Justice to pursue the investigation formally. Kopka was rearrested, and a search of his carpentry shop revealed a substantial cache of arms: machine guns, hand grenades, ammunition. On a tip from Kopka, a much bigger arsenal was found at the home of a fellow Communist, a railwayman named Opluštil. Also arrested, Opluštil confessed that the weapons were transferred to his house immediately after Kopka's arrest, by the local Party Secretariat. When he showed a reluctance to hide them, a Communist Deputy in Parliament warned him: "If you don't do it, or ever breathe a single word about it, you could be crushed between two cars, or fall off a train, without anybody ever knowing how it happened." From a chain of supporting confessions, it then came out that this Communist Deputy, J. Juri-Sosnar, had himself made the bombs for the plot, using explosives from the Olomouc depot, where a quantity was found bearing the same serial number. He had been instructed to make them by Gottwald's son-in-law Alexej Čepička.

The trial, scheduled for March, 1948, did not take place for obvious reasons. All those indicted as accomplices in the plot were released from prison immediately after the February coup; Deputy Juri-Sosnar was greeted as he came out by a large Communist reception committee and a brass band. Simultaneously, the non-Communist prosecutor handling the case for the Olomouc Court was arrested, as were all non-Communist witnesses for the prosecution. The last of these witnesses died on September 10, 1968, without uttering another word on the case; his tongue had been cut out in prison.

Among the non-Communists arrested in this connection was Viktor Krajina, the partisan hero and National Socialist Secretary, who later escaped. Once safely in the West, he revealed that Soviet NKVD agents had worked with local Communists from the start in the perfume-box plot. Of the five security police officers who came to arrest him personally, one, speaking Russian only, was obviously from the NKVD.

The judicial orders whereby the accused were freed and their accusers imprisoned were signed by Gottwald's new Minister of Justice, Alexej Čepička, whose juridical concepts were best summed up in his own words. "Yes, I admit it," he once said proudly at a public meeting. "I will violate the law as often as political interests demand it."

Here, then, was the background of those six Communist functionaries milling around in Masaryk's apartment on the morning of March 10, thirteen days after the Communist takeover. Whatever they may have done at Czernin Palace, they were not the men to confide their secrets; and by the spring of 1968, all but one were long dead. Vladimír Clementis was executed in the Slánský trials in 1952. Jindřich Veselý, fired from the Interior Ministry in 1950, ended by committing suicide. Jan Hora, thrown out of his state security post less than a month after Masaryk's death, died of natural causes later. So did Interior Minister Nosek and Klement Gottwald, the latter within two weeks of Stalin. Josef Gorner alone was alive, and reportedly he didn't stay at the palace long.

Still, Dr. Gorner should be well worth a visit. Vice President of Interpol in 1948 as well as national CID Director, he had apparently taken a shrewd look at the future early on. He resigned discreetly from both posts in 1951, withdrawing to peaceful anonymity in the offices of the National Historical Archives. That was where I found him, burrowing among stacked volumes of scholarly works, courteous though not visibly delighted to receive me. There was scarcely a whiff of the policeman about him now, flab setting in at the waist, hands indecisive and soft, gray eyes retreating behind rimless glasses. Considerably younger than Dr. Borkovec, he appeared to have left his youth behind years before, gratefully exchanging the hazards of an inquisitive mind for the autumnal comforts of security. He was plainly attached to his impersonal little office, puttering around it as we talked, shifting a metal chair, flicking dust from the leaves of a bristling rubber plant, straightening a corner of the linoleum matting.

"I hope you haven't been taken in by all this nonsense about Masaryk," he began, setting a box of cigarettes and matches between us. "Actually the case is *not* complex and never was. I tried to go to the core of the matter at the time, and I was satisfied then, as I am now. Of course my view seems pro-Soviet these days, because nobody is bothering to discuss *facts*. It was always the political side of this affair that created complications; when politics get into any case with criminal features, a criminologist is an unhappy being."

He was relieved, then, to be off the case before long?

"Well, yes, in a way, though I wasn't officially assigned to it. Borkovec was naturally called in, from our Prague headquarters, and I just went along, since it was so important. We both thought it incorrect for the security police to take over. But I was more or less expecting it under the circumstances."

And he was reasonably sure of suicide from the start? He didn't doubt it, knowing what Masaryk was up against. There was no plausible motive for murder, after all; the Communists had everything to gain by keeping him alive. Some people in the West were finally able to overcome their prejudice and accept this; the recent testimony of Masaryk's secretary in Glasgow, Dr. Soukoup, was especially realistic. "It was psychology that counted most. Masaryk was sensitive, with a deep feeling for music. He was a believer in God, a man who obviously disagreed with the February events, who had an extraordinary love for our people and was under extreme pressure from Western statesmen. His solution was quite understandable."

All the same, I insisted, an expert must evaluate factual evidence as well as psychological motivations. Dr. Gorner nodded gravely, apparently carried back to the days when he had done little else. He was not in the habit of making intuitive judgments, he said, although in this instance he did have to rely more on the observations of others than on his own. For example, he'd made only a cursory examination of the corpse, assuming there would be a full autopsy later, and he was only upstairs about twenty minutes. The disorder reported in the press was much exaggerated. The bedroom was about the way you'd expect an untidy bachelor to leave it; and the bathroom, with the broken glass and pillow in the tub, merely indicated that Masaryk must have gone to pieces at the last minute. Some things were photographed, he remembered, and a piece of the bathroom window sill was cut out, presumably for laboratory study of the excrement. Admittedly the procedure didn't seem as thorough as the CID's would have been. "Obviously the case was not expertly investigated, not enough was done, and I can't say if the security police really finished the job. But I had no reason to question their decision. I believe Borkovec agreed with me."

I had the impression, I said, that Dr. Borkovec thought there were unsettled questions about the appearance, or position, of the body. There were rumors that the police doctor, Teplý, was also bothered by this, and even that his own death was somehow connected to it.

"I see no connection whatsoever between Teplý's death and Masaryk's." Dr. Gorner abandoned his inspection of the rubber plant to drive his point home. "The fall did happen in an unusual way, but I'd already seen such suicides. The position suggested what we call the candle way of falling, upright and feet first—nothing exceptional about that. And the autopsy confirmed that his feet were crushed by the fall. I saw the feet myself: you couldn't fake that. So it excludes any manipulation on the ground afterward."

His own theory wasn't quite the candle way, I objected, puzzled. Wasn't there a difference between that and a backward somersault? There was a slight difference, because certain features had to be taken into account, he explained, moving to the cretonne-curtained window to demonstrate. "Masaryk's bathroom window was rather small, about one yard high and wide, I'd say, and the Minister was a big man—probably weighed two hundred pounds. He couldn't have just stood up on the sill and jumped. The smear of excrement on the window sill indicated that he was sitting down. There was a long abrasion on his abdomen, as you know" (I didn't know) "which suggested that he scraped against the wall as he fell. He couldn't have done this if he'd jumped face forward. So he would have had to go out backward, head over heels. The fingerprints confirmed this. . . ."

"Where were the fingerprints, exactly?" I interrupted, trying not to betray surprise. "On the sides of the window casing, I believe, or on the window frame—I don't recall, precisely. At any rate, the inward position was perfectly clear. I once had an almost identical suicide case: the man sat like that and let his body fall backward because he was afraid of looking down into the depths. I'm told Masaryk suffered from vertigo. . . ."

Had he also come across situations where a man lost control of his bowels before taking his life, I asked. Wasn't that supposed to be a symptom of intense fear, which a suicide presumably doesn't feel once his decision is made? Not at all, replied Dr. Gorner with the patient air of someone who must have explained this to laymen a good many times over. The symptom didn't show up often in suicides, but was known to happen, with people who were afraid of pain. He'd heard that Masaryk had inordinate fears of this kind. No doubt I would find it so, if I inquired.

I would ask about it, I agreed, wanting suddenly to end the conversation. I didn't know if Dr. Gorner shared the lurch of pity I felt as we sat there amongst his potted greenery, casually exploring the unknown terrors of a man within minutes of dying. Was that how Jan Masaryk left the world—cringing, trying not to look? I thanked Dr. Gorner, who was plainly anxious to get back to his work, and hurried out of the ugly red-brick building that had kept him safe and sound for all these years.

Prague was lovely in the soft gray light of a rainy spring afternoon, and I dropped in at the Café Slavia, overlooking the river, for a twilight view. The Slavia was crowded as always at this hour, bearded law-school students wedged into alcoves with improbable blondes in oversized sunglasses and mini-skirts, writers and journalists arguing politics over their Pilsner beers and evening papers. A radio commentator I knew waved from a corner table, making room for me on a stiff settee of Joan Crawford vintage. Had I heard the latest from Moscow, he asked, stabbing at the offending paragraphs with a vicious pen. Tass had hit the roof today, stung by a charge in the Czechoslovak Communist daily, *Rudé Právo,* that Masaryk was murdered by Beria's gorillas. "Some misguided people in fraternal Czechoslovakia . . . were spreading slanderous reports" on Jan Masaryk's death "to stir up anti-Soviet moods among politically unstable people," warned the Soviet news agency, and "echoing long-forgotten reactionary legends" about his father. Tomáš Masaryk, the Czechoslovaks' "so-called" Founder and Liberator, was actually an "anti-Marxist tool of the imperialists," who had organized an uprising of Czechoslovak troops in Siberia after the Bolshevik Revolution and paid a Russian terrorist two hundred thousand rubles to assassinate Lenin. "No matter how many wreaths may be laid on his grave, Tomáš Masaryk remains what he has always been: a dangerous enemy of the Soviet people."

"They're out for blood," my friend remarked, not having the palest idea of how right he was. Everybody at the table, and probably half the people in the room, had written about the Masaryk case, each word flicking the Russians on the raw. The Dubček regime, already under intense pressure from Moscow, was pleading for restraint. But talking to Prague's journalists in those days was like talking to the wall. They were going to find out whatever there was to know about Jan Masaryk and the Russians could like it or lump it. Yet the risk might be greater than the reward. There could hardly be a simple, straightforward solution to this mystery. No one whose path had crossed Masaryk's around the time he died was likely to have come through the next twenty years without emotional scars. There were my two star witnesses, for example, neither perhaps consciously lying but surely not telling all they knew. Both were political casualties, Dr. Borkovec muted by his broken career, Dr. Gorner's vision blurred by his Marxist faith. How many more, caught under the political wheels that had never stopped grinding since Masaryk died, were maimed in spirit? Could a single witness have escaped unharmed?

Chapter 4

Czernin Palace is more imposing than beautiful, with its lofty vaulted ceilings, vast, cold ballrooms, austere marble corridors encased in glass. It was a barracks for the Imperial Austrian Army in the Hapsburgs' day—fittingly, Masaryk thought. He would willingly have exchanged it for his snug Westminster flat in London, kept up for him until he died. Even in his private quarters, he lived mostly in the bedroom, disliking the heavily draped and upholstered formality of the adjoining drawing room. But he was no safer there than anywhere else in the last weeks of his life. His telephone was tapped, his walls were bugged, every spoken word was transmitted to the Czechoslovak security police (STB) and relayed to the Soviet NKVD. Security agents loitered in the palace grounds, scrutinizing visitors, trailing the Foreign Minister wherever he went; and what they didn't know they could probably pry out of somebody on his household staff.

The butler, Příhoda, an old family retainer in the Masaryks' service for twenty-eight years, was a tippler, garrulous in his cups. The household purser, Topinka, and his plump, rosy wife had come to him after eighteen years with President Beneš, but the wife in particular was too excitable to be altogether reliable.

The chauffeur, Dohnálek, seemed incapable of treachery except at the wheel—he was such an awful driver that Masaryk usually drove himself—but was slow-witted, easily pumped. Masaryk's personal bodyguard, Vyšín, though seemingly loyal, was officially on the STB payroll. His three private secretaries had been with him a relatively short while. Jiří Špaček, senior among them, was much the closest, a steadfast aide since the Minister's return to Czechoslovakia in 1945. Antonín Šum, young and inexperienced, had worked for him only six months, joining the staff in September, 1947; and Masaryk himself had been away for half that time, attending a UN General Assembly session in New York. Lumír Soukoup, a student in Edinburgh when Masaryk recruited him for part-time secretarial work during the war, did not come to Prague until December, 1947, barely three months before Masaryk died. If he had no reason to question the fidelity of all three secretaries, he took none fully into his confidence toward the last.

By then he wasn't confiding in anybody. Reticence and guile, new to him, were his last refuge. To his sister Alice, whom he cherished above all creatures, he said not a word about his plans. To others he said too much to reveal his true intentions. He was leaving the country; he would never leave; suicide was the only way out; it was no way out; he would go down fighting; there was nothing left to fight for—he told one thing or another, or hinted as much, to a score of people. He may have been trying deliberately to cover his tracks, or desperately to find comfort and counsel. The one certainty is that nobody knew what he really meant to do. He was utterly alone when the moment for decision came.

The decision could not be long delayed. Everybody on his staff at the palace sensed that. Yet they had not the smallest sign, seeing him hourly from morning to evening on Tuesday, March 9, that he would be dead the following day. This much at least they could agree on twenty years later—all but the chauffeur still alive, nursing their memories.

I started with Příhoda, the butler, very old now, eyes veiled by a milky film, grayish pallor on his trembling cheeks, fitful mind never far from thoughts of his own impending death. His small flat in Mala Strana was full of it, somber, silent, permeated with the musty odor of aging flesh. He used to cry a lot about Masaryk, he said, but not any more: it was so long ago. Something was wrong, he'd always known that. The Minister was absolutely normal all day before it happened, a little tired maybe, not as cheerful as he was before the February events, but cheerful enough. When Příhoda brought his breakfast, at eight on March 9, they chatted as usual. At nine, Pavel Kavan, Counselor of the Czechoslovak Embassy in London, called in briefly. Then General Hasal came by and the Minister left with him for Sezimovo Usti, the President's country house: the new Polish Ambassador was supposed to present his credentials that morning.

The Minister came back around two in the afternoon, ate a good lunch, and went to bed, asking to be called at four. When Příhoda woke him, he decided to stay in bed; he was just getting over a bout of bronchitis and hadn't quite recovered. One of his secretaries, Jiří Špaček, brought Dr. Kavan into the bedroom for another visit around five—the Counselor was returning to London in the morning—and returned after Kavan left, staying until about eight. Then Příhoda brought dinner on a tray: cold roast chicken, potatoes, salad. The Minister ate heartily, saying how much he enjoyed it. He seemed entirely himself. "He wasn't excited or nervous—nothing like that." At 9:30, Příhoda cleared away. Before leaving, he set a bottle of beer, two bottles of mineral water, and two sleeping pills on the night table, and opened the bedroom window, as was customary. The Minister was settled comfortably in bed, with a large writing pad. "And, Příhoda," he called out as the butler left, "tomorrow morning at half past eight! Thank you and good night."

The story came out haltingly, sentences left trailing, voice fading as Příhoda drifted into the mists of recollection. But he was firm enough about the facts, repeating them several times. Had he noticed anything unusual that day? Not that day, but the one before, yes. On Monday, Masaryk took him aside. "He tells me he has to burn something. I say all right, I'll take it down to the furnace and burn it there. 'Not like that,' he says, 'not like that. Can't you burn it someplace else?' I say, only in my kitchen upstairs, because we have a stove that goes with gas and coal there. So we take the trash basket, he has documents and packages in it . . . and he comes upstairs with me. I tell my wife to go away, because Vera isn't supposed to know what's going on, I send her to another room, and we stand there, burning everything. But it wasn't so easy, those packages were thick. I had to soak them in gasoline to get them all burned up."

Did Příhoda know what was in the packages? Dollars, he said, wads of dollars. And the Minister didn't explain? No, no, Mr. Minister wouldn't give away secrets like that.

I asked what he thought when he was told that Masaryk was dead. He didn't know what to think, he replied. His rooms were just over Masaryk's, but he had heard nothing during the night, not even the sound of the body falling. The first he knew of it was when he was called down around seven in the morning, to bring Interior Minister Nosek up in the lift. He was too upset to notice much. He couldn't understand the condition of the apartment, though, especially the bathroom—a pillow in the tub, another under the sink, razor blades scattered all over the glass shelf above the sink, pajama cords wound together in a rope hanging from the doorknob, everything else upside down, the window wide open there when it was always kept shut. Nothing like this had ever happened. "Mr. Minister would never take out his own razor blades. . . . They were in the hall, in a cupboard, I kept them there myself, I would always put a fresh one in his razor, every morning. And would he sleep in the *bathtub?* No, never, I never saw anything like it. . . ."

Might somebody have gotten into the apartment late at night, I asked. How could they? The staircase doors were closed, locked, there was only the private lift, and nobody had a key to it except the Minister and Příhoda. But into the palace, yes, anybody could get into the palace. Příhoda's son used to do it all the time when he'd sneak home late and didn't want to be seen: he'd just climb the back garden wall, hardly three feet high, get in the back door to the boiler room, go through the cellar and up the rear servants' staircase.

Nevertheless Příhoda didn't hear a sound that night. Footsteps, a scuffle, cars coming and going? Not a sound. He could never understand it, till he died. But it was not for him to pass judgment. . . . The knotted hands, brown-blotched and thickly veined, shook as we said goodbye. Too old for tears, he was not yet past remembrance.

It was different with Topinka, springy and bustling now as he was in the exciting times when the Minister would ask him, without batting an eye, to lay on a grand banquet for one or two hundred guests on forty-eight hours' notice. The Minister always made impossible demands, and Topinka, keeper of the household—and Masaryk's—purse, loved nothing better. Here, it was clear, was the kind of domestic pearl that a servantless generation has heard about but never seen: efficient, indefatigable, doggedly devoted, bossy. Masaryk couldn't even accept an invitation for a game of cards without consulting him, he told me proudly. "I'll come if Topinka will give me some money," the Minister would say, and the purser, big ears red with pleasure, quick little eyes beaming over a sharp tiptilted nose, would dole out the crowns with a scolding shake of the head for his employer's incurable extravagance.

Working for Jan Masaryk was the great experience of his life. Thrown out of the palace and every job he managed to land afterward, he had scraped through the next two decades on whatever his wife could earn, poring over yellowed clippings, photographs, and letters, reliving the past. "There!" he said, opening a treasured architectural volume on Czernin Palace. That was the corridor opening on to the flat, this the door of the lift, there the bathroom window, here the courtyard. "They didn't notice him at first, you see, because he lay behind this column, to the side—no, much farther to the side, yards away. They only saw him when they came back down, through the glass door. . . ."

Who were "they," I inquired. The palace stokers, Merxbauer and his brother-in-law Pomezný, Topinka answered, surprised at my ignorance. Ordered to lower a ceremonial flag at dawn, the two had gone up to the roof around five in the morning, getting the key from Příhoda's wife, and had seen Masaryk's corpse as they came down again half an hour later. They had at once informed the policeman on duty in the residence wing of the palace, who telephoned from the porter's lodge to tell Topinka that something terrible had happened. Topinka, rushing to Masaryk's apartment, was appalled by what he saw.

He was the first one there. The bedroom was a shambles, bed awry and wildly tumbled, sheets pulled from the mattress and pillows missing. The night table was tilted, *Good Soldier Schweik* and the Bible (unopened) hanging over the edge, broken bottles and glass flung to the floor. Chairs were overturned, closet doors and bureau drawers open, shirts and pajamas spilled out. In the bathroom, the medicine chest was empty, the floor covered with crushed glass, one pillow under the sink, another in the tub, bathmat tossed across the room, all the towels pulled down and crumpled, toilet bowl filthy with excrement, window sill smeared with it, window seat overturned, fingerprints on the wall around it.

Frightened, Topinka ran out of the apartment to look for the Minister, down the long corridor, through the loggia, until, rounding a corner and glancing downward, he saw the covered body below. As he reached the courtyard—it was then around six-thirty—Interior Minister Nosek arrived with Deputy Foreign Minister Clementis. "What's going on here?" Clementis asked Topinka. "I don't know what's going on," he answered, sobbing. They went up in the lift together: Nosek, Clementis,

Příhoda, Topinka. Once in the apartment, Nosek quickly sent the servants away and shut the door.

Just before seven, CID Inspector Borkovec came, followed shortly afterward by the police doctor Teplý. Around seven-thirty, Dr. Teplý had the body carried upstairs. Sometime near ten, Teplý told Topinka that the household staff might come to say goodbye. The body by then was not in Masaryk's bedroom but laid out in a guest apartment across the hall. Several officials were present as the servants filed in, among them Minister Nosek's *chef de cabinet,* Richard Spurný, and Dr. Teplý. "We all stood at the foot of the bed, crying," Topinka went on, crying himself as he recalled the scene. "Then the washerwoman Mařenka whispered to me, 'Why are his pajamas wrong side out?' Women notice that kind of thing, I wouldn't have seen it otherwise. And then my wife went right up to him—she couldn't believe he was dead, his eyes were open. 'Jesus Maria, what's this?' she said. There was this big blue bruise on the side of his head, his fingernails were full of plaster and paint, and when she bent to kiss his forehead she saw a little hole, like a pea, behind his ear, with dried blood around it. 'What's this, what's this?' she kept saying, and Dr. Teplý came over and told her, 'Clear out, all of you, you can't stay here any more.' "

Was Topinka sure about the hole behind Masaryk's ear? Not positive, he didn't see it himself, his wife was the only one who went close to the body and touched it. But he did suspect violence? How couldn't he, he asked, still in tears. His first thought, when the policeman phoned up to him, was that Masaryk must have fled the country in frantic haste. Nothing in the Minister's behavior the previous day had suggested the possibility of suicide. Topinka had been in and out on Tuesday, the Minister joking with him as always. He had seen him at lunchtime and again around eight in the evening, when he went in with Příhoda for a few words with the Minister. There was a new cook, Nezerka, young and not too self-confident, worried about the dinner. "Very good, excellent," the Minister reassured Topinka. "Tell the cook not to worry."

Later, around midnight, when Topinka was in his room going over the household accounts, he noticed that the lights were
still on in the Minister's bedroom. Though he had a clear view
from his own window across the courtyard, he did not see the
Minister there. Did he hear the thud of a body falling? No, he'd
heard nothing. Might somebody have entered Masaryk's apartment without Topinka's hearing or noticing? Of course, after
midnight, when he was asleep, he wouldn't have heard a thing,
his room was across the courtyard. Lots of people had keys to
the Minister's private lift: Příhoda, the cook, the laundress, the
charwoman, the Minister's sister Alice, the bodyguard Vyšín and
another secret policeman who used to be a second bodyguard,
Topinka himself—there were twelve keys in all.

Příhoda had said there were only two, I remarked. Topinka's
shrug needed no explanation. Did Příhoda tell him about the
mysterious papers that the Minister burned the day before?
Yes, he'd mentioned it—lots of dollars, he'd said—and Topinka
told him to shut his trap. The old butler was drunk again, he
said; he was at the bottle from morning to night, the Minister
was too softhearted to get rid of him.

I asked about the windows. Was it true that the one in the
bathroom was higher than the one in the bedroom? Not higher,
he answered: both were about four feet from the floor. But
there were two differences. The aperture of the bathroom window was half that of all the others in the flat because the upper
half was cut off by a glass inset in the bathroom ceiling, creating
storage space above (see photograph) . Also, the radiators under
the bedroom windows were set into the wall, while the one in
the bathroom stood out. There was always a screen in front of
it, and a window seat in front of the screen, so it was particularly awkward to get at. What with this and the fact that it
tended to stick, nobody bothered to open it except to clean it.
Certainly the Minister never went near it.

And then, it wasn't right, the way the body fell. Topinka
opened the book on Czernin Palace again, smoothing the pages
tenderly. "Here, you can see where the Minister lay. He must

have been four, five feet to the side of the bathroom window, and far out, maybe four yards. How could he jump like that?" And why the disorder in the flat, he went on, like a battlefield? People said Masaryk was untidy, a typical bachelor, I suggested. Topinka shook his head, indignant. The Minister often left his clothes lying around after undressing; and sometimes, when Topinka would leave salami and pumpernickel on the night table for him—he loved a snack like this when he was reading in bed—he would drop the salami skins lazily on the floor. But never, never would the Minister put his room in such condition. No, it didn't make sense. . . .

Eyes blurry with weeping, the tip of his tilted nose shiny red, Topinka showed me to the door of his bright, spotless flat. I apologized for upsetting him. He was glad, he said. Those were his best years, with the Minister. Just to think of them made him feel better.

He had gone on for hours, rambling but on the whole consistent. Several small details coincided with some I was already fairly sure of and, except for the lift keys, with Příhoda's as well. I doubted that this was prearranged: Topinka was too plainly scornful of the befuddled butler. Still, it was possible that he was magnifying the case for murder, carried away by his adoration for Masaryk. Could a man like Topinka conceive of a man like Jan Masaryk taking his life in such a state of animal terror? For that matter, could I?

At the Alcron lounge that evening, submerged in the famous fumes of cigar smoke and whisky for which it is known in Fleet Street as the Yellow Submarine, I fell into conversation with some older reporters who had known Masaryk well. They swapped stories until midnight: how he would destroy a celebrated bore at a party with a single mordant phrase; how he would play the piano when all but a few cronies had gone home, improvising brilliantly, his music at times wonderfully moving; how fond he was of pub-crawling in London, escaping the stupefying after-dinner talk of cardboard diplomats and their glass wives; how altered and sad he was, that last winter in Prague. The Czechoslovaks worshipped him in those days—they must have had a premonition of things to come—snatching at his clothes and stripping his car for souvenirs. He was bigger than life for them, a folk hero. But that only made him lonelier. He was always lonely, come to think of it, for all his hundreds of friends, especially toward the end, too high on a pedestal built for his father, too long away from home. However he died, it was a sad loss for everybody who knew him. They'd all loved him. Poor man.

Vyšín, the bodyguard, adored him, too. His three years with the Foreign Minister were the happiest of his life, he told me; he'd felt as if he were protecting his uncle. He was forty at the time and must have been very handsome, with his swaggering carriage and Mediterranean coloring—deep brown eyes, swarthy complexion, regular white teeth set off by one of gleaming gold. Masaryk often twitted him for being such a devil with the ladies. "How about *you*, Mr. Minister?" he would reply, delighted with his sally. Things went badly for him after the Minister died. Fired from the security police a year later, he had to start at the bottom of the ladder in the Health Service, washing laboratory glasses, working his way up just far enough to maintain his family in two tiny, cluttered rooms.

He had greeted me with ceremony, hurriedly donning a worn tweed jacket for the occasion, calling to his wife to bring slivovitz, a stealthy odor of cooked cabbage creeping toward us as she opened the kitchen door. Out came the tattered clippings, the signed picture postcards, the sepia photographs from the rotogravures. Here was the Minister holding a baby for a christening; there he was in the grandstand, reviewing a parade, in that flat-crowned, floppy-brimmed hat he would never part with; here he stood in cap and gown, receiving an honorary degree at Brno University, overcome with pride. Masaryk never finished university—did I know that? He was no genius at school, and his father finally packed him off to America to make his way in the world, when he was twenty. He'd gone off with fifty dollars in his pocket, Vyšín informed me, glowing with pride himself, and come back the biggest man in Czechoslovakia. Some said President Beneš was more important. But it was Jan Masaryk the people worshipped—he was one of them, he had the touch.

It sounded as if Vyšín had spent a good deal of time with Masaryk, I said. "Oh yes, I went everywhere with him, even abroad, right from the time he came back to Prague. There used to be two of us assigned to him from the STB. But the other fellow got taken off the job after the February events, and I handled it alone after that. I didn't mind. I'd have worked around the clock for the Minister."

All the same, Masaryk's mood changed a lot after the Communist takeover, Vyšín went on. "He tried to keep up his humorous mask in public, but he was very unhappy, more serious than before." He was lonely too, seeing only a few intimates: his sister Alice who lived on the Loretanska hill, five minutes' walk from Czernin Palace; the American authoress Marcia Davenport, who had a flat across the hall from Alice; Karel Čapek's widow, Olga Scheinpflugová, the actress. Marcia Davenport was especially close; the Minister saw her practically every day, though Vyšín refused to believe he meant to marry her as she claimed. Still, Masaryk was obviously attached to her, and relieved when she got off to London safely on the Sunday before he died.

"He stayed with her much longer than usual on Saturday night, at least two hours, and when he came out I could see he'd taken a drop more than he ordinarily did—he wasn't at all a heavy drinker, though some may say so. Then, Sunday afternoon, coming back from Lany, he kept asking me how the weather was for flying. I couldn't imagine what he was getting at, until I found out later that she left for London that day. He never told me she was leaving Prague. He didn't tell me he was going to join her in London soon either, like she says in her book. Maybe he was just making a promise to reassure her. You know how women are." The gold tooth glittered in a wise smile.

Did Masaryk seem upset or melancholy on that Sunday visit to Lany? Not at all, not on Sunday afternoon. It was in the morning that he was noticeably distraught, after the big rally in Old Town Square, when Communist leaders commemorated Tomáš Masaryk's birthday by saying that the President-Liberator would have approved their "new course"—and his son's presence in the Communist cabinet—if he were alive. The Minister was wild, Vyšín said. "How dare they, the bastards?" he'd muttered, coming away. But his anger seemed to pass after visiting his father's grave in the afternoon. Did Soukoup, the secretary, go along? No, Soukoup's story was drivel. Masaryk was alone in the car that Sunday afternoon, with Vyšín and Dohnálek, the driver. Was Vyšín sure, I pressed, knowing that Masaryk's sister Alice and niece Herberta had gone along. Positive, Vyšín replied, velvet eyes looking squarely into mine. And what happened on the last day, Tuesday?

"I got to the palace around eight, my usual time, to take the Minister from his apartment to his office in the other wing. General Hasal, the Minister of Transport, was with him on Tuesday morning, and he got into the car with us, about half past nine. We stopped off at Premier Gottwald's office in Krakovka Street, the Minister went up with General Hasal and came out alone, and we went on to Sezimovo Usti to the President's country house." Masaryk stayed on for lunch alone with the President after the ceremony with the Polish Ambassador, Vyšín continued, and walked in the garden with Beneš for about an hour afterward—it was such a nice day, you can have days like that in Bohemia in March. Was Vyšín sure, I asked, Příhoda and Topinka having both said that the Minister lunched at Czernin Palace. Yes, certainly. "Before two he came out and said, 'O.K., boys, let's go!' as he always did, and we left for Prague. A peculiar thing happened in the car, he fell asleep.

I'd never seen him do that before. He suffered from insomnia, had an awful time getting to sleep. He used to say to me, 'How do you do it? You sleep like an ox!' But he was fine when he woke up. 'Have a cigarette,' he says to me, and I tell him for the thousandth time that I don't smoke on duty. 'Smoke! I command you!' he tells me—he was pretty frisky. 'Do you want me to indulge my vice all by myself?' "

Back at the palace, Masaryk went straight to his bedroom. Vyšín, checking the day's schedule, saw that there were no outside appointments in the afternoon. Knocking at 4:30, he was dismissed for the day. The Minister had to prepare a speech for Polish-Czechoslovak Friendship Day, and would not be going out. Vyšín never saw him again.

What was his first impression when he heard the news? He was sure it was suicide, and hadn't changed his mind to this day. The sensational stories in the press were poppycock. "Take that chap Straka, the one who said he was working in the palace, and heard those cars drive up, the telephones cut off, all that nonsense. He's a pervert, Straka—a queer, schizophrenic —you can't take his word for anything. Maybe he *was* working that night, but his name wasn't on the register. As for Major Chlumský—! The man's a liar or a lunatic, pure and simple. I can assure you that the Minister did *not* leave Czernin Palace again that night, did *not* visit Clementis, was *not* accosted by a man waiting in a black Tatra. All made up, every word."

Furthermore, continued Vyšín, speaking more slowly for emphasis, nobody got into Masaryk's apartment after nine in the evening. It was easy enough to enter the palace at night, but impossible to enter Masaryk's rooms without a key to the lift; and the only people who had keys were Příhoda, Topinka, the cook, the driver, the three secretaries, and Vyšín himself. (This was the third list of key holders I'd been given.) None of these eight would turn a key over to an intruder, said Vyšín: he could vouch for that. How could he know all this, without having been at the palace himself that evening? He had ways, he said, giving me a cryptic look. And did he see the apartment the next morning? Yes, he was picked up in a police car and brought to Czernin Palace around eight.

"They told me the Minister was found about half past five. The fellows in the courtyard said he was lying three or four yards to the side of the bathroom window. The bones of his feet were splintered, they said, but there wasn't much blood. Apart from the feet, there was only a small wound on the back of the head, and a bruise on the side of the temple. I didn't see the Minister's body in the courtyard, myself. He was laid out on a table in his flat when I came, and that was all I had eyes for. I was crying, it was a terrible shock, I was too grieved to see the scene as a detective." There was "some" disorder in the bedroom, yes; no doubt it would seem odd to an outsider. But Masaryk was a typical bachelor who rarely noticed where he dropped his clothes; when traveling, his hotel room was always a mess. Did the Minister usually put pillows in his bathtub, I inquired. Well, yes, as a matter of fact, Vyšín answered: the Minister liked to rest up in a cool dry tub when he couldn't get to sleep. I mustn't be put off by peculiarities like this, the Minister was not a conventional man. Anyway, Vyšín, who knew him so well, didn't look for suspicious clues. Instinct told him it must be suicide. "He never showed a fear of being killed. And he was so sad. What else could he do?"

Yet Marcia Davenport had written in her recent book that Masaryk lived in terror in those last weeks, that he was convinced the Communists meant to kill him, that the new Communist regime had first withdrawn both of his bodyguards—Vyšín included—and then, after reinstating Vyšín on Masaryk's insistence, assigned "two thugs in leather jackets" to follow the Minister (and Vyšín) everywhere. She had seen them from her window several times, falling into line behind Masaryk as he left her door, and had caught one lurking in the lobby of her own house. Surely Vyšín must have noticed this? No, he knew nothing about it. Not even the Communist government's attempt to remove him, along with his colleague, as Masaryk's bodyguard? No. Really? Really. We smiled at each other, regretfully. No further questions.

Chapter 5

Vaclavske Namesti—Wenceslas Square—is the heart and soul of
Prague, a long, broad slope rimmed with sooty nineteenth-
century façades and crisscrossed with wheezing trams, meeting place for lovers, shoppers, children, journalists and poets,
peanut vendors and flower sellers, newsboys, whores, hawkers,
students, pop singers, idling under the benign bronze shadow
of Saint Wenceslas, munching delicious hot sausages at the
horké párky stalls, discussing life, sex, furniture, politics, skiing
conditions in the Tatra Mountains, the new French food store
around the corner. Here, Praguers made their defiant stand
when the Soviet invaders arrived in August, 1968, and here too
they cheered wildly, in February, 1948, at Klement Gottwald's
exultant announcement that the Communist Party was in
power. A generation had come of age in the intervening years,
challenging the frauds perpetrated by its elders as the same
generation was doing all over the world; and the elders,
ashamed of their failures, were trying to make amends. But
the years had told on them. They were not made of iron.
Who is?

Within a radius of ten blocks encircling Vaclavske Namesti
are the offices of newspapers and news agencies, radio, film, and

television networks, the Writers', Artists', and Journalists' Unions, whose imperious demands for truth generated the January revolution and sealed its fate. They were asking a great deal not only of the Kremlin but of their own people. It isn't easy to tell the truth in any society, and in Czechoslovakia, by 1968, fear was a conditioned reflex.

I was all too familiar with the symptom by the time I met Masaryk's secretaries. Lumír Soukoup, in Scotland, would have to be left for later. The other two were in Prague. But Jiří Špaček, more accessible, was anxious to be together with Antonín Šum for the meeting, and a fortnight went by before that could be arranged. It was evident, as we settled into comfortable armchairs in Špaček's office at Czechoslovenske Films, that their lives had taken very different turns.

Antonín Šum, just starting out on his career in 1948, had spent the next thirteen years in jail. After that, he put in five years as a chimney sweep and another with a subway construction company. It was only in the autumn of 1968 that he became a respectable citizen, rehabilitated by the Dubček regime and appointed as head of the Boy Scouts. He had not yet achieved those heights when I met him, and every faint twitch of facial muscles, every controlled gesture revealed the strained concentration of a man within sight, but not quite within reach, of his long-desired goal. Still fairly young, sandy hair clipped in a crew cut and figure spruce, his myopic blue eyes were restless behind thick lenses, his voice unexpectedly thin and high.

Jiří Špaček had been luckier. Due for a tour of duty abroad before Masaryk's death—this was why Lumír Soukoup came over from Scotland that December, to be broken in for his job—he was whisked off to Switzerland by Ambassador Jaromír Land, husband of Masaryk's niece Herberta and a Communist in good standing, to become Counselor of the Embassy there. When he returned to Czechoslovakia the early wave of arrests following the Communist takeover had subsided. Though fired from the Foreign Ministry, he was not arrested. After five bruising years as a factory hand in a textile mill, and later in a diesel plant, he had worked for Czechoslovenske Films from 1954 onward. Keeping out of jail for all those years, however, was hardly a less instructive experience than managing to survive a jail sentence: Dr. Špaček was not quite, but almost, as watchful during our meeting as Dr. šum. Nevertheless, one could see why Masaryk had relied most on Špaček, his senior secretary, altered by the years now, burly figure bloated, dark pouches under the eyes, heavy face pasty and lined, but still with a calm, sturdy quality that the Foreign Minister must have valued as the net drew tight around him.

The interview was choppy going, the younger secretary abrupt, irritated by insistent questions, coldly disapproving of his colleague's occasional lapse into conditional clauses. For Dr. šum, at any rate, the question was open and shut. Both seemed entirely sincere, however, in their belief that if ever a man was driven to take his life, Jan Masaryk was: his last seven or eight months were anguished, the last weeks an unrelieved nightmare.

Until the summer of 1947, they agreed, Masaryk had tried to believe that Czechoslovakia's postwar obligations to Russia could be reconciled with its independence in foreign affairs. He was even rather hopeful, as the summer approached, that the democratic parties could hold their own if not actually improve their position. But he lost the illusion irrevocably in Moscow, when Stalin forced him to veto the Marshall Plan. His senior secretary—his only one in those days—had vivid recollections of his return to Prague. "I knew what was going on in Moscow, naturally," Dr. Špaček began. "I'd been seeing the dispatches, and there were some telephone conversations, so I was aware of the details. But never, never would I have expected to see the Minister so physically—psychologically, yes, I'd have expected that—but *physically* destroyed. You must have read what he said, when I met him at the airport: 'I went to Moscow a free Minister and I'm coming back a servant of Stalin.' And then he added: 'You'll remember this date: my visit to Moscow.' "

The decision to participate in the Marshall Plan was made unanimously by the Czechoslovak cabinet with the Communists' full consent, Špaček continued, but Stalin couldn't have cared less. He put it bluntly to Masaryk: "We consider this a question of principle, on which our friendship with the Czechoslovak Republic depends. If you go to the Paris conference, you will demonstrate that you mean to collaborate in Western actions to isolate the Soviet Union." Masaryk, who had brought a personal and confidential memorandum from President Beneš on the subject, then tried to read it to Stalin. But the Soviet ruler interrupted brusquely, saying: "Don't bother. I've already seen it," and he waved a copy, there on his desk. The Czechoslovak President's memorandum had been drawn up in secret a few hours before Masaryk left for Moscow, its contents presumably known only to Beneš and his Foreign Minister. It was a staggering shock for Masaryk to discover—to be told so carelessly, indeed contemptuously—that even then, in an officially constitutional state governed jointly by the democratic and Communist parties, Stalin's spies were installed in the President's inner office, doubtless in the Foreign Minister's as well.

The situation deteriorated rapidly from that July to the following February. After the perfume-box assassination plot in September came vicious propaganda attacks on democratic leaders, merciless Soviet pressure on Masaryk at the UN General Assembly session in New York, accelerated Bolshevization of the regular and secret police. By mid-February, the democrats were helplessly trapped.

Dr. Špaček was present on February 19 when Stalin's Deputy Foreign Minister, Valerian Zorin, arriving in Prague unannounced to "check Soviet wheat deliveries," came to call at Czernin Palace an hour and a half later. Masaryk was in bed, running a fever, hoarse with the bronchitis that lingered until his death. He turned white as a sheet when Zorin was announced, Špaček said. Complete rupture was imminent between the democratic and Communist parties—would in fact become final the next day, with the resignation of twelve democratic ministers from the coalition cabinet. Zorin didn't waste words on Soviet wheat shipments. Stalin still trusted Masaryk, he said, but "events taking place in your country are intolerable and we shall not tolerate them." Anti-Soviet elements were endangering Soviet-Czechoslovak friendship, he warned, and must be eliminated from positions of influence. Masaryk perfectly understood what Zorin meant.

The next four days were hell—the coalition smashed, President Beneš wavering, democratic leaders in a panic, the Communists' armed Workers' Militia roaming the streets. Dr. Šum, down with the measles from February 19 to March 4, missed most of the crisis. (He neglected to mention this, and I didn't find out until much later.) But the senior secretary was at Masaryk's side from first to last. "I was in the office when Gottwald telephoned on February 24, asking the Minister to join the Communists in the new cabinet," Dr. Špaček told me. "At first, Masaryk tried to convince Gottwald that maybe it would be opportune to make somebody else Foreign Minister, somebody more in tune with the new situation. He wasn't in good health, he said: he had influenza, and this chronic bronchitis, and a sprained shoulder that bothered him, and probably couldn't carry out his duties properly for some while. Then Gottwald spoke for a long time—naturally, I couldn't hear what he said— but I gathered he was making promises, giving guarantees of some kind that this would be a democratic government and nothing would happen to anybody. Finally, the Minister answered, 'Yes, all right, but I must consult Beneš first.'"

Twenty-four hours later, Masaryk stood at a window of Czernin Palace, Špaček with him, as ten thousand students surged up the hill to Hradcany Castle to breathe spirit into the enfeebled President Beneš, and Gottwald's police opened fire before his eyes. Deeply shaken, Masaryk tried to rescue the two hundred students arrested that afternoon, and managed to get one hundred and eighty released. It was the last service he could do for his people.

On March 1, three days after the takeover, Communist employees in the Foreign Affairs Ministry formed an Action Committee, without consulting the Foreign Minister or even taking the trouble to inform him. "They acted entirely on their own, told the Minister nothing until it was done," Špaček went on. "Then, when they had the decrees drawn up, purging a long list of old Ministry functionaries and professional diplomats at home and abroad, they asked for an audience with the Minister."

"He was still sick then," Šum interjected.

"Yes, he received them in bed. They had everything ready, written down, he had only to sign."

"According to what I heard, he didn't want to sign," Šum said.

"He signed, though. . . . He made them understand he didn't want to—Gottwald had promised that nobody would be touched —but he signed."

Shortly before the Action Committee's ultimatum, a group of ex-army officers in the Ministry had come to Masaryk, men who fought with the British Army during the war. They had opposed the Communists' Action Committee, been threatened, begged the Minister to protect them. A few hours after he put his signature to the purge list, the spokesman for this group was arrested, his Minister already helpless to save him.

On March 5 Masaryk attended the first meeting of Gottwald's all-Communist cabinet. He came back undone. "It was terrible," he told Špaček. Communist ministers, reveling in their victory, had made no secret of their future plans. Several joked coarsely at the democrats' expense, a number made open and sinister threats, the Communist Information Minister, Václav Kopecký, attacked Masaryk personally in a grossly offen-

sive way. "And they call that a government!" Masaryk exclaimed to his secretaries. "I tell you, gentlemen, it's madness!"

Then came the rally in Old Town Square two days later, the
Communists' crude effort to make the dead Tomáš Masaryk
their accomplice, and his son's impotent rage. Was it true, as
their absent colleague in Scotland, Soukoup, maintained, that
after this rally Masaryk said he would never set foot in Parliament again? True, Dr. Šum answered firmly, spectacles gleaming with the vigorous nod of his head; Soukoup told him so.

"I never heard him say that." Dr. Špaček's heavy face was
impassive. There was a slight pause.

Anyway, Špaček resumed, Masaryk did not intend to go on
with the farce much longer. Whether or not he appeared before
Parliament on March 10 with the new cabinet, he had already
agreed with President Beneš that the two would resign together
soon; both recognized that they were merely being exploited by
Gottwald, could salvage nothing by collaborating with his
government. Certainly they would have broken with the Communists before the elections in May. In that case, I suggested,
was there a really urgent need for Masaryk to make a decision
before the meeting of Parliament on March 10? Most people
assumed that he'd joined the Communist government on the
insistence of President Beneš and was going to be stuck with it,
that he had no choice but to remain in this government or
break with Beneš, breaking a vow made at his father's deathbed.
If Beneš meant to let him off the hook, if he could look forward
to early release, perhaps in a matter of weeks . . .

"And what would *that* mean?" Dr. Šum's voice was acid.
"There could be no release for a man in Masaryk's position: he
was at the end of the road." The Communists were too strong
by then, the younger secretary argued, Masaryk would have no
remote chance of opposing them at home and was too old to go
abroad and start all over again. He had spoken of suicide several
times. They'd all heard him, in the office, especially after the
rally in Old Town Square. He'd asked Soukoup, when he got

home, "What do you think? Would it make sense if I should
end it all? Would people understand?"

I looked toward the senior secretary and he nodded. Yes,
it was true, Masaryk had spoken to Špaček about it as well:
"I'm nearly sixty-three, my life is finished, I don't see any other
solution."

"How can you say your life is finished, Mr. Minister," Špaček
had said. "Your father was sixty-four when he began his struggle
for Czechoslovakia. You must not do it. The country needs
Masaryk."

Yet a number of Masaryk's friends insisted that the fight
hadn't yet gone out of him, I said, that he meant to oppose
the Gottwald regime, either in Czechoslovakia or from London,
his second home—or, if nothing else, simply to retire there and
live out his last years in peace. He had sent secret messages to
this effect to several people abroad, and there were all sorts of
stories about his plans for escape. His personal physician, Oskar
Klinger, had put out the story years ago, for instance, that they
were going to leave the country together on March 10, in a small
plane.

"Bosh!" snapped Dr. Šum, crew cut bristling. "Why should
the Minister leave with Klinger? They weren't particularly
close. Klinger simply happened to be the Ministry physician,
who took care of all the personnel, not just Masaryk. None of
us believed his story."

"Klinger wasn't very serious," the senior secretary broke in,
apparently agreeing fully with his companion this time. "He
said a lot of things that weren't true, once he got off to America. For instance, he claimed he wasn't allowed to see the
Minister's body. That isn't so. I myself called Dr. Klinger, asking him to come to the autopsy. His secretary told me he didn't
have time."

Was Špaček himself present at the autopsy? Both secretaries
were, around noon on March 10. Šum fainted and was carried
from the room when the examining surgeon began to saw open

Masaryk's skull. But there was no doubt that the man wielding the saw was Dr. František Hájek, said in the *Student* article to have been kept three yards from the corpse. He had dictated his findings to his assistant, Dr. František Tesař, now Director of the Forensic Medicine Institute at Charles University. Šum and Špaček were quite close to the mortuary table, along with the bodyguard, Vyšín, and several secret police officers. The body had been washed sometime during the morning, when it was taken to a police station near Czernin Palace and then brought back again. They saw no bullet hole or other external marks, except for a large blue bruise on Masaryk's right temple and behind his ear, a small wound at the back of the head, and a sizable scrape on his stomach. There were no signs of injury on his arms or elbows, though there were visible welts on his fingers and paint or plaster under his fingernails. Šum told me that he was the one who later put a nosegay of snowdrops behind Masaryk's ear in the coffin, to conceal the hideous autopsy scar. He also suggested that the scrape on the stomach was the clue to how the Minister must have fallen. About a yard beneath the bathroom window was a cornice roughly two feet wide. The Minister, not wanting to look down, must have lowered himself onto this ledge facing inward, brushing his stomach against it as he let go.

I tried to visualize the scene. The window aperture was three feet by three feet. Masaryk was six feet tall, stout, flabby. Climbing onto the sill over the protruding radiator and starting from a sitting position, legs dangling inside the room, he would have had to hunch himself into a ball and swing his legs outward, twisting around to keep facing inward so as not to look down. It seemed an awkward way to jump. Didn't Dr. Šum think so? Perhaps, he answered dryly, but I seemed to forget that Masaryk was desperate, forced to take the only way out.

Again I glanced at the quiet senior secretary, his nod of agreement more diffident now. Yes, he said slowly, it was probably the only way out. They both knew that Masaryk was afraid of pain, quailing even at an appointment with the dentist. Yet as far as they could tell—or told me—the humblest filing clerk might have had a wider choice of suicide weapons than the Foreign Minister. He was under unrelenting surveillance by then, using the telephone solely for official conversations, writing on a pad to convey anything confidential to his secretaries. He owned a gun, but had told Špaček to lock it away in the office safe: he didn't like guns. There were only "two or three" sleeping pills left in the bottle, Špaček thought. It was no simple matter to slip out and buy poison. The window was there . . .

They both took it for granted, then, that he did jump?

"If you'd seen what he was like in those last weeks, you couldn't doubt it." Dr. Šum leaned forward, voice not querulous now, nearsighted blue eyes fixed earnestly on mine. "His life's work—everything he stood for—was gone, in ruins. He was exhausted, ill, depressed. Believe me, you would have had no doubt."

But Dr. Špaček was troubled. Twenty years of uncertainty were written on his broad, stolid face—nagging little questions he could not quite put out of mind. "Yes, he must have jumped," he said thoughtfully. "He was sick, disgusted. We took it for granted, yes." Nevertheless, the senior secretary added, Masaryk was no more depressed on Tuesday, March 9, than on any other day since the February events, had shown no sign of a gathering nervous storm. Šum was with him from 3:30 to 5:00 in the afternoon, Špaček himself from 5:30 until 8:00. "We went over routine business, he signed some photographs and documents, and then we arranged the schedule for the next day. He had Parliament in the morning, and he'd made an appointment to see the new Polish Ambassador, and in the evening he was going to make a speech for the first anniversary of the Polish-Czechoslovak Friendship Treaty. I could see he meant to prepare the speech carefully; I gave him some background material and he asked for more. He was behaving normally, not distracted or tense. When I left him, he was settling down in bed with a pencil and paper to write the speech." And he did write it. Špaček found the draft on top of the bureau the next morning, short but complete. He gave me a copy.

Did either secretary find anything else—a suicide note, a message of some kind? No. Šum reached Masaryk's apartment after 9:00 A.M. on March 10, long since overrun at that hour by secret police and Communist functionaries. Špaček, arriving around eight, was kept waiting well over half an hour before being admitted. Obviously the police could have appropriated a suicide note by then, if there was one.

What about the opened Bible which their colleague, Sou-koup, spoke of in his *Scotsman* article, the verses from St. Paul which, according to the third secretary, were underlined by Masaryk on the night he died? Yes, Šum affirmed at once, the verses must have been circled by the Minister that night: Soukoup had seen the page only a couple of days before, the lines unmarked.

"I don't think so." Dr. Špaček did not look at his younger companion, but for the barest instant a crackling current passed between them. "There were hundreds of verses marked in the Bible, by the Minister's father, years and years ago. I saw them dozens of times, and I'm pretty sure these two were among them —especially Verse 24, the one about the crucifixion of the flesh."

"At any rate, you yourself didn't see the Bible lying open to the page that morning?"

"No, I did not," Špaček answered flatly.

"Did Soukoup see it there?"

"He was out sick all week." An amused glint came and went.

The absence of a message was curious. If Masaryk was contemplating suicide for weeks, talking it over with his secretaries, wondering whether his people would understand, surely he might have found some way to leave a note—if not for the nation, or his friend Marcia Davenport, at least for his beloved sister Alice—in some place where the secret police would not be the first to clap eyes on it? Both men assented. The Minister could easily have smuggled a note out through any of his three secretaries, or the purser Topinka, or the butler Příhoda; he was fond of the old man, and trusted him. "Maybe he just couldn't think of things like that, when he came right down to it," Špaček suggested. But there were other loose ends, not so readily dismissed.

Dr. Špaček scarcely mentioned the condition of Masaryk's bedroom, so crowded with functionaries by the time he arrived that he couldn't tell whether the disorder there was the Minister's work or theirs. The bathroom was harder to account for, however. He saw the broken glass on the floor, the two pillows, the excrement, the fingerprints standing out clearly on the dusty wall around the window and on the outside and inside of the window frame itself. Frankly, the senior secretary admitted, he didn't understand it.

The bodyguard Vyšín told me that Masaryk often rested up in a dry bathtub, I observed. Might that explain the pillows? Dr. Špaček smiled for the first time, doing wonders for his tired eyes and pallid face. Vyšín generally accompanied the Minister only as far as the door, and wouldn't have been in and out of the flat much. He himself had never seen Masaryk resting in the tub. I turned to Dr. Šum, who shot me a sharp look. No, nor had he.

Yet for all the senior secretary's evident reservations—Dr. Šum appeared to have none—neither seriously suspected murder. There were undeniably some odd circumstances. Nothing in Masaryk's behavior during those last tense weeks, or in all the time they'd known him, would have prepared them for the insane panic which, judging from the appearance of his bathroom and the manner of his fall, must have seized him just before he died. The official explanation offered by Interior Minister Nosek at the time was absurd. According to Nosek's statement in Parliament on March 10, the Foreign Minister's self-control had snapped after reading "reproachful telegrams from his for-

mer friends in England and America" during the night, bringing on an attack of "sudden insanity." Actually there were very
few telegrams of this kind, and Masaryk had never seen them:
his tactful secretaries were careful to keep them out of sight.

Still, seeing them or not would hardly have made much difference. In March, 1948, Masaryk was under a crushing weight
that few men would have the strength to bear. He had no need
of written evidence to demonstrate that his position, on the
night he died, was unworthy of his illustrious name, and un-
tenable.

He had been bitterly aware of this since February 20, when
the twelve democratic ministers resigned from the National
Front cabinet and he refused to join them. He had considered
their decision senseless, and worse; his admired friend and colleague Justice Minister Prokop Drtina had considered Masaryk's a betrayal past all understanding. They were both right.
The departure of these democratic leaders from the government
was their last voluntary act as politicians. Masaryk, remaining
behind, was haunted by remorse in the few weeks left to him.

Chapter 6

"I knew I'd get them in the end, but I never thought they'd hand me their asses to kick, on a platter," Gottwald remarked to Jan Masaryk when the twelve ministers resigned. In fact, they were wonderfully obliging. Nothing in the Constitution—Tomáš Masaryk's Constitution—required Gottwald to resign when the democrats went. He still had a majority in the cabinet. President Beneš could not constitutionally demand his resignation without a vote of no confidence in Parliament. Nor could the President withhold approval indefinitely for his Prime Minister's list of new cabinet members to replace those departing. "The parties of order, as they call themselves, die by the legal state which they created," Friedrich Engels once wrote. So they did, in Prague.

Nowhere else, before or since, has a Communist minority come to power by Parliamentary means. The Czechoslovak Communists later described their triumph accurately in a handbook that has become a Marxist classic: "The representatives of the bourgeoisie . . . were replaced in the government, absolutely legally and in accordance with the constitution valid since 1920, by new representatives . . . recognizing the leading role of the Communists in the state. The government was nominated by the President of the Republic and unanimously approved by Parliament."

It is frivolous, but interesting, to speculate on what might have happened if Jan Masaryk had walked out with those twelve ministers. Gottwald would thereupon have lost his majority in the cabinet; President Beneš would have been entitled to demand his resignation, dissolve Parliament, and call for immediate elections; Valerian Zorin, directing operations in the Czechoslovak Communists' map room, might have had to marshal his forces for a more conventional assault. Gottwald, while losing nothing else, might have been cheated of his unique niche in Communist history.

But Masaryk stayed and Gottwald found his niche, an unimportant if poignant historical footnote. The Communists would have won anyway. The democratic parties were much too far gone by February, 1948, to put up effective resistance. One might even argue that they were dead before they started, stricken mortally at Yalta and finished off in Moscow, where Stalin administered the last rites in 1945. All the same, Gottwald contributed greatly to their speedy burial. "While, prior to the elections in 1946, the bourgeoisie had a relatively strong mass basis," says this Communist handbook, "a short time of under two years of people's democratic government was sufficient for the disintegration of the political army upon which the bourgeoisie could formerly count." It certainly was.

The whole plan is there, in that handbook with its musty Marxist title: *How Parliament Can Play a Revolutionary Part in the Transition to Socialism and the Role of the Popular Masses.* It is still in use, attentively studied by Communist parties all over the world. For the Czechoslovak Communists, with their "peculiarly Czechoslovak road to socialism," were years ahead of their time, nearly a decade ahead of even Palmiro Togliatti, the Italian Communist leader whose ideas about a relatively peaceful conquest of power—the Italian road to socialism—were supposedly a spectacular breakthrough in Communist thinking. "The Czechoslovak example," the handbook notes, "proves that an apparently slower progress of socialist revolution, by gradual transition, was actually the *faster* way, because the two-in-one task of the revolution began to be fulfilled simultaneously. When the dictatorship of the proletariat was realized, the state apparatus already existed in principle; the working masses had already gained experience in state, organizational, and educational work; new forms of working-class organizations were in existence, vital to the proletarian dictatorship. All this is achieved by the proletariat only *after* its victory, if it attains socialism violently, through civil war."

The handbook explains precisely how the Czechoslovak Communists managed their gradual transition: through a "pincer movement operating from above and below," closing implacably around the bourgeois necks Gottwald had spoken of so long ago. Both forms of pressure were planned in Moscow before the Red Army set foot on Czechoslovak soil. Those from below would be organized by local "National Committees," formally elected, in practice selected by Soviet military commissars as the Red Army advanced. Those from above would be generated through the Ministries that Gottwald collected at the 1945 Moscow conference.

The Moscow agreement indicated in general that Czechoslovakia was, politically speaking, already slightly pregnant. Delivered to Hitler by the Western powers in 1938 and delivered from him by the Red Army in 1945, the Czechoslovaks were hardly in a position to resist Russian proposals. The agreement they signed provided for a National Front government of democratic and Communist parties, the formula immutable, the relative strength within the Front dependent on free elections. The government's program was laid down in advance: nationalization of insurance, banking, electric power, armaments, steel, and other key industries; redistribution of seven million acres confiscated from two and a half million expelled Sudeten Germans; an advanced social welfare plan; guaranteed human rights (an afterthought good-naturedly written in by Gottwald on the democrats' suggestion) ; a school system cleansed of "anti-Bolshevik propaganda"; a foreign policy based on "the alliance with the Soviet Union and a vigorous Pan-Slav policy in Eastern Europe," while permitting "friendly relations with the Western powers." It wasn't bad for a starter, from the Communists' point of view.

Neither were the political arrangements. All the more conservative prewar parties were abolished. Furthest to the right in the Front were two moderate parties: the Catholic Populists in the Czech lands, polling 16 percent of the national vote in 1946; the nationalist democrats in Slovakia, whose 62 percent of the Slovak vote (against the Communists' 30 percent in that region) marked them for early extinction. The other three Front parties were socialist, one and a half of them the nice law-abiding kind, the rest the other sort. President Beneš's National Socialist Party, embedded in democratic Masaryk traditions, had 18 percent of the national vote. The Marxist Social Democratic Party, with 13 percent, had one literally democratic wing and the other led by its abjectly pro-Communist chairman Zdeněk Fierlinger. Then came the Communists with their 38 percent, democrats to the manner born by the look of them, strolling down "a quiet road to socialism . . . without further revolutions," as Gottwald put it, accepted by a great many voters as merely a leftish branch of the Social Democratic family.

"The very conception of this broad National Front," as that handbook justly observes, "contributed greatly to attaining our end." So long as Fierlinger could eventually control the whole Social Democratic Party, the Communist minority could count on a block of 51 percent in Parliament; and all of Gottwald's ministers (including Fierlinger's) did their bit to see to it that "the bourgeoisie, with numerical superiority in the decisive organs, would be impotent to isolate the Communists and stop the revolution." Most of them presented provocative bills to manipulate the democratic parties into "either giving in or showing their anti-people's face." The Minister of Industry was particularly good at it: with two-thirds of industry already nationalized under the Moscow agreement, says the handbook, "the claws of the pincer bit deeper into the bourgeoisie's flesh . . . by tearing another 13 percent from the hands of private enterprisers in 1947." While most private fortunes were wiped out by postwar inflation, furthermore, the Minister of Finance proposed to take care of the remaining few with a "millionaire's levy" to compensate peasants for losses in the severe 1947 drought—a millionaire, in Czechoslovak crowns, being anybody with $20,000. The Minister of Agriculture "liquidated the Kulaks" with a bill limiting landholdings to a hundred acres, and swelled the "pressure from below" with his uncommon largesse: cheap farm credits, cut-rate farm machinery and seed, judicious redistribution of rich Sudeten farmland to a million and a half deserving peasants, four out of five of whom thereafter voted for the Communist party.

The Information Minister, controlling typographical workers from below and newsprint—not to mention the radio—from above, reduced the democrats to helpless silence at the suitable moment. The "independent" but pliant Defense Minister, Ludvík Svoboda—the same, no longer so pliant, who became President of the Republic in 1968—fired high-ranking democratic officers and confined his troops to barracks on the day of the *Putsch,* declaring that "the army goes with the nation: whoever disturbs the nation's unity is a menace and must be removed." But the "signal role," it says in the handbook, "was played by the Ministry of the Interior, which was led by the Communists, and the units of State Security directed by them."

President Beneš had been reassuring about the Interior Ministry on leaving London for Moscow: he would never let the Communists have it, he told Masaryk. Bemused by a Stalin at his charming best, and preferring to remain above the fray as Head of State, he let it go. He hadn't much choice in any case. His delegates were prisoners. His Foreign Trade Minister in

London could only communicate with them by broadcasting messages over BBC; and had they held out against Moscow's demands, "there would have been no train to take them home" —or so they were told later by the Social Democratic quisling Zdeněk Fierlinger.

They did not grasp the enormity of this concession until January, 1948, when the Communists were already poised for the kill. "Creative application . . . of the pressure-from-below principle," says that remarkably candid handbook, had led quickly to "arming the proletariat" in an illegal Workers' Militia, organized by Interior Minister Nosek and his Deputy Minister Jindřich Veselý. By pressure from above, on the other hand, "the nucleus of a new armed state apparatus, especially the security apparatus, was formed under the control of the Interior Ministry." Nosek, a fast worker, soon had a luxuriant variety of regular and secret-police units, armed and empowered to make arrests: his own political STB, the regular National Security Corps (SNB), the "special security" ZOB, the army intelligence OZB, and a paramilitary formation of mobile police that would be used to occupy Prague in February, 1948. His right-hand man, coordinating these units, was the one found dangling from a tree near Brno twenty years later, Major Bedřich Pokorný.

Major Pokorný's career shows what a good technician can do, given the proper equipment. A specialist in suborning witnesses and manufacturing evidence, he was equally skilled at blackening the names of democratic leaders and frightening the wits out of their followers. Working through the Communist Interior Ministry's "Defamation Section," he had only to make one of two charges—wartime collaboration with the Germans or postwar espionage for the capitalist West—to fill the prisons with rank-and-file democrats and damn their leaders as political delinquents. By early 1946, he was already at work among inmates of Pankrac and Ruzyne, persuading former Gestapo agents to help him defame the democratic underground resistance. His prime target was Viktor Krajina, Secretary of Beneš's National Socialist Party, whose heroic partisan work during the war had been commended by Churchill and Stalin both.

In April, 1946, Major Pokorný announced at a press conference that, whereas the Communists had performed gloriously in the underground resistance, most democratic partisans had collaborated with the Gestapo, Krajina included—a fine specimen of rewritten history in the making. The Communists themselves had a scandalous record of wartime collaboration. They had methodically betrayed democratic partisans to the Germans not only from August, 1939, to June, 1941—the period of Stalin's pact with Hitler—but throughout the war, with a view to liquidating their postwar political rivals. German documents captured after the war provided a wealth of detail, including at least three egregious cases of Communist agents specially trained in Moscow, turning hundreds of democrats over to the enemy. Viktor Krajina, whose reports to London on these Communist betrayals had incurred their special wrath, was arrested by the Gestapo on a tip from them in 1943. Three parachutists sent from London to help him were intercepted by Communist agents, who disarmed them and arranged for their arrest as well; two of the three were executed by the Gestapo.

In 1946 it was still too early to frame a celebrated partisan fighter like Krajina. He called Major Pokorný's bluff and was formally exonerated, while Pokorný was demoted temporarily. The following year, however, the Major came up with a superb conspiracy charge against the Slovak Democratic Party, whose intolerable electoral strength had led a Communist leader to say *publicly* after the 1946 election, "We must at all costs prove the Democratic Party guilty of treasonable activities, and then disband it." Pokorný produced the proof that the Democrats were plotting to form a breakaway state under Western patronage. Two radio transmitters, thirty-six kilos of explosives, thirteen hundred cartridges, nine revolvers, and a hand grenade were "found"; three hundred and eighty Democrats were arrested, including their Party chairman, a Vice Premier; scores were tortured into fake confessions. By late October, 1947, the Democrats' chairman was obliged to resign as Vice Premier, and the Slovak Democratic Party was practically out of business. One down and two to go.

With Major Pokorný's help, the Communists then went on to what the handbook calls "the further disintegration of our political opponents." The Catholic Populists, more conservative and therefore less competitive, were left for last, unmolested until January. The National Socialists had their turn in November. The charge in their case was the formation of an anti-Communist espionage network in Western Bohemia. Major Pokorný outdid himself for the occasion, with a parade of witnesses as beautifully drilled as the Bolshoi *corps de ballet*. But he ran into trouble with his *prima ballerina*, a convict borrowed from Ruzyne by the name of Podivín. Given a choice between release from jail for "rendering certain services" or having his mother and brother join him in prison, Podivín tried to be serviceable. He helped to frame another ex-convict named Reichel as a Western spy, whereupon Reichel was promptly arrested and offered his release on similar terms. The two went through a week of intensive coaching, holed up in a Prague apartment with Pokorný's agents. But once on stage, alas, Reichel sang. The secret police, he said in court, had offered him acquittal on the rigged spy charge if he would accuse the National Socialists' three top leaders—Chairman Peter Zenkl, Secretary Viktor Krajina, and Justice Minister Prokop Drtina—of "plotting forcible action against the Communist Party and the State."

In this instance, as in all others, it was Prokop Drtina who brought Major Pokorný's work to light. His detailed report to the cabinet about the Reichel-Podivín affair, on January 27, 1948, was the second within a week to expose the Interior Ministry's activities. On January 21, he had risen in Parliament to reveal the full details of the Communist perfume-box plot to assassinate Zenkl, Masaryk, and himself. Naming names, sparing nobody, he was told at this dramatic session, though he didn't need telling, that he was a marked man. "Your Drtina is rushing straight to his doom," a fellow National Socialist was warned by a Communist deputy. He didn't stop, but his time was running out.

On February 13, Drtina addressed the cabinet once more to deliver what was to be his last report as Minister of Justice. His theme was the systematic Communization of the police. All the important posts in the Interior Ministry were now occupied by Communists, he said. Five of the nine departmental heads in the security division were Communists. The three chief posts at Central Headquarters of the political police were held by Communists. The three branches of the National Security Corps were headed by Communists. Sixty of the seventy high-ranking officers in the regular police were Communists; and the eight remaining non-Communist divisional commissioners in the SNB's Prague section—the only rank authorized to issue arms and ammunition to the police—had been replaced by Communists just that morning. Drtina thereupon demanded cancellation of the promotion order for these last eight Communists, and an investigation into Interior Minister Nosek's personnel policies. For once, the fellow-traveling Social Democratic ministers voted with their democratic colleagues—sixty of their own party members were among the police officers kicked out by Nosek— and the Communists, in a minority, could not block Drtina's motion. Even he, clearsighted as he was, failed to realize that this would be the end of him, and of democracy in Czechoslovakia.

Interior Minister Nosek didn't even bother to attend the February 13 cabinet meeting, or the next one on February 17, when he was supposed to give an account of himself. No sooner was Drtina's motion approved in the cabinet than "the million-member colossus of the Communist Party with all its transmission belts to mass organizations was set in motion," as our old friend Jindřich Veselý, Nosek's Deputy, later noted. By then, Premier Gottwald had a deadly assortment of weapons to command the streets and terrorize an opposition with nothing left but bows and arrows.

Democratic leaders had noticed this happening without really comprehending it. Almost to the last, President Beneš maintained that Czechoslovak Communists were "not like other Communists," that Gottwald was "a reasonable man who believes in Parliamentary democracy." The average democratic deputy drifted along with this comforting view until Parliament, as that lucid handbook says, "became a direct instrument for establishing the dictatorship of the proletariat."

It was on the basis of Drtina's irreproachably constitutional demand, rudely ignored by the Communists, that the twelve democratic ministers resigned, perfectly unconscious of the ambush they were walking into. None of them, apparently, had considered the possibility of bringing on a Communist *Putsch.* "The Communists thought of a *Putsch* in September, 1947," President Beneš told Josef Korbel, then his Ambassador to Yugoslavia, on January 12. "But they abandoned the idea and will not try any more. They found out for themselves that I enjoy a certain authority in the nation. And not only that. They know that I have numerous supporters among the working class, even among the Communist workers. They have come to realize that they cannot go against me. A *Putsch* would be directed against me as well, and they cannot afford it. I shall not move from my place, and therefore there will be no *Putsch.* Besides, the police are not fully in their hands. Half of them stand behind me, and the army is fully behind me."

Incredulous, Ambassador Korbel asked Beneš what he thought of General Svoboda, the Defense Minister. The President answered that Svoboda was reliable, as were some forty younger generals. He was astonished to hear from Korbel that the Air Force Commander was a Communist Party member, but considered him reliable all the same. "Don't worry," he concluded. "The danger of a Communist *Putsch* is past. Return to Belgrade and carry on."

Five weeks later, President Beneš was confronted by the reliable General Svoboda, along with Premier Gottwald and Interior Minister Nosek, arrogantly demanding his surrender. They had "conclusive proof"—Major Pokorný's scenario and other unimpeachable documents—that the twelve democratic ministers were plotting "a vast armed conspiracy" against the Communists and the state: the President must accept their resignations and the replacements proposed by Gottwald for a "regenerated National Front." The next day, a delegation of fifty-five loyal workers stormed into the President's office at Hradcany Castle: "Mr. President," said their spokesman, "I am a simple worker, but I know this much: if the majority of the nation wants something, you as President must submit." Beneš replied sharply that he wasn't going to "let the streets decide" for him, but his power of decision was already gone. When he wanted to address the nation that evening, the Communist Information Minister remarked with full confidence, "We will not allow Beneš to appear before the microphone again." He never did.

Long after the *Putsch* was over, Czechoslovakia's democratic leaders sheltering in London were still meeting weekly, trying to decide what hit them. They bickered over this as over everything else, never wholly clarifying the cloudy events of that day when Gottwald got what he wanted on a platter. They did agree, though, that they had decided to resign without any assurance of carrying a majority in the cabinet with them. The majority would have depended either on the vacillating Social Democrats, or on Jan Masaryk.

The Social Democrats were not lost to democracy by any means. In fact, they had overthrown the quisling Fierlinger as party chairman the previous November. He had gone too far by signing a joint-action pact with Gottwald, without so much as consulting his party. During their short fling at freedom, Social Democratic leaders openly denounced Communist terrorist tactics, especially in the factories. "Meetings are usually called after working hours, when the majority of workers have left, and methods of voting are controlled by direct intimidation," said their daily, *Pravo Lidu*. But Fierlinger wasn't finished. "Don't play with the Communists. They won't tolerate it, nor will the Russians," he had advised his rebel colleagues, adding: "You'll see—I'll be back in four months." He made it in three.

Nevertheless, he was still out in the cold on the day the crisis began. Only the evening before, Gottwald had offered the Social Democrats two-fifths of the cabinet posts if they would join him in a two-party government in the event of a democratic walkout, and they turned him down. Their three cabinet ministers even showed a fleeting interest in joining the walkout when they were approached, rather late in the day, on the afternoon of February 21. But Gottwald dissuaded them. "If you don't march with us, you will be liquidated with the others," he said. Marching with him, the Social Democratic Party was liquidated two months later.

Jan Masaryk was a different story. He was a democrat to his bones, he had that name, and he had that deciding vote in the cabinet. Yet he was not informed of the twelve ministers' decision until they told him on the telephone, *after* they resigned. Apparently they were expecting President Beneš to take care of him, and everything else.

What they were banking on was the President's refusal to accept their resignations, whether or not they carried a majority of the cabinet. This, they reasoned, would force Gottwald to cave in on the issue of Communizing the police—a splendid trophy for the May election, which they were sure of winning. It did not occur to them that there wasn't going to be a free election in May, since the Communists were equally sure of losing.

Stalin had lost interest in that sort of contest as early as the previous July, when he had vetoed the Marshall Plan. His decision to cut short Soviet Russia's postwar dalliance with the West was clear by then, and clearer still when he revived the prewar Comintern as the Cominform, in September, 1947, to coordinate Communist operations abroad. The Czechoslovaks' coalition government, with its bridge-building foreign policy, milktoast reforms, and Western parliamentary procedures, was never more than a temporary expedient for him. It was useful for a while: Gottwald, who could easily have taken power in 1945 with the Red Army's help, was allowed instead to tinker with an experiment which soothed the West and cost the Kremlin nothing but a little time. The Czechoslovak Communist leader had long hankered after that historical niche of his, insisting in 1945 that "with the proper skill, the Communists could gain a majority of the nation," which was "the most important thing for all revolutions and all progress." Why not let him try?

But Gottwald, too, was running out of time. By September, 1947, every one of Stalin's newly acquired states in Eastern Europe was securely under Communist control except Czechoslovakia. At its opening meeting in Warsaw that month, the newly reorganized Cominform sharply criticized the Czechoslovak Communists for their weakness and ordered them to take measures for the seizure of power. The orders were underlined at the Cominform's next meeting in northern Italy. At the same time, the Communists' electoral prospects were worsening. The electorate's early postwar enthusiasm for the Soviet liberators was wearing off. Rejection of the Marshall Plan was a shock. The tactics of the Communist police were arousing suspicion. In November, Fierlinger lost control of the Social Democratic Party with its indispensable 13 percent of the vote. And judging from their private sampling of public opinion, the Communists themselves might poll no more than 28 percent.

So Gottwald had no choice but to prepare for a *Putsch,* merely looking for a suitable pretext. He didn't even wait for the twelve democratic ministers to resign. The Communists began to mobilize a full week before that, within hours of the February 13 cabinet meeting where they were outvoted on the police issue. "We will never allow the police to be taken out of our

hands," Gottwald said, and that was that. On the afternoon of
February 13, the Communist Politburo submitted a full report
to the Cominform, and decided to meet twice daily in Gottwald's villa and to install at once direct telephone lines from
there to the Interior Ministry and the Soviet Embassy. Plans
were made for a mass Congress of Workers' Councils and
another of peasants to converge on Prague: the "pressure from
below." Simultaneously, the Interior Ministry moved in from
above.

On February 15, fresh contingents of Russian secret police
were flown in from Moscow, deployed within the week to all
district commands of the Czechoslovak secret police. A sizable
group of NKVD agents was stationed in Prague—twenty-three
at the Hotel Flora, sixteen at the Grand Hotel Steiner—to work
with the Czechoslovak military intelligence. On February 19,
Valerian Zorin arrived. By February 20, the day of the twelve
resignations, eighteen thousand fresh Red Army troops had entered Austria from Russia for deployment along the Czechoslovak border, while Czechoslovak Interior Minister Nosek had
police regiments stationed in all "sensitive areas" and the illegal
Workers' Militia organized in "alert squads."

Before nightfall, the Party was mobilized down to the last
neighborhood cell. Detailed directives went out from the Politburo to "make preparations for purging the National Front
of reactionaries." By midnight, couriers were leaving the capital in all directions, braving bitter frost, snowdrifts, blizzards.
Teletypes transmitted hourly orders to regional and district
committees. In Prague, the Deputy Commander of the Workers' Militia, Josef Smrkovský—a far different breed of hero
when, as head of the Czechoslovak National Assembly, he defied
the Russian invaders twenty years later—reported to the Party
that he had proclaimed "a state of battle from 6:00 A.M. tomorrow, when Prague Militiamen will receive two hundred cartridges each."

The pincers closed during the next four days, holding the

democrats in a steel vise. Convoys of trucks escorted by a battalion of SNB police rumbled into Prague, bearing ten thousand rifles and two thousand submachine guns for Smrkovský's
Militiamen. Nosek's police sealed the borders, occupied all public buildings, bridges, crossroads, and main thoroughfares in the
capital, raided National Socialist and Catholic Populist headquarters, arresting secretaries and staffs, impounding documents. The twelve democratic ministers, their resignations not
yet accepted by the President, were trailed by secret police, man-
handled by street mobs, forbidden to enter their ministries,
warned by letter: "If you do not obey, we shall use all the means
which the working class has at its disposal." Fierlinger's pro-
Communist followers forcibly occupied the Social Democratic
Party's headquarters, threatening the lives of his opponents,
backed up by the police. Communist action committees sprang
up in all government offices, newspapers, and mass organizations, taking command, purging the staffs, their moves synchronized by another old friend: Gottwald's son-in-law Alexej
Čepička. All non-Communists were barred from broadcasting
studios and thrown out of the Information Ministry. Hundreds
of journalists, publicists, civil servants, and local democratic
party leaders were arrested. Democratic newspapers were shut
down, their printing plants occupied by police, deliveries of
newsprint cut off by workers who refused to produce it for them
and railwaymen who would neither load nor unload it. *Mlada
Fronta*, the Communist youth daily, announced the good news:
"For the first time in the history of the Third Czechoslovak Republic, newspapers which undermine the confidence of the
people in their government cannot be published. We must hail
with joy these measures which, at last, have freed our press from
traitors to the nation." It was quite another kind of press freedom that *Mlada Fronta* fought for, with desperate courage,
when the Red Army occupied Prague in 1968.

Meanwhile, the Communists took over the streets. Fifteen
thousand armed militiamen paraded through the capital. Mon-

ster rallies of one and two hundred thousand people were held on February 21, 22, 24, and 25, overflowing Vaclavske Namesti and Old Town Square. Busloads of workers rolled into Prague for the Trade Union Congress on February 22, eight thousand delegates shouting for Beneš to accept the twelve resignations and "clean up political life." On February 24, two and a half million workers staged a one-hour general strike. "If someone thinks he can toss our people's demands to the winds, when they have so spontaneously—nay elementarily—demanded that these agents of foreign and domestic reaction ought not to return to the government," cried Gottwald to a wildly cheering crowd, "then that someone is damned wrong."

If President Beneš might have thought so on February 20, he realized by February 25 that he was indeed damned wrong. The demand certainly wasn't all that spontaneous. The tremor of revolutionary excitement spreading among workers and intellectuals was undeniably strong: plainly a great many believed ardently in the Communist cause at the time. But they were demonstrably a minority of the population, a third at most, more likely closer to a quarter, overpowering only because the instruments of power were already in their leaders' hands. Even among the workers, the Communists controlled less than 60 percent of the trade-union organization, URO. There were eleven hundred delegates from the democratic parties among the eight thousand otherwise handpicked for the February 22 Workers' Congress, seven hundred of them daring to vote against the final resolution, surrounded as they were by a howling, exalted mob. Thousands of other workers who refused to join in the general strike were fired on the spot, many beaten up and thrown bodily out of their factories. The overwhelming majority of students had turned against the Communists, who polled only 25 percent in university elections just two months earlier. The Czechoslovak youth had been deserting the Communists wholesale throughout the previous year, membership in the Communist youth organization dropping from six hundred thousand to less than half that figure. Democratic leaders, fanning out through the country over the weekend of February 21–22 to prepare for the election campaign they thought was coming up in May (!), found thousands of their constituents eager to resist, pleading for organization and guidance. They were abandoned then, as they had been after Munich in 1938, and would be after the Soviet invasion in 1968, by leaders who preferred surrender to bloodshed.

At eleven in the morning on February 25, Gottwald drove to Hradcany Castle, bringing with him the names of one hundred sixty-six deputies—a majority in Parliament—who would vote for his new list of cabinet ministers. Half the portfolios were allocated to Communist Party members, the rest to renegades from the democratic parties, and Jan Masaryk. At four in the afternoon, Gottwald returned to the castle for the President's answer and, a few minutes later, drove back to Vaclavske Namesti, where two hundred thousand followers waited in the biting cold. He wore a Russian sheepskin cap, and he was drunk. He thanked President Beneš for respecting the will of the people. The great square thundered with applause.

Chapter 7

Were the democrats cowardly? Stupid? Blind? Perhaps some, surely not all. They were caught in one of history's traffic accidents, to use a French premier's phrase when Czechoslovakia suffered its next misfortune twenty years later: law-abiding citizens knocked down as they crossed the zebra line.

From beginning to end, these sound democrats put their faith in Parliament and Tomáš Masaryk's beautiful Constitution, assuming, incredibly, that the Communists would do the same. As early as June, 1943, the Czechoslovak Communists' Central Committee defined its postwar aims: "Our supreme revolutionary goal is the establishment of a Czechoslovak Soviet Republic and its attachment to the Union of Soviet Socialist Republics. The revolution must break and destroy the whole bourgeois, capitalist system to the last molecule. . . . No matter if after the war we must deport one hundred, two hundred, or eight hundred thousand tainted individuals to forced labor camps outside the boundary of our new state. There is only one way, the way of revolution. Revolution—and to the East. To the East to our Slav tree trunk. To the East to our proletarian union. To the East, the best that the toiling people of the whole world have created. To the East, to the East, to the East!"

Yet as late as February 20, 1948—with Stalin's emissary already in Prague, fifteen thousand Communist Militiamen alerted, and crack police regiments ringing the capital—Czechoslovakia's democratic leaders were still talking about those elections. When President Beneš received the twelve letters of resignation that afternoon, he said to his last caller, head of the Catholic Populists: "It was the only decision to take. This time the Communists have calculated poorly. Now it is important to speed up the elections. The Communists' losses will surpass their own forecasts. You can count on me entirely."

Czechoslovak émigrés have been snarling at each other for two decades over the question of whether Beneš did or did not approve of the resignations in advance. His fellow National Socialists insisted that he did. His Chancellor, Jaromír Smutný, swore he didn't. Nevertheless he was closeted with National Socialist leaders for several hours on February 18. It is hard to believe they would have gone ahead and resigned without his tacit consent. It is also hard to believe—but beyond question in this instance—that neither they nor he, good constitutionalists all, included Jan Masaryk in their calculations.

Having made an egregious tactical error by leaving Gottwald with a majority in the cabinet, they might at least have tried to rectify it. Masaryk, with his deciding vote, could still break Gottwald's majority by resigning. The President could then constitutionally dissolve Parliament and call for new elections. The democrats, going under, might if nothing else have branded Gottwald as the outlaw he was. But not once from February 20 to 25 did National Socialist leaders communicate with Masaryk. Nor did the President personally advise him to resign. In fact, Beneš claimed afterward that he sent away the man bound to him by the most solemn vow without offering any advice at all. "That Jan!" he remarked to his counselor, Jan Jína, when Masaryk left the castle after their sole meeting during the crisis. "He actually wanted me to make up his mind for him!"

Was it possible that President Beneš didn't care how Masaryk made up his mind on this momentous issue? And was it conceivable that Tomáš Masaryk's son would have agreed to be Gottwald's Foreign Minister in the next government, alone among democratic leaders, on his own initiative, without a word from the President he had promised to stick by until the end? He knew what would be expected of him in the future government. "The engagements we have undertaken toward the Soviet Union are sacred," Gottwald said midway through the crisis. "Always and for everything we will be at the side of the Soviet Union and nowhere else. The law must strike all those who undermine our foreign policy. . . ." Nobody close to Jan Masaryk could imagine his assisting voluntarily in the final destruction of his country's independence—the scepter of nationhood, crowning achievement of his father's life.

Masaryk never revealed what the President said to him in the castle that day. Nor did Beneš, who, whatever he said, obviously made no effort to grasp the one constitutional opportunity he might have had to resist the Communist assault. Indeed, the President's behavior in the crisis was mystifying all along.

His support for the twelve ministers was apparently unreserved, once they moved. "At last!" he said, when the National Socialists telephoned to inform him of their resignations. "And now, careful—no blunders!" He would not accept their resignations under any circumstances, he declared, and "I shall insist that the government be based on all the National Front parties. . . . I will nominate a new government only in agreement with the leadership of all parties."

By February 22, with thousands of identical telegrams flooding his office, the Trade Union Congress at its deafening height, the President began to waver. Through Counselor Jína, he sent word to the four National Socialist ministers, asking if it wouldn't be better "to appease the Communists" by accepting the resignations, facilitating his negotiations with Gottwald. Stunned, they refused. He seemed to have taken fresh heart

when, on February 23, he received the four ministers of his own
party: National Socialist chairman Peter Zenkl, Justice Minister
Prokop Drtina, Foreign Trade Minister Hubert Ripka, and
Education Minister Jaroslav Stránský. None of them, on leaving him, was remotely prepared for the decision to come within
forty-eight hours.

The meeting was deeply moving. "The five men had known
each other for thirty years," wrote the former Czechoslovak
diplomat Josef Korbel. "Zenkl was former Mayor of Prague and
a cabinet minister many times over, inmate of the Buchenwald
concentration camp for six years, a relentless fighter against
totalitarianism. Stránský, publisher of the distinguished daily
Lidove Noviny, deputy and professor, was sensitive, cultured,
the greatest orator of his day. Drtina, quiet, determined, a rock
of faith and stubborn guardian of justice, had been the President's political adviser and spokesman for years. Ripka, journalist, diplomat, seasoned negotiator, was the best tactician of them
all. And there was Beneš, statesman of world fame, Foreign
Minister for seventeen years and President for thirteen, cold
analyst, trained sociologist, a democrat to his soul, dedicated
to reason and peaceful methods, but a victim of Munich,
a political stroke from which he never recovered, and now of
two physical strokes, his alert intellect housed in a broken
body."

Beneš opened the conversation by saying, "I told Gottwald
flatly, 'What you are doing is a coup d'état, a *Putsch,* but I will
not be pushed around. . . . What you are preparing is a second
Munich, and I'll have no part of it.' " Then the President assured his party colleagues, "I will never sign my name to the
list of puppet ministers that the Communists are trying to impose on us. If they insist, if we do not reach an understanding,
I will abdicate. I will not be their accomplice."

They went on to speculate on the Communists' future moves,
possibly including intervention by the Red Army. "I cannot
rule that out," Beneš said. "In that case, what would we do—
what in God's name would we do?"

"Obviously we'd be beaten," replied Ripka, the best tactician of them all. "But the whole wide world would know that the Communist regime was imposed on us, that Czechoslovakia was the victim of aggression, defenseless against it. . . . This defeat would lead us to a new victory."

"Perhaps," said Beneš. "But no one will help us. The West won't help us. Moscow knows that."

Then, overwhelmed with bitterness, the President renounced the lifelong belief that had led him into such tragic error. "I know them, those people in Moscow. I've had occasion to observe them more closely than you. You overestimate their intelligence and farsightedness. I overestimated them, too. They take themselves for realists; at bottom they are only fanatics. They are as blind as Hitler. . . ."

"You say that!" exclaimed Stránský. "You, who have done more than anyone else in the world to achieve honest cooperation with Soviet Russia?" Beneš smiled sadly, and they left. They never saw him again.

They heard the news by telephone on February 25. The President no longer had the strength to tell them, face to face, of a decision for which he should perhaps not be judged too harshly. He was grievously ill, nearing death. He was given a disproportionate share of the burden by democratic leaders who precipitated the crisis with unbelievable lack of forethought and then left him to deal with it. There was little or nothing more he could do. It was much too late to resist the Communists by force. The army, sturdily loyal only two years before, had long since slipped through his trusting fingers; and democratic leaders, far from organizing a vast armed conspiracy against the Communists, were so pitifully disarmed that the one rally they tried to hold in Vaclavske Namesti was broken up in no time, at gunpoint, by the Communists' police.

But he might have abdicated. He had said he would. He chose instead to maintain the Communists' fiction of legality, lending them his name and Presidential seal. "The state must survive," was his only explanation before dying the following

September, "and if it has to survive it must have some form of government."

There had always been a contradictory streak in Eduard Beneš. If democratic leaders were so grossly unprepared for the *Putsch*, it was in good part his fault. Few men in his time did more to encourage the belief that Czechoslovakia would be safe for democracy on Stalin's side of the Yalta line. And he knew better—had known better since his first visit to Moscow in 1943, long before the war was over, well before the Yalta conference. But he did not tell his fellow democrats so, nor did they know he knew until five years later.

Like a great many of his countrymen, Beneš was a fervent Pan-Slav, strongly drawn to Russia by ancient ties of blood and the powerful impulse of Czechoslovak history. Living at the very heart of Europe, overrun through the ages by predatory neighbors to the north and south, the Czechs of old Bohemia looked hopefully toward the great nation of fellow Slavs to the East. Someday they believed Russia would take her rightful place at their side, shielding them from their classic enemy. Germany had been the enemy for fifteen centuries, ruling the Czechs through its own Bohemian settlers or the Austrian Germans, who appropriated the territory for the Hapsburgs after the Battle of the White Mountain in 1620 and held on to it for three hundred years.

The Munich Agreement made Russia look incomparably more attractive. Tomáš Masaryk's Republic, liberated from the Austro-Hungarian Empire at last after the First World War, had basked in the glow of Western friendship until its friends casually signed it over to Nazi Germany two decades later. The British Prime Minister had assured Hitler in Munich that he would answer personally for Czechoslovakia's submission, remarking on his return to London that he saw no need for concern over a "quarrel in a faraway country, between people of whom we know nothing." He was wrong about that, the careless disposal of this faraway country having led directly to the

Jan Masaryk, his mother Charlotte Garrigue, and his sister Alice, 1916.

Jan Masaryk; his niece Anička; his father, Tomáš Masaryk; and his sisters, Alice and Olga, 1935.

Jan Masaryk as a young man. *Wide World Photos*

Jan and Tomáš Masaryk, 1933. *Courtesy, Czechoslovak News Agency*

Jan and Alice Masaryk,
his sister.

Masaryk at a public demonstration, 1947, months before the Communist
Putsch. Courtesy, Czechoslovak News Agency

Masaryk with puppet Socialist Democrat Zdeněk Fierlinger (left) and Stalin's emissary Valerian Zorin (right), who came to Prague, February 19, 1948, to direct Communist takeover of February 25. Photo taken February 28. *Courtesy, Czechoslovak News Agency*

Members of the Czechoslovak Parliament who resigned after February, 1948, Communist *Putsch* and fled to England to plan a government-in-exile: (from left) Štefan Rocvara, Viktor Krajina, Blazy Vilim, Adolf Procházka, Adolf Klimek, May, 29, 1948. *United Press International Photo*

Masaryk at his last public ceremony at the Old Town Square, Prague, March 7, 1948: the ceremony commemorated his late father's 98th birthday and the anniversaries of two victorious battles, from World Wars I and II. *Wide World Photos*

Masaryk (extreme right) at Sezimovo Usti, President Beneš's country house, on the morning of March 9, 1948, the last day of his life: (from left) Eduard Beneš, Vladimír Clementis, Deputy Foreign Minister; Jozef Olszewski, Polish Ambassador. *Courtesy, Czechoslovak News Agency*

Dear Mr. Minister, my dear friend,

   We are celebrating today an anniversary which is very important for our nations and states--the 1st anniversary of the signature of our Treaty of Friendship and Mutual Aid. The Poles and Czechoslovaks have definitely found themselves on their place in the family of the slavonic popular-democratic states.
   In the last year we have done a good work. We shall continue in this work and intensify still more our social, economical and cultural relations, as it should properly be between brothers and neighbors.
   Our greatest common problem is Germany. We remember the past and look with open eyes towards the future.
   Strong, working and faithful we shall resist to all snares and become a firm fortress of peace and democracy.

                              Jan Masaryk

Photostat and translation of the draft of a speech for Polish-Czechoslovak Friendship Day, written by Masaryk after dinner on the night of his death, March 9, 1948.

Czernin Palace, Masaryk's residence and headquarters of the Ministry of Foreign Affairs in Prague, scene of Masaryk's death. *Courtesy, Czechoslovak News Agency*

Masaryk's bedroom and adjoining sitting room, as furnished in 1969 (used as a guest apartment) : door to left of bed leads to bathroom.

Masaryk's bathroom window, from which he allegedly jumped.

Ledge outside Masaryk's bathroom window. *Courtesy, Czechoslovak News Agency*

View from Masaryk's bathroom window down to the courtyard below, where his body was found. *Courtesy, Czechoslovak News Agency*

Members of Czechoslovak Parliament standing beside Masaryk's empty chair with its floral tribute, on the morning of March 10, 1948, shortly after Masaryk's death. *Courtesy, Czechoslovak News Agency*

Members of the Communist regime at Masaryk's funeral: (from left) **Mrs. Klement Gottwald; Klement Gottwald,** Premier; Václav Nosek, Interior Minister; Antonín Zápatocký, Trade Union leader. *Courtesy, Balkan Universal Press*

Masaryk in casket: the nosegay behind his right ear allegedly placed by his third secretary Lumír Soukoup. *Courtesy, Czechoslovak News Agency*

Troops and dignitaries escorting Masaryk's bier in the funeral procession in Prague, March, 1948. *Wide World Photos*

Czechoslovakian people mourn Masaryk's death at funeral procession. *Courtesy, Czechoslovak News Agency*

Masses of bereaved Czechs: Old Town Square, Prague, March, 1948. *Courtesy, Czechoslovak News Agency*

Pavel Straka, government clerk, allegedly on duty at Czernin Palace the night of Masaryk's death. *Harry Redl, Life Magazine © Time Inc.*

Dr. Jaromír Teplý, who was called to examine Masaryk's body, with his wife after their wedding in 1929. His death, which occurred mysteriously soon after Masaryk's own death, is said to be the key to the Masaryk mystery. *Courtesy, Czechoslovak News Agency*

Masaryk's second secretary Antonín Šum (top) and third secretary **Lumír**
Soukoup (bottom).

Russian invasion after Czechoslovak liberal reforms, August 21, 1968, town of Liberec.

Jiří Kotlar, State Prosecutor, in charge of reinvestigation into the Masaryk mystery. *Harry Redl, Life Magazine © Time Inc.*

Second World War. But that wasn't much help to the Czechoslovaks.

Prime Minister Chamberlain did answer personally for their
submission. President Beneš mobilized his army only to de-
mobilize under pressure from London and Paris, and Hitler
moved in with no trouble at all, spending his first night in
Tomáš Masaryk's apartment at Hradcany Castle. Had he won
the war, the Czechs would have been wiped off the map. The
official Nazi plan for them, approved by Hitler, was "to assimi-
late half the Czech population and eliminate the other half."
The candidates for elimination were particularly "the racially
Mongoloid part and the major part of the intellectual class."
The plan had to be postponed: grave bomb damage to Germany's industry and an acute labor shortage throughout Nazi-
held Europe obliged Hitler to treat Czech workers and peasants
more mildly. But the six years of occupation were bad enough.

Hardly a family escaped the searing touch of the German
Gestapo, and every area of national life came under brutal
Nazi control: the Sokols (a patriotic group of gymnasts), sports,
the churches, the arts, the theater, the press and radio, the
schools. All Czech universities remained closed from 1939 to
1945, the Nazi Gauleiter's reply to Czech protests being: "If
England wins the war you can open your own universities; if
the Germans win, five years of elementary school will be enough
for you." Domestic farm animals were inventoried for delivery
to the master race, and the lifeblood of Czech industry was
drained off to the Third Reich. Economic losses by German
theft or destruction came to $14 billion at the war's end, while
the inflated Czech currency was next to worthless by then. Some
thirty-eight thousand Czech underground fighters were executed by the Gestapo, and another two hundred thousand—at
least half of them Jews—did not return from Belsen, Dachau,
Auschwitz, Terezin, and other concentration camps. The exquisite symbol of the Nazi occupation was Lidice, a mining
village of five hundred inhabitants selected at random for re-

prisals when Czech partisans assassinated the Gestapo Chief and Protector of occupied Czechoslovakia, Reinhard Heydrich. The village was razed to the ground, all its male adults were executed, its women and children were deported. One in every sixty Czechs lost his life under the occupation, and nobody could have come through those six years of terror, subservience, humiliation, and physical and intellectual privation without lasting psychological damage.

President Beneš never got over the shock of Munich. Even when wartime Britain did its best to make amends, he was convinced that his people would be insane to trust this or any Western power ever again. Realizing that Czechoslovakia was too small to survive alone after the war, he turned instinctively eastward. To his mind, Munich sealed the bond of union between Soviet Russia and Czechoslovakia. Russia was the only European power that "kept its word" in 1938, he wrote in his memoirs. His own country and Russia were the only two consistently following an "anti-Fascist policy." Only they were ready to fight Hitler in September, 1938, and they were "left alone." Western betrayal was the work of European reaction, Soviet loyalty the proof of democratic solidarity.

In an experienced and sophisticated statesman, the view seemed singularly ingenuous. The Russians could easily talk of leaping to Czechoslovakia's defense, knowing perfectly well they wouldn't have to. They weren't supposed to, by treaty, unless the French did; and the French, signatories to the Munich Agreement, predictably didn't. Furthermore, Stalin's democratic solidarity was none too evident in the next two years. Barely a month after the Nazi *Wehrmacht* completed the dismemberment of Czechoslovakia in March, 1939, Stalin opened secret negotiations with Hitler. Soviet Foreign Minister Molotov's talks with Hitler, surely the most grotesque in modern history, centered on the total destruction of Great Britain and her empire—Molotov was frankly enchanted by the prospect—and division of the spoils between Germany and Soviet Russia, with some crumbs for Hitler's junior partners. A ten-year Soviet-German Pact along these lines was signed in September. During the two years it lasted, the Kremlin did its best to demoralize and betray resistance fighters throughout occupied Europe. It also withdrew diplomatic recognition from independent Czechoslovakia, according it instead to the Nazi Protectorate over the Czechlands and the puppet Slovak state collaborating with Hitler—which is more than the Western states did. The behavior of Czech Communists during these two years may be imagined from the fact that not one of Gottwald's speeches in this period was ever published.

Nevertheless, Beneš was sure Soviet Russia would end up on the Allied side. In fact, he maintained secret contact with the Soviet Ambassador in London all through those two years. Vindicated by Hitler's invasion of the Soviet Union in 1941, he was greatly heartened by the apparent changes coming over Russia thereafter: the dissolution of the Comintern in 1943, suggesting an end of Bolshevik ambitions for world revolution; recognition of the Russian Orthodox Church; a mighty revival of Pan-Slavism, rank heresy to Bolshevik old-timers, now patriotic Russia's answer to Hitler's foaming hatred for the Slavs. The Kremlin's sponsorship of Pan-Slavism was spectacularly successful, a promise for all Eastern Europe's 145 million Slavs of enduring protection from thrusting Germany. The Czechs, westernmost of the Slavs, never in their history having come into direct contact with the Russians, were the movement's most enthusiastic supporters.

Beneš wasn't alone in his pro-Russian policy in those days. Most of his democratic ministers-in-exile felt that postwar Russian friendship was indispensable. But many, especially Jan Masaryk, had reservations which Beneš did not share and did his best to overcome. Masaryk, who liked the Russian people but detested their government, was full of premonitions as he watched his fellow Slavs sliding downhill. He was desperately anxious to have his homeland liberated by the British and

American armies, haunting the White House and Pentagon during the war, offering almost any terms: "Send us your troops," he told President Roosevelt, "and you can have a blank check to do as you like."

President Beneš, wholly committed to the closest possible collaboration with Russia, did not throw his considerable diplomatic weight behind his Foreign Minister. The West had not yet consigned his country to Moscow when he went there in November, 1943, to negotiate a Friendship Treaty, against urgent British advice. The Big Three had not yet met at Teheran, where they were to decide to let the Red Army liberate Prague; and they were still nearly two years away from the Yalta Conference, where they were to agree that all Eastern European states must have "democratic postwar governments friendly to the U.S.S.R." Nobody made Beneš go to Moscow. It was his idea.

Welcomed as Head of State, royally dined and deferentially toasted, he was immensely impressed by Stalin and Soviet Russia. "I did not expect such prospects of cordial and harmonious cooperation for the future," he cabled Masaryk. "Progress here in the development of ideas is great, real, and definite. To imagine that the present outlook toward the Comintern, religion, cooperation with the West, Pan-Slavism, is merely tactical would be a fundamental error. . . . I regard it as certain that all treaties not only with us but also with the British and Americans will be kept. . . . Throughout our discussions, our partners repeatedly stressed that they are not concerned with our internal affairs and would not interfere with them."

On his return to London with a Friendship Treaty guaranteeing "mutual respect of sovereignty and noninterference in internal affairs," President Beneš was radiant. He had talked with Gottwald and other Czechoslovak Communists in Moscow, too, and was delighted with the outlook for postwar political collaboration. "The Soviet Union does not request anything special from us," he said in a secret message to the democratic underground in occupied Czechoslovakia. "Our policy will simply be that of our democratic majority."

His private impressions were something else again. Among the papers found after his death were scribbled notes of that first visit to Moscow in 1943. He wrote:

1. The National Committees to be set up after liberation are in fact Soviets, in the Communist understanding.

2. The Communists' totalitarian tendencies remain: under the guise of the National Front, in fact, one party should govern.

3. The Communists' participation in the government has one aim: to get hold of positions and have decisive influence in preparation for seizing all power in the state.

Not only was Beneš quite sure of this, but he had a pretty good idea of how the Communists meant to go about it: he came back to London with the written proof in his pocket. On leaving Moscow, Gottwald asked him to carry a confidential letter to the Czechoslovak Communists' leader in England—the future Interior Minister Václav Nosek. Whether as a courtesy or by deliberate intent, he gave the letter to Beneš in an unsealed envelope. The Czechoslovak Communists, polling only one in every ten votes before the war, would "in all probability be the strongest party after the war," Gottwald wrote to Nosek. "So we consider it obvious that Communists must be able to play a truly effective role in the new government. This means, among other things, that the portfolios of Interior and Defense must be held by the Communists. The new Prime Minister, of course, must be a man of the bloc." The pincers were already in place when an accommodating future victim carried the letter to London.

How could President Beneš, a democrat to his soul, have failed to warn his government-in-exile of these hazards, concealed them from his friends of thirty years' standing, remained above the fray when his democratic ministers signed the fatal Moscow agreement two years later, let another three years go by without lifting a finger to prepare them for self-defense? He may have been hoping against hope, unable to accept what his analytical mind told him, clinging in spite of everything to his lifelong faith in Russia. Described by Lloyd George as "impulsive, clever, but much less sagacious and more shortsighted than Tomáš Masaryk," Beneš was not the penetrating thinker and scholar his mentor had been. Tomáš Masaryk, who probably understood the Russians better than any European statesman of his day, also realized the importance of their friendship: he would never have pursued an *anti*-Soviet policy. But he had no sentimental illusions about them. He had studied the Russian language since childhood, visited the country often, and been present during the Bolshevik Revolution, whose leaders he knew well. Lenin, he wrote later, was brilliant but spiritually crude and half-educated; and the new revolution destroyed ruthlessly without ceasing to be Byzantine. "Uncritical, wholly unscientific infallibility is the basis of the Bolshevist dictatorship. A regime that quails before criticism and fears to recognize thinking men stands self-condemned." The Founder and Liberator would not have been taken in by Stalin.

Perhaps Beneš wasn't really taken in either. He may simply have been stalling for time. Though the Big Three never told him about their decisions at Teheran and Yalta, he must have guessed, at least by May, 1945. Nothing else could explain General Patton's failure to sweep into Prague from nearby Pilsen during the anti-Nazi uprising, when the Red Army was still tied up at Teschen, a hundred and twenty miles away. Other Eastern European states assigned to the Soviet orbit were getting brisk treatment, their democratic leaders left to languish in exile while the Red Army went about its business. If Czechoslovak democrats showed the smallest anti-Soviet inclinations, they might never have gotten back to Prague at all. Perhaps, Beneš may have thought, their loyal cooperation then and later might persuade Stalin that he needn't destroy them to the last molecule. Certainly the President was inordinately fearful of offending Stalin in the slightest way, refusing even to recall the traitorous pro-Communist Zdeněk Fierlinger as his wartime ambassador to Moscow—a rare instance when Jan Masaryk actively intervened, begging him to do so. If he did know more than his fellow democrats about Stalin's real intentions, he might have been that much more anxious to avoid incurring Stalin's displeasure; and if this was his reasoning, he was entirely capable of keeping it to himself. He never went in for collective leadership.

The one certainty was his horror of civil war. If President Beneš could not face bloodshed to defy the Germans—admittedly a hopeless case—he was still less willing to pit Czech against Czech, Slav against Slav—also a hopeless case. Whether deliberately or not, his people were kept in ignorance of a situation that might rouse them to resistance while they still had time. The average Czech was left undisturbed in the reassuring assumption that the country's home-grown Communists were Social Democrats at heart, militant but patriotic, earnest disciples of the Founder and Liberator they praised so loudly, committed to the Constitution they glorified to the last. The first shocking evidence to the contrary was not made public until Prokop Drtina revealed the true nature of the Interior Ministry's activities in January, 1948, much too late to do anything about it.

Some were still ready to fight even on the last days of the *Putsch,* recognizing the hopelessness of the case. The ten thousand students marching to Hradcany Castle were as defiant then as they were when Hitler came: "Defense also means a readiness to fight—even if we know the results will be the same as in 1939," they said in their manifesto. In rejecting their appeal, President Beneš did not spare his countrymen the bloodshed he dreaded. The Communists' Interior Minister had said shortly before the coup, "We are accused of Gestapoism, and I do not deny it. On the contrary, we shall show our opponents that we can do this better than the Germans." He was as good as his word. Within six months of the *Putsch*, the new Communist regime had a hundred and twenty-four forced-labor camps in full swing, the inmates treated with no less savagery than the Gestapo's; and the Czechoslovaks suffered more from the Stalinist purges in the next three years than any of the hundred million Eastern Europeans absorbed into Soviet Russia's postwar empire. It wasn't the first or last time that many Czechoslovaks asked themselves whether hopeless defiance would not have been better than none.

European history might have taken a different course if the Czechoslovaks had resisted the German invaders after Munich. They hadn't a prayer of overcoming the German forces. But they had an excellent army, and Nazi officers arriving in Prague were astounded by the strength of their unused military defenses. Abandoned though they were on every side, their resistance might have brought the Allies into the Second World War before Hitler was ready. "Where Beneš failed—and it cost him and his country much—was in not taking violent decisions at a supreme moment," wrote Winston Churchill in his history of the war. "He was too experienced a diplomatist, too astute a year-to-year politician, to realize the moment to stake all on victory or death. Had he told his cannons to fire at Munich time the Second World War would have begun under conditions far less favorable to Hitler."

Czechoslovak history might also have been different if President Beneš had taken a violent decision at a supreme moment in 1948. Unlike the other Eastern European states—Poland, Hungary, Rumania, Bulgaria, Albania, Yugoslavia—his country was a borderline case at Teheran and Yalta, still more so at the Potsdam Conference in the summer of 1945. Prague, after all, lies well to the west of Vienna. President Truman, replacing the dead President Roosevelt, took a much tougher line at Potsdam against the Russians' westward advance. Disregarding the Yalta agreement, he refused to withdraw General Patton's Sixth Army from Czechoslovak soil until the Red Army agreed to withdraw simultaneously, the following December. His distrust of Russia was explicit when he announced the Truman Doctrine in the spring of 1947: the Kremlin was no longer pretending by then to keep its end of the Yalta bargain by holding free elections in the rest of Eastern Europe. The United States had the atom bomb at the time and Soviet Russia didn't. Having failed to press this advantage for three years, President Beneš had naturally lost it by February, 1948, far too late to request, or expect, American help against the Communists. But it wasn't altogether out of the question that Czechoslovak democrats might have had some American support if they'd thought of asking for it sooner.

And Communist history might have been changed if Czechoslovakia's Communist leaders, trying to humanize Communism, had ordered their army to fire on the first Russian soldier crossing their borders in 1968. They didn't have a hope of overcoming the Russians either. But Soviet leaders, divided amongst themselves and struggling to keep a hold on their disintegrating empire, might have been forced to retreat by an aroused international Communist community if the Czechoslovaks had fought and died, kept the issue open like a running sore, instead of treating with the invader, trying to outwit him like the Good Soldier Schweik, making the best of the worst. Having lived for months in occupied Prague this last time, I have no doubt that hundreds of thousands of Czechoslovaks were prepared to give their lives in a direct confrontation with their assailants. For the third time in thirty years, their leaders wouldn't let them.

Chapter 8

"Are you going to write one of those cheap anti-Communist tracts?"

"I don't think so."

"Well, then, a vulgar thriller?"

"Not if you mean what I think you mean."

"Do you know anything about Czech history? Hus? Žižka? Comenius? Are you going to say They Did Him In, whatever anybody tells you? Because if that's your game, don't count on me."

"Actually, I'd thought of getting all the evidence together, and then feeding it into an IBM computer . . ."

"Computer?" A pause. "That's got style! All right. Where do we begin?"

It was the first of my many meetings with Anna Masaryk, in her office at the National Gallery overlooking Old Town Square, at her sister Herberta's Mala Strana flat, small but furnished with some Biedermeier pieces and a few choice rugs, and in her own attractive mansard rooms around the corner, near the river: "If you stand here, no, *behind* the desk and right against the wall, and bend your head *just* a little, you'll get *quite* a decent view of Charles Bridge." The living room, carved out of an attic, oddly shaped and decorated with flair, was full of surprises. So was Anička. The frail-looking frame, feet, hands, did not prepare you for the square aggressive jaw, the mischievous blue-gray eyes for the soft, tremulous mouth, the spiky pepper-and-salt hair for the delicate complexion, fresh as a spring fruit. At fifty, she might be sixty or thirty, depending on her thoughts from moment to moment. Daughter of Jan's brother Herbert, she had not married, nor had she left Prague for more than a month or two at a time, not even under the Nazi occupation. She was as resolutely Czech as Smetana, Pilsner beer, and her grandfather, whose thin gold spectacles she loved to pop on (and off) her short nose, making her look, as she said, like a nineteenth-century lady Bohemian owl.

Herberta, mother of a grown son and daughter, was more matronly, tall and plump, auburn hair brushed smooth, hazel eyes level over broad Slavic cheekbones. She could hardly be more different from her sister, her handsome face sedate, thoughts composed, crisp voice cutting through Anička's little follies: "Nonsense, my dear, you know very well that isn't *art nouveau*. It's simply a hideous middle-class coat rack. Perhaps if you cover it in something it won't show."

Yet they were plainly linked, regnant the two of them, Masaryks both. You could tell by their superb self-assurance, indifference to social distinctions of any sort—money, class, political rank—indestructible sense of clan. They didn't have an easy time, with their name, in a Communist state. The family country house went, of course; they had no income and not much in the way of a choice of jobs; there were long years when even old family friends were afraid to be seen with them. But they never thought of going away, strongly disapproved when Aunt Alice went to live in America after her brother Jan died. If a Masaryk couldn't live in Czechoslovakia, who could?

For Uncle Jan, though, it would have been different. They wouldn't have blamed him for going to live in London. "Dry realism" was a prime Masaryk quality, after all, dictating a choice for Jan as it did for his father in the First World War. Tomáš Masaryk was bent on hastening the fall of the Austro-Hungarian Empire and went into four years of voluntary exile at the age of sixty-four, hating every minute of it. His wife was under house arrest in Prague, his daughter Alice was in prison, he himself was a fish out of water away from his homeland. "I often consider whether I ought not to go home again," he said to Eduard Beneš in 1916. "Of course they'd hang me. But at least I should see my wife once more. . . ." And later, he wrote: "I'd heard rumors that my wife had fallen ill; I was afraid Alice would not be able to stand prison life; there was a report in the American papers that our Jan, serving in the Austrian army, had been, or was to be, hanged on my account. All this, and a great deal more, was a trial to my nerves, but they did not give way." Tomáš Masaryk stayed abroad, thinking it best for the national Czechoslovak cause. Jan, too, might have reasoned this way.

Not that he was a replica of his father—not at all, both women agreed. Grandfather had a gaiety and a fund of wry humor that outsiders rarely detected. But he was ascetic, a gifted scholar, incurably addicted to politics. Jan worshipped him and never dreamed of becoming like him. Jan had more of a genius for living, but not for doing anything particular with his life. He hadn't his father's drive. Left to himself, he would have been happy just to play the piano, perhaps to become a professional musician. He never sought responsibility, though he rose to it.

He was anything but a diplomat—at any rate, anything but "a born *Middle European* diplomat," as Herberta put it—fuming at protocol, impatient with formalities, irritated beyond words by "stupid third secretaries with university degrees" who kept telling him "that wasn't the way one did things." In this he was very much like his father: the President-Liberator was in perpetual hot water with his protocol officer for the same reasons. What Jan did have was intuitive diplomatic skill, in handling people and grasping the essence of a question. Eduard

Beneš, as Tomáš Masaryk's Foreign Minister, had insisted on making a diplomat of Jan, sending him first to Washington as Chargé d'Affaires and then to London as Chancellor, and later Ambassador. The President was dubious, because Jan was his son: Tomáš Masaryk was a democrat, as a biographer once observed, not a dynast. But Uncle Jan came through marvelously well. Toward the end, he was the most popular foreign diplomat in London. The British used to cheer him as he drove through St. James's Park or Piccadilly during the war; and nobody but Winston Churchill could top his wartime broadcasts.

But he never fell irretrievably into the diplomatic mold, "thank God," said Anička. He could be acid-tongued, when provoked, without a thought for diplomacy. One of the best stories was his reply to an American Senator who asked, "How's your father? Does he still play the violin?" "Sir," said Jan, "I fear you are making a small mistake. You are perhaps thinking of Paderewski and not Masaryk. Paderewski played the piano, not the violin, and was president not of Czechoslovakia but of Poland. Of our Presidents, Beneš is the only one who played. However, he played neither the violin nor the piano, but football. In all other respects your information is correct." He could also be irreverent, bawdy, rebellious, moody, changeable as the weather, which was why, continued Anička, a lot of people got him all wrong.

"They'd say he had a 'streak of melancholy,' " she went on, watching me carefully for the smallest sign of apostasy, "or he was 'oversensitive,' or 'complicated.' People are in love with romance, they like to think of their heroes as brooding Byronic figures. But none of us in the family are like that, you know. We're peasant stock, country folk; Grandfather's father was a coachman, remember. Uncle Jan wasn't really so complicated: he was sensuous, and felt things on many different levels. It's absurd to say he was melancholy. If you're intelligent you've got to be sad some of the time; only vegetables are never sad. But he wasn't 'sad underneath,' as the soppy romantics would say. He could be sad one minute, gay the next, his mood could change quickly. Why not? Life can flip upside down in a matter of seconds, why shouldn't we?"

He could be pigheaded, too, even with the parents he adored. They were severe with him. Charlotte Garrigue, his American mother, was *very* severe. She was an enigmatic figure, cultivated, elegant, dressed in fine gray batiste with high lace collars, setting off her lovely gray hair, china-blue eyes, and porcelain complexion. She was a beauty, but so closed in by her strait-laced Protestantism that you couldn't see through to her soul. She'd had a hard time with the Czechoslovaks, was never really accepted, for all her left-wing political opinions, which should have been popular in her day: she'd march in May Day parades as a Social Democrat, wearing that fine gray batiste, but she didn't have "the touch." She was too direct, and therefore strange, for Prague's nineteenth-century bourgeois society.

Anyway, it was family history that Charlotte was even more exacting with Jan than Grandfather was; and Jan, "who didn't want to rebel and couldn't help it," would always say "do excuse me," sincerely penitent, when he crossed them. He was a big disappointment to them at school. His teachers used to din it into him that he *must* learn because his father was the most distinguished intellectual in Prague; and he stubbornly refused. Finally his father took him out of Charles University and sent him to the United States, with enough money (barely) to live for a month, and not a single introduction to smooth his way.

He had some bad years in America, working as a messenger, an insurance clerk, in a steel foundry, with a dance band, quite ill for a time. His health was poor and—unlike his father, a rigorous gymnast—he was physically lazy, which didn't help. But it wouldn't occur to him to complain about his parents' decision. He was always a small boy with them. They loved him but were a little afraid of him, and therefore stricter, because he was too emotional. And he—whatever they did to or for him— was unfailingly grateful, therefore defenseless. It was very moving, Anička said.

With his sister Alice, continued Anička, the roles changed: he was the defender, she the defenseless one. Alice was the eldest child, forced to grow up too soon, never as beloved as Jan, who "had only to enter a room—this enchanting, great-eyed boy—and society fell at his feet." It was Alice who took over when their mother's nerves gave out. Charlotte was broken in spirit during the war years, under constant police surveillance, her eldest daughter in prison, while Tomáš Masaryk fought the Hapsburgs from abroad; and she became a shadow when her son Herbert (father of Anička and Herberta) died in 1915 of typhus contracted while working among Polish refugees. (Rumors that Herbert committed suicide were persistent, but untrue.) By the war's end, Charlotte was a nervous wreck, in and out of a mental home. She died in 1923. From wartime on, Alice was everything, and did everything, for Grandfather. She "never created her life or dared to," said Herberta, "she was always living for somebody else." When Tomáš Masaryk moved into Hradcany Castle as first President of the Republic, it was she who managed the whole affair—the furnishing, the receptions, the food and servants, the right admixture of the pomp her father loathed and the simplicity he demanded. She alone could interpret the needs of a man who, living amongst the splendors of a castle built for ancient kings, slept on an iron camp bed, covered with army blankets. Alice was plain, good, selfless. Her brother Jan treasured her, and did all he could to protect her.

Next in his affections, said Herberta, were his two nephews, sons of his younger sister Olga, who had married into the old Swiss Revilliod family and settled in Geneva. A year apart, her sons were the last males in the Masaryk line. The younger one, Leonard, was "very Masaryk," said Anička, "brave, sensuous, engaging, a natural leader." It was shattering for Uncle Jan when Leonard's RAF plane was shot down in World War II. Then he was stricken again when Leonard's brother Herbert died soon afterward of tuberculosis: Olga, a Christian Scientist, had refused to let her son undergo conventional medical treatment. Jan, who loved children and longed for some of his own, was crushed by the loss of both nephews and never entirely got over it.

He'd had only one other truly deep attachment: for his wife, Frances Crane Leatherbee. Daughter of Tomáš Masaryk's great American friend, the millionaire industrialist Charles Crane, she was a widow with three children when Jan married her in 1927. She looked, said Anička, uncannily like Jan's mother—beautiful, stately, blue-eyed, with that same breath-taking complexion. But she was a much haughtier woman—an unspeakable snob, the nieces thought—and utterly humorless to boot. She'd expected to be treated like royalty and, to the apparently malicious pleasure of Jan's nieces, wasn't. By 1932, she'd had enough, and left Uncle Jan for good. It hit him hard. He was rapturously happy when he married her. Never before or since was he so in love with a woman. "He wasn't very clever about his lady friends," Herberta observed.

Evidently his nieces thought him none too clever about Marcia Davenport either. "*She* certainly wasn't one of your heroic Masaryk ladies," said Anička, slipping on Grandfather's gold spectacles to give me a properly quizzical look. "But maybe Uncle Jan was relieved to get away from heroic ladies for a change." The American authoress, then in her mid-forties, had come along late in his life, at a time of sharpening loneliness. Returning to Prague in 1945, he was almost a stranger in his own country. He'd gone to the United States at twenty-one and stayed nearly a decade. He might have remained forever if, by chance, he hadn't been in Austria on vacation when World War I came in the summer of 1914 and hadn't been pressed into service as a cavalry officer in the Hapsburgs' army. Then, soon after the war, he'd been sent to Washington, and not long thereafter to London, where he'd remained without a break from 1925 until the end of the Second World War. He had left his country a callow youth and come back a diplomat of international fame, on first-name terms with the greatest men of his day. The masses idolized him: he did have "the touch." But the Czechoslovaks who might have grown close to him held back, too proud or shy to cultivate his friendship.

With Marcia Davenport, he could be comfortable. He'd known her for years in the States, they shared a passion for music—her mother was the famous opera singer Alma Gluck— and she was unmistakably devoted to him. One gathered that the nieces found her a trying woman, cloying in her affection, emotive, short on style. But Aunt Alice liked her, and whether or not Uncle Jan meant to marry her—as she wrote after he died, though he'd occasionally made fun of her behind her back —he needed the qualities she had. She was a marvelous cook and an instinctive nest-builder; Uncle Jan was starved for a family life of his own. "You know," said Anička, with an oddly guilty sidelong glance at Herberta, "that's the main reason why I believe he really intended to go to England at the end. If everything else was lost, he could still have finished out his last years as normal people do. He might have just played the piano, and spent careless evenings with people he really enjoyed, and cooked divine dishes with Marcia, and been cosseted. He always longed to do that, all his life. He used to be so happy in his London flat. And Marcia would have known how to take care of him there."

Why, I asked, might he decide to stay in Prague and take his life instead? Again Anička stole a glance at her sister. Herberta plainly disapproved of loose speculation on this subject. "There was a lot we never did understand about his last days," she said firmly. "We didn't know why he stayed on in Gottwald's cabinet after the twelve ministers resigned, how much say President Beneš had in that. We didn't know why he made Marcia go to London—she took forty suitcases with her, at a time like that!— just a couple of days before he died, whether he meant to get her out of the way or join her. We didn't know if he meant to fight or surrender. It could have been either. He had a fierce temper, you know. He didn't lose it often, but when he did, it could be frightening; he'd just *close down,* go icy on you, he could be ferocious."

He might also have been torn between two concepts of resistance, the nieces thought. President Beneš was traditionally opposed to violence, bloodshed, whatever the provocation, choosing to rely on reason. But Tomáš Masaryk, wrestling with his conscience all his life on this issue, had concluded that nonresistance to evil was in itself an evil. "If somebody attacks me with the intention of killing me," he once said in a heated argument with Tolstoy, "I shall defend myself and, if there is nothing else for it, I shall kill the aggressor. If one of the two has to be killed, let it be the one who has an evil purpose." Later, on the eve of Czechoslovak independence, he had said in a memorable declaration: "We condemn violence. We do not wish to use it, nor shall we do so. But against violence we shall defend ourselves, if need be, by iron methods." Which way, coming to his last great crossroads, would Tomáš Masaryk's son decide to go?

For a moment the two sisters were silent, Anička visibly yielding at last to the younger but less impetuous Herberta. "We don't 'know' anything, really," Herberta said, "except that nobody could 'know' without a shadow of a doubt that Uncle Jan committed suicide." Was she thinking of his secretary now in Scotland, Soukoup? She nodded, hazel eyes snapping scorn. Soukoup was merely trying to make himself count for something—he didn't, otherwise—by exploiting Masaryk's death, she said. Uncle Jan didn't really think too much of him, in fact considered him rather vain and more than a little boring. His pretensions to have Masaryk's intimate confidence were ridiculous. There was his preposterous story about accompanying Masaryk to the family cemetery at Lany on March 7. "Uncle Jan called me on his private line to invite me along," she explained. "He sent Dohnálek with the car for me first, we picked up Aunt Alice, then went on to Czernin for Jan. We stayed at the cemetery five minutes—certainly not *an hour*—and Jan behaved just as always. Naturally Soukoup wasn't there. Why on earth should he be? Uncle Jan didn't go in for public display in family matters. And could anyone who knew him well imagine him playing that comedy Soukoup describes? 'God and father will forgive me,' for goodness' sake, and kneeling to touch the earth! Uncle Jan!"

Neither niece ruled out the possibility of suicide. What had troubled them for twenty years was the *way* Masaryk supposedly committed it, like a beachcomber in a Joseph Conrad novel, or the black sheep of the family in a story by Somerset Maugham. Above all, they could not understand how he would deliberately leave the world without a message for Alice. Everybody else might conceivably be forgotten at such a moment: the rest of the family, Marcia Davenport, the Czechoslovak people as an impersonal whole. But his protective tenderness for his sister Alice was something one had to have lived with to understand. It was all but unthinkable that he would wound her so deeply by taking his life without so much as saying goodbye.

And then, to jump out of a window, in pajamas, barefoot—such a primitive, messy, undignified and *uncertain* way to die. Uncle Jan had wept when Minister Drtina jumped out of a third-story window just after the Communist takeover. Not only was it a servant girl's way out, he'd said, but as poor Drtina had learned, one could not even be sure of succeeding. The ignominy of trying to take your life, only to be picked up by Gottwald's police and bundled off to a prison hospital! The ignominy, too, of being found in that squalid, graceless state! Jan himself, perhaps because he was overweight and physically ungainly, was exceptionally fastidious about his person; and he had such an easy elegance in everything he said, did, wore. Surely, if he'd decided suicide was necessary, he would "do it the right way"? It was hard to believe he didn't have, or couldn't procure, enough sleeping pills. He could have "left quietly" like that instead of falling to the ground like a sack of meal. What the nieces could not accept, at bottom, was the suggestion that their delightful Uncle Jan—supremely civilized, urbane, witty, polished, sensual, elegant—could be reduced by whatever external pressures to a witless animal state.

If nothing else, they felt, the memory of his father would have given him the moral force to leave the world "as a Masaryk would." Grandfather had been strongly opposed to taking one's own life. He'd written his thesis on the subject and had gone back to the haunting theme in many later works. He'd maintained that there was a "definite link between suicide and the German cult of the Superman," adding that "the German 'Nation of Thinkers and Philosophers' had the greatest number of suicides, developed the completest militarism, and caused the world war." Still, the old man did recognize that suicide could come about through loss of faith. "With this book I have said that life without belief loses certainty and strength—with this I have said everything," he pointed out.

Jan may have been facing a crisis like that, his certainty and strength gone. Yet he must have thought of the father he venerated, before choosing his way out. Would he have left without a word for the nation Tomáš Masaryk had liberated? Wasn't that supposed to be the idea of his despairing gesture, after all —to convey something, encouragement, solidarity, defiance, passive resistance, to his people? Wouldn't he have tried, at least, to go with a meaningful dignity befitting his name, with the quality that counted so much in the family—with that indefinable but recognizable thing called style?

Tears, which came easily to Anička, were in her eyes as she went over this painful ground. Herberta, briskly handing brandy around in glasses of aged Bohemian crystal, restored emotional order. "Yes, it's hard on us to remember; we grieve for him still," she said. "And it all came and went so quickly, we could never get it straight in our minds."

Anička recalled how they'd heard the news. They were at the family country house, where they had gone immediately after Herberta's visit to the Lany cemetery with Jan. The car came for them from Prague on March 10, and they rushed back, to Czernin Palace. "We got there about eleven in the morning, but they wouldn't even show us where he fell. 'You can't see anything,' the police told us. We couldn't get into his flat upstairs; they'd taken him away for the autopsy, and they didn't want us around.

"We went over to tell Aunt Alice, and came back in the afternoon. He was laid out in his room, on the bed. The room was still in disorder. For a little while, I was alone with him. I felt I must know more—whether he had injuries, bruises, something hidden we hadn't been told about. I went to pick up the sheet. I wasn't afraid. And then, looking at his face, so full of dignity, I thought: he's already suffered so much pain. Leave him in peace."

Chapter 9

The air was electric with tension when Jan Masaryk died, a quarter of a million Czechoslovaks winding up the Loretanska hill and through the grounds of Czernin Palace for a last look at him, kneeling in the streets, sobbing as the coffin went by. Gottwald was terribly nervous. His secret police were everywhere, mingling with the crowds, and the armed Workers' Militia was out in full strength. The population had had barely two weeks of Communist rule, enough to get an acrid taste of it, possibly not enough to be cowed by it. The emotional charge running through that mass of weeping mourners could have blown the Communists and their still shaky regime sky-high.

Did they want him dead or alive?

"Alive. Obviously." State Prosecutor Jiří Kotlar hunched forward over the thick sweet coffee he'd brewed in the office himself, cup teetering, ticking the question off in a notebook balanced on his knees. "He died just when the Communists needed him most. He was being surprisingly cooperative, what's more. You'll have heard that he joined in with the Ministry staff in the one-hour general strike, the day before Gottwald's new cabinet was formed? When a French reporter asked him why, he just said, 'I'm always with the people.' What more could they ask? We haven't found a scrap of evidence to suggest a motive for getting rid of him. Why in the world should they? The last thing they wanted was Masaryk's death."

Under the circumstances, the last thing I might have expected was a different answer. It was September, 1968, when I first called on the State Prosecutor in charge of the Masaryk case. The Warsaw Pact armies had invaded Czechoslovakia some weeks before. Prague was occupied by the Red Army; and while the progressive Dubček regime was still pretending that nothing had really changed, everything had in fact changed. Formally, State Prosecutor Kotlar was going right ahead with his investigation into Masaryk's death, authorized the previous April. Supposing he should produce evidence of murder, though: what would the Russians think?

Still, it was hard to think of Jiří Kotlar as dishonest. Wary, yes: he could no more afford an incautious move than a sapper handling a land mine. Yet he looked as if he wished he could put his feet up and talk things over without these annoying restraints: an unpretentious and restful man. His welcome was informal, when I had threaded my way to his door through a honeycomb of corridors in the administrative wing of Pankrac prison. The room was bright, cluttered, homey, a travel-worn typewriter nestling among heaped files and books piled helter-skelter, a pink plastic instant water heater perched on a portable tape recorder, a large blackboard covered with chalky squiggles, wedged in among volumes of criminological works lining the wall from floor to ceiling—a room very much like my open-faced and slightly rumpled host.

He started from the beginning, explaining with a glint of humor in his frank, wide-set eyes that contrary to popular expectation, he did not set out to expose a murder but to clear up a mystery. People were bound to be disappointed: he appeared to be the one Czechoslovak in fourteen million who was determined to examine the case on its merits. He hadn't finished yet, far from it. But he had carefully studied the Interior Ministry's archives. They contained no facts suggesting anything but suicide. Czechoslovakia's Criminal Code distinguishes between "clarifying" and "investigating" a case with possible criminal features, he explained. A case must be clarified to determine the existence of a crime, investigated to find the miscreant. In the Masaryk affair, Dr. Kotlar was limited to clarification because there was no valid cause to presume a crime in advance. So far, he'd found nothing whatever which, from a criminological or legal viewpoint, could be taken as evidence of violence.

"My first problem was to find out if the 1948 investigation was correct, and you know—nobody is going to like this—it was. At least the part I've checked carefully was. We've found no irregularities in the proceedings. Take the autopsy. I've interviewed several witnesses who were present. One of them is Dr. Tesař, who took the official notes; he's Director of the Forensic Medicine Institute now. They all say the autopsy was done according to the regulations. The physiological examination showed no bullet holes or other marks of violence. The chemical analysis showed no signs of poison. Professor Tomíček, who did the chemical analysis in the laboratory, was head of the Institute of Chemical Medicine, obviously a reputable professional. He's dead, but we have no reason to doubt his word. In short, the post-mortem was in order. It showed conclusively that Masaryk was not shot, or strangled, or poisoned. So you see, we don't even have a reason to exhume the body, though no doubt the press would enjoy that. We take it as established that Masaryk died from injuries caused by falling directly on his feet, while alive and conscious. There is no evidence that he was given, or took, any drugs. . . ."

"Not even the two sleeping pills his butler left for him?"

"No, no sleeping pills. There was nothing at all in the stomach." Dr. Kotlar gave me a rueful look. "I can see you're going to find this pretty dull, but there you are. The investigation showed beyond reasonable doubt that Masaryk was fully conscious when he fell; and the injuries corresponded to the manner of his death."

I'd seen several qualified experts who didn't appear to agree on this, I observed. There were some uncharacteristically athletic theories to account for the manner of Masaryk's fall, and sinister suggestions as well. Why all these efforts to explain? What was wrong with the position of the body?

"Nothing. Masaryk dropped from a height of ten yards. A deviation of half an inch from that height could mean a yard's deviation by the time he hit the ground. That would explain why he lay considerably to the side of the window. Aside from that there were no particular problems. We often have cases of people falling without losing much blood, or even suffering many external injuries. Of course, we're going on guesswork so far. We'll be doing a reconstruction of the fall—I'd like to wait until next March 10 for that, so we can have the right light and weather conditions. We won't only be checking on the position of the body; we'll station people where those in the palace were supposed to be at the time, to check on the sounds that may or may not have been audible. Funny that nobody heard the body land, don't you think? It's something we'll be looking into."

I wondered if he'd also be looking into the case of the police doctor, Teplý, said to have died under curious circumstances after his initial examination of Masaryk's corpse. Some witnesses had assured me that I could never solve the mystery of Masaryk's death without solving Teplý's, I said. Could the State Prosecutor help to clear this up?

"Here's Teplý." Dr. Kotlar rummaged among the folders on his desk, held one up, regretfully put it down again without giving me a glimpse of the contents. "Can't show it to you at this stage. Sorry. You see, if I let this stuff leak out now people will get ideas from it, and then I'd *never* get a truthful word out of them. I've got trouble enough as it is. You'll have to believe me when I say that Teplý's report fits with the rest.

He described the broken heels, knees, hips, and the scrape on
the abdomen, and said the death was caused by the fall. He
estimated the time of death as from two to three hours before
examination—say, between five and six in the morning. His report confirms Dr. Hájek's autopsy findings. And it *was* Hájek
who did the autopsy. Not the slightest question about it."

I already knew that much, I said. What puzzled me was why
so many people should come forward voluntarily only to tell
stories that were so easily disproved. Except for Masaryk's
nieces Anna and Herberta, I doubted whether a single witness
I'd seen so far had failed to lie to me about something or other.
I was beginning to find this the most interesting part of the
case. Yes, Dr. Kotlar agreed, patting the fuzz where his hairline
used to be, forehead crinkling in irritation. Though one got
used to the phenomenon in criminal investigation work, it did
seem exaggerated in the Masaryk case. He was almost tempted
to believe people were doing it just to waste his time and the
government's money. As a small sample, there was this witness
who swore that Hájek claimed he'd never gone near Masaryk's
body. The witness was perfectly respectable—indeed, an outstanding scientist—Professor Karel Kacl, Tomíček's successor as
President of the Institute of Chemical Medicine. Why he should
make up such a tale Dr. Kotlar could not imagine. Maybe he'd
had political ambitions, after the January revolution. Anyway,
Professor Kacl couldn't be taken seriously.

Stories about Teplý, the police doctor, were a bigger head-
ache. The State Prosecutor had gone into the Teplý rumors
exhaustively. There was simply nothing to them. "You can
take it as safely ascertained that Teplý committed suicide, and
did it for personal reasons," Dr. Kotlar said, drawing a thick
black line across Teplý in his notebook. "We know his motives.
I'm not at liberty to disclose them yet, maybe I can tell you in
a few months. I've spoken with witnesses who claim they saw
Teplý write a secret testament before he died, which was supposedly smuggled out to the *New York Times* a year or two

later. The *Times* people helped me look for the testament, and it turned out that the letter was 'not available.' Teplý also used to have connections with the Monastery of Merciful Brethren here—he was going to be a monk at one time—so we asked for their help too. From what we learned at the monastery I can state unequivocally that no such testament existed. This much I can tell you: Teplý had troubles with his wife, and troubles with his office colleagues; he was a bundle of troubles. His wife tried to kill herself two or three times. He was seriously ill, too. That's why he used barbiturate injections for his suicide. . . ."

It was the *Student* article that sent so many Czechoslovaks off on a wild-goose chase, continued Dr. Kotlar, shaking his head in mild wonder at humanity's infinite capacity to be gulled. *Student*'s editors never bothered to check a word of that story. They just lifted it whole from the one published by *Der Spiegel* in West Germany in 1965. In fact, they did worse: they picked out the material that sounded most plausible, omitting the more far-fetched items. The byline in *Der Spiegel* was a fake, of course. The writer calling himself Michael Rand was Benno Weigl, a Czechoslovak émigré now free-lancing in London; and where *he* got his material was a question Dr. Kotlar didn't care to waste any more time on. That man! Recalling the time he'd wasted on Weigl already, his gentle voice took on a faint rasp.

"After weeks and weeks of hunting for some of the witnesses Weigl named, I went to London to see him. I put it to him that those people never existed and—would you believe it?—he said maybe I was right. There was the palace guard he wrote about, Václav Sedm, who allegedly gave this gang of NKVD agents a key to Masaryk's elevator and then went home with a toothache. You can't imagine the trouble we went to, looking for Václav Sedm. We combed the police registers covering a thirty-year period. We questioned the two surviving policemen of the four on duty at the palace that night. We went to every jewelry shop

that was functioning in 1948, because Sedm was said to have
gotten a lucrative job in one after he did his dirty work, and
we questioned all the older employees. We put out a dragnet
for a widow of that name. We searched records of birth, baptism, marriage, death, burial, not only for the name but anything sounding like it, or a combination of its letters. Not a
trace. I can only believe Benno Weigl when he says he invented Václav Sedm.

"Naturally, once you take out Sedm, Benno Weigl's case
more or less falls apart. Sedm was his sole link to the so-called
NKVD agent, Major Schramm, in the Masaryk case. Without
Sedm, Weigl had no proof of any connection at all between
Masaryk's death and Major Schramm—and certainly none involving the NKVD. I haven't even tried to ask the Russians
about this. I wouldn't know what to ask them." I imagined the
Russians would know what to answer all right. We both grinned
and let that pass.

At any rate, the unhappy Mr. Weigl appeared to have put
up a poor show all around. "I asked him what documents he
based his article on," continued Dr. Kotlar. "All he would tell
me was that the information came from people who left
Czechoslovakia after 1948. Part of it, he said, was taken from
written documents that he was 'permitted to see,' deposited in
a bank vault in London, to which Weigl has access only 'with
the permission of somebody else.' He promised to let me see
this material. In fact, his last word when I left London was that
he was going to send me photocopies. So far I've had several
letters from him, asking for official statements on his behalf
because he's suing the London *Times* for libel. He hasn't sent
me any photocopies though."

Still, the State Prosecutor seemed to me to be going rather
far in dismissing Benno Weigl's article merely as "facts that
must be rejected and deductions that cannot be confirmed."
My own impression was that Weigl had picked up some extremely pertinent information, however garbled some of it

came out in print. Indeed, if he'd learned all that from just a glimpse of those documents locked away in a London bank vault, the documents ought to be exceptionally valuable. Writing in *1965*, when nobody in Prague had an inkling of any details in the Masaryk case, he had mentioned several important facts confirmed by eyewitnesses I saw myself in 1968. He did get some names wrong, and apparently primped up the material for publication. Nevertheless, his article included a more or less full description of Masaryk's last day, fairly accurate testimony from perhaps a dozen people, the discovery of excrement on Masaryk's body, the disorder in the apartment, the broken glass and pillows in the bathroom . . .

Dr. Kotlar listened attentively; he was a very good listener. "Yes," he said at last, jotting down a few notes, lounging back in his chair. "We've gotten all sorts of reports about the condition of the apartment. Opinions aren't uniform about that. But the disorder has been greatly exaggerated. You must keep in mind that Masaryk was a bachelor. The majority of witnesses suggest that he didn't pay much attention to order . . . he seemed to live in typical bachelor style. Several witnesses tell me they often saw his flat in the state it was in on the morning of March 10. We have the photographs of the rooms —sorry, I can't show you those right now either; you'll have to come and see me when I'm further along. They do show the pillows in the tub and broken medicine bottles on the bathroom floor. I have the broken glass right here, in that box. . . ." His lips twitched as I looked at the box. "Don't worry, you'll get to see it all by and by. But these things alone don't carry much weight. If the disorder was abnormal, it would have to be related to *something*, some sign of struggle, or forcible action. We've found nothing to prove this."

How about the excrement? Wouldn't that indicate fear, forcible action?

"I doubt it, in Masaryk's case." Dr. Kotlar lit a fresh cigarette from the dying butt of another, an incongruous habit, it occurred to me vaguely, for somebody with such apparently bottomless inner calm. "Naturally we'll need some expertise about the excrement, a psychiatric opinion. Offhand, though, I'd say it wouldn't mean much in this instance. A suicide isn't afraid when he makes the decision for purely personal reasons: inner disequilibrium, an inability to adjust to the outside world, and so on. In Masaryk's case, the decision would have been more or less political, external, a reasoned intellectual decision made in spite of his love of living. He might still be frightened, knowing he had to do it. We don't rule out physiological causes either, of course. I've ordered laboratory tests on the laxative effects of the mineral water he drank that night. Krandorf, it was called."

Was I right, then, in gathering that the State Prosecutor was already reasonably sure it was suicide? Reasonably sure, not positive, he agreed, the smallest crinkle appearing on his placid forehead again. It was not yet established whether Masaryk went out, or anybody entered his flat, in the evening, after dinner. Indeed, there were still gaps in the time schedule for the whole of his last day. Dr. Kotlar had managed to fit several people into the schedule who weren't mentioned in the original investigation. He couldn't show me the list—sorry again, all in good time. But he could tell me that Masaryk did stay to lunch at Sezimovo Usti on March 9 with Present Beneš and his wife. Hana Beneš was alive, very old but vigorous still, and she remembered the occasion clearly.

"I spoke to her myself," Dr. Kotlar went on. "She told me definitely that there was no talk at the table about plans for Masaryk's departure. The three were alone together at lunch. After they'd eaten, the President and Masaryk walked in the garden by themselves, but not for long, because it was cold out. I asked if her husband would have told her of Masaryk's plans to leave—assuming there were such plans—and she excused herself from answering, as the question was too intimate. She implied, though, that he would not have kept such news from her."

So far, I'd been told by Masaryk's butler and household purser that he came back to Czernin Palace for lunch; by the two secretaries that he returned to Prague by three, and so must have left Sezimovo Usti quite early after lunch; by the bodyguard Vyšín that he'd walked in the garden for an hour with President Beneš after lunch, the weather being fine; by the State Prosecutor that the walk didn't last long because it was cold out. While these smaller discrepancies didn't seem to matter much, there was an important point involved: Masaryk's opportunity for a reasonably long private talk with President Beneš, presumably having to do with his plans either to resign from the Communist government, or leave the country, or both. Either would provide what was missing so far—a motive for murder. Did Dr. Kotlar exclude the possibility that the two men discussed such plans at Sezimovo Usti that day?

On the whole, yes. It was most unlikely that Madame Beneš, who was present at the lunch, would have had no hint of Masaryk's plans, either from him or later from her husband. Where was the need for secrecy, after all? "Masaryk didn't need to 'escape' at that time. As Foreign Minister he could easily have found an excuse to travel, and simply not return. Lots of other Czechoslovaks were leaving the country in an entirely normal way that March, even as late as the following July and August. . . .

"No proof whatever could be found to verify any of a dozen stories about Masaryk's plans to escape," Dr. Kotlar went on. "None of his close friends testified that he intended to leave. On the contrary, they said he felt obliged to remain, miserable as he was, because of Beneš." He'd spoken of suicide to several, and almost literally said goodbye to at least one. On Friday, March 5, he'd suddenly called his old friend John Ennals, Secretary of the British United Nations Association, who was in Geneva at the time. Once on the line, he seemed to have nothing to say. When Ennals heard of Masaryk's death the following Wednesday, he concluded at once that the telephone call was an unspoken farewell. He'd confirmed this to Dr. Kotlar, who thought it most revealing of Masaryk's state of mind. There were many other indications along these lines: his lonely vigil at his father's grave on March 7, his search for an apt quotation from the Bible some days before he died, his conversations with his staff toward the end. Masaryk's secretary, Soukoup, had supplied invaluable information on the subject. . . .

Had the State Prosecutor really found Soukoup a useful informant? Oh yes, possibly the most useful of the lot. When Dr. Kotlar had visited him in Glasgow, they had talked for eight hours. He'd brought back a tape of the conversation, much of it extremely significant, if not decisive. And had Dr. Kotlar cross-checked Soukoup's information with Masaryk's other two secretaries, in Prague? Actually, he hadn't seen them personally; he'd left that to an assistant. Soukoup had appeared to be the one who was best informed. I had a somewhat different feeling after seeing the other two secretaries myself, I said. Not only was Soukoup very much the junior member of Masaryk's staff, but he had a lamentable habit of telling fibs. Dr. Kotlar didn't seem very interested. Fleetingly, and not for the first time in our lengthy interview, a tiny stab of doubt pierced my mind.

He seemed to sense it. "All the same, we're not taking anything for granted," he said reassuringly. "Masaryk was too important in our country's history. We don't intend to leave anything unexplored in this affair." That was why the State Prosecutor had been so meticulous in investigating the story of Pavel Straka, the night clerk on duty at Czernin Palace during the crucial hours before and after Masaryk died. Straka was the witness who claimed to have heard several cars drive up to the palace before midnight, leaving again around three or four in the morning. In the interval, his office door was allegedly locked and the telephone line cut; and upon rushing to the courtyard after his release, he had found Masaryk's body, and later described the details to Masaryk's actress friend Olga Scheinpflugová—after which he'd spent the next twelve years in jail.

Straka's report, said Dr. Kotlar, was similar to Benno Weigl's, "with the difference that some of Straka's assertions are correct." His claim to have telephoned and later visited Madame Scheinpflugová to relate this story was confirmed by the actress herself, before she died in April, 1968. But Straka appeared to have shifted times a little: he said he had called her on the phone around seven in the morning, whereas he did so two hours later, when he might already have had some picture of what was going on at the palace. Other things Straka said had yet to be verified. One was the technical possibility of cutting the Ministry telephone lines, for example. Several details were almost certainly wrong, the noisy arrivals and departures in particular.

Sluing around in his chair, Dr. Kotlar rubbed a careless tweedy elbow over the chalk squiggles on the blackboard, and drew a fresh diagram. Here, on the mezzanine floor toward the back of the palace office wing, was Straka's office. His windows overlooked the first courtyard, separated from the second in the residence wing by a broad ceremonial staircase. In March, when it was still cold and the central heating was still on, the palace windows would be closed. The distance between the office and residence entrance was a hundred and thirty-five yards (see sketch on page 144), so it would be rather difficult for Straka to hear anything going on around Masaryk's side of the vast building. Both entrances of Czernin were guarded by police constables, furthermore, relieving each other every three hours. Of the four taking turns throughout the night, none had heard or seen cars arriving and departing. Two of the four policemen on duty were alive: Josef Klapka and Jaroslav Filipovský, both stationed in the office wing that night. The other two, Emmanuel Jindříček and Václav Staněk, now dead, were interrogated by security police on the morning of March 10, and their testimony was included in the archives. Not only did they hear and see no cars on the palace grounds, but they noticed nothing else unusual throughout the night. Pavel Straka's reference to a meeting with the porter in the residence wing could not be ac-

curate. There were two porters in the palace, for the first and
second wings, both dead. But they did not work at night, reporting for duty around nine in the morning. Since it was Straka
alone who spoke of mysterious midnight visitors at Czernin, the
story did not appear to hold water.

The constables seemed hard of hearing, I observed. Not even
the two alternating on duty in the residence wing—less than

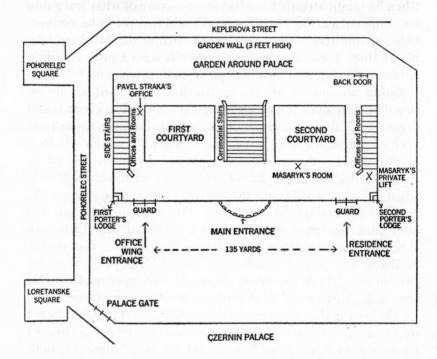

ten yards from the courtyard where Masaryk fell—had heard the
thud of a two-hundred-pound body striking the ground, in a
walled-in area so acoustically constructed that you could hear a
pebble drop. Dr. Kotlar nodded, admitting the enigma. Furthermore, how about the *back* entrance of the palace, I inquired.
The butler's son used to get in that way without the slightest
trouble; and Straka, working in a room at the rear of the office

wing, might perhaps have heard these sounds coming from Keplerova Street, running along the rear garden of the palace from Pohorelec Square, which he specifically mentioned (see sketch). Here the State Prosecutor was on more solid ground. "Out of the question. There was a policeman on duty at the back entrance of the residence wing. Not a soul went through there." Who was the policeman, I asked, the existence of this fifth constable never having been mentioned before. Dr. Kotlar gave me another of those kindly, regretful looks. All in good time.

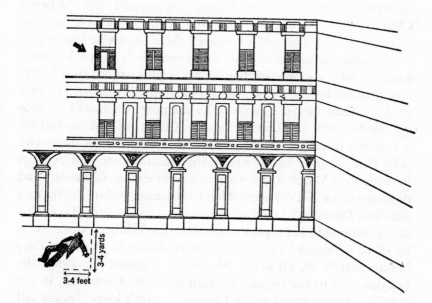

3-4 yards

3-4 feet

"You understand that Straka's credibility is open to question," he said. "He doesn't seem to have quite a normal personality [a euphemism for Straka's obvious homosexuality] and he apparently has an abnormal desire to be in the limelight. He claims he was a close friend of Masaryk, for instance, and to prove it shows us a book with the Foreign Minister's autograph. Masaryk autographed thousands of books; and the secretary, Soukoup, says it's ridiculous to imagine he would have more than a nodding acquaintance with an unimportant clerk like Straka. Still, we don't want to reject Straka, or say he's inventing his story. We want to prove it one way or another."

There was, however, a witness whom the State Prosecutor did reject, with a vehemence so out of character that I marveled later at my failure to make more of it. The witness, undeniably shady, was Major Chlumský. "You will recall," said Dr. Kotlar, lighting another cigarette, resolutely calm, "that Major Chlumský's appearance on the scene last spring was preceded by anonymous letters to the Prague papers and me. 'Where's Chlumský?' the headlines said. Believe me, wherever he was, he'd have been better off if he stayed there. When he finally presented himself, he turned out to be somebody called Vítězslav Kadlcák, who announced that *he* was getting anonymous letters too—threatening ones, at that—and wanted protection. Protection! Then he led us around by the nose. He wasn't Chlumský but he knew all about Chlumský. Chlumský had worked for a Western intelligence service and had the goods on the Soviet NKVD. Chlumský had firsthand information that Masaryk was in danger on March 9 and warned him to escape. Chlumský had dossiers on the NKVD agent Major Schramm, and on Schramm's assassins. Chlumský knew all about the police doctor Teplý, his secret testament, his report to the Interior Ministry, the reasons he died. Chlumský knew every move Masaryk made for days before March 10, all about his visit to Premier Gottwald the last day, and to the Deputy Foreign Minister, Clementis, in the evening. There wasn't much Chlumský didn't know, let me tell you.

"I can't bear to think of how much time we wasted on Major Chlumský. Eventually we found out that all those anonymous letters to the press, to me, and to himself, posted from every corner of the Republic, were written on his own typewriter. I questioned him myself three times, and each time he changed his story. First he said he got his material from an important politician, who died years ago. Then he said he passed the stuff on to somebody abroad, thinking we couldn't find the man. But we did find him, and he never got information from Chlumský-Kadlcák. Then he kept producing *new* material, as if we didn't have enough to worry about. The man was sick. He had a disturbed personality. You might say he was deranged. If we hadn't been strictly objective about him, we would have gotten into really bad trouble. Take it from me: you can forget Chlumský."

I very nearly did forget Chlumský. It was pure luck, when I came across his initials in an obscure item on the inside pages of a Roman newspaper some months later, that his unpronounceable name hadn't slipped from my memory entirely.

At the time, however, I was inclined to take the State Prosecutor's word on this and most things. I had to take somebody's word, after all; and despite the obvious limitations imposed upon him, I found it hard to question his honesty. He was helpful and apparently as candid as he could be to the last, rising apologetically when a harried secretary put her head in for the fifth or sixth time to remind him of a waiting caller. "Come back just before Christmas," he said cordially, round face friendly as he ambled along at my side through a network of corridors until I could see my way clear to the exit. "By then I should be far enough ahead to give you most of the documentation you want—unless another Chlumský-Kadlcák comes along." We both smiled, a small joke shared. He waved, noticed the chalk dust on his sleeve, gave it an absent-minded rub, and strolled back into the maw of Pankrac prison.

Chapter 10

Rain was falling in sheets as I dived into the dreary vestibule of a tenement in the Holesovice district, assailed by the stench of gas, urine, garbage, coal dust, and rancid cooking oil that infests the slums of Europe. I was discouraged before climbing the littered staircase, and more so coming down again half an hour later. I didn't learn much from the retired police constable living in a shabby one-room flat above, except that I'd been told at least one outright lie by State Prosecutor Kotlar.

Josef Klapka was tall and bone-thin, his face emaciated and corrugated with wrinkles, his eyes unexpectedly lively in their deep brown sockets. His living-dining-bedroom was spotless, furnished with odds and ends of the 1930's, walls decorated with a string of medals for his service in France with the Czechoslovak Foreign Legion during the First World War. One of the two surviving policemen guarding Czernin Palace on the night of March 9, 1948, he was fired from the service three months later, and thrown out of his apartment. Nobody explained why. He told his story simply. As he said, there was little to tell.

"In the first entrance—that's the office entrance—there was me and Filipovský; he was on duty from one to four in the morning, me from four to seven, and so on through until past noon. Then, on the other side, where the Minister lived, there were these two other policemen, Staněk and Jindříček, they're both dead. No porters at night. They'd go off at eight and come back next morning; we used the porters' lodges at night.

"Anyway, I was there, in the first porter's lodge, until 1:00 A.M. Then I came back on at 4:00, and sat down in my usual place, to the left of the entrance, in that big marble hall. I could see out through the glass doors into the courtyard, but it was the first courtyard, on the left of the main entrance as you go in, not the one the Minister fell in. About twenty past six in the morning, the palace stoker Merxbauer came running over with another fellow. He was all excited, he said he just saw Minister Masaryk's body in the other courtyard. These two fellows were up on the roof to take a flag down, and they saw the body when they came downstairs again. Right away I rushed over there. I had to see for myself, I couldn't believe it, you know how it is. He was lying on his back with his head turned a little to the right side, his left hand was folded over his heart, his right arm was stretched out straight; I could see he was dead. His face was all dark like, and his eyes were wide open. . . . I tried to breathe into his mouth, no good, I felt his heart. . . . I didn't have a mirror, but you can tell when somebody's dead. The bones of his heels were scattered around, I picked up a piece and kept it. Then I ran to the telephone in the second porter's lodge, next to that courtyard. The guard there, Jindříček, he didn't know a thing about what was going on, he was snoring away. I was the one who had to tell him.

"So I called the Home Minister, Nosek, and then Dr. Hora of the security police, and they came in five minutes, with the ambulance. Then the police doctor Teplý came, and he said the Minister must have died three, four hours ago. . . ." From a bureau drawer, Klapka pulled out a tattered and yellowed sheet of notebook paper on which he had written that same day: "Minister Jan Masaryk died of suicide on March 10, about three o'clock in the morning. He was found at 6:30."

If the time of death was set so early, I said, then he, Klapka, would not yet have been on duty when the Minister fell. It would have been his colleague, Filipovský, wouldn't it? That's right, said Klapka. The timing might also fit part of the story told by the Ministry night clerk Pavel Straka, I went on. Straka spoke of seeing the body around three or four in the morning, and his description of the corpse seemed to dovetail with Klapka's. Right again, said Klapka. Could Straka have seen or heard something that Klapka or Filipovský didn't hear or see? Klapka couldn't speak for Filipovský. He himself saw no cars, the way Straka said. "No, I didn't hear a sound, nothing at all, when I was on duty. The only odd thing—I was a fool, not noticing, I was so upset—was when they put the body on the stretcher, I realized there was no blood, just a little on the right side, after he was on the stretcher. That was funny, I said to myself. That's all."

Shortly after 7:00 A.M., he continued, the body was carried to the police station fifty yards away in Loretanske Square, washed, and brought back again, up to the apartment. Klapka was questioned by the secret police around ten, remained on duty until one, then went home. He had no other information.

But there was one more thing I wanted to know. "Who was the policeman guarding the back door of the residence wing?" I asked casually.

Klapka looked blank. "Back door? No one. There wasn't any policeman at the back door."

Drenched as I walked home through the pelting rain, I thought back over my last talk with State Prosecutor Kotlar. "Out of the question," he'd said, relaxed, on solid ground. "There was a policeman on duty at the back entrance of the residence wing. Not a soul went through there." It might be a minor point; maybe not a soul did go through there. What worried me wasn't so much the accessibility of the back door as the probity of Dr. Kotlar. If he'd deliberately lied on one question, what about the rest? I had better make sure.

The other constable, Jaroslav Filipovský, was too sick to see me for more than a few minutes. Paralyzed by a stroke, speaking with difficulty, he told me what he could. He'd seen the Minister passing, on the evening of March 9, sometime while he was on duty in the office wing between seven and ten. Masaryk was in good humor, joked with him about how grand he looked in his new uniform, seemed altogether normal. Filipovský couldn't believe it was suicide when he heard the news next day. He had replaced Klapka in the porter's lodge at 1:00 A.M., staying until 4:00, and heard nothing. "But how could I hear anything?" he asked. "From my side of the palace to the Minister's apartment was a great distance—maybe a hundred and fifty yards—anything could happen there, I wouldn't hear it. Besides, if somebody got into the palace that night, they wouldn't have to come through the front entrance. There are lots of ways to get into Czernin from behind. You could come over the back wall and through the garden, or from Pohorelec Square through the Ministry garages. You could even drive a car through that way, and from where I was, you wouldn't hear a sound. Anybody could have got in the back way, without my knowing."

Wasn't there a policeman guarding the rear door of the residence wing?

"Rear door? Not that night. Nobody at all."

To be doubly sure, I called a colleague on the Czechoslovak television team which had prepared four lengthy documentaries on Masaryk's death. Had the team, by chance, looked into the question of who was assigned to guard duty at Czernin Palace on the night of March 9? Yes, there'd been a check of the police register at the Loretanska Headquarters. And who was on the register for night duty? Klapka, Filipovský, Jindříček, Staněk. No guard stationed at the rear door? No.

Although Jindříček and Staněk were long dead, the TV crew had managed to track down Staněk's widow, a tired, faded woman in her sixties who made a small sensation in her minute or two on the television screen. It wasn't true that none of the

policemen on duty had heard or seen any late visitors at Czernin
that night, she said. Her husband did. He was guarding the
residence wing from 1:00 to 4:00 A.M. "About half past one,
some cars came, and some men got out and stood under the
portico. My husband didn't dare say a word, they told him to
be quiet, and all the cars had government license plates, so he
thought he'd better shut up. Afterwards, I couldn't understand
it, he never heard the body drop. I said to him, 'Imbecile!
Where were you?' 'Nothing,' he says to me, 'it was nothing . . .
I was just . . .' He was just outside, walking up and down.
'Fine,' I tell him, 'you can walk up and down as much as you
like, who's to stop you? You weren't forced to stay in the porter's lodge all night long, just so you kept the lodge door
locked; nobody could get into it while you were outside, could
they? That's all right then.' All the same, my husband was
supposed to be in the porter's lodge and he wasn't there."

How interesting, I suddenly thought:

1. *Václav Staněk:* police guard officially on duty in residence
wing during crucial hours; absent from porter's lodge at decisive moment; now dead; widow says he knew of late-night
visitors, kept mouth shut.

2. *Václav Sedm:* police guard allegedly invented by Benno
Weigl in *Der Spiegel,* said to have been on duty in residence
wing during crucial hours; absented himself at decisive moment
pleading toothache, presumably after giving NKVD agent
Schramm the key to Masaryk's elevator; reportedly dead; widow
quoted in Weigl's article *(in 1965)* as having confided to somebody: "If my Václav were alive, he could say how five men got
into Czernin Palace the night Masaryk died."

Well, well.

In describing his long search for Benno Weigl's witness,
State Prosecutor Kotlar did not mention the widow Staněk to
me. She had appeared on television, was therefore available. I
wondered if he'd tried to find her, during those weeks when he
was combing police registers, searching birth, baptism, marriage,

and death records, casting a dragnet for the missing guard's widow, hunting for any combination of the letters, or something similar to the name, of Benno Weigl's Václav Sedm.

I found myself wondering more and more about Dr. Kotlar as time went by. He hadn't been straight with me about the police guards; and I quickly discovered that he had been none too forthright about the autopsy proceedings either.

There was no question that the post-mortem on Masaryk's corpse was done personally by Dr. František Hájek, then Director of the Forensic Medicine Institute at Charles University. All the eyewitnesses confirmed this. So did Dr. Hájek's close friend, Professor Karel Kacl, the outstanding scientist whose testimony was dismissed by the State Prosecutor as merely a matter of political self-interest. Contrary to what the Prosecutor told me, Dr. Kacl never claimed that his friend Hájek did not perform the autopsy; his point was that Hájek signed the official autopsy report under duress.

Dr. Kacl was one of the few witnesses I did not see personally: he was either not at home, or not in Prague when I was there. But he was interviewed by several Czechoslovak reporters and appeared on television, his story always the same. He had known František Hájek well since long before the war, was intimately associated with him at Charles University, where both were science professors, had done him a particular service after the Nazi occupation. Dr. Hájek, he said, was "an honest and decent man" and a sound progressive who "fully understood" Soviet Russia's struggle during the war. But Hájek had fallen from grace, through no fault of his own, when the German Gestapo forced him to participate in a team of inspection examining the mass graves of Polish soldiers allegedly massacred by the Red Army in Katyn forest. Dr. Hájek tried everything to get out of this, even attempting to undergo an intestinal operation. Although he couldn't avoid it in the end, he'd said as little about Katyn as he could get away with: just that he saw several hundred dead soldiers wearing Polish uniforms.

"After the liberation," continued Dr. Kacl, "Hájek was accused of collaborating with the Germans, and arrested. I and several other members of the faculty exerted all our efforts to get him released and rehabilitated, and we succeeded. This further strengthened our friendship, which is why I could speak so confidentially with him about a delicate matter like Jan Masaryk's death. As the court's expert, the Director of the Forensic Medicine Institute, Dr. Hájek was always extremely reserved in discussing any case, even with his colleagues; and because of the Katyn cloud hanging over him, he was still more cautious. Several fellow physicians suspected that he could be blackmailed, misused in the Masaryk post-mortem, because of this dark spot in his past, and perhaps he was. In any event, he was clearly not convinced it was suicide.

"Our conversation took place soon after Masaryk died. I can't say precisely when—three weeks later, a month—but fairly soon. At that time, when the suicide version was official, I didn't ask Hájek straight out if Masaryk was actually murdered or committed suicide. That isn't done. Given the official verdict, I had to put the question indirectly: what pointed to suicide, what to murder, and so forth. Hájek answered with great delicacy, just listing facts and letting me draw my own conclusions. These were the points he stressed:

"1. A man committing suicide usually jumps with his face outward and back to the room, therefore falling on his face and the front of his body.

"2. A man committing suicide is not afraid, and never shows physiological symptoms of fright, such as loss of sphincter control—that is, the excrement.

"3. The investigation indicated that Masaryk fell from the window backward. There was no trace of alcohol in his blood, so that he would not have fallen by accident—when drunk, for instance. This leads to the conclusion that he was pushed.

"These things, told to me by Dr. Hájek in a most difficult political situation, were an expression of great confidence in me.

I have kept silent all these years for his personal safety and, after his death, the safety of his family. I feel that I am justified in speaking out now, and even that it is my duty to tell the public all I know."

This was the testimony, from a professional of high repute—Professor Kacl was, after all, head of the Institute of Chemical Medicine—dismissed by the State Prosecutor as a made-up tale. The Prosecutor had accepted the exactly opposite view of another expert instead.

Dr. František Tesař was the man to whom Dr. Hájek dictated his autopsy findings, and who became Director of the Forensic Medicine Institute after Hájek died. It was exam time when I called on him, and several students were waiting their turn in his outer office, pale amongst test tubes, blood slides, gap-toothed skulls, and the pungent breath of small creatures pickled in formaldehyde. A gruff, stubby-legged man with a stiff crest of silvery hair, white lab coat starched to the nines, relentlessly scrubbed fingers stained with nicotine, Dr. Tesař had only a few minutes to spare for me. But he was concise in the short while we had.

As far as he knew, there was only a minor technical irregularity about the Masaryk autopsy. In cases with possible criminal aspects, the law required that the first examining physician on the scene should formally request a court order for the autopsy and then do it himself, in a local hospital. Afterward, if there were questions, the results should be verified by the Forensic Medicine Institute. By rights, Teplý, the police doctor, should have asked for this court order, and he didn't. The autopsy was therefore performed directly at the Institute. Nevertheless, it was all open and aboveboard.

"Dr. Hájek, who handled the examination, clearly favored the theory of suicide caused by a jump from the window, because there were no signs indicating that Masaryk might have been pushed. A push might be indicated if the Minister was attacked and trying to defend himself, or if he were somehow deprived of consciousness. There were no indications of an attack. The body was not scratched and bruised all over; and excrement isn't necessarily a sign of violent fear—I've often seen it in suicides. The Minister was clearly not unconscious either. The chemical analysis showed that he wasn't poisoned or drugged. There were only traces of one or two sleeping pills in the stomach contents. That couldn't possibly cause a state of unconsciousness. . . ."

"I beg your pardon?" I wasn't sure I'd heard that right. "The chemical analysis showed what, did you say?"

"Traces of one or two sleeping pills," Dr. Tesař repeated impatiently. "Not at all enough to knock a man out, you know."

I didn't keep Dr. Tesař long. He had those students waiting in his anteroom, and he'd given me a lot to think about. In the first place, somebody was lying about the autopsy report. Dr. Tesař himself, heading the Forensic Medicine Institute, claimed the report was authentic. The equally reputable Dr. Kacl, heading the Chemical Medicine Institute, claimed it was signed under duress. Which of them had a better right to speak for their dead colleague, Dr. Hájek—the court's foremost expert in 1948? Did Hájek believe, when he signed the autopsy report, that Masaryk jumped or was pushed?

Secondly, State Prosecutor Kotlar had lied to me about the sleeping pills. That made *two* outright lies I'd caught him in, I reflected, breasting an upward human stream to get down the Institute's narrow stairway, beginning to feel professionally aggrieved. "No, no sleeping pills," he'd said with that rueful look, when I asked about the chemical analysis of the internal organs. "I can see you're going to find this pretty dull, but there you are." In fact, I wasn't finding it a bit dull. The more deception I ran into, the more engrossed I became.

Within a month or two of my first talk with the State Prosecutor, I could be quite sure that he had misled me, willfully or otherwise, on the following points:

1. The investigation in 1948 was correct. . . . "We've found no irregularities."

2. "We haven't found a scrap of evidence to suggest a motive for getting rid of him."

3. None of Masaryk's close friends testified that he intended to leave the country.

4. Masaryk lunched with the President and Hana Beneš on March 9, and almost certainly did not discuss plans for his departure.

5. There was no need for secrecy. Masaryk could have left the country normally in March, and as late as the following July and August.

6. No proof whatever could be found to verify any of a dozen stories about Masaryk's plans to escape.

7. "There was a policeman on duty at the back entrance of the residence wing. Not a soul went through there."

8. There was nothing wrong with the position of the body in the courtyard.

9. "No, no sleeping pills. There was nothing at all in the stomach."

10. The majority of witnesses described the disorder in Masaryk's flat as "typical" of his bachelor habits.

11. Rumors concerning the police doctor, Teplý, were investigated exhaustively.

12. Dr. Teplý set the time of death at somewhere "between five and six in the morning."

13. Masaryk's state of mind at the last was best revealed by his lonely vigil at his father's grave on March 7, and his search for an apt quotation in the Bible.

14. The presumably nonexistent palace guard Václav Sedm was the sole link to the so-called NKVD agent Major Schramm in the Masaryk case.

15. The pseudo would-be ex-Western intelligence agent, Major Chlumský, was too "sick," "disturbed," and "deranged" to deserve serious attention. "Take it from me: you can forget Chlumský."

Not one of these points was in itself necessarily conclusive. But taken together, in the State Prosecutor's version, they made up an appreciably more satisfactory case from the Russians' point of view than the facts allowed. On all fifteen points, the facts were available to Dr. Kotlar long before they were to me. I couldn't really blame him for withholding them: he had a monkey on his back. He could hardly anticipate—I didn't myself— that I would stumble on certain documentary evidence which he must have thought was safely under lock and key.

It wasn't only toward the State Prosecutor that my thoughts turned when I finally set eyes on this evidence. One by one, phrases and sentences came back to me from a score of witnesses I'd seen in Prague since the spring of 1968, some nervous, others composed, several engagingly direct, a few visibly reserved, a number touchingly eager to help, if only in the smallest way. It was saddening to see how far twenty years of fear and blurring memory had led them all astray. It seemed fitting, too, that the only ones who did not appear to have strayed from the truth at all should bear the name of Masaryk.

Chapter 11

Czechoslovakia has 3,553 miles of frontier, all but 150 miles of no use whatever to an escapee in March, 1948. To the northwest, north, east and south lay, respectively, the Russian zone of Germany, Poland, Soviet Russia, and Hungary, all under Communist management. To the south and southwest lay Austria, jointly administered at the time by a four-power military mission including the Russians. The only escape route was a short strip of Bohemian forest land giving onto the American zone of Western Germany. Some fifteen thousand Czechoslovaks crossed this strip clandestinely in the first weeks after the Communist coup.

They left clandestinely because, contrary to what the State Prosecutor told me, they couldn't go legally—not if they were in politics, that is. Political émigrés are rarely a nuisance to anybody but each other after ten or twenty years of exile. But they can be irritating in the formative stages of a police state. None of Stalin's surrogate governments in Eastern Europe wanted its nationals abroad, consorting with Westerners, communicating with their countrymen back home, encouraging resistance from privileged sanctuaries in Paris, London, Rome. Like his opposite numbers in every capital of the expanding Soviet empire, Premier Gottwald wanted his opponents where he could lay hands on them.

Those who did not try to slip across that strip of border quickly discovered their error. No democratic leader of even minor status remained at liberty long. Some were executed; others simply disappeared; a great many spent years in jail, often without ever coming before a court. Even those who fled were sentenced to life imprisonment or death in their absence. It is impossible to believe that Jan Masaryk would have been left alive and free for more than a few months had he stayed on in Prague.

Considering the Communists' efforts to prevent the escape of much less important politicians than Jan Masaryk, one can imagine the precautions they would have taken to keep Czechoslovakia's folk hero from getting away. Among those who fled the country in the early weeks of Communist rule was Hubert Ripka, one of the National Socialist ministers closest to President Beneš. He described his flight this way:

"During the fortnight following the coup d'état, the Communists told me several times, very discreetly of course, that I had nothing to fear. They went so far as to let me know that though the authorities had relieved me of my post as lecturer at Prague University, they might possibly reverse that measure. Communist leaders knew me well enough not to count on my conversion, from which I deduced that their message was above all an indication of their anxiety to dissuade me from continuing my political activity abroad. For me that was one more reason to hasten my departure. . . .

"Immediately after the coup I thought about escaping. It was extremely difficult for anyone to leave Czechoslovak territory. Even before February 25 the frontiers had been hermetically closed, and passports were no longer valid without express authorization from the Interior Minister. The frontier between Czechoslovakia and the American zone of Germany was comparatively short and easy to watch. Not only had troops been massed along the frontier, but a corridor twenty kilometers wide running alongside it was subjected to strict surveillance by police and soldiers constantly asking for your papers. A few days later, it was not permitted to move about in this territory at all without a special permit. A few people succeeded despite everything in passing into Germany, mostly on skis. Not being too good at sports and, moreover, too tall and well known to pass unnoticed, I had to seek other means. The preparations for my flight were complicated by the fact that I was watched day and night by police. The watch became more and more strict: after a short time, a plainclothes detective was assigned to ride with me when I went out in my car. . . ."

Managing to shake off the detective tailing him, Ripka was able to keep a rendezvous with friends organizing his escape. They drove him to a spot in the Bohemian woods, where he and several companions were told to wait in an improvised hut of branches until the next morning, when a small plane would fly in from abroad to pick them up. At dawn, however, "we were thunderstruck to see a score of men approaching the field. They spread out at the edge of the woods, keeping in the shelter of the trees. 'It's the police!' I exclaimed. 'We've been betrayed!' " No, said a companion, it was only a unit of the Labor Brigade. But it was in fact the police, led by Security Chief Jan Hora in person. He was apparently lying in wait to capture the plane first, then the fugitives. When the small plane came on schedule, its pilot flew over the meadow twice, spotted the police and flew off again. Ripka's companions in the branch hut were thereupon seized and hauled off to prison. He himself, by a ruse, managed to evade arrest and, after considerable hardship, get across the frontier on foot.

Hubert Ripka wasn't the only democrat who had trouble getting out. There were nightly dramas along that short strip of frontier for months after the coup. I learned something of this from an old friend, an officer attached to the American CIC (Counter-Intelligence Corps) at Regensburg, in the American zone of Germany, not far from the Czechoslovak border. A center of United States counterintelligence operations, Regensburg had a refugee camp for émigré Czechoslovaks and special training units for those willing to go back on intelligence missions. My friend, Colonel X, was himself going in and out of Czechoslovakia from the war's end until late in 1948. His sources of information were rather good.

Long before the takeover, he told me, he had instructed his border guards to watch out for signs of a *Putsch*. Informants from the Czechoslovak security police (STB) and army intelligence (OZB) had told him the takeover was bound to come, probably in early spring. They'd first spoken of this in September, 1947, advising Colonel X that the lives of President Beneš and Jan Masaryk would be in danger once the *Putsch* began. He had transmitted this information to the Pentagon, which passed it on to the State Department. United States Ambassador Laurence Steinhardt thereupon warned Beneš and Masaryk. President Beneš replied that he wasn't worried, saw no chance of a Communist coup, and in any case had full confidence in the Czechoslovak Defense Minister Ludvík Svoboda, a "loyal ally and friend."

The first moves to seal the border, said Colonel X, came on February 20, the day the twelve ministers resigned. Over the next five days, heavy reinforcements were pulled up to the frontier, closed tight by February 25. "For the next two months we had our hands full." As thousands of people tried to flee the country, the new Communist regime doubled the border guard, erected lookout towers, set up heavy log barricades, and established military roadblocks on every road leading to airports and the frontier.

"It was somewhere around then, shortly after the *Putsch,* that we were alerted to the chance that Jan Masaryk might be coming across the border," said Colonel X. But early on March 10 a Czechoslovak army officer told him that Masaryk had died "under mysterious circumstances." After that came a total security clamp-down on Masaryk's death, "so airtight that none of my agents could get anywhere near the information. The security precautions were unusual even for the Communists—utterly effective. I was absolutely stuck." Whether or not Colonel X knew more than that, he wouldn't say.

Two reports published soon after Masaryk died maintained that he was, in fact, planning to escape—not by land, but by air. The *New York Times* carried the first report on March 10, the day his body was found. The source was "a former Czechoslovak official" who had crossed the border secretly into Germany on Monday, March 8, and asked that his name be withheld "to avoid possible reprisals against his wife and children in Prague." The reason he'd left the country, he told the *Times,* was that he was one of a group preparing to smuggle Masaryk out of the country by plane. The preparations were thwarted "because twenty-three secret police were assigned to guard the Foreign Minister," he said. When the project broke down, he was advised to make his way over the border alone. He was driven to within a four hours' walk of the frontier, and did the rest on foot.

The second report appeared in the *Saturday Evening Post* on August 21, 1948, written by O. Henry Brandon. There was nothing fake about this byline: Mr. Brandon was, and is, a distinguished diplomatic correspondent for the London *Sunday Times.* President Beneš and Jan Masaryk were his personal friends. So was their physician, Dr. Oskar Klinger.

Dr. Klinger, who fled to the United States soon after Masaryk died, made a big splash with the story he told Henry Brandon. Apart from himself, he began, "there is nobody else alive who lived hour by hour with Masaryk and President Beneš through the last dramatic days of democratic Czechoslovakia." He had seen Masaryk daily since the start of the crisis, the Minister having been down with a cold and bronchitis. He had also seen President Beneš regularly, since the President required constant care after two strokes. He was present in Hradcany Castle on the morning of February 25, when Masaryk asked Beneš about joining Gottwald's new cabinet. The President, according to Klinger, "wanted at least one reliable man in the government," and so replied that "he would have nothing against it." Dr. Klinger and Masaryk had waited in an adjoining room when Communist Premier Gottwald came with his list of new cabinet ministers, and the President agreed to sign it. They'd both seen Beneš directly afterward, "face twisted with pain, staring into space, walking slowly toward an easy chair in a curiously stiff manner, as if with the last physical strength left in him."

Nine days later, on Saturday, March 6, Dr. Klinger was present at the President's country seat in Sezimovo Usti when Masaryk came to lunch. The talk at the table was mostly about Justice Minister Prokop Drtina, who had tried and failed to take his life after the coup. Masaryk "violently disapproved of Drtina's desperate act," said Dr. Klinger, observing that jumping out of a window was what a servant girl would do. "It's a stupid way to go about it," the Minister had said, "and besides, there's no guarantee of success. Furthermore, suicide doesn't absolve anybody of his responsibilities. It's a very poor escape." It was after this lunch that Masaryk broached the question of flight to Dr. Klinger. "Everything I've done, I did so long as I could justify it to my conscience," the Minister reportedly told him. "Now I can justify it no longer. Beneš himself has given up the fight. And if even Drtina, one of his most faithful friends, considered suicide the only solution—which I condemn—then I can leave Czechoslovakia to fight against Communism. Let's leave together."

It wasn't the first time that Masaryk had spoken to Klinger about leaving for good. He was already thinking of this in late September, 1947, when he took off for New York to attend the UN General Assembly session. He had said explicitly before leaving that he might not return, instructing Dr. Klinger in that event to escort his sister Alice to Geneva, where she might stay with his other sister Olga Revilliod. But he did return to

Prague, however reluctantly, doubtless through a sense of duty toward President Beneš; and things seemed much calmer and safer on his return than he had expected. At the year's end, said Dr. Klinger, Masaryk was looking forward hopefully to the next general elections, which he was convinced the Communists would lose. Addressing a large open-air meeting of Czechoslovak war veterans on Zofin Island, in Prague, he made one of his most courageous speeches, suggesting how secure he still felt. Many people were being criticized in those days as "bourgeois reactionaries," Masaryk said. "I proudly declare that I am one of the reactionaries and bourgeois. . . . The word 'reaction' derives from the Latin word 'reagere.' If your opinion is different and you act against something—you react. As long as I live and my mind works, I shall react, and if I do not agree with others, I shall say so. That is why I am one of the reactionaries, people who react, and I shall always react against evil in an orderly manner. 'Bourgeois' is the French word for citizen: I am proud to be a citizen of the Czechoslovak Republic, and I claim and accept all my civic rights and duties."

Masaryk's speech, reported in these words by *Lidová Demokracie*, brought down the house. But a few days later, said Dr. Klinger, Premier Gottwald warned the Foreign Minister that if he didn't behave better in public the Communist press would tear him to pieces. It was vividly clear even then that the Communists deeply distrusted him and were merely using him as long as he might be useful. His conversation with Dr. Klinger after that lunch with the President, on March 6, indicated that he did not intend to be useful to Gottwald any more.

On Monday morning, March 8, when Dr. Klinger came to give Masaryk his usual injection, the Minister was in a fury. The day before, he'd attended that rally in Old Town Square where Communist leaders spoke of Tomáš Masaryk as one of their own kind. It was the ultimate outrage. "While most of his actions in the past weeks were prompted by his sense of obligation towards Beneš," said Klinger, "his most crucial decision—

to return from New York in December, 1947—was due first of all to a profound respect for his father's memory, and his own duty to live up to the Masaryk name. . . . The Communists' abuse of that great name proved in the crassest manner that he, too, had been used as a puppet. He reproached himself for having joined the new government," and told Dr. Klinger that he was now making final plans to leave the country. "We must leave together, Oskarku," he said.

The following morning, March 9, Dr. Klinger saw Masaryk shortly after nine o'clock, just before the latter left for Sezimovo Usti. Masaryk had spent the entire previous day making preparations for the flight. "Oskarku," he said in a subdued voice, "everything is ready. Are you?" Klinger nodded. He had no family, his preparations were simple. "Well, then, I'll ring you tomorrow morning at seven o'clock and ask you for an injection. You understand? But you won't come here. This will be the signal that all is in good order. You jump into your car and drive straight to Brezany. I'll wait for you there." Brezany, Klinger recalled, was the country seat of the German Gauleiter Reinhard Heydrich during the war. There was no real airfield nearby, but a vast meadow, big enough for a good-sized plane to land. "We will be flown to England," Masaryk continued. "Take only the barest necessities with you."

When they parted, Masaryk added: "And don't contact me any more from now on, even by telephone. Should the plan fail and I don't ring you tomorrow, come and see me as usual in the morning." That was the last time Dr. Klinger saw Masaryk alive.

Later in the day—Masaryk's last day—Dr. Klinger called Madame Beneš to ask how the President felt after the Polish Ambassador's ceremonial visit. She said her husband was depressed, and remarked that Masaryk did not stay for lunch as he'd originally promised. At the last minute, he'd said he had an appointment with the American Ambassador in Prague. Klinger said nothing more. He made his preparations to leave as soon as the phone rang the next morning.

When it did ring, around eight, the voice was not Masaryk's but that of President Beneš's Chancellor, Jaromír Smutný. "Masaryk is dead," Smutný said. "He jumped out of the window. Will you go to Sezimovo Usti at once and prepare the President gently, before Gottwald brings the news officially?" Klinger left immediately for Sezimovo Usti. The President was surprised to see him. "Why are you here so early, Klinger?" he asked, a slight undertone of suspicion in his voice. Klinger hedged, finally came out with it. "Masaryk has committed suicide," he said at last, adding slowly, watching the President's reaction: "He jumped out of a window."

"And—?" Beneš asked.

"He is dead," Klinger said.

The President seemed stunned. After a long pause he spoke in measured tones: "I don't believe it was suicide. Will you investigate the cause of his death and attend the post-mortem examination?"

But Dr. Klinger did not attend the post-mortem. Permission was not refused: he was simply notified too late, in a telephone call from Prague to Sezimovo Usti, seventy miles away, fifteen minutes before the autopsy was to take place. Neither was he given any other opportunity to see Masaryk's body. Though he had been the Minister's personal physician for many years, he was not summoned to Czernin Palace when the body was found. He saw it for the first time only when Masaryk was already lying in state.

Dr. Klinger did not linger in Prague. But before leaving, he claims, he did investigate Masaryk's death on his own. He was convinced of murder, for these reasons:

1. Masaryk died on the day he had arranged to flee the country; obviously the security police must have discovered his plans.

2. Few people loved life as much as he did. He would never choose death of his own accord, and if he did, would never jump from a window. First of all he would be afraid of not succeeding, and so living on to suffer terribly, as Justice Minister Drtina did. He was so frightened of pain that he recoiled even from a

hypodermic needle, or boiling water, having once been blistered by it. He always carried fifty to sixty sleeping pills on his person, more than enough for a lethal dose, and kept a loaded revolver by his bed. The sleeping pills, in particular, would have been his logical choice.

3. If the authorities had nothing to hide, they would have summoned Dr. Klinger to examine the body in the morning, and would certainly have notified him about the post-mortem in time. Everybody on Masaryk's staff, and the police, knew Dr. Klinger had been the Minister's personal physician for years.

4. Normally people who commit suicide leave letters behind. Justice Minister Drtina did, for instance.

5. The fecal excretions on the bathroom window sill indicated that Masaryk was in a panic. A man who decides to commit suicide would not lose control over his sphincter. Also, the fact that he was found in his pajamas and barefoot argues against suicide. He was clearly dragged out of bed.

6. According to "two of my patients in a position to know," shots rang out in Czernin Palace on the night of March 9, and four coffins were carried from the palace early the next morning.

This last rocambolesque flourish didn't do much for Dr. Klinger's credibility. Of all the chilling tales coming out in the spring of 1968, not one breathed a hint of gunfire and coffins at Czernin. In 1948, however, Western correspondents in Prague did receive anonymous letters to this effect the day after Masaryk died, I discovered. Whether the information in these letters came from Dr. Klinger's two patients or the other way around, I could not ascertain. Nor could I question him personally about his story in general, since he was in New York and I in Rome. Nevertheless, my editor talked with him early in 1969. He insisted not only that the details in Brandon's *Saturday Evening Post* article were precise, but that his own life was in danger after he left Prague. In London, before coming to the United States, he was lured by a ruse into the Czechoslovak Embassy, where an attempt was made to kidnap him; he came to the United States because his friends indicated they could no longer protect him in London. Repeated efforts were made in New York to trick him into going back home.

Considering the date of publication, Dr. Klinger's story as told to Henry Brandon certainly couldn't be tossed aside. He was speaking in August, 1948, barely five months after Masaryk died, at a time when not a single detail of the scene at Czernin Palace was known to the public, and most eyewitnesses were either in prison or too terrorized to open their mouths. There were details in his story that he couldn't possibly have dreamed up. Yet that was more or less what State Prosecutor Kotlar suggested. So did Masaryk's two secretaries in Prague. "Bosh!" Šum had snapped when I asked about Klinger's story of the planned escape. "Why should the Minister leave with Klinger? They weren't particularly close. Klinger simply happened to be the Ministry physician, who took care of all the personnel, not just Masaryk. None of us believed his story." And the senior secretary, Špaček, had agreed: "Klinger wasn't very serious. He said a lot of things that weren't true, once he got off to America. For instance, he claimed he wasn't allowed to see the Minister's body. That isn't so. I myself called Dr. Klinger, asking him to come to the autopsy. His secretary told me he didn't have time."

Yet the two secretaries left out several items of information about Dr. Klinger, leaving me with a distinctly pejorative impression of this not very serious gentleman. Among the things Špaček and Šum must have known but failed to mention were these:

1. Dr. Klinger literally did not have the time to attend the autopsy because he was seventy miles away in Sezimovo Usti when the telephoned invitation came. I later found proof of this myself.

2. He was in fact *not* summoned to the palace when Masaryk's body was found, despite his longstanding position as the Minister's personal physician, nor was he even informed of the death until Chancellor Smutný telephoned—a curious omission on the part of the Communist authorities.

3. He was President Beneš's longtime personal physician as

well as Masaryk's, suggesting a professional status more imposing than the one implied.

4. He often lunched or took tea with the Beneš family, and
played cards or chess with Masaryk; surely he was more than a
casual acquaintance.

5. He did visit Masaryk on Tuesday morning, March 9.
Though neither Šum, nor Špaček, nor the State Prosecutor included his name on the list of callers they gave me, I later found
proof of this as well.

6. If Masaryk's supply of sleeping pills was actually down to
"two or three in the bottle," as Špaček told me, he could easily
have gotten more from Dr. Klinger that morning—assuming he
was contemplating suicide rather than escape on this last morning of his life.

Why should Masaryk's secretaries withhold these facts? Did
they have a private grudge against this card-playing and perhaps
frivolous bachelor crony of the Minister's, whom they seemed
deliberately to be putting in such a poor light? Had they forgotten such significant details? Was it more convenient not to
remember?

For all the slighting comment in Prague, I did find partial
confirmation of a sort for Dr. Klinger's story, from the least
likely imaginable source. On April 25, 1949, somebody calling
himself Bohemicus wrote an article published in *Le Figaro*,
saying that Masaryk had *two* plans to escape abroad. But the
Minister told Bohemicus that he had changed his mind at the
last minute, deciding instead to sacrifice his life "because actions
speak louder than words." With a touching faith in Bohemicus,
Masaryk then confided that he was going to jump out of a window, and meant to write two testaments beforehand, one political, the other personal. According to Bohemicus, Masaryk was
occupied in writing these testaments from 9:30 p.m. to 12:30
a.m., consuming most of his private writing paper supply in the
process. That done, he picked up his father's Bible, opened it to
St. Paul's Epistles to the Galatians, circled verses 22, part of 23,

and 24, laid the Bible on his bed, "opened the window, and jumped." As simple as that. Helpful to the last, Masaryk presumably left his two written messages lying around so that the Communist secret police could find them first thing in the morning. Supposedly, also, he completed his orderly preparations by first taking two sleeping pills, and then knocking over some furniture in his bedroom, trailing his pillows to the bathroom, and grinding his medicine bottles underfoot—barefoot— before jumping.

Guess who Bohemicus was. That's right.

Apart from this one impulsive reference, the apodictical Soukoup, Masaryk's third secretary now in Scotland, did not speak again of Masaryk's "two plans for escape." There wasn't a word about it in his presentation of the suicide case in the spring of 1968, either in the *Scotsman* or in his interviews with the international press. Did he mention the escape plans to State Prosecutor Kotlar during their eight-hour conversation in Glasgow? If not, why not? If so, why should the State Prosecutor ignore such testimony from Soukoup, his most useful informant? "No proof whatever could be found to verify any of a dozen stories about Masaryk's plans to escape," Dr. Kotlar had told me. "None of his close friends testified that he intended to leave."

As a matter of fact, two of the closest friends Masaryk had in the world did testify that he intended to leave—or so he told them.

Chapter 12

The answer to Jan Masaryk's intentions on March 9, to leave Communist-dominated Prague or to stay, to escape by suicide or to escape his country to fight in the court of world opinion, lay in the kind of man Jan Masaryk was. His closest friends are the best witnesses to that. Yet even they do not agree.

Sir Robert Bruce Lockhart was nearing seventy when, in 1951, he put his personal memories of Jan into writing. Coming to Prague as Commercial Secretary of the British Legation in 1921, he had met Jan without taking much notice of him until they lunched alone one day, in Jan's rooms at Hradcany Castle.

For a young man with a few crowns in his pocket and no wife to wait up for him, Prague in the early twenties was a captivating mistress, flashing with intellectual wit, its theater magnificent, music glorious, wine cheap, fiddlers tireless, cabarets open till dawn. Nowhere on the Continent except for Paris was there a capital at once so handsome and romantic, luminous, gay.

"It had been a long luncheon even for those festive days of Prague's new birth," Sir Robert wrote. "As I came away from it, I felt that here was a man whom I could confide in and who in many respects shared my likes and dislikes. Nor was I mistaken. Our first meeting was to ripen into a friendship which was proof against all the abasements and upheavals of our time."

Masaryk enchanted him that day, talking "with disarming frankness" of his early life and hard struggle in the United States, telling war stories "with inimitable artistry and garnished with the spice of half-a-dozen languages," playing the piano. "Musically, he was a 'middle-brow', but he could produce the same effects from a piano that a Hungarian gypsy draws from his violin, and for an amateur his gift of improvisation was remarkable. I yielded immediately to the charm. At luncheon he had been gay, ribald, and, in language and manner ultra-American. At the piano he was a Slav of Slavs. Then and ever afterwards I marvelled at his sudden changes of mood which still remind me of the race between sun and clouds in a Highland sky. Years later, whenever we had a vodka or one of his dreadful slivovice and vermouth cocktails, he used to say 'Over the hills' as he raised his glass. 'Over the hills' meant his dreamland of escape: a cottage under the Tatra Mountains, a Slovak shepherd's reed, and the music of a running stream.

> "Where is my home? Where is my home?
> Brooks are running through the meadows,
> Pines are whispering on the hills,
> Orchards dressed in spring's array
> An earthly paradise portray,
> And this land of wondrous beauty
> Is the Czech land, home of mine."

So runs the opening verse of the Czechoslovak national hymn, which Jan played after lunch, putting "more longing into it than Talich and the Czech Philharmonic ever did. He never found his home, although he made many attempts to discover it."

"For the hills of his own Slovakia," continued Sir Robert,

"he had an abiding passion. During the war he mentioned them constantly in his broadcasts and always with longing: 'I am sometimes sick at heart when I realise that Gestapo agents go over the hills of Turiec. . . . For me Turiec is home. There I spent the most beautiful days of my youth, and there I want to return in my old age.' . . . There was a certain shyness about Jan's sentimentality, and if he felt that he had revealed his soul too nakedly the mood would pass like a flash, and he would be shouting for drinks, insisting that he was the bad member of the Masaryk family, and proclaiming that from his drunken Slovak grandfather, a jovial child of nature who liked his dram of plum vodka, he had inherited an incurable capacity for enjoyment."

In his youth it seemed true, wrote Sir Robert. Jan was light-hearted, rarely serious, never solemn, loved to sit up till dawn in the *nachtlokals* lingering on from the Hapsburg days, "listening to Wolf, a gifted pianist . . . and to the sobbing violin of Bureš, and drinking more than was good for us." Their friendship deepened from 1922 to 1925, the one interlude in Jan's diplomatic career when he stayed continuously in Prague, as mender of human relations for the then Foreign Minister, Eduard Beneš. The two friends were often together in those years, Jan revealing all the complexity of his personality, his gaiety, exuberance, romanticism, boredom, irritation, melancholy. "There was a separate Czech Jan, a Slovak Jan, a Polish Jan, a Hungarian Jan, a noisy American Jan, a romantically sentimental Scottish Jan, and even a reserved English Jan, and I do not think that anyone knew all the Jans."

Born on September 14, 1886—his father died on a September 14, blighting his birthdays forever after—Jan inherited his liberalism and Western outlook from Tomáš Masaryk. With him, Jan was always at his best. "I had several opportunities of seeing them together, for in those early 'twenties' the President liked to talk to me about Russia [where Lockhart had headed the British Mission before coming to Prague]. Jan's attitude was always the same. Regarding his father as a saint and scholar to whose heights of thought and asceticism he himself could never climb, he took no part in the conversation, but sat listening intently and watching eagerly for an opportunity to minister to the great man's needs, which were few. He always spoke of, and to, his father with an affection revealed more by the respect and admiration in his eyes than by any words." His devotion was the strongest influence in his life, coming from the heart, tolerating no criticism. "Indeed, the only time that I ever saw him really angry was when, at a small dinner-party in Prague, a young foreign diplomat, newly arrived and not realising who Jan was, made some foolish remarks about the boredom of coming to a country of which a coachman's son was President and lorded it luxuriously in the castle of ancient kings. Jan said nothing at the time, but his veins swelled with wrath."

From his frail and beautiful mother, on the other hand, Jan inherited the sensitive and somber streak running through all the children of the marriage. Not many saw that other Jan in his younger years. "Few, if any, of his compatriots took him seriously. None, I think, saw any signs of future greatness in him. Those who knew him intimately liked him, but others, resentful of his rapid advancement, regarded him as the privileged son of the President and muttered against favouritism in high places. In those days, his nickname was 'Playboy of the Western World.' "

If not for Munich and the war, he might never have been known as anything else. He'd become enormously popular in London during his thirteen years there before Munich, lifted out of the ruck of ordinary diplomats by his charm and unconventional flair. But it was still a rather inconsequent career. Those were the years when the new Central European states emerging from the ruins of the Austro-Hungarian Empire were crude fare for polished diplomats in Ten Downing Street. " 'I spend most of my official time in there explaining to the gentle-

men inside that Czechoslovakia is a country and not a contagious disease,' " Jan used to say.

Munich changed him. Some of the gaiety was extinguished,
new stature added. He accepted the weight of responsibility that
came with his father's name. If British appeasement of Hitler
was an agonizing shock for him, it did not throw him off balance. He still thought Great Britain was the most civilized
country on earth; and he was generous enough to say publicly,
shortly after Munich, that he " 'wanted nothing better for the
world than that all countries should have the same qualities
as these islands of Britain.' "

When the Second World War broke out on September 3,
1939, he came back to London after a long American lecture
tour, and Eduard Beneš joined him. Lockhart, appointed as
British liaison representative to the Czechoslovak government-
in-exile, grew very close to them both, watching Jan's performance with growing pleasure. On September 8 of that year he
made his first BBC talk to the Czechs, in a series that made
him, with the single exception of Winston Churchill, the most
effective Allied broadcaster of the war. His technique was
simple, and his instinct sure. The Czechs at home were his
valiant and long-suffering people, to whom he always spoke with
humility, sympathy, admiration. Not only did he win their affection, but he probably did more than anybody else of his time
except Winston Churchill to restore their shaken confidence in
Britain.

" 'The people here go quietly about their business,' he
would say over BBC. 'There is no clamor, no excitement, no self-
glorification such as we hear daily from Germany. . . . The
British people know anxiety; they do not know what fear is.' "
He never forgot that for a year Britain faced the enemy alone;
and describing the nation's courage, he liked most to talk about
the workers. Once, he said in a broadcast, he'd passed a grocery
store in a working-class quarter with nothing left but its shop
front, the rest bombed to splinters, and a sign on the door:

"Open for business as usual—a little more than usual." On another occasion, he had tried to console a British worker for the loss of his wife and child in an air raid, giving him his hand and saying, as Lockhart reports, " 'In spite of everything we must hold out.' " The worker answered: " 'Whatever happens, I shall certainly hold out a week longer than Hitler.' " And Jan would end his broadcasts saying: " 'The spirit of the British is magnificent—magnificent!' " The Czechs listened raptly, even though the death sentence was the official Nazi penalty. He was no longer a playboy for them but *"naš Honza* ('our Johnny') ," trusted, leaned upon, loved.

His contribution during these years was more human than political. When asked what his war aims were, he would say: "I'm fighting for the right of Jew and Gentile to read *Das Kapital* and *Mein Kampf* in Prague streetcars—every citizen must have the right to shout in the streets 'I don't like my Prime Minister.' " Or, simply: "I want to go home." He left the politics to Eduard Beneš, whose effort was "stupendous," wrote Lockhart. "I had every opportunity of studying the relations between the two men, for I spent almost every weekend at Beneš's country house at Ashton Abbots in Buckinghamshire, and Jan was frequently present. Beneš continued to make the policy, develop the arguments, prepare every detail of the new constitution to be introduced after liberation. Jan remained aloof from detail. . . . His attitude to Beneš was one of personal affection and duty. He recognized in Beneš an intellect vastly superior to his own, and rarely questioned his political judgement. Only in regard to Soviet Russia did Jan have doubts and here too, his hesitation was more psychological than rational. He recognized the necessity of an understanding with the Soviet Union. On more than one occasion he said to me—in rather coarse language—that he would rather go to bed with Stalin than kiss Hitler's behind. On the other hand he was instinctively suspicious. . . ." Like his father, he regarded the Russians "spiritually as Asians and politically as a reactionary power built on imperialism. As a defender of small nations he could not find any sign of liberty, equality and fraternity in the Communist dictionary. 'For me Russia after the revolution remains the same imperialistic Great Power that it was before,' " he would say. And, on Lenin, he observed, " 'Once Lenin said that people must stop listening to Beethoven, because he has the power of making people too happy. He was afraid lest they would become too soft to make the revolution. There you have the whole of Lenin.' "

Otto Friedman, a Czech émigré, writing in *The Break-up of Czech Democracy,* says that Masaryk once told him in his London flat, "I am a Liberal. And I don't want to be governed either from Berlin or from Moscow."

And his address before a students' meeting in the Cambridge Union Society, quoted in the Cambridge *Daily News* (February 23, 1940), included these words: "I am the last one to criticize the inner politics of Russia, but I also must respectfully submit that just as there is a high wall round Berchtesgaden, so there is a high wall round the Kremlin . . . the dictators are not informed properly. . . . Don't tell us that Hitler is going to save us and that Stalin is going to save us. We are either going to save ourselves or be lost. This fight is for one thing—the sanctity of the human soul. In totalitarian countries, they would interfere with my improvising on the piano, if I played two bars of a certain tune. If you make politics out of art or religion or out of the innermost freedom, I don't want to live."

Leaving with Beneš on the fateful journey to Moscow in 1945, the war nearly over, Jan was full of premonitions. He understood that the only hope of independence, for a country in Czechoslovakia's geographical position, lay in an amicable understanding between East and West. But he could already see the hope dwindling. Stalin and his Foreign Minister Molotov, forgetting their assurances in 1943, talked of the Czech's "second liberation" as the exclusive work of the Red Army and Czechoslovak Communist Party; and with no compunction, they imposed a government on Beneš in which all the key posts were in Communist hands. The fruits of victory were already turning sour; the second liberation, which had promised so much, might end with Moscow proving to be a second Munich.

Several people who were there on that Moscow trip have told me about it. Dubious before he came, they said, he detested the Czechoslovak Communist Gottwald on sight and deeply distrusted Soviet leaders; and for all his considerable skill at dissembling, the Russians knew it. "I've been moving mountains to convince Stalin that I'm on his side," he told Italian Ambassador Pietro Quaroni in Moscow, "but he refuses to believe me." When Mrs. Davenport asked him soon after his return from Moscow how Stalin had treated him, he had replied lightly, "Oh, he's very gracious. Of course he'd kill me if he could. But very gracious."

Sir Robert did not see Jan again until two years after the latter's return to Prague. Then, in May, 1947, after Czechoslovakia's brief period of freedom with the departure of the Red Army, he spent a week at Czernin Palace. "During my six days at Czernin Palace, I had seen more of Jan than in all the years I had known him. He gave me much of his time. Every night at the end of our work we sat up late and talked like brothers. . . . Politically he was much happier than he had been. He did not like Soviet leaders and was still afraid of them. Above all, he dreaded a rupture between the United States and the Soviet Union. He was irritated by the Americans who, he felt, did not understand Europe." Yet he hoped against all reasonable hope that an understanding with the Soviet Union could be achieved. He had genuine faith in the United Nations and was convinced that, in spite of all difficulties, it could restrain the ambitions of the Great Powers.

This was true despite his own harrowing experience at the San Francisco meeting of the UN in 1946, described by the Czechoslovak UN representative, Ján Papánek, in a letter of May 16, 1958. Soviet Foreign Minister Molotov had pressed Masaryk to sponsor membership for the new Polish Communist government, which he agreed to do at the opportune time. Impatient, Molotov sent a note in Russian through his interpreter, Pavlov: "Mr. Masaryk: Mr. Molotov asks me to advise you that if you do not act it will be a gross violation of the agreement between you and him. Pavlov." Masaryk was so shocked by the threat that he gave Dr. Papánek the note, saying, "Keep it, one day we will need it."

Lockhart wrote that Masaryk had "complete trust in his own countrymen who, he always said, had too much sense ever to be deceived by Communism, and though the 1946 elections, which returned the Communists as the largest Party with thirty-seven per cent of the votes, were an unpleasant surprise to him, he was confident that reason would prevail and the Communist tide recede. He was a man of peace who believed that it could be achieved by the spoken word. Of his own Communists, who he was sure were on the down grade, he was not afraid. Indeed, he told me he could handle them with ease, and I certainly saw him do it."

To a large Communist meeting in Prague, for instance, Jan had said bluntly, " 'I may not agree with the policy of Mr. Churchill to-day, but I say here and now that for the winning of the war and for our liberation we owe more to Winston Churchill than to any other man.' The Communists cheered him vociferously." Again, one evening during Lockhart's visit, the two went to the National Theater to see Leoš Janáček's *Kát'a Kabanová*. Lockhart, desperately tired, rose to go at the end of the long opera, but Jan pulled him back. "Then going to the front of the box he stood up and called for Talich, the conductor, who was under fire from the Communists on a charge of collaborating with the Nazis and had been re-instated mainly by Jan's efforts. The whole audience, which included President and Madame Beneš, followed Jan's example, and, when in response to the insistent calls Talich appeared on the stage, he received an ovation such as I have never heard in any other theatre. It was, in fact, an anti-Communist demonstration, and Jan had led it."

Privately, however, Masaryk was not happy. "He hated to hurt and, preferring postponement to decision, made more promises than any man could fulfill. He did his best to keep them, especially to the humble and meek to whom he was always accessible and whom he never failed, but the day was not long enough for all to benefit. It started on the telephone in his bedroom at eight a.m. Sometimes he was kept so busy that he could not get dressed before eleven.

"Physically he was a tired man who lived on his nerves and slept badly. Although he liked to say that his coachman grandfather was a roaring drunkard, he himself drank only beer when we were alone. While I was with him, his doctor gave him an overhaul and the result, he told me, was completely satisfactory. But I knew not only that he was tired but also that in the mornings he had a racking cough. I was convinced that if ever a man was suffering from nervous exhaustion, it was Jan.

"I had always regarded him as a lonely man whose gaiety was a mask, but never before had I realized how pitiably alone he could be in a city where he knew everybody. His work was a labour of duty to his country. Cabinet meetings were an irksome imposition. . . . He belonged to the public and whoever belongs to the public rarely leaves it willingly. Yet almost his last words to me in Prague were 'I wish to God I could be rid of it all.' "

Before Lockhart left Prague on May 20, he went to a Communist rally in Mnich, eighty miles from the capital, with Jan and Marcia Davenport, who had come to stay in Prague earlier that spring. Jan was to speak in commemoration of the southern Bohemian partisans fallen in the resistance against the Nazis. "It was raining, and Jan was tired and depressed. . . . When we reached Mnich we saw in the distance the site of the manifestation. The setting was imposing. The monument, which was waiting to be unveiled, was still draped in black and stood on a small plateau half-way up a gently undulating hill. Here in a large grassy rectangle were assembled some 20,000 people: peasants in their national costume, legionaries of the First World War, troops and officers and military bands, and the diplomatic representatives of the Soviet Union, Poland, Yugoslavia and Bulgaria. . . .

"We took our seats . . . behind the Slav ambassadors. Jan was as nervous as a frightened puppy, fidgeted incessantly, and kept asking me for cigarettes. His turn to speak came rather late. . . .

"Jan began slowly. He was, he said, a minister without a party. Some might say that he was above party. He could assure them that he was very much under the parties. There was laughter and loud applause. . . . His language was simple and came from the heart.

"On the widows' and mothers' benches two old women wept quietly and continuously. Below the tribune was a group of peasant girls whose bright national costumes made a colourful ring around Jan. The sun was now shining from a clear sky, and I watched one pretty girl whose eyes were fixed on Jan in adoration. Her face was transfigured with a faith that one sees only in pilgrims to Lourdes.

"Then Jan spoke of the pan-Slav manifestation. He paid his tribute to it. Every time there was a war, it was the Slavs who had to pay. This must not happen again. He went on to say what the Slav brotherhood must be. It must work for good and not for evil. Its corner-stone must be love. There must be no militancy, no hate. Then he quoted the text from Šámal's Bible about mercy and humility. He spoke of the brotherhood of man, and the United Nations. There was one more reference to the men who had died that others might live. A final exhortation to *makat*—a Czech slang word meaning 'to work' which he illustrated vigorously with his whole body. Then he sat down.

"When the end came with the singing of the impressive Hussite hymn *All Who Are God's Warriors,* the vast crowd surged round Jan, and Marcia Davenport and I had some difficulty in following him to his car. It was his greatest triumph. No one else counted, and at every village on the way back from Mnich to Tábor the peasants came to greet him."

Barely six weeks after Lockhart left Prague, Jan was summoned to Moscow by Stalin and forced to drop the Marshall Plan. On Jan's return to Czechoslovakia, President Beneš had his first stroke.

Hubert Ripka, a member of the Beneš cabinet, wrote of Masaryk's mood after the Moscow debate: "He seemed even graver than usual, and as soon as we were alone he allowed his anger to burst out. 'There was nothing to be done,' he said, even before he sat down. 'You may congratulate yourself that you were not there. It was frightful, and horribly humiliating! Do you know what discouraged me most? The fact that some members of our own delegation did not even realize that we had just been slapped. And you won't believe this: there were even some who showed their pleasure. I blushed for shame! . . . They backed us up against the wall while pretending to treat us as friends. Stalin was, as always, very friendly, almost jovial; but he did not give way an inch. The game was clear: he had come to an understanding with Gottwald; the interview with us was nothing but a formality. . . .

" 'My dear friend, we are nothing but vassals! The saddest thing is that there are people of our own blood who are doing this dirty work. The Communists have not an ounce of patriotic pride. They are slaves of Moscow, and they rejoice in their servitude.' "

Still, he could be lighthearted that summer, in public, about the ever-present threat. He told a Congress of the International Organization of Journalists, "Now you will be touring Czechoslovakia, if you come across an iron curtain, ring me up, and I'll come and have a look at it." Soon afterward, on September 11, came the Communist perfume-box plot to assassinate Jan and his two democratic colleagues. Then the secret police, orchestrated by Major Pokorný, produced their democratic "plot" in Slovakia, a rehearsal for the *Putsch* to come the next February. After that came the discovery of the National Socialist "spy network" in Bohemia. Obviously the Communists were beginning to close in.

Since the end of September, Jan had been representing

Czechoslovakia at Lake Success. In Washington, in November, 1947, he received a fierce blow. He had gone there expecting to see President Truman or Secretary of State Marshall or both. He was hoping for some assurance that the United States would stand behind his country's democratic forces in the coming showdown. President Truman had recently pronounced his courageous Doctrine to save Greece and Turkey from Soviet absorption; and while Chechoslovakia was on the wrong side of the Yalta-Teheran line, Stalin's broken promises might just conceivably stiffen the American position there. But it was much too late. Masaryk was not even received by the American President or his Secretary of State. Czechoslovakia was written off, finished. (Later, and only a few weeks before his death, he was to say, according to the *New York Times,* "The United States treats us as though we had already been sold down the river, but we haven't yet.")

When Masaryk called on Mrs. Davenport in New York that November night, she wrote, he was "deathly pale." He sat down slowly in a chair. He seemed to be in shock. "We sat in dead silence for I cannot imagine how long. Finally he looked at me as if I had asked him a question and with a small, quick motion, almost imperceptible, he shook his head. Thereafter I believe he was never the same again. From then on, he was a frightened man. . . ."

Returning from the UN Assembly session in New York, early in December, 1947, Jan stopped off in London. "On December 3rd my telephone rang," wrote Lockhart. "It was Jan. He was at his flat in Westminster Gardens. Could I come to see him?

"It was a dull and gloomy afternoon, and I found him depressed and terribly tired. He was in a dressing-gown with his left arm underneath the sleeve. Shortly before leaving for Lake Success, he had dislocated a muscle in his left shoulder. It still gave him pain. His American friends, he told me, said that he had hurt his shoulder leaning too hard on the Iron Curtain. He had been unhappy in the United States, where he was forced to follow the Soviet line. Inevitably some Americans misunderstood his attitude. There had been published rumours that he had made a fortune on the Black Market and was not going back to Czechoslovakia. The truth was, he said, that some American friends had tried to persuade him to give up politics and become an American citizen. He had been tempted. Then he looked at me as though seeking my approval and said: 'You can leave your country twice or as many times as you have the strength to fight. You can't do it to fight your own countrymen.' "

Several others close to Masaryk have spoken of the pressures on him during that stay in New York. Dr. Ján Papánek, then head of the Czechoslovak delegation to the United Nations, said in a letter to me: "My wife and I were among the many who tried to convince Jan Masaryk to remain in the United States in the Fall of 1947. He was determined to return to Prague. The night before he left, he had dinner with us in our home and we sat and talked for a long time. In the course of the conversation he repeated that he must return to keep a promise he had made to his dying father—that he would stay close to Dr. Beneš and support him. . . . Then he said firmly that he knew 'they' would kill him, but that he must return. . . ." He said the same to others.

To the American columnist Dorothy Thompson, a good friend for twenty-five years, he wrote during that last stay in New York: "I have been toying with the idea . . . to let myself go at one of the closing sessions of the General Assembly and call out a warning to all those self-centered nationalists assembled in the Flushing-Success area. . . .

"For the time being I am persona most grata with my people at home. It is very touching how they hang on to me, as if expecting things from me. *How will I fail them least?* That's the question. Because, things being as they are, I cannot deliver the goods they so deeply deserve. . . . I will do the best I can.

"I must go home as soon as possible *to give my fairly passionate support to those* who are trying to carry on the lovely

Bohemian tradition against cynical and well-organized material dialectics.

"For the time being we can hold our own. How long I know not. Somewhere, sometime, somehow, I am going to stand on my hind legs and shout to the Great Powers, 'Gentlemen, your fly is open!'

"But the timing—that's the problem!"

Yet even then, Masaryk had not lost hope altogether. "Somewhat to my surprise," wrote Lockhart of that last encounter in London, "Jan was not pessimistic about the coming Czechoslovak elections in the Spring. The Communists were not nearly so strong as people thought. He himself was going to enter the contest, and was going to attack as soon as he arrived in Prague. To me this was cheerful news, but he spoilt the effect by adding gloomily: 'of course, if the Russians interfere, we are finished.'

"He was quite frank about Beneš's health which, he said, was much worse than official statements implied. There had been something in the nature of a real stroke. It had left an impediment in his speech. It was only slight perhaps, but it was dangerous in a man who worked as hard as Beneš did."

Jan had told Marcia Davenport, as she wrote in her autobiography, *Too Strong for Fantasy,* that Beneš had had symptoms of arteriosclerosis for some time; and Dr. Klinger, the President's physician, explained how much this would account for marked changes in his personality, his sudden indecision, fluctuations of extreme obstinacy and weakness, typical refusal as an arteriosclerotic to admit his condition. President Roosevelt had been much the same.

"He, Jan, was going back to take some of the load off Beneš's shoulders," Lockhart went on. "I looked at him with fear in my heart. He was in no physical state to carry his own burdens, let alone somebody else's. . . . As we said goodbye, he made a great effort to be cheerful, clapped his hand on my shoulder and smiled. 'Never mind, old boy. We'll beat the b . . . . s yet.' They were the last words I heard from his lips."

When the coup came, and Masaryk remained in Gottwald's

government, he was criticized by his Czechoslovak admirers and some of his Western friends, though the extent of reproachful letters, later made much of by the Communists as having been a prod to suicide, is disputed by other friends.

There was no mystery about Masaryk's decision to remain in Gottwald's Communist government temporarily. Masaryk told Papánek in New York and Mrs. Davenport that his response to Beneš fulfilled a promise he had made to his father. Later, he told Marcia Davenport he'd stayed in Gottwald's cabinet because Beneš, "bludgeoned and without his full faculties," had not left. Gottwald, as Masaryk told her, had met every demur of Beneš's with threats of civil war. By implication, any war would bring in the Red Army. "Munich all over again," said Beneš to Gottwald, and then, to Masaryk: "In 1938 I had to bear the brunt of Munich alone when you were abroad. Now you must stay and help me and the country." But Masaryk knew that Beneš was beyond giving help, or receiving it.

Sir Robert did not expect Masaryk to stay at his post long. "At the end of February I received a message from him, begging me to do my best to keep his name out of all broadcasts and newspapers. He knew, the message said, what he was doing."

"On Monday morning [March 8]," Sir Robert Lockhart wrote, "I was called to the telephone in my Hove apartment. It was Marcia Davenport. She had come straight from Prague with messages for Sir Orme Sargent [at the Foreign Office] and me. She had instructions, she said, to see me first. I told her that I would be in London on Wednesday morning, but offered to come at once if the matter was urgent. She hesitated for a moment, then said quietly: 'Wednesday will do.' She told me on the telephone that the situation was much worse than the outside world realised, and that the plight of Beneš and Jan was terrible.

"On the Wednesday morning I caught an early train to London and arrived in my club before half-past ten. I was called to the telephone at once. A voice from the *Evening Standard* said 'Can you tell us something about Jan Masaryk?' 'Why?' I asked tremulously. 'What has happened?' Back came the answer: 'He has committed suicide. He was found dead outside Czernin Palace at 6:30 this morning.' "

Masaryk's death was announced by the *New York Times* in the morning paper of March 11: "Masaryk Killed, A Suicide, Reds Say; UN Shelves Czech Plea for Inquiring." The prospect of his empty chair in the new cabinet of Communist Premier Klement Gottwald was said to have delayed the public announcement. The foreign press had spread the news before the people of Prague were notified.

The Communist regime ordered a state funeral, the draping of public buildings with black streamers, and the flying of the national flag at half mast. Premier Gottwald was to deliver the funeral oration; Communist Deputy Foreign Minister Vladimír Clementis would give an address at the grave. The official report referred to "a disturbance of the mind," brought on by insomnia and a nervous disorder. Ironically, another story in the *Times* that day quoted Masaryk's note to Lord Halifax on September 25, 1938, protesting Munich: "The nation of St. Wenceslas, Jan Hus and Thomas Masaryk will not be a nation of slaves." In Prague, the Parliament took a five-minute recess.

Sir Robert heard the news with "a heavy heart" and went to Claridge's to see Marcia Davenport. "She was shattered and at first incoherent. . . . I stayed with Marcia for two hours, and she told me all she knew." The sequence of events seemed to be this:

On February 19, Valerian Zorin, Deputy Foreign Commissar and Molotov's trusted lieutenant, had flown from Moscow to Prague. An hour and a half after his arrival, according to Josef Korbel, a member of the Czech UN delegation, who wrote of it later, Zorin visited Masaryk, who had been confined to bed. Masaryk told the Secretary General of the Ministry, Arnost Heidrick, immediately afterwards, that Zorin was cordial "telling him that Stalin had full confidence in Masaryk but that on the other hand he must understand that the Soviet government cannot follow passively all the extravagances of the political parties in Czechoslovakia." Hubert Ripka, a member of Beneš's cabinet, heard later that Zorin had gone even further and had stated to Masaryk, "The events which take place at this moment in your country are intolerable and we shall not tolerate them."

Zorin visited the Minister of Transportation, Pietor, and Václav Majer, the Minister of Food, who was ill at home. Majer, who led the anti-Communist wing in the Social Democrat Party, was convinced that the visits, ostensibly to discuss grain delivery, were a camouflage to Zorin's real purpose in Prague. Zorin sat up until dawn making plans with Communist leaders Gottwald and Slánský, Workers' Militia leader Smrkovský, Interior Minister Nosek, and the fearsome General Bedřich Reicin, directing the army's counterespionage service with a cadre of Soviet NKVD agents (the information supplied later to the UN by the Czechoslovak representative Ján Papánek). Although this maneuver was not known at the time, Masaryk, nevertheless, unlike the other democratic leaders, at once suspected the worst. He was appalled when, on February 20, the twelve ministers sent their resignations to the President, Sir Robert said.

The most Masaryk could do was to use his diplomatic sore throat and bronchitis to stay in bed through the next four days, denying Gottwald a quorum for a cabinet meeting.

During those four days, the Czechoslovaks waited for President Beneš to give them leadership, while the Communist pincers closed. For three days people appealed to Beneš to take a public stand. But Beneš did not. Marcia Davenport wrote later in her autobiography, which remains the only source for all of Masaryk's last conversations, that she asked Jan why Beneš was unresponsive. "Does it mean that he can't?"

"He nodded.

" 'You mean—he can't, physically—or they won't let him?'

" 'Both,' he said. His face was ghastly."

On the afternoon of February 25, Masaryk called her from

Hradcany Castle, to say he had something to tell her. He came to her house on the Loretanska, a few yards away from Czernin Palace, as he did almost every day she did not come to the palace. His face, she said, was "like a mask. . . . He said, 'Lost. Utterly lost.' Beneš had given in. . . ."

"The state must survive," Beneš had said, according to other reports, "and if it has to survive it must have some form of government." Gottwald went to a mass meeting in Wenceslas Square to tell the crowd: "The President did not arrive at his decision easily, but in the end he accepted the will of the people."

Early the next morning, Masaryk's butler, Příhoda, brought Mrs. Davenport a note: "Am staying in this 'govt' for time being. It breaks my heart for you to receive these shocks, which you deserve less than anybody in the world. Do not be too sad. Be bitter and be proud—of yourself. I am very proud of you. You believed in a decent hope—so did I. It could not be. But this is not the end."

On Thursday, February 26, the day after the coup, Masaryk told her he wanted her to go to London and wait for him there. He could always go out by attending a conference abroad, and "intended to get out" at the next scheduled one, she said. "When he joined me, we would be married. . . ." She reserved a flight to London for March 7.

On Saturday, February 28, he came to her flat straight from Hradcany Castle to tell her that Beneš had left the Hrad for Sezimovo Usti. I learned in Prague that President Beneš was terrified for his own personal safety during this move, allowing only the oldest members of his own staff to pack his things—especially the kitchen equipment and food.

On Tuesday, March 2, Příhoda brought Marcia Davenport another note from Masaryk: "Slavik has resigned and denounced this govt. Extremely bad." Václav Slavik was the Czechoslovak Ambassador to Washington, and his action touched off a frenzied hue and cry. Slavik's resignation brought Masaryk quiet distress. Masaryk never used the phone after the

Slavik thing. Marcia Davenport said: "I begged him not to come to see me since it was obviously dangerous for him, and he burst into tears and said if he could not see me he would break." When she observed to Masaryk that he wouldn't be able to see her if she were in London either, he tried to smile.

" 'I know,' he said, 'but if I have to choose between knowing you are locked up here or knowing you are safe at Claridge's it had better be London. If I know you are there waiting for me it gives me something to live for.' "

After Slavik's resignation two men in leather jackets, like members of an American motorcycle gang, followed Masaryk wherever he went. When he protested the withdrawal of his own men, his personal guard was restored, and Mrs. Davenport wrote, "Jan thereafter never moved a step without him. He went nowhere on foot except to see his sister Alice and me." But the men in leather jackets persisted. (Papánek told the UN Security Council later, on March 22, 1968, that "during his last days" Masaryk "could not make a move without the two special guards assigned to him after the coup.")

Sir Robert wrote that "on Saturday [March 6], Jan had been to Sezimovo Usti and Beneš had said to him: 'I had to bear the brunt of Munich when you were abroad. Now that I am old and ill you must stay and help me and the country.' Jan had come back from this meeting in a deep depression, and had told Marcia that Beneš would never see the Hrad again. He was a broken man. When the crisis came, Jan had stayed at his post, partly to support Beneš and partly to help others who were in danger. He had failed. Now this was the end."

Jan went to say goodbye to Mrs. Davenport on Saturday evening. He made her burn every scrap of paper in her possession down to repair and food bills, gave her a dozen last-minute instructions, and the messages for Sir Robert Bruce Lockhart and Sir Orme Sargent of the British Foreign Office. "He said, 'When you get to Claridge's tomorrow, don't go out. Do not go out of the hotel. Do not leave your rooms at all. Stay there all the time until you hear from me.'

"I said yes," Mrs. Davenport wrote. "I did not ask him a question. He said, 'Very soon . . . few days . . .' " She watched him as he crossed the street, the bodyguard beside him and a man in a leather jacket behind them.

Sir Robert took up the story: "Jan sent her [Marcia] to England on Sunday, March 7th. The message to me was that he would escape later at some conference. . . . He wanted us to think well of him. . . . He was being spied on by his own people. On no account was I to come to Prague. My life would be in danger." Writing later in *Foreign Affairs*, Sir Robert noted that sometime after February 20 he had received another similar message from Masaryk.

The Communists might easily have discovered Masaryk's departure plans. If Mrs. Davenport's flat was bugged, for instance, Masaryk's last conversation with her would have revealed his intention to go in just a few days. Even if not, however, his reported conversation with President Beneš on that same Saturday, March 6, would have been more than enough.

For example, a man who had joined Beneš, Mrs. Beneš, and Jan at that lunch told Mrs. Davenport what he had heard:

"Jan asked Beneš what his intentions were, for himself and for Jan. Beneš said that he wanted to resign but that Gottwald would not permit it. Beneš did not answer concerning Jan; he was in no condition to answer. Jan told Beneš that he could no longer stay on in the false position he had assumed. Beneš was indifferent. Jan said he felt he had discharged his final obligation and that further compliance with the situation was impossible. It was now necessary to extricate himself. Beneš became rather excited but said nothing that was to the point. Jan was endeavoring to learn whether Beneš had any wishes or intentions which in Jan's mind would still bind him to Beneš. It was impossible to get an answer. Finally Jan asked Beneš what he proposed they should both do now that Beneš had got them out on the end of a limb. Beneš lost his temper and said he did not care what Jan did. Jan should solve his own problems, get himself out of his own difficulties. Jan replied that he meant to do that if he could. He intended to leave."

Ján Papánek, in an address on March 22, 1948, to the UN Security Council on the Communist seizure of Czechoslovakia, reported a similar but even stronger intention on Beneš's part to resign: "I believe that President Beneš would have resigned immediately if he were a free man. I know positively that on Saturday, 6 March 1948, the Foreign Minister, Jan Masaryk, visited him at Sezimovo Usti. I know that on that day the President said he was going to resign."

The Russians could well have known of the substance of this conversation then or at the later meeting between Beneš and Masaryk on March 9. In Moscow the previous July, Stalin had picked up from his desk the copy of a secret memorandum dictated by President Beneš on the Marshall Plan—its contents presumably known only to Beneš, his secretary, and Masaryk himself. Evidently the Russian NKVD had excellent possibilities of knowing exactly what was going on in the President's quarters.

For Sir Robert, writing in 1951, Masaryk's death was "still an unsolved mystery, and the whole truth known only to a few Communists and perhaps not even to them." It was obvious, he wrote, that "if the Communists had discovered Jan's alleged intention of leaving the country, they had every motive for silencing him for ever. His arrest might have provoked civil war. Once abroad and free, he would have been a formidable opponent, for his voice, known to the whole population, might have made an irresistible appeal."

On the other hand, Lockhart went on, the Czechoslovak Communists seemed caught off guard by the tragedy. Chancellor Smutný was with President Beneš, for instance, when Premier Gottwald and Interior Minister Nosek came to announce the news of Masaryk's death officially; and Smutny "has told me that the two men were visibly shaken, and that there were tears in M. Nosek's eyes. If murder it was, then I think M. Nosek had no part in it and that the directive may have come from a more distant authority, and was carried out by agents who took their instructions from abroad." Nosek, in his public announcement of the death, had said, according to the *New York Times* of March 11: "That good man and patriot and friend of our people, that man who just a few days ago said he was going on by the side of the people, has voluntarily put an end to his life."

Plainly the Communists could not admit murder, and in announcing Jan's death as suicide they released a spate of propaganda fixing the blame on the West. Nosek made this point, and so did a government radio announcer, reported in the *New York Times:* "J. Masaryk was a sensitive man who suffered under the attacks of the foreign press. He had become the object of invectives and attacks and reproaches and accusations. The more painful and sorrowful is his loss to all of us."

A story from London the day of his death quoted an unnamed friend who had left Prague only two days before as saying that the theory that reproachful messages from friends in the United States and Great Britain had hastened his death was false, that Masaryk was not worried about such letters. "But, whatever traces and clues remain will have been cleaned up by now. The police move fast in Czechoslovakia these days," the friend told the *New York Times.*

"In point of fact," wrote Sir Robert in 1951, "there was no hostile or abusive criticism from Britain and very little from the United States, where Jan's friends were well aware that he was trying to save something from the wreck of the Masaryk democracy. Moreover, the instinct of the Czechoslovak people was sound. They knew he was no Communist. 'No man shall dictate to me what books I shall read, what music I shall hear, what friends I shall choose.' This and similar phrases they had heard from him too often from his lips to be deceived, and to every Czechoslovak his death following hard on the commemoration of his father's birthday, told his own story. There was no place for the son of Thomas Masaryk in a Government which had used violence in order to seize power."

Sir Robert had no doubt that Masaryk did make plans to escape and would have been happy to live again in England, his second home. "Klima, who served him for twenty-four years, told me that on Jan's last visit to London in December, 1947, his parting words were: 'I'll be back here in the flat in February. It's the only place where I can get a real rest, and I need a long one.' "

Masaryk told two people that he would escape by plane early on March 10, Mrs. Davenport says she was told by those involved. The day before, he told one he had changed his mind and would take his life. It seems reasonably clear, from Mrs. Davenport's description, that the two men in question were Masaryk's third secretary now in Glasgow, Lumír Soukoup, and Masaryk's personal physician, Oskar Klinger. The man who opted for the theory of suicide told Marcia Davenport that Masaryk had said he would write a personal letter to her, as well as a political message. But none was ever given to her, though Clementis did return several gold pieces she had once given to Masaryk. She herself was convinced of murder.

There was no actual evidence of late visitors to Masaryk's flat on the evening of March 9, but Mrs. Davenport has pointed out how simple it would be for any to get in unobserved, since there were "innumerable entrances to the Cerninsky Palace other than the main ones," and many means of access to Masaryk's own rooms: "Jan and I had not failed to explore these features, and we used to shudder after we had counted a total of *eleven different means of access to his private rooms. It was possible to enter Jan's bathroom from a service passage without crossing his bedroom; and it was possible to enter the bedroom without using the main hallways and doors which gave access to it.*" [Italics added.]

Marcia Davenport felt that the description of the body and the disordered apartment indicated violence. She thought the razor blades and knotted pajama trouser cords were planted "to give an impression of suicidal hysteria and indecision about the means to be used. . . ." Further, she thought Masaryk's fear of pain and his "peculiar physical modesty and fastidious-ness" would have made a choice of such a suicide impossible. He would have used pills, if anything. Mrs. Ján Papánek agreed, in a recent interview in New York, that Masaryk would never have jumped from a window—he would have used pills.

On the other hand, when Arnost Heidrick, then Secretary General of the Czechoslovakian Foreign Office and now dead, escaped to the West in January, 1949, he told James Reston of the *New York Times* that Masaryk had "committed suicide—without the slightest doubt." Heidrick, who had seen Masaryk each day during his last weeks, said he talked constantly first of escaping to the West and then of suicide.

John Gunther, who last saw Masaryk at his apartment in New York in November, 1947, said later that Masaryk spent his last days and nights burning his private papers; he was told so by someone who helped him burn them. But this, as he said, could have meant a decision either to escape or to commit suicide.

In the United States on the day of Masaryk's death, his old friend Ján Papánek had called a special press conference. Said the *New York Times:* "First, he said that he could not believe that Mr. Masaryk had committed suicide. Then, with his hands trembling, he read a formal note he had sent to Trygve Lie, the Secretary-General of the UN. The note said: 'It is very clear that the coup by the Communist minority by force was ef-fectuated successfully only because of the threat of the use of military force of the Union of Soviet Socialist Republics.'

"The note asked the Security Council to look into the Czecho-slovak question as a threat to 'peace and security.' That eve-ning Mr. Lie announced that he could not forward the note to the Security Council. His reason was that Dr. Papánek had him-self cut connections with Prague and, therefore, spoke as an individual."

He told the UN Security Council twelve days after Masaryk's death: "For myself, I cannot accept the official explanation of his death as suicide. I know that he planned to leave Czechoslo-vakia and begin to work all over again for a free Czechoslovakia."

And on August 30, five months later, Dr. Papánek charged that Masaryk had been murdered and cited a secret medical report as evidence. At the same time General František Morovec, former Czech Army intelligence officer, said there had been a burst artery in Masaryk's neck, evidence of a struggle. Moreover, he said, there was plaster under Masaryk's nails, and the leg and body bruises were "incompatible" with suicide.

In 1969, in New York, Dr. Papánek, now directing the American Fund for Czechoslovak Refugees, said in an interview that he became "more and more sure as time went on that it was murder." Masaryk, he said, told him many times during that last trip to America that he was certain that he was going to be killed soon after his return to Prague. As Dr. Papánek wrote in a leaflet *Ten Years: The Czechoslovak Question in the United Nations* in 1958: "He did not want to talk to the Soviet delegates and when contacts and discussions with them were necessary I often had to go in his place. At the end of the General Assembly session in December, many of us advised him not to return home, but he emphasized he was needed and it was his duty to return even though he knew and said—that they would kill him."

"He had an intuitive sense," Dr. Papánek said. "And the greatest danger to the Soviets would have been for Jan to escape. He had a way of reaching the minds as well as the hearts of people. There was no man more loved in Prague, and he was very popular in the United States as well, a man of tremendous warmth."

Papánek himself was harassed by the Communist government after his friend's death. A forged letter allegedly signed by Beneš attempted to replace him as Czech representative to the United Nations after he refused to surrender the office to the Communists. He was able to obtain an affidavit which proved that the letter was a forgery. He was never formally recalled, nor did he resign. The Prague Communist regime simply announced that Vlado Houdek, who had been the secret link of the Communists in the chancery of the President of the Republic, had been named in his place. Also, in August when Papánek was in France for the General Assembly of the UN, the Czech government sought his extradition. France refused and, instead, offered him protection.

We come to the fascinating realm of speculation. Robert Bruce Lockhart believed the message that Masaryk sent to him through Marcia Davenport, and so did she. Three friends—Sir Robert, who had known him since 1921, Ján Papánek, who had been a close friend since about 1923, and Marcia Davenport, who had known him since 1941—were among perhaps a dozen people in the world with more than an outsider's knowledge of Masaryk's way of thinking, his tastes and taboos, habits, reactions, emotional reflexes. Why, then, did Lockhart conclude that Masaryk committed suicide after all, whereas Ján Papánek and Marcia Davenport were convinced that he must have been murdered?

Sir Robert, maintaining that Masaryk decided at the last moment to take his own life "in protest," would have us believe his friend died a hero's death, faithful to an ancient and noble Czechoslovak tradition. The Protestant martyr Jan Hus deliberately chose such a death in 1415, when he went to the stake to protest the depravity, dishonesty, and corruption of the Catholic Church; so did Jan Palach, the young Czechoslovak student who set himself aflame five hundred and fifty-three years later—the names of Jan Hus and Jan Masaryk on his lips— to protest the new Soviet military occupation. However, other friends like Marcia Davenport and Ján Papánek thought Jan wanted to live, and that, too, was a sturdy Czechoslovak tradition. The friend who said he knew Masaryk planned to escape because he had arranged to accompany him—Dr. Oskar Klinger —refuses now to elaborate on his earlier statements except to say that he had dictated the full story in London in 1947 working two days with a secretary, and that its publication now could not bring back the dead. Perhaps later he would, when those still living in Czechoslovakia who mattered could not be injured further.

Chapter 13

"A great epoch calls for great men. There are modest unrecognized heroes, without Napoleon's glory or his record of achievements. An analysis of their characters would overshadow even the glory of Alexander the Great. Today, in the streets of Prague, you can come across a man who himself does not realize what his significance is in the history of the great new epoch. Modestly he goes his way, troubling nobody, nor is he himself troubled by journalists applying to him for an interview. If you were to ask him his name, he would answer in a simple and modest tone of voice: 'I am Schweik.'

"And this quiet, unassuming, shabbily dressed man is actually the good old soldier Schweik; that heroic, dauntless man who was the talk of all citizens in the Kingdom of Bohemia when they were under Austrian rule and whose glory will not pass away even now that we have a Republic.

"I am very fond of the good soldier Schweik . . . and I am convinced that you will sympathize with this modest, unrecognized hero. He did not set fire to the temple of the goddess at Ephesus, like that fool Herostrate, merely in order to get his name into the newspapers and the school reading books.

"And that, in itself, is enough."

Thus did Schweik's creator, Jaroslav Hašek, introduce the hilarious antihero who, from the instant he appeared on the Czechoslovak scene in the twenties, became folklore, the image of a nation, a way of life. It is not clear whether Schweik made the Czechs what they are today or whether they, being what they are, made Schweik. Either way, one has only to pass a day with him in the rear lines—where else would he be?—of the Austrian Army during World War I to perceive that Schweikism is man's best, if not sole, defense against heroism, patriotism, militarism, idealism, Boy Scoutism, totalitarianism, causes of whatever kind, and all plots, schemes, blandishments, injunctions, and exhortations leading to any form of death save the tranquil sort that comes of old age and, if you're lucky, overdrinking and overeating. This last is Schweik's supreme concern: to stay alive and therefore, with the entire force of a mighty empire concentrated on getting him to the front, to keep away from it. His stunning success may be measured by the fact that he manages in the end to be taken prisoner by his own army.

Jan Masaryk was never long out of Schweik's company. Hašek's book customarily lay on the bedside table next to his father's Bible, and he wouldn't move a foot out of Prague without taking the book along. He'd been drawn to Schweik by bonds of the tenderest affection from the start, his feelings deepening over the years, the nieces Herberta and Anička told me: the Good Soldier was such a cosmic joke on the gods and their earthly representatives, "such a help against something that cannot be helped." For a country as small as Czechoslovakia, so geographically situated as to be a perennial temptation to the Continent's giants, Schweikism was—is—a last refuge.

Masaryk himself resorted to it until almost the very end. There was a noticeable tinge of Schweikism in his relations with the Communists from the time he went to Russia with President Beneš, in 1945, and realized that anything like a frontal assault on these people, and this country, was out of the question. Even his decision to remain in Gottwald's Communist cabinet had a certain Schweikian quality—a forlorn hope by then, but still a faint one, of outwitting an invincible opponent by appearing to embrace him like a brother. He could never have done it with Schweik's peculiar talent; he was too obviously polished and openly witty to carry off his exacting role. Nevertheless, his long and intimate association with the Good Soldier gave him a considerable knack. "With this government I shall enjoy governing," he told Western reporters, referring to that Communist cabinet of Gottwald's, the irony almost imperceptible in his smile. Schweik would have stood him a glass of rum for that, if he happened to have the money on him.

Schweikism is not easily defined, still less easily imitated. It requires a saintly composure, deep craft, unflinching hypocrisy, an unconquerable lack of false pride, an unerring sense of self-preservation, careful avoidance of outright defiance, just the right degree of studied mental deficiency—well short of transcendental imbecility—that alone can outwit an otherwise insuperable opponent. Even Schweik, unexcelled at making a stupefying botch of an order he has set out with cheerful alacrity to obey, is satisfied with his performance only rarely, after "doing something so appalling that he could never be allowed to discover what it is."

Sunny-tempered, unendurably talkative, his intentions irreproachable at all times, the guileless Schweik with his "broad, smiling countenance, bounded by a large pair of ears projecting from underneath his cap, pressed down tightly on his head . . . gave the general impression of a man who is altogether at peace with the world and blissfully unconscious of any transgressions on his part." Never does Schweik suggest for a moment that he isn't longing to get to the front, and the quicker the better: "I'm as glad as I can be," he tells his lieutenant on hearing that they are both to go; "it'll be a grand thing if you and me was to fall together fighting for the Emporer and his family." Nor has he anything but the warmest enthusiasm for the Hapsburgs and their imperial interests. "Long live Franz Josef! We'll win this war!" he shouts shamelessly as he's trundled across Vaclavske Namesti in a wheelchair, brandishing crutches, to report to his draft board; and the maundering lunacy behind both sentiments is at once apparent.

"What's wrong with you?" asks the medical officer, who has just ordered a previous malingerer to be taken away upon ascertaining that the man was dead. "Beg to report, sir, I've got rheumatism but I'll serve the Emporer till I'm hacked to pieces," Schweik replies modestly. "My knees are swollen."

"Aha, rheumatism—a frightfully troublesome disease," says the doctor, giving instructions for Schweik to receive the standard malingerer's treatment: "absolute diet," stomach to be rinsed out twice daily, clyster once daily.

"Don't spare me," Schweik urges the myrmidon administering the clyster. "Remember, you've sworn to serve the Emperor. And if it was your own father or your brother who was lying here, give 'em the clyster without turning a hair. Remember that Austria stands as firm as a rock on these clysters and victory is ours."

"The best thing to do," explains one of his cell mates, "is to squirt paraffin oil under the skin on your arms. My cousin had a slice of good luck that way. They cut off his arm below the elbow and now the army'll never worry him any more."

"Well," says Schweik with good nature, "you see what you've all got to go through for the Emperor."

"How do you like it?" the prison doctor asks malevolently after wrapping Schweik in a wet sheet to knock the hypochondria out of him.

"Beg to report, sir, that it's like being in a swimming bath or at the seaside," is his happy rejoinder.

"Has the state of your mind ever been examined?" the doctor inquires.

"In the army, the military doctors officially reported me as feeble-minded," he answers solemnly and proudly. "I'm no malingerer, I'm feeble-minded, fair and square. You just ask them, in the Ninety-First Regiment. . . ."

"You misbegotten whelp," rants a regimental colonel maddened by his limpidly innocent gaze and pure sweet smile, "you scabby ape, you wretched blob of scum, you skunk of a Socialist, you! . . . Are you an idiot, or ain't you?"

"Beg to report, sir, that I'm an idiot," Schweik answers, beaming.

For an idiot, our antihero has exceptional qualities. In civilian life, for instance, he'd made rather a good thing out of peddling curs with forged pedigrees. "There was a lady came one day . . . and said she wanted to buy a parrot," he recalls. "Well, what was I to do, not having any parrot and not knowing where to lay hands on one? But I had a bad-tempered bulldog, quite blind he was, too. And I give you my word, sir, I had to talk to that lady from four in the afternoon till seven in the evening before she bought the blind bulldog instead of the parrot."

In his first army job, furthermore, he is a surprisingly efficient batman to the sodden, irreligious ex-Jewish army chaplain who must frequently be scooped up and propelled homeward under arduous conditions. There is a memorable occasion when the chaplain has everything set up to say a Field Mass for departing troops, only to find he's forgotten about getting a ministrant to replace the one who'd left for the front.

"Never mind, sir," says Schweik. "That's a job I can manage."

"Do you know how to do it?"

"I've never done it before," replies Schweik, "but there's no harm in trying. . . . All that silly stuff about *et cum spiritu tuo* after your *Dominus vobiscum*—I'll see to that, all right. And afterward it's a pretty soft job to walk around you like a cat on hot bricks. And then to wash your hands and pour out the wine from the goblets. . . ."

"All right," says the chaplain, "but don't pour out any water for me. . . ."

The whole matter passes off without a hitch.

He can, too, be uncommonly generous in taking the rap for superior officers, among them the philandering lieutenant to whom the chaplain loses him at cards. Also, despite his usual amiability, he can be stern in the face of iniquity, as he was when his landlady, Mrs. Muller, lent his bed to a nightclub porter while Schweik was in detention for malingering. Stricken by remorse upon his return, Mrs. Muller leaves a note for Schweik saying, "Pleese sir forgiv me for not seeing you agane, becos I shall jump out of the winder."

"Liar," says Schweik, and waits.

Half an hour later the unhappy Mrs. Muller creeps into the kitchen, evidently expecting words of comfort from the tenant she has callously betrayed.

"If you want to jump out of the window, go into the bedroom," says Schweik. "I've opened the window for you. I wouldn't advise you to jump out of the kitchen window, because if you did, you'd fall into the roses in the garden and squash them and then you'd have to pay for them. If you jump out of the bedroom window, you'll land nicely on the pavement, and if you're lucky, you'll break your neck. If your luck's out, you'll just break all your ribs, arms and legs, and then it'll cost you a pretty penny in the hospital."

From time to time, what's more, Schweik can lapse into something dangerously like coherence. Walking through a field of recent battle where the stench of improperly buried soldiers is oppressive, he observes with his usual cheerfulness: "There'll be a fine harvest here after the war. They won't have to buy any bone meal. It's a good thing for farmers when they've got a whole regiment rotting away in their fields. There's no manure can beat it." Then there was the day when, during a stay in the guardhouse for attempted desertion—he'd walked in the wrong direction, searching earnestly for his regiment—he tried to "foster the military spirit" by singing lustily through the bars of his cell:

"And by his gun he stood
And kept on loading, loading,
And kept on keeping on.
A bullet came up quickly
And took his arms off slickly,
He never turned a hair
But kept on loading, loading
As he kept standing there,
And kept on keeping on."

If not for Schweik's nice sense of proportion, he might often have gone too far. As it was, he sometimes cut things rather fine: "I'd like to know what you think you're up to, you porpoise, you!" yells the chairman of an army medical commission whose views on Schweik are remarkably divergent.

"Beg to report, sir, I don't think at all," he replies with his childlike smile.

"Himmeldonnerwetter!" bellows a commission member, clanking his sword. "So he doesn't think at all, doesn't he? Why don't you think, you Siamese elephant?"

"Beg to report, sir, I don't think because soldiers ain't allowed to. Years and years ago, when I was in the Ninety-First Regiment, the captain always used to tell us: 'Soldiers mustn't think. Their superior officers do all their thinking for them. As soon as a soldier begins to think, he's no longer a soldier, but a lousy civilian.' Thinking doesn't lead . . ."

"Hold your tongue!" the chairman interrupts fiercely. "We've heard all about you. You're no idiot, Schweik. You're artful, you're tricky, you're a humbug, a hooligan, the scum of the earth, do you understand?"

"Beg to report, sir, yes, sir."

In matters of importance, though, Schweik's idiocy is consummate. The sublime example comes when his regiment is leaving for the front and Lieutenant Lukash, to whom he is orderly, is hunting for the books—copies of the second volume of *Sins of Our Fathers*—which his colonel has just informed him will be needed to decipher a new military code.

"Schweik," says Lieutenant Lukash, "I want to know more about those books you mentioned to me yesterday."

"Beg to report, sir, that's a very long story, and it always seems to sort of upset you, sir, when I tell you all the ins and outs of anything. . . . You see, sir, it was like this:

"They wanted to send these here books to the battalion office but everyone there was away, because they had to be in the canteen when they're off to the front and nobody knows whether they'll ever get another chance of going to the canteen. Well, sir, there they all were, drinking for all they was worth, and I couldn't get hold of any of them by telephone. . . . The regimental office kept kicking up a row because they couldn't get any answer and so they couldn't pass on the message that the draft office was to fetch some books for the officers of the whole company. Well, sir, you told me that things have got to be done promptly in wartime, so I telephoned and said I'd fetch those books myself. There was a regular sackful of 'em and I had quite a job to get them into the company office. Then I had a look at those books . . . and you see, sir, this book was in two volumes. One volume separate and another volume separate. Well, sir, talk about laugh! I never laughed so much in all my life. Reading ain't exactly in my line, you might say, but I never heard of anyone starting to read the second volume of a book before the first. . . . So I thinks to myself, why, they must all be dotty, because if anyone's going to read a book like this *Sins of Our Fathers* or whatever it is from the beginning, they got to start with the first volume, because we don't read books backward like what the Jews do. So then I telephoned to you, sir . . . and I asked you whether, being wartime, things was all topsy-turvy like and books had got to be read backward, second volume first . . . and you told me I was a silly chump. . . . Are you feeling queer, sir?"

Lieutenant Lukash has turned pale. His countenance, white

as a sheet, shows no trace of wrath. But there is something of
sheer despair in his expression.

"No, no, Schweik, that's all right. Get on with your story."

"Well, sir, as I was saying, it didn't take me long to see that
there was no need for the officers to start reading Volume One
afterward. . . . I at once telephoned to ask you whether you
wanted the two volumes at one go, and you told me to stop talking twaddle and did I think they were going to lug a lot of extra
books about with them. . . . And then I asked our quartermaster . . . and he said the officers seemed to think the war
was a sort of damned picnic, taking a regular library with them
as if they were going away for their summer holidays. . . .
Well, after that, I thought I'd better get your opinion again so
I telephoned to ask you what I was to do about those books and
you said that once I got something into my silly fat head I never
let go until I got a smack across the jaw. So then, sir, I only
took the first volume to the battalion office and left the rest in
our company office. My idea was that when the officers read the
first volume they could have the second served out like in a
lending library, but suddenly the order came that we was leaving, and a message was sent all over the battalion that the rest
of the books was to go into the regimental stores. . . . They've
got all sorts of stuff in those stores, sir. Why, there's the top
hat belonging to the choirmaster at Budejovice . . ."

And so, his childlike smile and golden disposition never failing, Schweik bungles and bamboozles his way to salvation. His
regiment having departed for the front despite his ardent assistance, he is sent ahead with the quartermaster to find billets
for the night. "It strikes me that we've taken the wrong road,"
he says, inspecting the landscape and announcing that they
should turn left.

"Don't be a fool, Schweik," says the quartermaster. "You can
see from the map that we've got to go right, like I said."

"Maps are wrong sometimes," answers Schweik serenely.
"Anyhow, this is the way I'm going. It's a more comfortable

road than yours. I'm going along the stream where the forget-me-nots grow, and if you want to traipse along in the broiling heat, you can. I stick to what Lieutenant Lukash told us. He said we couldn't miss the way. So I'm going to take it easy across the fields and pick some flowers."

Late in the afternoon, Schweik reaches a small pond where an escaped Russian soldier, stark naked for bathing purposes, sees him and runs off, leaving his uniform behind. Schweik tries it on, and lingers at the brink of the pond for a good look at his reflection in the water until he is discovered there by a field patrol from his own army, hunting for the Russian fugitive. In spite of his protests, he is carried off by the patrol and put to work with a gang of Russian prisoners, repairing a railway line. The whole thing is so sudden that Schweik doesn't realize what has happened to him until the next day, whereupon he writes with a piece of charred wood on a wall of the schoolroom he's quartered in:

"Hear slept Josef Schweik of Prague, Company Orderly of the 11th Draft of the 91st Regiment who while looking for Billets was taken prisoner . . . by the Austrians by Misteak."

The man is far gone who doesn't feel a powerful urge stealing over him to behave like Schweik after spending a little time with him. Whoever and wherever we are, the victimized part of us must rejoice in the triumph of this intrepid fellow victim who, as the Czech writer Antonín Liehm says, "recognizes the grotesque logic of his situation, adapts to it, enters into it, carries it to the absurd, and in the end survives." But it isn't really true that in parlous times fourteen million Czechoslovaks become Schweiks overnight. In the first place, not even Schweik's countrymen can perfectly master his style. Many tried, when the Germans occupied Prague in World War II and again when the Russians did thirty years later. But they could not resist an un-Schweikian display of loathing for the invader; and Schweikism without Schweik's peculiar saintliness—that seraphic smile, that unfurrowed brow, those incomparably innocent eyes beaming with kindly affection—lost much of its original savor. At best, they could only follow his elementary rules:

1. Always try to outlive the enemy; dying will get you nowhere.

2. Never offer open resistance to an irresistible force.

3. Always offer to cooperate.

4. Never actually do so, despite your most valiant efforts.

5. Always misunderstand what is wanted of you, the more so when what is wanted is transparently clear.

6. Never lose heart: the irresistible force is bound to dissolve into frustrated impotence before you do.

Naturally these rules are attractive to a small country lying at the crossroads of Europe, directly in the path of all history's conquering armies. The Czechs have in fact thought along these lines for a long while. Karel Havlíček, a nineteenth-century leader of the Czech awakening under the Hapsburgs, once wrote: "Elsewhere men have died for the honor and welfare of their fatherland; the same reasons impel us to live for it." The greatest of Czech historians, František Palacký, put it more succinctly: "We were here before Austria and will be here after Austria is gone." Yet where older Czechs take instinctively to Schweikism when calamity strikes, younger generations have grown dissatisfied with their lovable antihero and even ashamed of him. Students, in particular, find this national image of a determined dimwit humiliating. They prefer Jan Hus.

As anti-antiheroes go, they could hardly do better. A hundred years before Martin Luther, Jan Hus was openly resisting the irresistible force of the Papacy, obstinately courting death with his inflexible defense of the truth. Death came to him as he chose it. But the Hussite Protestants fought on after he was burned at the stake, beating back wave after wave of attacking Catholic crusaders, until their final defeat at the White Mountain two centuries later. The Catholic Hapsburgs were pitiless in victory, urged on by their court preacher, Friar Sabinus, with his vengeful text from the Psalms: "Thou shalt break them with a rod of iron; thou shalt dash them in pieces like a potter's vessel." Even so, whipped, humbled, hunted, ravaged physically, spiritually, financially, politically, culturally, socially, the vanquished Czechs gained something through resistance they probably would never have had without it: an independent Czechoslovak Republic, if only three centuries later.

The kingdom of Bohemia was a sovereign nation long before Jan Hus appeared. Its kings were native Czechs for four hundred years, starting in the late Middle Ages; and even afterward, tied dynastically to German princes of the Holy Roman Empire, it was independent internally, never a vassal state. The national Czech spirit was already alight in the early 1300's. The poor embraced the simple, evangelical Waldensian sect, demanded preaching in the vernacular, and deplored the clergy's scandalous immorality and merciless extortion of fees and taxes. Czech nobles at court—the enlightened court of Emperor Charles IV—publicly denounced the whoremongering, gambling, simony, drunkenness, sloth, and *luxuria* debasing ecclesiastical life. Emperor Charles himself, large-minded and devout, longed to make his native Prague a true city of God. By founding Charles University in 1348, he gave form to this movement, as well as a scholarly tradition fine enough to astonish the patronizing Petrarch. The men of Charles's Court, wrote the Italian poet after a visit in 1356, were "so mellow and urbane that one would think they were Athenians born and bred." Before the century was out, Charles University ranked with Bologna, Paris, and Oxford among Christendom's centers of learning.

Bohemia was prosperous and strong then, stirring with humanist thought and nationalist pride, ripe for the reformation when Master Jan Hus took the pulpit of Bethlehem Chapel in 1402. He was marvelously eloquent, a glowing Czech patriot, compassionate, cloaked in rectitude, steeped in the defiant doctrine of the great Oxford reformer John Wyclif. With Wyclif, he believed that a sinful authority ceases to be an authority. The quickest way to riches, he said in his sermons, was to become an abbot or bishop; all of society's abuses were caused by priestly greed. "The cowsheds on the church estates are more imposing than the lords' castles or the churches," he wrote. "Rain does not wet the prelates, mud does not get into the monasteries, hunger and thirst have been held at bay by their wealth. The Church is the receiver of gifts, the Church buys while the poor are everywhere in need." Further, he said, the Church treated all religious ceremonies as goods to be sold to the faithful. From cradle to grave the common people had to pay the priests and prelates: for baptizing children, for weddings, for the saints' intercession, for blessing eggs and salt. "One pays for confession, for mass, for the sacraments, for indulgences, for churching a woman, for a blessing, for burials, for funeral services and prayers," he said. "The very last penny which an old woman has hidden in her bundle for fear of thieves shall not be saved. The villainous priest will grab it. . . ."

He had the love of his people and therefore the favor of his sovereign, Wenceslas IV, who rightly estimated the popular temper; and so, for some years, he was shielded from hierarchical wrath. When the Archbishop of Prague induced the University masters to condemn Wyclif's teachings as heresy, King Wenceslas provoked the German Rector into quitting and put Jan Hus in his place. When the Archbishop personally burned Wyclif's books in his palace courtyard, the gesture so inflamed the populace that he was forced to retire discreetly from the city—and excommunicate Jan Hus from a safe distance. Master Hus thereupon consigned his own works for public burning, but did not stop defending Wyclif's work. It wasn't until two years later, in 1412, that the Archbishop managed at last to drive him from the city, by threatening all Prague with an interdict. The climax came when Pope John XXIII, later deposed as a "devil incarnate" for his simony and infamy, sent envoys to Prague to sell papal indulgences. He needed the money for his war with the King of Naples: any Christian paying the required sum was absolved of all sins and guaranteed a smooth passage to heaven. Master Hus thundered from the pulpit against this desecration of the people's simple faith. Three journeymen inspired by his sermon protested openly in church, and were summarily executed. The Czechs took up arms and gathered around the Town Hall in Old Town Square: Prague was on the threshold of revolution. When peace was restored, with great difficulty, Hus had to leave the city. His friends feared for his life: no Christian was allowed to offer him food, drink, or lodging, and wherever he lived, all religious ceremonies—baptisms, masses, and burials—were forbidden.

He went to southern Bohemia, worked among the pious Waldensians, preaching in the Czechs' native tongue and popular idiom, closer to his people than ever. Synods, public condemnations, censorial sermons, and ecclesiastical edicts could not budge him. Nor could the cardinals who, in 1414, summoned him to the Council of Constance. He arrived in Constance with a safe-conduct from Sigismund, ruler of the Holy Roman Empire and archdefender of the papal cause. He had no faith in Sigismund but much in his ability to plead his own case. Soon after his arrival, he was arrested and thrown into prison, fettered hand and foot in a castle tower exposed to the winter winds. For the next eight months he endured calculated tortures of mind and body; he was interrogated, badgered, ridiculed, wheedled, menaced. He would not even renounce heresies that he had never espoused. Again and again, responding to whatever pressure, he answered simply, "I will not recant."

He was calm when, on July 6, 1415, he was led through the streets of Constance to a meadow beyond the city walls, and bound to the stake with a rusty chain. In a farewell message to Charles University, he had written: "I, Master John Hus, in chains and in prison, now standing on the shore of this present life and expecting on the morrow a dreadful death, which will, I hope, purge away my sins, find no heresy in myself, and accept with all my heart any truth whatever that is worthy of belief." To his "dear pupil and beloved brother in Christ," Master Martin of Volyn, he wrote: "Do not be afraid to die for Christ if you would live with Christ. . . . Ponder always what you are, what you were, what you will be. Mourn the past, mend the present, beware of the future: I speak of sins." At the stake, faggots of straw ready to be set afire, messengers of the Council came and asked him to recant. Hus answered: "The prime endeavor of all my preaching, teaching and writing and of all my deeds has been to turn people from their sins, and this truth that I have written, taught and preached in accordance with the word of God and the teachings of the holy doctors I willingly seal with my death today." God's truth would prevail, he said.

His death raised a storm in Bohemia, already very nearly lost to Rome. "The abominable Czech heretics" mobilized for defense, pronounced their right to worship as they pleased, and worked out their Protestant creed in four Articles:

1. The word of God must be freely preached in the kingdom without opposition from the clergy.

2. The sacrament of the Eucharist under the species of bread and wine must be administered to all the faithful who are not guilty of mortal sin.

3. The worldly wealth and temporal goods now in the hands of the clergy must be taken from them and they must be compelled to live in apostolic poverty.

4. All mortal and open sins and other uncleannesses contrary to the law of God must be punished, without respect of person or class.

They were, inevitably, divided amongst themselves, the more conservative aristocracy inclining toward compromise with Rome, the more radical plebians toward the sword. Their open revolt broke out four years after Jan Hus died, when Praguers armed with spears and clubs stormed the New Town Hall, liberated the Hussites held prisoner there, and hurled the Mayor and city fathers from the window. That was the origin

of another ancient and enduring Czech tradition: death by defenestration.

Bohemia nearly went up in smoke then, the flames of revolt
fed by revolutionary peasants and the urban poor. The Taborite
Hussites, as they called themselves, preached that "no man
should be subject to any man," that "robbing of the poor shall
cease," that no rents or taxes should be collected, that "once
the lords were burnt up in ovens like stubble" Christ would
descend and "place supreme power in the hands of the people."
Private property would be abolished, everything would be held
in common, Christ's millennial kingdom would bring "a golden
age . . . a paradise on earth."

From Rome, and from Emperor Sigismund's court, the call
went out to all Catholic Europe to rescue Bohemia from the
renegade Hussites, for the lords, the Holy Roman Empire, the
Pope. Crusaders and mercenaries were recruited from Spain,
Italy, France, Hungary, and Germany, attacking in armies of a
hundred thousand and more, incited to sack and burn, kill all
Czech-speaking citizens, Hussite or not. Again and again they
were driven back by the Hussites' military genius, Jan Žižka.
The Hussite wars lasted twelve years, the Czech reformation
almost another two centuries. For even after an uneasy truce
there was no peace. Only in 1620, after the Battle of the White
Mountain, was peace imposed at last, Bohemia's religious freedom lost, sovereignty gone, the Hussites crushed.

Toward the end they were in pathetic disarray, divided by
sharp internal quarrels, abandoned—as usual—by their allies.
The beginning of the end was the celebrated Defenestration
of 1618: a hundred Czech noblemen made their way into
Hradcany Castle and threw three envoys of the Catholic Emperor Mathias from a high window. The three envoys survived,
as it happened, landing on a soft mound of refuse. But everybody knew the final war had to come, and the Czechs were
utterly alone. Later, the story was told in Vienna of a messenger
who said that even after defeat the incumbent Bohemian King

Frederick could muster a great army. The King of Denmark was his uncle, the Hollanders his friends, England's James I his father-in-law; and each would send him a hundred thousand. Someone asked: a hundred thousand what? "The King of Denmark will send a hundred thousand red herrings," was the reply, "the Hollanders a hundred thousand cheeses, the King of England a hundred thousand ambassadors."

Nothing, nobody, was spared after 1620. All Bohemia became the hereditary property of the Hapsburg family. Every non-Catholic priest was banished from the kingdom, and by 1627, not a soul, even of the nobility, could live in the kingdom who was not of Catholic faith. The property of all Protestant nobles was confiscated, and four out of five of them went into exile. Taxes and special levies bled the Czechs white. "How rich was our ancient kingdom when first you had it all men know," wrote a Czech Jesuit to his Hapsburg rulers, "and you have brought it but ruin and disgrace. The nobles you have oppressed, great cities made small. Of smiling towns you have made straggling villages, of pleasant towns rows of wretched hovels. Where before happy craftsmen labored, now hungry starving wrecks of men stalk the weeded paths. . . . The court at Vienna, its appetite whetted by the sweet savor of Czech money, cries out daily 'Give us more, Give us more!' "

Still, they'd fought the good fight. It brought them closer together in language, custom, and thought, detached them further from their Germanic neighbors, made indelible lines of their Slavic ethnic markings. The very memory of their ultimate degradation kept their sense of nationhood alive. From 1620 to 1918 they nursed the memory, clinging to the promise of the illustrious Comenius, their last Hussite Bishop, who wrote before dying in 1670: "After the tempest of God's wrath shall have passed, the rule of thy country will again return to thee, O Czech people."

Chapter 14

"No thanks, there's really nothing you can do for us. Excuse me, but this is our business."

"I meant you, personally. Could I do something, get something for you in Rome?"

"Not unless you can bring my best friend back with you."

"Your best friend? Is he in Rome?"

"Rome, Paris, Vienna—anywhere out there." A broad sweep of the arm.

"I don't know. I'll try. Who is he?"

Not the shade of a smile. "A Smith & Wesson. Thirty-eight, with a shoulder holster. I'd never forget you."

He was a Czechoslovak Communist, in the secret police. It was late in the autumn of 1968 when I met him in occupied Prague, living in such carefully contrived obscurity that few Czechoslovaks knew he existed. It took weeks to trace him and delicate negotiations to arrange a meeting. Not a thing could be done by telephone. I was meticulously screened, and elaborately instructed in how to avoid being followed. Soviet KGB agents would have given a lot to find him. If the Russians were still blocked at every turn in the Czechoslovak Interior Ministry, two months after the invasion, it was at least partly because of him and a few like-minded secret police officers. On their own initiative they were taking turns around the clock, gun in hand and telephone at arm's reach, to handle any Czech security officer collaborating with the Russians. As far as I knew, they went on with this self-appointed mission until the end of 1968, when the Dubček regime ordered them peremptorily to "return to legality."

Let's call him Karel. I can't say more about him except that he would plainly be just as nervous without a gun on him as I was when—to explain why he would prefer a Smith & Wesson —he showed me the one he had. He'd been with the security police since 1945, during the preparations for the Communist coup, the coup itself, the Slánský trials, the purges. He'd been highly placed in the service, demoted, reinstated, jailed for a while, released with a warning. He knew the secret police structure inside out. Whether his information was altogether reliable or not, I was able to confirm at least part of it. He carried an astonishing amount in his head, reeling off names, dates, positions, and interlocking directorates in the Czechoslovak and Soviet secret services as an English country vicar might rattle off old cricket scores. Apparently he never forgot a name or face; I could *see* him fixing mine in his memory. I took it for granted that he wouldn't forget anyone who talked too much either.

What I wanted to learn from him mainly was this: if a Communist kangaroo court had condemned Jan Masaryk to death by defenestration, who might the executioners be and how would they go about it?

That would depend partly on who was passing sentence, he began. If the decision were made by the Czechoslovak Communists, they would have consulted the Russians first. But that wouldn't necessarily be so the other way round. If the Russians had concluded that Jan Masaryk had to go, the matter could have been handled in a few hours, without informing Czechoslovak party leaders at all.

In March, 1948, Karel continued, the Czechoslovak Ministry of the Interior was not yet openly and wholly under Soviet control. That didn't happen until more than a year later, after Lazslo Rajk was imprisoned in Hungary and the Stalinist purges were well under way in other Eastern European states. Slow to produce candidates for a purge trial in his own party, and distressed by nasty Russian hints on the subject, Premier Gottwald admitted in 1949 that his secret police were not as "professionally qualified" as, say, the Hungarian Communists'. Stalin's security boss, Lavrenti Beria, accepted the implied invitation at once, sending four Russian "counselors"—soon to become twenty-six—to take the Interior Ministry in hand.

But this didn't mean that Czechoslovak security matters were left to the Czechoslovaks until 1949. A sizable contingent of Soviet NKVD agents had stayed behind when the Red Army withdrew at the end of 1945, working in key districts with Communist-controlled units of the secret police. Starting in mid-February, 1948, substantial reinforcements came from Moscow. Several dozens were stationed in Prague, working with military intelligence, training interrogators for the secret police, overseeing street activities during the takeover through the armed Workers' Militia, carrying out independent assignments emanating from the Soviet capital. The newcomers, operating from the Soviet Embassy, were called "coordinators." Though still obliged in those days to ask the Czechoslovak Interior Ministry for dossiers, they were already in a position to bypass the Czechoslovaks when necessary.

This much was confirmed by several sources, including Dr. Ján Papánek, head of the Czech UN delegation in 1948. I didn't need Karel to tell me, furthermore—it is documented history—that once the Czech coup was carried off, Stalin set the course of Czechoslovak history on the basis of "intensifying the class struggle *after* the conquest of power by the working class." From the moment the Czechoslovak Communists were in control, the Soviet ruler set out to eliminate all traces of

Popular Frontism, class collaboration, East-West bridge-building, social-democratic sentimentality, nationalism, and every other aspect of Masarykism from the Czechoslovak scene. Within a few months of the coup he had already presented the Czechoslovaks with a plan to wage "pitiless war" not only on the class enemy, but on "all presumed enemies of the Party and the Soviet Union" inside and outside the party's ranks; and he personally selected the two authoritative local party leaders to carry it out: General Secretary Rudolf Slánský and the longtime Comintern agent Bedřich Geminder. It was called Plan TB (tridni boj, or class struggle), and it laid the original premise for a twenty-year reign of terror, striking down anti-Communists and Communists alike. From Plan TB derived the "law for the protection of the Republic" in October, 1948, providing legal cover for the most numerous and monstrous juridical crimes in any Communist-controlled state except Russia itself.

For grotesque horror, not even the Rajk trial in Budapest compared to the Slánský trials in Prague, for which preparations began the very year Masaryk died. As always in these matters, the accused were selected in Moscow beforehand by card index (Jewish origin, time spent in a Western country, relatives living in the West, service with the Loyalists in the Spanish Civil War). Their testimony was invented by their interrogators and given to them to be memorized by heart, their crimes recognized by the Czechoslovak party two decades later as "imaginary and prefabricated," a mosaic of supporting "evidence" extracted by unspeakable tortures of body and mind. Describing his experience as one of Rudolf Slánský's thirteen codefendants, Arthur London has conveyed something of the peculiar nightmare—scientific dementia, controlled insanity—that went into procuring confessions: methodical denial of sleep, eighteen hours in a standing position for interrogation, permanently manacled hands so monstrously swollen that he was reduced to lapping food from a tin plate like a dog, sly hints of arrest and

torture for his wife and children, appeals to his political conscience ("the Party needs your confession; do it for the Party's
sake"), gloating assurances that there were too many supporting
"confessions" for him to deny anything in court, bland promises
that a confession would bring deliverance from an otherwise
unavoidable death sentence. His description of the shock to
Rudolf Slánský and ten other defendants when they heard the
sentence of death pronounced was memorable. The truly unforgettable part, however, was his explanation of how the interrogators of these eleven doomed and innocent men persuaded
them to accept the death sentence without making a legal appeal—or even a personal protest in the courtroom.

The technique, developed by Russian interrogators in the
1930's, was standardized and easily mastered. By the time the
Slánský trials opened in December, 1952, Czechoslovak Communist *apparatchiks* and security police had learned to work
smoothly under Russian supervision. Soviet inquisitors could
come and go, in their swings around Eastern European capitals
to coordinate the purges in progress, leaving details to be
handled by their colonial security forces. In the preparatory
phase of Plan TB, however, the Russians preferred to rely on
their own cadres for certain matters.

Beginning in February, 1948, Karel told me, there were three
distinct groups of secret agents operating through the Soviet
Embassy in Prague. The "executives," made up of Soviet "counselors" and "coordinators," worked in the open with the Czechoslovak Interior Ministry. The "offensives" were submerged,
anonymous, relying on their own communications, informers,
liaison operatives, gunmen: the notorious Beria gorillas. The
Rote Kappella (Red Band) was the most secret and lethal of all.

Much shrunken since wartime, when it became a legend for
its exploits in Nazi Germany, the Rote Kappella still had romantic emanations for those who loved spy stories. Operatives
for this celebrated Soviet espionage network were no common
lumpenproletariat thugs. They were cultivated, resourceful,

superbly brave and coolheaded, wholly and ardently committed to the Communist cause. Most of them had been recruited by the prewar Comintern, from all over Europe, and still owed their allegiance to its successor, the Cominform, the Kremlin's executive branch for Communist operations abroad. There was rarely a professional killer among them, and killing was not their main purpose. They were, principally, intelligence-gatherers at the highest level. They killed only when necessary, always with an exquisite sense of political purpose, and in utter secrecy. Had their group received an order to kill in Prague, nobody else—neither the other Soviet secret service units in the Embassy nor Czechoslovak Communist leaders—would have known about it.

For Czechoslovak security officers of Karel's rank, the Rote Kappella might have been operating on a different planet. He knew only that a skeletal structure had been retained in Prague after the war, presumably getting orders from the Cominform. He had a considerably better working knowledge of the next most secret Soviet group in Prague: the "offensives," Beria's gorillas. Even here, his information was limited. "Eventually, we got to know who their Czech operatives were," he told me. "But we never found out who *they* were. We used to call them the Centrum."

All these units had excellent facilities, continued Karel, as did the Czech secret services. "We inherited the German security apparatus after the war, including some marvelous radio communications built for the German Navy," he said. In addition, the Soviet Centrum had a flawless system for picking up information quickly from the Czech Interior Ministry: the Ministry's Chief of Radio Communications worked for the Centrum as well. Among other Czech agents working for the Centrum in 1948, to Karel's knowledge, were:

1. Bedřich Geminder, head of the Czech Communist Central Committee's International Section, known as Moscow's man in

top Czech Party circles, coadministrator of Plan TB. Executed with Rudolf Slánský in 1952.

2. Bedřich Reicin, Deputy Defense Minister, head of the army's Second Department for counterespionage. Executed in the Slánský trials.

3. Major Augustin Schramm, liaison officer between Bedřich Reicin's Army Counter-Intelligence Bureau and the Centrum. Rumored to be Jan Masaryk's assassin. Murdered in Prague, May 27, 1948.

4. Major Bedřich Pokorný, coordinator of the Interior Ministry's security services. Murdered near Brno, March 31, 1968.

5. Jarin Hosek, liaison between Major Pokorný's security services and the Centrum. Said by Karel to be the murderer of Major Schramm. Alive, residing thirty miles from Prague.

6. Captain M. Pich-Tůma of the Czech security police (STB), one of seven former security officers arrested by the Dubček regime in June, 1968, for murders committed twenty years earlier. His trial, which opened in the Higher Military Court on December 12, 1968, was adjourned indefinitely on Russian insistence.

These operatives were answerable to the Soviet Centrum independently of their responsibilities to the Czechoslovak secret services. As a rule, Beria could count on perfect loyalty and discretion from such people, whose personal histories were known to him in capillary detail. For instance, he had a useful dossier on Major Pokorný, who had been an army spy before the war, and another on Bedřich Reicin, who was sent into wartime Russia as a Gestapo agent. Reicin's record in particular was so egregious that several hundred Czechoslovak army officers wound up in jail for questioning his moral title to office after the war.

It was not Karel who told me but Chancellor Jaromír Smutný, and Marcia Davenport respectively who wrote, that President Eduard Beneš and Jan Masaryk both feared Bedřich

Reicin more than anybody else in the Communist security network. The President, according to his Chancellor, realized that he could do nothing about the army during the February crisis so long as the implacable Reicin stood in his way. Masaryk, certain that the Communists meant to kill him sooner or later, was convinced that Reicin would get the assignment. Even in Reicin's far-from-squeamish circles, he was distinguished for his brutality. To be arrested by his Army Second Department was to be beaten up automatically on arrival and systematically thereafter before so much as getting around to being questioned. It was for this Second Department that a special contingent of Soviet NKVD agents was flown in from Moscow shortly before the coup.

Nobody knows how many Czechs were liquidated secretly by one or another branch of the local security police, or the Soviet Centrum in Prague, after the coup was completed. Judging from books written by survivors and published since the January, 1968, revolution, the figure must run into thousands. Karel himself, keeping score from 1948 until Stalin's death and Beria's execution in 1953, had a list of well over two hundred. Not all were dispatched on the Centrum's orders, by any means. But from what Karel told me of Captain Pich-Tůma alone—and most of the details were confirmed publicly in the Captain's unfinished military trial—I got a fairly good idea of how the Centrum used its Czechoslovak operatives.

Captain Pich-Tůma, a young Communist activist when World War II began, had fled to Soviet Russia to escape arrest by the Germans. There he was trained as a parachutist by Major Augustin Schramm, responsible for training Czechoslovak partisans in Russia. Later, he was dropped into the Bohemian-Moravian highlands as a commissar of a partisan unit. He risked his life repeatedly and became one of the country's partisan heroes. At the war's end, Pich-Tůma told the court, he went into rather special police work: party leader Klement Gottwald asked him to organize a supersecret security force parallel to existing forces in the Interior Ministry, which Gott-wald didn't entirely trust. Pich-Tůma's special security unit was therefore directly answerable to the Czechoslovak Party's Central Committee; and Pich-Tůma personally was directly answerable to the Soviet Centrum.

In June, 1948—three months after Jan Masaryk died and a few weeks after Masaryk's alleged assassin, Major Schramm, was murdered—Captain Pich-Tůma killed at least one Czech and ordered the death of another. He confessed to both mur-ders twenty years later. His personal victim was Engineer P. Konečný, Prague Secretary of President Beneš's National Socialist Party. The other victim was a security officer in the STB named František Novotný. According to the state's formal charges, both victims had been arrested "illegally" and inter-rogated "inhumanly." Konečný was bound so tightly with wire that blood poisoning set in. He was then crammed into the trunk of a car, alive, and transported to Banska Bystrica in cen-tral Slovakia, where Captain Pich-Tůma fired two bullets into the back of his head. Afterward, his corpse was slung into a potato sack and carried to a steel smelter in Ostrava, where it was "liquefied" in the blast furnace. The security officer, František Novotný, was also stuffed alive into the trunk of a car and taken to a wood near Benesov, twenty-four miles from Prague, where he too was shot "while escaping." His body was buried on the spot.

Captain Pich-Tůma spoke rather frankly to the military court before the Russians got the trial called off. He had habitually used physical violence to interrogate prisoners in 1948, he said, since it was "the official opinion in higher Party circles that force could be used when there was danger of delay." There was no such thing in those days as security-service regulations. "Orders were given orally, and we often didn't know what our subordinates were doing when, without our being informed, they would get instructions from higher quarters." As for the two victims named in the case, he had decreed their deaths with-out formal charges, still less a judicial order, or authorization from any Czechoslovak source. He was not conscious of violating any law, he told the judge: "The laws, often dating from feudalist times, did not apply to us in the revolutionary period. I recognized and respected only one law: the class law."

His two victims had to be "liquidated physically," Captain Pich-Tůma testified, because they were a "threat to the Communists' security." František Novotný, a fellow partisan fighter, security officer, and Communist Party member, had to die because "he knew too much" about certain secret-police operations. "It was impossible to bring Novotný before a court because we feared that he would disclose a number of dangerous facts regarding our transgressions of the law." The Prague secretary of the National Socialist Party, Engineer Konečný, apparently had still more explosive information. He was important enough for Captain Pich-Tůma to shoot personally because, as the Captain said in court, "we suspected that Konečný knew who killed Major Schramm."

Apart from unverified rumors, the court knew nothing of Major Schramm in December, 1968, except that he'd been a hero of the partisan resistance, leader of the Communist Party's partisan organization, and editor of a review on partisan affairs. For all the rumors in the press after the Masaryk case was reopened, no proof was yet forthcoming of Major Schramm's other activities. Nor did Captain Pich-Tůma offer any at his trial. He was not asked, and did not try, to explain why it was so urgent to conceal, rather than expose, the identity of Major Schramm's murderer. He said nothing of the fact that he and Schramm were both connected with Beria's Centrum in Prague, or that Schramm was the Centrum's liaison with Bedřich Reicin's infamous Second Department in the army. He did not suggest that Schramm himself might have gotten to know too much and thus become a threat to the Communists' (or the Russians') security. Certainly he made no reference at all to a possible connection between the deaths of Major Schramm and Jan Masaryk. Yet there was a tantalizing hint of this at his trial.

Among the witnesses in Captain Pich-Tůma's trial was a

former security agent named Zdeněk Řípa, who claimed merely
to have driven the car carrying the Captain's victim, Konečný,
in the trunk. According to my informant, Karel, Zdeněk Řípa
actually directed the operation. Far from being a nondescript
driver, Řípa was a close and trusted aide of Major Pokorný's,
coordinator of the Interior Ministry's secret services, and also
a Centrum operative. When Pokorný was found with a noose
around his neck (and almost certainly with his throat cut) in
the spring of 1968, the Czech news agency Ceteka reported that
he'd been a star investigator into the deaths of both Jan
Masaryk and Major Schramm. When Pokorný was called in on
the Masaryk case, around eleven in the morning on March 10,
1948, it was Zdeněk Řípa who accompanied him to Czernin
Palace. When Pokorný was called in on the Schramm case two
months later, Řípa not only assisted him but—as Řípa himself
told the court—was then asked by the Party's Central Committee to *lead the search for Schramm's killer.* When Centrum
agent Pich-Tůma shot somebody suspected of knowing who
killed Schramm, it was Řípa who drove the death car to Banska
Bystrica and thence to the Ostrava blast furnace. And when
Major Pokorný disappeared twenty years later, on the eve of
the Dubček regime's decision to reopen the Masaryk case, *it
was Řípa who stumbled on Pokorný's body hanging from a tree*
—or said he did, when he so informed the Brno police on April
9, 1968, nine days after Pokorný was reported missing.

Karel paused, when we had covered the ground this far, to
apologize. He was giving me only fragmentary information on
this point because it was all he had, he explained: he had never
been able to get a more complete picture. Řípa was a thin
strand connecting Major Pokorný (Czech Interior Ministry and
Soviet Centrum) to Major Schramm (Czech Army Counter-
Intelligence and Soviet Centrum) to Jan Masaryk. Karel knew
of another possible connection, more interesting. Frankly, he
would not advise me to explore it.

The precautions to ensure secrecy in the security forces after

Masaryk died were stricter than any in Karel's experience before or after. Even the highest-ranking Communists involved
in the case were picked off in one way or another, sooner or
later. Vladimír Clementis, Masaryk's Deputy in the Foreign
Ministry, ended up if only coincidentally on the gallows with
Slánský. Josef Gorner, the National CID Chief, retired in
1951 and never opened his mouth again. Security Chief Jan
Hora was thrown out of his job barely two months after
Masaryk's death. Jindřich Veselý, Deputy Interior Minister,
was the object of an assassination attempt by agents of Beria's
Centrum in 1949; he survived despite the nine bullets in his
body, only to commit suicide later. Major Pokorný alone, the
Interior Ministry official who was in fact given top authority
in the Masaryk case, went unmolested until his murder two
decades later. Knowing what they knew about his past, the
Russians could supposedly rely on Major Pokorný's discretion.

Naturally, Karel went on, the official version of Jan Masaryk's
death was for public consumption. Very few ranking Czech
security officers believed it was suicide. Most knew better than
to question the verdict openly. A handful tried to find the
truth secretly. Between 1948 and 1951, four separate groups
of security officers in the STB, very restricted and highly
clandestine, set out to investigate the case from the inside.
Karel was not sure how far they got. Three of the officers involved were assassinated. Most of the others ended up in Ruzyne
and Pankrac. Not many came out alive. From those who did,
however, Karel was able later to piece certain things together.
In each instance, the groups were stopped just as the trail was
leading to Jarin Hosek, the liaison officer between Major
Pokorný's security services in the Interior Ministry and the
Centrum. Reconstructing the evidence that Karel knew they'd
found, he was personally certain that Jarin Hosek had killed
Major Schramm on the Centrum's orders. He was not certain,
but strongly suspected, that the Centrum wanted to eliminate
Schramm because it had used him to eliminate Masaryk.

If so, continued Karel, there'd been a fast bit of footwork involved. Two young Czechs working for the American CIC (Counter-Intelligence Corps) had been arrested, tried, and executed for the murder of Major Schramm. It was a fact that both were at Major Schramm's door when he was shot. The Centrum, informed of their every movement, had sent Hosek in to finish Schramm off and frame these young CIC agents for the crime. Thus, the Centrum got rid of an agent it wanted to silence, got the case officially closed in short order, and managed to put the blame for everything on the Americans—a master stroke.

Of course there was no conclusive proof, Karel said, nor was any likely to turn up. Although Jarin Hosek was still alive, this in itself suggested the futility of approaching him. If Hosek didn't have such a prodigious talent for silence he would have been dead long ago. Did I want Hosek's address? No, I didn't. All things considered, I was sure Karel was right in advising me to leave Hosek alone. I didn't realize how right he was, though, until some months later.

Chapter 15

"The Security Police network in the Soviet orbit is really international, with a concomitant convict's international. Although at times, mainly during the early stages of imprisonment, the Security Police take great care to keep prisoners apart, after the sentence they get mixed up. As a precautionary measure they often transfer convicts from cell to cell, from wing to wing, and even from prison to prison. The various 'national' Security Police organizations make arrests on each other's behalf, and convicts having some particular information are frequently exchanged. In the preparation of the Rajk case, for instance, Istvan Stolte, one of the principal false witnesses, was kidnapped by the Soviet M.V.D. (Interior Ministry) from Wasserburg, near Munich, then taken to Baden in Austria. From there, the Russian General Bielkin brought him personally by car to Budapest. Noel Field, the American Unitarian Service Committee official, was arrested with his wife in Poland and sent to Budapest to be another state witness in the Rajk trial. Stolte was then sentenced to imprisonment for life (I shared a cell with him for a while) and Noel Field to fifteen years. In a larger rigged trial, most of the Soviet orbit usually contributes incriminating witnesses. If there are not enough witness-candidates, say, in Rumania for a Zionist plot, then Zionists from Hungary, Poland and Russia are 'loaned' to the Rumanian security police. Nine copies of all Security Police minutes, files, testimonials, trial reports are prepared (we all had to sign nine copies of our confessions) . One copy of everything is sent to the Moscow M.V.D. headquarters, the nerve-center of the Security Police network. The many millions of files enable the producers of the large and small rigged trials to have a wide choice of actors.

"This system enables the convicts to get inside information about the Security Police International. In one of the large cells in a Security Police headquarters one might meet a convict who had been loaned for interrogation by, say, the Czechoslovak security police. In a week or two this man could pass on the collective knowledge of the convict population in Czechoslovakia. As the communist old guard generally has a large role in the rigged trials, former party secretaries, members of Central Executives and Politburos, can clear up mysteries of party history which have puzzled communists for years. The 'suicide' of Jan Masaryk, the Foreign Minister of Czechoslovakia, may for instance be a mystery to the outside world. Inside Czech prisons, convicts even know the names of the two Security Police thugs who threw him out of the window."

The writer, George Paloczi-Horvath, was a reputable Hungarian journalist imprisoned in Budapest from 1949 to 1954. I didn't meet any Czech convicts who admitted to knowing the names of those security-police thugs he talked about. But his description of prison life in the fifties was unmistakably familiar. From 1948 to 1960 and later, Pankrac, Ruzyne, Leopoldov, and other Czech jails teemed with prisoners whose pooled political knowledge would make fascinating reading. Isolated in solitary confinement until they "confessed," they could then communicate with each other, though rarely with the outside world, and usually only by guarded means: snatches of illicit conversation in the prison courtyard, code messages tapped through water pipes, smuggled notes on scraps of paper.

A good many people among them must have known—or claimed to know—something about the Masaryk case:

1. Rudolf Slánský, ex-Secretary-General of the Communist Party, member of the Party's Commission on State Security.

2. Karel Šváb, ex-head of the Party's Commission on State Security.

3. Bedřich Reicin, ex-Director Army Counter-Espionage (Second Department), agent of Soviet Centrum.

4. Bedřich Geminder, ex-head of the Party's International Section, member of Commission on State Security, agent of Soviet Centrum.

5. André Simon, ex-head of the Czech Information Service, said by some experts to have been an agent of the Soviet Centrum *in Moscow*.

6. Vladimír Clementis, ex-Deputy Foreign Minister, present at Czernin Palace in the early morning of March 10.

7. Josef Pavel, future Interior Minister after January revolution, member of Commission on State Security.

8. Benno Weigl, author of *Der Spiegel* articles which led to reopening Masaryk investigation.

9. Ivan Sviták, author of the *Student* article based on the *Spiegel* article.

10. Antonín Šum, one of Masaryk's three private secretaries.

11. Pavel Kavan, Counselor of the Czech Embassy in London in 1948, Masaryk's last known caller on March 9, 1948.

12. Zdeněk Borkovec, head of the Prague CID, in charge of Masaryk investigation until security police took over.

13. František Borkovec, Zdeněk's brother.

14. Pavel Straka, the Foreign Affairs Ministry clerk on night duty on March 9.

15. Vladimír Sis, an editor of Catholic Party paper *Lidová Demokracie,* intimate friend of police doctor Jaromír Teplý.

16. Vítězslav Kadlcak, alias Major Chlumský, who claimed to have documents proving Masaryk was murdered, by Major Schramm.

17. Miloslav Choc, alleged murderer of Major Schramm.

18. Slavoj Sadek, Choc's alleged accomplice.
19. Vávra-Stařík, leader of Choc's anti-Communist underground.
20. Václav Provazník, member of Choc's group.
21. M. Černoušek, another member of Choc's group.
22. Jindřich Doležal, cell mate of Vávra-Stařík's.
23. Eva Dušková, Choc's fiancée.
24. Vlastimil Kaplan, an STB investigator of Schramm's death.
25. Major Bedřich Pokorný, coordinator of Interior Ministry secret services, star investigator in the Masaryk and Schramm deaths, arrested briefly in the fifties for abuse of power.

No doubt there were other convicts, remaining in obscurity, who had some knowledge in regard to Masaryk's death. Of the twenty-five on this list, ten were executed, one died in prison, one died a few weeks after release, one committed suicide, one disappeared, one was murdered. How many of these and the remaining ten did exchange notes, and what they may really have told each other, we will probably never know. Believing themselves sealed off forever from the outside world, knowing they might be hanged at any moment, they talked amongst themselves as they would never have done before their arrest, and would not do after their release. Once outside again, some miraculously regained their Communist faith. Others preferred not to make a point of having lost it. Nearly all rediscovered some need for circumspection, their knowledge filtering now through anxieties, fears, rancors, and ambitions that came of being back among the living.

Most of the rumors about Major Schramm emanated from these circles. Though hardly known to the public, he was well known to Czechoslovaks who had been behind bars, having helped to put so many of them there. That was his business, or his cause, as he would have called it.

Augustin Schramm had no particular lust for cruelty and was certainly no professional killer. He was a passionately committed Communist, altogether at Moscow's service. The son of Sudeten German peasants, he spoke Czech with such an execrable accent that he shunned public appearances, which weren't to his liking anyway. Tall and bony, his Teutonic features and pale-blond hair setting him apart from his Slavic comrades, he was by temperament aloof, taciturn, dour. But he was efficient, rising above the handicap of his German blood to become Secretary of the Czechoslovak Communist Youth Union in the thirties. When Hitler invaded, he fled to Soviet Russia, where he worked as a blacksmith in a kolkhoz for a while, then received special military training as a partisan instructor, with the rank of Major in the Red Army. There, under Rudolf Slánský's direction, he trained Czechoslovak partisan paratroopers, lectured, looked after their weapons, sent them into occupied Czech territory. He returned to Prague after the war as a trusted Soviet agent and the Czechoslovak Communists' supreme arbiter on partisan affairs.

In this dual capacity, Major Schramm acquired immense power. He had access to secret wartime documents, the authority to commandeer dossiers from the secret services, and inquisitorial instruments at hand in Bedřich Reicin's Second Department of the army, through which he worked with the Soviet Centrum. For the Communist Party, he undertook a vast purge of the army and security forces, arranging the expulsion of democratic partisans as wartime collaborators and/or postwar spies for the West: many wound up in Ruzyne's security cells, tortured as brutally by fellow Czechs as they'd been by the Gestapo. At the same time, he collected confidential information for the Centrum about a lot of other people, including his own Communist colleagues. He had enough of it by the time he died to blackmail half of Prague, most Communist leaders included.

He lived in the Vinohrady district, just opposite his good friend and coworker for the Centrum Bedřich Geminder, with his Hungarian wife Anna Bebrits, whom he had met at the

Partisan School in Russia. Early on the morning of May 27, 1948, as she described it twenty years afterward, the Schramm doorbell rang and her husband answered. "I heard a few words, then four shots, and he fell. I rushed to him from the bedroom. He was bleeding heavily. In a few minutes he was dead."

Mrs. Schramm couldn't see her husband's assailant very well. The vestibule was dark, and all she'd noticed when she got there was a departing back in a light raincoat. Nevertheless, she was sure that the two youths executed for the crime were guilty: the twenty-three-year-old Miloslav Choc, and his accomplice Slavoj Sadek. Both were "fanatical admirers of the former bourgeois parties," she said, who left Czechoslovakia after the February events and landed up in the United States Army camp at Regensburg. There, under the auspices of the American CIC, they'd plotted against "the new workers' power." The CIC then sent them back to Prague "to kill personalities of our new political life," including her husband and Ludvík Svoboda, then Defense Minister. Their gesture had no connection whatever with Jan Masaryk's death, "an absolutely absurd suggestion." Major Schramm had no clandestine side to his work. "My husband was not an employee of the Interior Ministry and had no secret mission. . . . Though we lived an exciting life, there was not a single night when he was not at home. . . . Certain forces are interested now in putting events in a false light, trying to evoke an anti-Soviet spirit. I must protest against the dirt and calumny touching the memory of my husband."

The Major's widow said all this in a letter to the Czechoslovak press from Budapest. A correspondent in London for the Hungarian Communist daily *Népszabadság*, she was recalled to Budapest twenty-four hours after Czech authorities announced that they wanted to question her in relation to the deaths of her husband and Jan Masaryk. She did not leave Hungary again.

The Major's secretary, Růžena Fišerová, also denied that he could have anything to do with the Masaryk case. A former partisan herself and a Communist militant still—blown-up

photographs of Lenin, Fidel Castro, and Che Guevara decorated her walls—she insisted that Schramm had nothing to do
with the Soviet NKVD either. During the war, yes, he had
worked "very closely" with the Red Army. But that was different. "I knew him simply as a just and energetic man who
hated Fascism. I don't believe he would have lent himself to
murder. . . . We once talked about Masaryk's death, soon after
it happened. Major Schramm said there'd been a mysterious
visit to Czernin Palace during the night—a Western agent who
came to criticize the Foreign Minister for going over to the
Communists. We both felt that must explain it."

Schramm himself had many enemies, she went on. It was true
that he had collected dossiers about many people and worked
hard to "purify partisan ranks." Authentic partisans admired
and respected him. But he had exposed many as frauds, who
were trying to build a career on a falsified resistance past: he
had no mercy on such people, and they held a grudge against
him. "I myself esteemed him," she explained. "But he wasn't
sympathetic, not popular. He lived only for the movement. He
was very severe."

Like Schramm's widow, his former secretary was sure that
the young Miloslav Choc was his killer. So was a former security
officer named Jaroslav Bouda, who had helped to investigate
Schramm's death. Though Bouda was thrown out of the STB
directly after this investigation—he spent the next twenty years
working in a stone quarry in northern Bohemia—he did not
suggest that one thing might have led to the other. "I knew
Schramm personally after the war," he told the press in 1968.
"He was an exemplary functionary, a wonderful man, I would
have given my life for him. It was on his request that I left the
Defense Ministry in 1947 to work for state security, to help him
liquidate some old matters with Gestapo agents." Because he did
know Schramm, Bouda continued, the STB asked him to help
track down the Major's killer. "That I did. We found Choc in
Olomouc, in Central Moravia. We caught the whole group,

not one got away. Choc admitted that he was trained by the
CIC in Regensburg and sent back to create disturbances in the
May election. He was supposed to carry out acts of sabotage,
kidnap the Social Democratic Minister Lausman, assassinate
Defense Minister Svoboda, things like that. . . . He had
bleached his hair, but the taxi driver recognized him as the man
he drove from the place of the murder to the railway station.
Choc was never tortured, not even a slap on the face. He behaved very well in the hearings. Once he said: 'There's no
point to all this. In six weeks there'll be a countercoup, and
you'll be sitting here and me there.' He was no coward. He
never thought he was going to be executed, though. . . ."

Nevertheless, another security officer on the same case was
full of doubts about Choc's guilt. The evidence of identification was flimsy, the procedure extremely hasty, a great deal left
unexplained. Troubled throughout the months of Choc's interrogation and trial, STB officer Vlastimil Kaplan was "very
depressed when they telephoned to tell him that Choc would be
executed shortly," his wife said two decades later. He was
arrested directly after Choc's execution, and imprisoned in
Ruzyne. He committed suicide soon after his release.

The trial of Miloslav Choc and his alleged accomplice Slavoj
Sadek was held in public. Choc admitted freely that he'd been
sent back into Czechoslovakia by a committee of anti-Communist émigrés in the United States Army's Regensburg camp.
He testified, too, that he and Sadek did go to Major Schramm's
house that morning. But somebody else had gotten there first,
he said. Whoever it was did the killing. Choc's group was not
supposed to kill Major Schramm. The instructions were to kidnap him and carry him back to Regensburg. The reason, Choc
said in court, several times over, was that Major Schramm
killed Jan Masaryk and was wanted alive in Regensburg so that
he could be made to confess.

Choc and Sadek continued to protest their innocence until
their execution, not only to the outside world but also to their

fellow prisoners. About a hundred and thirty Czechoslovaks were arrested on suspicion of belonging to Choc's anti-Communist underground, twenty-seven of whom got long prison sentences, nine sentenced to life. Among the latter was the Prague physician Václav Provazník, accused of having given Choc medical treatment. "I am persuaded that Choc did not kill Schramm," said Dr. Provazník in 1968. "I myself was given a life sentence, and while in prison I met other members of the group who informed me about the case. I was told that Milan Choc and Slavoj Sadek went to Schramm's home, and there they found another illegal group also charged—I don't know by whom—to kill Schramm. It was somebody from that group who did it. I spoke with Sadek in the shadow of the gallows, and he swore solemnly that neither he nor Choc killed Schramm. . . . I know that Schramm was a very important collaborator of the NKVD. . . . Many state security investigators involved in the Schramm case were later investigated themselves, some were tortured, a few committed suicide. . . ."

Another ex-convict called Jan Fischer said: "I shared a cell for a long time with Dr. Černoušek, a significant member of the Choc illegal group. According to Černoušek, Masaryk was either stunned or killed directly by Major Schramm. . . . Černoušek was sentenced to twenty years in prison; he managed to escape and was caught again. His further destiny is unknown."

Yet another ex-convict, Jindřich Doležal, was the cell mate of the Czech who sent Choc and Sadek to Prague on the Schramm mission: Vávra-Stařík, leader of the anti-Communist Czech émigré committee in the Regensburg camp. According to Doležal, Vávra-Stařík said repeatedly in prison that he'd been the avenger of Masaryk's death, but claimed he would never be executed because he could give the security police such valuable information. On this last point, at any rate, Vávra-Stařík was wrong. Though he did give valuable assistance to the secret police, he was hanged all the same.

The story of Vávra-Stařík himself was rather spicy. I learned more about him from a friend who had known him for many years, before, during, and after the war, and had been with him briefly in the Regensburg camp after the Communist takeover. The friend, B.L., was a high-ranking Czech democratic leader who escaped to the West in April, 1948, and was later sentenced to death in his absence. He did not want me to use his name. This is what he told me:

Vávra-Stařík started out in life as a schoolteacher in southern Moravia. When the Germans came, he joined the partisan resistance, ending up later in Slovakia. There, during the Slovak uprising in 1944, he met Major Schramm. The two were friendly until 1947, when they fell out sharply over politics, whereupon Major Schramm expelled Vávra-Stařík from the partisan organization. In April, 1948, Vávra-Stařík escaped to Regensburg, where he at once offered his services to the American CIC. The following month, he sent eight young Czechoslovak democrats back to Prague, led by Miloslav Choc. His friend B.L. had already left Regensburg by then, and did not see Vávra-Stařík until they ran into each other in Paris, early in 1949. Choc had just been hung when they met—Vávra-Stařík himself was condemned to death *in absentia* at Choc's trial—and B.L. criticized him bitterly for that suicide mission. "I told him it was a crazy thing to do, sending these poor boys in to assassinate some Communist criminal, as if that could possibly bring anything but grief for us or our country. Didn't he remember what happened when the underground assassinated the Nazi Gauleiter Heydrich during the war? It was a catastrophe for the Czechs, I reminded him. What was the good of killing Schramm? To my surprise, Vávra-Stařík agreed with me. He told me solemnly—he swore it—that he never gave Choc instructions to murder Schramm. The group's assignment was to kidnap Schramm and get him to Regensburg."

Although B.L. did not entirely trust Vávra-Stařík, he was inclined to believe this. Then, some six months later, Vávra-Stařík was kidnaped in Vienna by the Russian secret police and taken back to Prague. There, he became a star witness in the trial of thirteen Czech democrats for high treason, in June, 1950. His testimony was decisive in sending a woman to the gallows: Milada Horáková, a socialist deputy very much admired by her colleagues. Three codefendants were hanged along with her, five more imprisoned for life, the rest sentenced to jail terms up to twenty-eight years.

Outraged when he heard of this, B.L. could not decide whether Vávra-Stařík simply betrayed his own side to save his skin, or was acting all along as a double agent. "I couldn't exclude the possibility that he'd been working for the Communists, or the Russians, from the day he showed up at Regensburg," said B.L. "I was even more suspicious when news reached me that his own death sentence was commuted to thirty years' imprisonment after he testified against Milada Horáková; I assumed this would be a pretext allowing him to slip away. Not until many years later did I discover that Vávra-Stařík was executed after all. Even so, I couldn't swear *today* that Vávra-Stařík sent the Choc mission to Prague on his own initiative, or the CIC's. It's possible that some Czech Communists, or the NKVD, wanted to get Major Schramm out of the way, and arranged with Vávra-Stařík to organize the Choc mission so that a group of Western agents could be framed on the spot for Schramm's murder."

Whoever was giving him orders, it is fairly sure that Vávra-Stařík did instruct Choc to bring Major Schramm to Regensburg alive. The most moving confirmation of this came from Choc's fiancée, Eva Dušková.

She was not yet eighteen when Miloslav Choc asked her to marry him. She'd been fourteen, he seven years older, when they met and fell in love at sight. She must have been fresh as a primrose in those days. There was still a freshness about her when I met her in 1968, her flesh rosy and firm though by then there was too much of it. She was living in the outskirts of Prague with her mother, husband, and two children, a matronly woman with a pleasant, placid face and heavy hips, long past romance. Though her love had brought blight for her and everybody around her, she betrayed not a sign of resentment or self-pity.

In the years just after the war, Eva's mother used to rent rooms to students, one occupied by Eva's present husband, Dušek, another by Miloslav Choc, who was studying law. After Schramm's murder, the entire household was arrested: Eva, her father and mother, Dušek, Choc. Her mother spent the next twelve years in prison, Dušek seven years, she herself five, though she'd been sentenced to ten. Choc was proud, a patriot, and a democrat, she said, and in March, 1948, just after the Communist coup, he left Czechoslovakia. She knew nothing of his plans, he'd simply sent her a farewell letter after leaving, saying he was going to look for work in Slovakia so that they could get married. She heard nothing more from him, nor did she see him again except for a weekend late in April when he returned to Prague only—or so she thought—to leave again. Then, at the end of May, the police came. "Where's Choc?" they demanded. "In Slovakia, but I don't know where," she answered. "Do you know he killed Schramm?" they asked brutally. She didn't know it then or believe it ever.

They were both sent to Pankrac, Choc kept in solitary confinement and then in the death wing, she in a cell with several other women. She was not allowed to see him until after his trial, in December, 1948. Then she was taken to his cell three times before he died. "We might have talked of important things," she told me, "but I was too young. I didn't understand anything about politics, and I was afraid to even mention things like that. So we talked about our love, how much we'd always loved each other. I kept asking him if he still loved me. . . . The guards told me he wouldn't be hanged. But on February 18 they took me to his cell to say goodbye: he was going to be executed in the morning. I stayed with him more than an hour. We cried all the time. I begged him to tell me, because it wasn't important any more, if he did kill Major Schramm. And he told me: 'Never believe that it was me who killed Schramm. I am innocent. But one thing is sure: it was Schramm who killed Masaryk.' "

The next morning, after Choc and Sadek were hanged, the prison chaplain came to her cell: many people were still religious in those days, she explained half-apologetically. "My children, you must pray—pray for two innocent boys who died this morning," Father Tellini told her and her cell mates. He had been with Choc and Sadek just before they went to the scaffold, Eva said. He'd given them their last words of comfort and heard their confessions. "Naturally, as a priest, he couldn't reveal the secrets of the confessional. But we understood: he wanted us to understand that they were innocent."

Choc had a close friend called Fiala, one of the eight chosen for his mission, condemned to life imprisonment but liberated eventually. Later, when Fiala and Eva were both in the outside world again, he spoke to her of this mission. "Fiala told me their assignment was to capture Schramm alive," she said. "They were supposed to get him into West Germany, and bring along whatever documents they could find. The whole idea was to prove that Masaryk was murdered, and that Schramm did it." According to Fiala, she continued, one of the eight on the mission, by the name of Opletal, betrayed the others to the secret police soon after the group re-entered Czechoslovakia from Regensburg. So the police knew exactly when Choc was supposed to show up at Major Schramm's house. It would have been simple for them to arrest Choc and Sadek on the spot— and save Major Schramm at the same time. Evidently, somebody preferred to liquidate Schramm and pin the crime on Western agents.

Eva did not know if Vávra-Stařík had proof that Major Schramm killed Masaryk. She knew only that he'd told Choc and the others so, when he sent them back to Prague on their mission. Did Vávra-Stařík have the proof? Was he using the charge as an excuse to strike at Schramm because of a personal vendetta? Was he acting on his own? Taking orders from the American CIC? The Czechoslovak Communist party? The Soviet Centrum? Eva gave me a gentle smile, the smile of a shy young girl not yet overtaken by prison, heartbreak, motherhood, excess weight, fifteen years behind a loom in a textile mill. "If I'd only had some sense then, I might have found out. But I was a child. I loved him and except for that I was a child. I couldn't understand anything. And now, of course, it's too late."

Wasn't it hard to live with such a past, I asked, to be the wife of a man who had spent seven years in prison because of Choc, whom she'd loved? Things weren't as I might think, she answered. People who've been in prison have complexes when they come out; they don't really feel at home except with others who've been inside. "Something happens to us, in jail. We're never the same again."

Chapter 16

I'm not even sure exactly when he died. A close friend of his told me it was barely eight days after Masaryk's death. President Beneš's Chancellor said it was "a couple of months after." The *New York Times* said "three or four months"; ex-CID Inspector Zdeněk Borkovec said "about a year"; Masaryk's senior secretary, Jiří Špaček, said "at least two years." An ex-British intelligence agent said it was June 6, 1947 (sic). The Czech television documentary said it was January 3, 1949. State Prosecutor Kotlar asked me to come back: he'd have to look it up.

I'm not sure of very much else about him either. Some say he was murdered with an injection of gasoline, others that he injected the gasoline himself, still others that the hypodermic contained an overdose of morphine. State Prosecutor Kotlar said it was an injection of barbiturates. There were reports that he'd left a secret testament to be smuggled abroad, but no suicide note. Dr. Kotlar said he left a suicide note but no secret testament. His wife was reported to have committed suicide soon after he died, a year after, seven or eight years after, not at all. Not many of the Czechs speaking out in 1968 had anything useful to say about police doctor Jaromír Teplý. Nor, alas, did most earlier reports in the foreign press. The one thing I don't doubt, because I found proof of that much, is that Dr. Teplý knew more about Masaryk's death than he admitted officially.

His close friend was Dr. Josef Kazil, a curiously foreshortened figure of a man with an inordinately long face and broad forehead, his smile unexpectedly sweet, a look of perpetual surprise in his round gray eyes. At a colleague's suggestion, Dr. Kazil came to call on me. He'd been a personal friend of Dr. Teplý's for years, he said, and the two were professionally close as well: Dr. Teplý was head of the Interior Ministry's medical staff, Dr. Kazil chief of the Prague Municipal Health Service. He had seen Dr. Teplý only once after the critical morning when Masaryk died. "He was in a terribly nervous state, too shaken to go to his office. He would just pace around the house and go out for long walks. I could see that something grave was preying on his mind." Soon after Teplý died, the widow Teplý came to see Dr. Kazil in his office. "She told me her husband killed himself because he'd 'made an error' in his report on Masaryk's death, had kept saying he should never have let that report get out of his hands. She said he told her a lot about it before he died. She was very worried for her own safety. She asked me over and over again what she should do if the police came for her. She wouldn't tell me any details, though, and it was hard to make out what kind of error Teplý might have made. Knowing him as I did, I doubted it would have been an error in diagnosis. He was a very competent professional. I could only guess that he didn't write the full truth about the cause of death."

But there were certain irregularities that Dr. Kazil did not have to guess about. Teplý and he were both thoroughly familiar with the procedure in suicide cases, he himself being responsible at the Health Service for the official registration of suicides in Prague. Whenever there was any doubt about suicide, he explained, the law required the first examining physician to perform an autopsy, in the mortuary of the nearest hospital.

Then, if there were further questions, this physician should request a court order for a final autopsy, to be made *by a different physician*, at the Institute of Forensic Medicine. In other words, Dr. Teplý himself should have performed an initial autopsy, at a hospital near Czernin Palace, and Professor Hájek a second one at the Forensic Medicine Institute. It was most irregular that Teplý should have been bypassed and a single autopsy performed at the Institute—without a court order, by a doctor under a political cloud since the Gestapo made him take part in the Katyn forest investigation during the war. Furthermore, there should have been two separate signatures on the burial certificate (Ohledacti List) : Dr. Teplý's on the front page, as the first examining physician, giving the probable cause of death; Dr. Hájek's on the back page, summarizing the final autopsy findings. In the photocopy published in 1968, *neither signature was on the Ohledacti List.* Only the back page was signed; and it was signed by Hájek's then assistant, now Director of the Forensic Medicine Institute, Dr. Tesař.

Dr. Kazil had little more to say, and no way of proving what he said. He'd had a letter from Teplý's widow partially confirming his story, but when he was arrested some years later the police searched his flat and took everything away. After he left, I went back over the notes of my short conversation with the Institute's Director, Dr. Tesař. Though firmly defending the official finding of suicide, Dr. Tesař did mention the irregularity of an autopsy done directly at his Institute, without a court order. He also said explicitly that it was Dr. Hájek who performed the autopsy. Why, then, didn't Dr. Hájek sign the back page of the burial certificate? And why was Teplý's signature missing from the other side?

The police doctor had had a still closer friend, Vladimír Sis, who died in prison and so could not tell his story in person. A schoolfellow of Teplý's, Sis had kept up the warm friendship during the war and after, when he became an editor of the Catholic daily *Lidová Demokracie*. Shortly after Masaryk's death, Sis and his wife talked it over, she reporting a conversation with some of Masaryk's artist friends who claimed he meant to leave for London on March 10. "Yes, I know," Sis remarked to her. "Teplý told me it wasn't suicide." Then, *on the very day Teplý died,* Sis was arrested. When news of his friend's death reached him in prison, some time later, he wrote to his wife: "So Teplý too has died; I think I know why." Mrs. Sis kept the letter.

Not long afterward, Teplý's widow tried to kill herself and, failing, came to see Mrs. Sis in search of spiritual comfort. "We talked about both of our husbands," Mrs. Sis told *Lidová Demokracie's* editors in 1968. "Mrs. Teplý did not believe her husband actually committed suicide at police headquarters. What made her most suspicious was that, in spite of her desperate requests, *she was not allowed to see her husband's corpse.*" According to Madame Sis, Teplý's widow succeeded in her next attempt at suicide a year later.

There was little to go on, in Prague, apart from such hearsay evidence, and insistent press reports that Teplý wrote a secret testament before he died which was smuggled abroad. On December 29, 1951, nearly four years after Jan Masaryk's death, the *New York Times* did publish a document purporting to be Dr. Teplý's secret testament. The document's authenticity was vouched for personally by the *Times'* roving columnist, C. L. Sulzberger. "Less than five weeks ago a new report on the death of M. Masaryk reached the West," he wrote. "It has been carefully analyzed and cross-checked by at least one intelligence service and at least one foreign ministry. Perhaps it cannot be considered as irrefutably correct but it probably is as close as one can get to the detailed truth these days, with the situation what it is behind the Iron Curtain. This correspondent believes the present account to be substantially accurate, based on the account of Dr. Teplý, said to have been taken down by a responsible associate before Dr. Teplý's death.

"At five A.M. on March 10, Dr. Teplý received an urgent telephone summons from the Ministry of the Interior to go immediately to Czernin Palace. The doctor arrived at the Foreign Ministry shortly after 5:15. There he found a handful of secret police and uniformed national police agents. . . . [He] was taken into the palace courtyard where a policeman pointed to a lump lying under a blanket, the account said. It added that a security agent pulled back the cover and to Dr. Teplý's astonishment he'd seen a body clad in pajamas, whose face he recognized as that of M. Masaryk.

"The record of the account attributed to him said:

" 'I ordered one of the policemen to open the pajamas and I noticed all over the body traces of blows and scratches that appeared to be marks of violence. After a moment I requested that the corpse be lifted. I saw in the nape of the neck the mark of a wound, probably made by a projectile of 7.65 caliber. All around the wound were traces of scorching, indicating that the shot had been fired from very close range. I don't know whether I reflected to myself, or aloud, or if the policemen heard. I only know that I thought: this is infamous, a bestial assassination!'

"Examination of the body in a courtyard by artificial light would necessarily be cursory. Nevertheless, Dr. Teplý was said to have found that the heel bones had been smashed but he had not attributed the fracture to the body's fall. Instead Dr. Teplý was reported to have said it appeared that the heel bones had been beaten 'repeatedly with a very heavy instrument, for example a hammer.' The account said he had pointed out there were no traces of bruise or fracture evident on the soles of the feet or the toes.

"Furthermore Dr. Teplý was reported to have noted marks on M. Masaryk's hands as if he had fought desperately to protect himself before his death.

"M. Masaryk habitually lived a simple bachelor's life. Was there anyone in his apartment? A servant? The latest account said Dr. Teplý merely noted that while leaving after dawn someone had whispered to him that two employees of Czernin

Palace had been taken away by the police. The doctor noted that after his initial examination, Masaryk's body had been placed on a stretcher and carried upstairs to the third floor apartment. As Dr. Teplý walked through the courtyard behind it, he saw a black automobile draw up at the gate. M. Nosek (the Interior Minister), Dr. Vladimir Clementis (then Deputy Foreign Minister) and a Foreign Ministry Counsellor named Hora were said to have emerged. They were pictured as having rushed silently to an elevator while Dr. Teplý walked. When the doctor arrived in M. Masaryk's study, he found M. Nosek and M. Clementis busily rearranging the furniture and rugs which were in a great state of disorder.

"M. Nosek was trying to put together a footstool from which one leg had been broken off. The police stretcher bearers entered with their macabre burden. Dr. Teplý, on entering Masaryk's bedroom, was said to have noticed even greater signs of disarrangement. The bedside table was topsy-turvy; beside it was a broken cup and bottle. M. Nosek was said to have smoothed out the bed and M. Masaryk's body was laid upon it. According to the account, the Interior Minister then went to a window with Dr. Teplý, looked down into the courtyard gravely and muttered 'suicide.' Dr. Teplý was pictured as having demurred quietly, objecting that he thought the evidence was to the contrary. He was said to have recalled later that this had been utterly foolhardy, but 'I was truly furious and nothing mattered to me.'

"M. Nosek was said to have then ordered Dr. Teplý into Masaryk's study and instructed the police to bar all visitors from the bedroom. About twenty minutes later a man dressed in civilian clothes and carrying a towel on his arm entered the apartment and said something in a low voice to M. Clementis and M. Nosek. The man was then said to have moved on toward the bedroom where the body lay, but a policeman barred the way. Dr. Teplý said he had heard the newcomer mutter in Russian: 'Don't be stupid, fellow, let me pass.' M. Nosek and

M. Clementis were reported to have ordered the guard to stand aside. The visitor was said to have remained a half hour. . . . M. Nosek then summoned everyone present and warned them quietly that they had not 'seen a thing or heard a thing.' The Interior Minister was said to have ordered everyone out save for one policeman who was instructed to bar the door. According to the report, Dr. Teplý asked to be allowed to examine the part of the courtyard where the body had been discovered. He found, in the growing daylight, that the place had been completely scoured. . . . Either three or four months later—the date is not available—the doctor died as a result of having taken a 'wrong injection.' "

By 1968, so many other reporters had gleaned their own accounts from Mr. Sulzberger's account of Dr. Teplý's account of what he saw on March 10, 1948, that nobody seemed to recall where the original details came from. Unfortunately, neither did Mr. Sulzberger. His reply was courteous when my letter reached him in Pakistan, forwarded by his secretary in Paris. I'd asked him two questions about the article he wrote on Teplý seventeen years before: (1) Did Czechoslovakia's State Prosecutor Kotlar ask Mr. Sulzberger for help (as he'd told me he did) in tracing the source of this article? (2) Could Mr. Sulzberger tell me who the source was?

In his answering letter Mr. Sulzberger said: (1) No, State Prosecutor Kotlar had not communicated with him in any way. (2) He had no information about this article apart from that appearing in a forthcoming book of his, which I was welcome to quote. In its section on the Masaryk case, the book did not mention a secret testament of Dr. Teplý's. Instead, it referred to a French intelligence report:

"Before me while writing is a report made by SDECE, then a branch of the French Secret Service, classified as TRÈS SECRET and marked for reference purposes A/11.0/21.1/4903/526.454/ 25.2.7. This claims that a certain Dr. Teplý was summoned to the Czernin before dawn on March 10, 1949 [sic], where he was met by agents of two Czech police, the STB and SNB. In the courtyard, under a blanket, lay the body of Masaryk dressed in pajamas with different colored top and bottom. The corpse showed bruises, scratches and other signs of violence." From there on, the details in Mr. Sulzberger's book were identical to those published in his *New York Times* story. Since it was unlikely that the French secret service would base a top-secret report on material taken from the *Times,* I could only assume that the material in the *Times* was taken from the French top-secret report.

Among those borrowing generously from Mr. Sulzberger's story was a former British secret-service agent named E. H. Cookridge, who, in 1955, wrote a book on the Soviet secret-service network abroad. Mr. Cookridge's chapter on the Masaryk case depended almost entirely on the 1951 *New York Times* article. But he did add one arresting detail. The unnamed Russian-speaking man mentioned in the *Times,* seen by Dr. Teplý at Czernin Palace, wearing civilian clothes, with a towel on his arm, who spent half an hour alone in Masaryk's bedroom, was—said Mr. Cookridge—a notorious Czechoslovak agent of the NKVD named Otto Katz. Mr. Cookridge knew all about Otto Katz, who had served the Soviet Centrum in Moscow for twenty-two years before returning to Prague at the war's end. Once back, Katz took the name of André Simon, worked for a while as editor of the Czechoslovak Communist paper *Rudé Právo,* and was, in March, 1948, the Communist government's Director of Information. As André Simon, Otto Katz was hanged with Rudolf Slánský in 1952.

Mr. Cookridge did not say who told him that Otto Katz was the man Dr.Teplý saw at Czernin Palace. Nor did he say any more than Mr. Sulzberger did, still less the French secret service, about where the initial information on Dr. Teplý came from. But there was yet another secret serviceman who claimed to have gotten his information directly from the source. Announcing himself as a longstanding Western intelligence agent,

Vítězslav Kadlcák, alias Major Chlumský, told the Czechoslovak press in the spring of 1968 that he personally had seen Dr. Teplý's secret testament:

"After Teplý died, certain envelopes were smuggled abroad," he said. "I remember very well the photocopy of Dr. Teplý's official medical report on Masaryk, with his conclusion that it was suicide. But when I turned this photocopy over, I saw the letter Dr. Teplý had attached to it. In this letter, he had written: 'My official report on Jan Masaryk's death was not literally true. I wrote it on the orders of the Interior Ministry; it carried the seal of PI 7.' Later, it turned out that PI 7 was the code name for Richard Spurný, the Interior Minister's private secretary. Then Dr. Teplý went on to say in his secret letter that Masaryk's death had occurred in a state of horrible fear—one might even say of insane anguish. Teplý did not dismiss the possibility of suicide, not *normal* suicide, but suicide provoked by immediate fear, some dreadful terror. He said Masaryk must have been so frightened that even the banging of a door could make his nerves crack."

Attached to this secret letter of Teplý's, continued Major Chlumský, was a detailed description of how Masaryk spent his last day. "It listed what the Minister did hour by hour. I even remember it saying that on Masaryk's way home from the President's country house in Sezimovo Usti, he stopped at a crossroads near Benesov for a glass of beer. It described his visit to Clementis [the Communist Deputy Foreign Minister]—or rather, two visits, one in the afternoon, another on the evening of March 10; and it also noted an evening visit to Premier Gottwald. It said that when Masaryk left Gottwald's villa he was holding his head with both hands, and a policeman on guard there heard Masaryk mutter: 'This is betrayal, this is a new White Mountain.' That was about a quarter to eleven in the evening. . . ."

It was roughly here that Major Chlumský drew the line for the press, explaining that he had a wealth of additional material which he would rather turn over privately to the State Prosecutor's office. I never had a chance to question him myself because he was no longer around by the time I looked for him, shortly after the Soviet invasion. When, during our first conversation in the administrative wing of Pankrac prison, State Prosecutor Kotlar advised me to "forget Major Chlumský," he neglected to mention that Major Chlumský was already consigned to the official state institution for those to be forgotten, in a cell below.

I had no idea at the time that Major Chlumský would become so interesting half a year later. In September, 1968, he seemed merely one of those baffling witnesses emerging from nowhere, soon to melt away again. The State Prosecutor having assured me that the man was mentally disturbed—in fact, deranged— his version of the secret Teplý testament hardly seemed worth attention. Mr. Sulzberger's did, though: he was one of the best-known American journalists abroad. Still, there was something odd about his story in the Times, at once too well informed to be dismissed, and not quite credible.

In the first place, it included Dr. Teplý's flat statement that he saw the marks of a 7.65 caliber bullet, fired at close range into the nape of Masaryk's neck. A bullet of that size, fired point-blank, would surely have left a noticeable opening. I personally had met half a dozen eyewitnesses who got a fairly close look at Jan Masaryk's corpse on March 10: Masaryk's two secretaries Šum and Špaček, and his bodyguard Vyšín, all three present at the autopsy; ex-CID Inspector Borkovec and his superior, Dr. Gorner; and the present Director of the Forensic Medicine Institute, Dr. Tesař, who took notes of the autopsy findings. Not one confessed to having seen a bullet hole. The only such report came secondhand, from the household purser Topinka, who told me his wife saw "a hole the size of a pea" behind Masaryk's ear as she bent over the corpse in the bedroom. Could she alone be telling the truth? Were *all* the others lying?

Then there were the reported "traces of blows and scratches all over the body that appeared to be marks of violence." None of the eyewitnesses I'd interviewed described anything of the sort. At most, they spoke of a longish scrape on the abdomen, and a blue bruise on the temple and behind the right ear. On the other hand, several witnesses did mention having noticed white paint or plaster under Masaryk's fingernails, among them Topinka's wife, Dr. Gorner of the CID, and Masaryk's secretaries Šum and Špaček. This strongly suggested that Masaryk had grappled desperately to hold on to a wall or window frame, possibly confirming Dr. Teplý's alleged assertion that there were "marks on Masaryk's hands as if he had fought desperately to protect himself." On this and several other points, details published for the first time in Mr. Sulzberger's article, in 1951, were at least partly corroborated by eyewitnesses seventeen years later.

This was so, for instance, of Dr. Teplý's supposed statement that Masaryk's heel bones appeared to have been shattered not by a fall, but by being beaten "repeatedly with a very heavy instrument, for example a hammer." There supposedly were no traces of bruise or fracture evident on the soles of the feet or the toes. The implication was that Masaryk was tortured, shot, and *carried* to the courtyard to simulate suicide. Implausible as the theory sounded in many ways, it seemed to fit several otherwise unaccountable facts. It was evidently true, for one thing, that only Masaryk's heel bones were shattered. Not a single witness in 1968 referred to bruises or fractures on the soles of his feet or toes. Only by the weirdest of freak falls would a man jumping from a window alive and conscious land on his heels alone. If he did, the jar of such a landing should by rights telescope his lower limbs into his trunk which, as all witnesses agreed, did not happen. Furthermore, Masaryk's two-hundred-pound body was supposed to have fallen thirty feet to an enclosed and echoing courtyard; yet not a soul —from his butler and household purser, whose windows overlooked the courtyard, to the constable on duty ten yards away —heard the thud of the body landing. State Prosecutor Kotlar confirmed this. What's more, all eyewitnesses agreed on two singular circumstances: *there were no other visible external injuries on the corpse except a bruise at the back of the head; and there was little or no blood on the cobblestones under or around it.*

The internal injuries should have settled the matter one way or another. But the evidence on this point was by no means as solid as it might be. Dr. Teplý, unlawfully bypassed in the autopsy procedure, was not allowed to make an internal examination. Neither was Masaryk's personal physician, Dr. Klinger. Among those present at the post-mortem, in the laboratory of the Forensic Medicine Institute, only two were professionally qualified to understand what they saw when the corpse was cut open. One was the physician performing the autopsy, Dr. Hájek, who had lived under a political cloud since the war and was therefore susceptible to blackmail. The other was his assistant, Dr. Tesař, later his successor. Dr. Hájek's official autopsy report was never published. What purported to be a summary of it on the burial certificate (Ohledacti List) was given in photocopy to the British press in 1968 by Masaryk's third secretary in Glasgow, Dr. Soukoup. The text of this photocopy read: "Cause of death suicide; manner of death leap from second floor of Czernin Palace. During the fall suffered burst aorta, heart, kidneys, fractured ribs, backbone, pelvis." But the document as published had two striking irregularities: the regulation front page, requiring Dr. Teplý's signature, was missing altogether; and the back page, with the above summary of the autopsy findings, did not bear the required signature of Dr. Hájek.

As far as I knew, the only men alive in 1968 who had actually seen the original autopsy report were Dr. Tesař, to whom Hájek dictated his notes, and State Prosecutor Kotlar, who supposedly found a copy in the Interior Ministry's archives. I had already caught out the State Prosecutor in a number of misleading statements. And what did I or the public in general know about Dr. Tesař? Only that he was a competent scientist and a Communist in good standing, who swore that his now defunct superior believed unreservedly in Masaryk's suicide. An equally reputable scientist, much closer personally to Hájek—Dr. Kacl, head of the Chemical Medicine Institute—swore that Hájek believed it was murder. In any event, Dr. Hájek was peculiarly vulnerable to occult pressures when he performed the autopsy. Would there be anything in Dr. Tesař's past that made him vulnerable, too?

Whatever the autopsy revealed, however, it was hard to accept a theory excluding any possibility that Masaryk either jumped, or fell, or was pushed from a bathroom window ordinarily closed but on that morning flung wide, fingerprints on the wall around it, window seat overturned. Indeed, the more I examined the *New York Times* version of Teplý's secret testament, the more perplexing it seemed. Again and again, I was bound to discard an improbable detail, only to come across another that nobody could have known in 1951 without access to what was then inside information. Not a word had yet been published at the time about the fact that Masaryk's feet were intact and only the heel bones splintered; the names of the first Communist functionaries to arrive on the scene; the condition of Masaryk's flat. This last was particularly intriguing. The household purser, Topinka, who saw the apartment before any officials arrived that morning, assured me that he'd spoken about the "great disorder there" to nobody but his wife and the household staff, until after the January revolution. Yet the description of Masaryk's bedroom in the *New York Times* came uncannily close to Topinka's, down to the tilted bedside table and the broken cup and bottle beside it.

Passing almost unnoticed, besides, was the testimony of an obscure taxi driver who had worked for the security police in 1948, going under the initials B.J. It was unlikely that B.J. either supplied information for the *Times* article or borrowed

from it: he'd been in prison for two years preceding publication
of the Sulzberger story, and the *Times* was banned in Czechoslovakia throughout the Stalinist era. When he spoke to the
Czech press on April 7, 1968, furthermore, none of the details
he volunteered were yet known to the public. Claiming that
he'd driven three security officers to Czernin Palace sometime
around four in the morning on March 10, 1948, B.J. said he'd
followed the three into the palace courtyard. On seeing the
corpse, he noted that "the heels of the feet were badly damaged"
—it was he who scooped up the bones in a neat little mound—
while "there was very little blood." He also clearly remembered
"that the bedroom was in a state of extreme disorder" when
the stretcher was carried upstairs, on Dr. Teplý's orders. Then,
he went on, "we were told to guard the Minister's study and,
after a while, an unknown person came, demanding to be let in.
I refused. But then the Interior Minister, Nosek, gave me a
hint to let the man in, and I couldn't prevent it. He remained
in the study about half an hour, and came out with a briefcase
he didn't have before." Might that have been Mr. Cookridge's
Russian-speaking NKVD agent Otto Katz? Or Mr. Sulzberger's
unidentified gentleman carrying a towel?

I wasn't able to question B.J. either. While giving his full
name and address to the editor interviewing him, he wanted
nobody else to know who he was except State Prosecutor Kotlar.
Now that I'd gathered these bits and pieces of information
about police doctor Teplý, however, I did go back to see the
ex-CID Inspector who had been so insistent about this: Zdeněk
Borkovec.

The hallway was dank as ever, but his welcome was friendlier
this time, the astonishing blue eyes warming at once to trans-
parent aquamarine when he answered my ring. He asked how
I was getting on with the case, as we sat down at his square table
over coffee, and I said it was like trying to walk under water. I
wouldn't have believed so much effort would have to go into
covering so little ground. "You'll get used to it," he remarked,

amused. "We all do." He seemed relaxed, more curious now than cautious. Yet that shuttered look of his was still there. I wondered, watching the otherwise bold face under the bright cap of white hair, how much ground I could expect to cover even with him.

In our last talk, I reminded Dr. Borkovec, he'd said that I probably couldn't get to the bottom of Masaryk's death without looking into police doctor Teplý's. I had tried, and not gotten far. State Prosecutor Kotlar assured me, for instance, that there was no mystery at all about Dr. Teplý, that he had never written a secret testament, that he'd killed himself because of his health, or his wife, or both, for reasons having no remote connection to the Masaryk case.

Dr. Borkovec, skeptical, said nothing.

On the other hand, I continued, the *New York Times* had published in 1951 a secret testament attributed to Dr. Teplý, presumably based on a report of the French secret service, strongly implying that Teplý was murdered. The motive, supposedly, was Teplý's firsthand observation that Masaryk must have been beaten, tortured, and—since the powder-scorch marks of a 7.65 caliber bullet were clearly visible—shot.

"Is *that* what the *Times* said?" Dr. Borkovec's eyebrows went up. "Nonsense!"

Maybe, I assented. But I had yet to find somebody who either had, or would part with, more reliable information. Would Dr. Borkovec tell me more about what he himself had in mind?

He wouldn't tell me much. After sifting through the whole Masaryk case, he said, he still found the Teplý case "the more fascinating of the two." He scarcely doubted that Teplý killed himself. He'd spoken with the nurse who was with Teplý after the fatal injection: she told him Teplý took an overdose of morphine, leaving a note to indicate the exact dose—whether to make it plain that he was beyond saving or to arrange to be saved, nobody knew. It was true that Teplý's wife was not allowed to see his body, which needn't mean much: she was reportedly not at home when the police called to break the news, and once a body is taken to the mortuary relatives are not customarily allowed to see it. It was also true that she killed herself, perhaps a year afterward, more likely than not for personal reasons.

As for Dr. Teplý's motive, however, Dr. Borkovec still thought it should be sought within the context of the Masaryk case. There were several specific irregularities that Dr. Borkovec knew of. First, Dr. Teplý should by rights have performed the initial autopsy on Masaryk's corpse, and didn't. Second, Teplý's signature should have been on the burial certificate, and wasn't. Apart from this, Dr. Borkovec had little to go on. He'd been told by some of Teplý's closest friends that the police doctor did dictate a secret testament before dying, and that "certain documents got abroad." He, Dr. Borkovec, could surely not vouch for the accuracy of any statements in it. State Prosecutor Kotlar, who must have seen Teplý's report to the security police, was in a better position to guess at the secret testament's contents than Dr. Borkovec, who never saw the report and didn't like guessing anyway. Dr. Borkovec had offered to go over all the evidence with Dr. Kotlar, a perhaps useful offer considering his lengthy criminological experience, but had not yet been invited to do so. He really had nothing else to tell me.

Still, Dr. Borkovec was present when Teplý examined Masaryk's corpse. He was reasonably sure he would notice any serious discrepancy between what Teplý actually saw and what might be written in Teplý's formal report—or between that report and the official autopsy findings. Dr. Borkovec had discussed some confidential details concerning this with the State Prosecutor. So far, though, nobody had shown him either the Teplý report or autopsy findings. Without a chance to study and compare the two, he could go no further.

Would he say, from the summary I gave him, that the *New York Times* version of Dr. Teplý's secret testament might have been dictated by Teplý?

"Not if it says anything about a 7.65 caliber bullet hole." Dr. Borkovec's shrug was impatient.

How about the blows and scratches all over the body, as reported in the *Times?* The signs on Masaryk's hands of desperate self-defense? The suggestion that Masaryk's heel bones were crushed by a hammer and not a fall? Dr. Borkovec shook his head, though not quite so testily. No, that didn't sound like the right track, all in all.

"As I've told you before, I didn't examine the corpse closely. But I'd have noticed blows and scratches on such a scale, not to speak of a bullet hole. The hands now, yes, they were dirty, especially the fingernails; it might have been paint, or plaster, or wall dust—you couldn't reconstruct the whole case on it. As for the heel bones, I can't imagine Teplý dreaming up that bloody hammer. . . ."

In short, Dr. Borkovec doubted that the testament published in the *Times* was authentic? He did. And he believed, nonetheless, that there *was* such a testament, somewhere? He did. Had he any idea where I might look for it? His eyes were suddenly a seraphic blue, and his smile, on a man of meaner physical stature and less dignified bearing, might have been a grin. "Why not go to Glasgow and ask that secretary of Masaryk's—the one who knows everything?"

Chapter 17

So this was Lumír Soukoup. Having seen him on television in Prague, I recognized him at once, to his evident pleasure. "How did you know it was me?" he asked, gratified when I went straight up to him in the crimson plush lobby of a Glasgow hotel, sudden fame still warming him. He was subtly different off screen, handsome surely but a bit shorter than I'd expected and a shade less trim, the hands not quite as firm or the features as crisp, the general outlines blurred. He looked younger than he was, with his fair coloring and sprinkling of freckles, until you noticed the inelastic step and slight puffiness under the skin. His eyes were too small, a fleck of spite darting out in unguarded moments, and there were complaining lines around the mouth—self-pity? blighted expectations?—which, oddly, invited compassion. He hadn't a grain of humor.

He ordered a simple steak and salad, when we were settled in the old-fashioned hotel dining room, and I waited for him to add a voluptuous dessert, which, elaborately casual, he did. No wine: he didn't drink.

"You've seen them all, I suppose?" he began, gaze wandering over the roomful of city burghers and hearty commercial travelers.

"In Prague, do you mean?"

"No, no, in London . . . the people on the Czech desk at BBC, the old crowd, the class of '48, you might say."

I'd seen a good many, graying, dulled, incorrigibly Middle European after two decades in the Anglo-Saxon heartland, brooding over intramural quarrels that had roiled the Czechoslovak émigré community for twenty years. Few had a kind word for Jan Masaryk's third secretary in Glasgow, or one another: a tribal custom in any community of exiles. Many despised Soukoup as a ninny playing the Communists' game because he had insisted since 1948 that Masaryk took his own life. Often they were men for whom Masaryk's death was a mirror reflecting their own image. "What would I have done in Jan's place?" they'd ask themselves, deciding that he wouldn't have jumped—they didn't, after all—and must have tried to escape only to find the NKVD barring his exit. Or else, fuming at their impotence, they'd concluded that Masaryk deliberately chose an ennobling death, as Jan Hus did half a millennium earlier. But even these had little use for Dr. Soukoup, a mediocrity, they said, who'd cashed in on Masaryk's death to make a name for himself. He couldn't win, in those quarters.

"There's a lot of them I don't speak to, haven't for years," he told me, tucking into his steak. "I've never forgiven some of them for telling me it was my *political duty* to say Masaryk was murdered, whether I believed it or not. They ought to be ashamed, I said to them. Was that why we left Czechoslovakia, to tell lies like the Communists?"

I'd already realized how lonely Dr. Soukoup must be in his remote teaching post, cut off from his fellow exiles in London not just by physical distance but by bleak wastes of malice. He'd left Prague for Scotland on July 6, 1948, his pregnant English wife some months earlier. His first public pronouncement on suicide, soon after, established him at once as a softliner. The fact that he and his wife were both able to emigrate legally, through the intervention of Vladimír Clementis,

Masaryk's successor as Foreign Minister, inevitably made for sinister rumors. Some émigrés accused him of buying his way out of Communist Czechoslovakia with his suicide story. Others spoke darkly of unnamed British diplomats who, for reasons none too clear, got Soukoup his teaching job—an enviable advantage for a political refugee in those days—in exchange for unspecified services. Marcia Davenport, convinced that the Communists intended to kill her, sent private detectives up from London to keep both Soukoups under surveillance, driving his wife close to nervous collapse. He had accepted isolation, how willingly I didn't know, living quietly in a little country house in Stirlingshire, teaching Slavonic languages at Glasgow University, keeping himself to himself. He'd been out of things, forgotten, until the Masaryk case was reopened and his name turned up in the London press.

Yes, I told him, I'd met the London émigrés, divided as always about Masaryk's death and Soukoup's declarations on the subject. He wasn't surprised; almost none of them had firsthand knowledge of the case, he observed, putting the dross where it belonged. I suggested we go back to the beginning of his own connection with Masaryk. He was an ordained Protestant preacher, I'd heard. How did he drift into Jan Masaryk's politico-diplomatic world?

"It was in 1938, just after Munich, when I was a graduate student of theology at Edinburgh. Masaryk came up to make a speech and asked to meet me. We took to each other at sight, talked for hours. He needed somebody to help out with private secretarial work. Gradually, he fell into the habit of sending me documents for safekeeping, right on through the war and after. They piled up, I've got a mountain of them. Going through it all, you can see how Czechoslovakia lost its sovereignty step by step, and what that must have done to Masaryk."

He went on at length about Masaryk's dealings with Russia over the years. He talked well (better than he wrote, I reflected), and I didn't interrupt until we were almost through dinner. It was more than clear that Masaryk was under intolerable pressure, I said finally. What seemed less obvious was how he decided to face it in the end. Dr. Soukoup's arguments for suicide were well known to me, of course, and to everybody in Prague; the State Prosecutor directing the formal investigation thought highly of them—in fact, appeared to think they all but settled the question.

Dr. Soukoup was glad to hear it. All this talk of Beria's gorillas murdering Masaryk was extremely shortsighted as well as irresponsible, he said. "It has already exasperated our eastern neighbors and endangered our security, which is one reason I'm against it. The other reason is that it isn't true."

Still, I'd come across apparently creditable witnesses who disagreed with Dr. Soukoup on several counts. For instance, there was the visit to Tomáš Masaryk's grave in Lany on March 7, the Sunday before Jan Masaryk died. We'd all read Dr. Soukoup's account of how he accompanied the Minister on this lonely pilgrimage, Masaryk's solitary hour-long vigil at the cemetery, his melancholy silence on the return drive to Prague, his murmured hope that God and his father would forgive him. State Prosecutor Kotlar attached great importance to this trip as Dr. Soukoup described it, giving a moving glimpse into the anguished state of Masaryk's mind. Yet, in a conversation with Masaryk's niece Herberta . . .

He broke in before I could finish. "Actually, you know, I didn't go to Lany with the Minister that day. I'd asked if I could, and he said yes, but then I sensed that he would rather be alone. So I drove up to Lany by myself, and kept out of his way, just to be there if he needed me. It was his driver, Dohnálek, who told me about the trip back and how the Minister whispered—three times, Dohnálek said—that God and his father would understand."

I might have nailed Dr. Soukoup then and there. In the *Scotsman*, just five months before we met, he'd stated flatly that he did go to Lany with Masaryk; Herberta, and the bodyguard

Vyšín, who were unquestionably with Masaryk that afternoon, had told me Soukoup was nowhere in sight; and both said that Masaryk, not especially melancholy, spent no more than five or ten minutes at his father's grave. Apart from a reference in the Communist government's official announcement of Masaryk's death, the sole witness who testified to that compelling hour-long vigil at the cemetery was Dr. Soukoup; and he wasn't there. Yet glancing at the weak, handsome face, I felt I couldn't put all this to him: he was too vulnerable.

Then there was the farewell message in the Bible, I went on. Dr. Soukoup maintained that the Bible was found lying on Masaryk's bed, opened to the fifth chapter of St. Paul's Epistles to the Galatians, verses 22, part of 23, and 24 encircled in pencil:

But the fruit of the Spirit is love, joy, peace, quietness, fidelity, meekness, temperance . . .
. . . And those that are Christ's have crucified their own flesh.

The evidence on this was confusing. Although Dr. Soukoup had written that he saw the Bible lying there, hadn't he been out sick on March 10? Yes, actually, he was down with a raging fever all that week. Then he didn't see it himself? No. Frankly, I couldn't find anybody else who saw it either. I knew the story was published the day after Masaryk died, in the Communists' already captive Catholic daily *Lidová Demokracie.* While I'd interviewed most surviving eyewitnesses in Prague, however, not one remembered the Bible lying open on the bed. Two or three said they'd noticed it lying on the bedside table, closed, next to *Good Soldier Schweik.* Masaryk's senior secretary, Špaček, had the impression in any case that the verses in question were marked by Masaryk's father years before.

Besides, wasn't the choice of a message strange? St. Paul was dealing in this instance with the Jewish laws on circumcision, hardly apposite; and if Masaryk had searched among those lines nevertheless, he might, as Marcia Davenport remarked later, have found the first verse more to the point:

Stand fast therefore in the liberty wherewith Christ hath made us free, and be not entangled again in the yoke of bondage.

Dr. Soukoup's expression was tolerant, patient, knowing, resigned, faintly suspicious, honestly perplexed. "I can't think why everybody finds it so hard to understand those verses. You all ask the same question. Even the State Prosecutor, Kotlar, wanted me to explain what they meant. And they're so transparently clear! To me, those verses simply mean the antithesis of Marxism, a sublime assertion of spiritual over material values. It's a mystery why you all don't see it!"

Maybe it was because we didn't think of Masaryk as particularly spiritual, I suggested. From what I'd heard, Jan Masaryk had earthy tastes, a blasphemous tongue, and an irreverent if sensitive soul, had worshipped only his father while, in effect, paying his formal respects to the Lord, was no churchgoer and at most an indolent believer. According to his nieces Anna and Herberta, he had nothing like the austere faith of his sister Olga, a Christian Scientist who refused to permit medical treatment that might have saved her son Herbert. He wasn't even drawn to his sister Alice's more accommodating Unitarianism. If he'd thought of looking for a farewell text in the Bible, wouldn't he be likely to choose something more pertinent to worldly matters?

A faint pink flush crept up under the light freckles. "Jan Masaryk was far, far more religious than most people realized. You would have had to know him intimately—be with him day after day, hour by hour—to grasp that." He hesitated, then added with that tiny dart of malice, "You really shouldn't take everything the nieces tell you as gospel, you know."

I was intrigued, and a little shocked. Was it their word or their judgment I ought to worry about?

"That's up to you. I never had much to do with the nieces, of course; we moved in different circles. But they weren't all that clever. They both have exaggerated ideas about their talents, and the family's—that artistic streak they're forever

harping on. Jan was the only Masaryk who was truly humble;
he knew he wasn't a great musician, just as his brother Herbert,
the nieces' father, wasn't a great painter, or Anna an original
art critic. Naturally they cover up for each other. You'd do well
to keep in mind that Herberta used to be a red-hot Communist
in those days."

I knew that, and thought it irrelevant. Whatever Herberta's
political past, she'd struck me as too proud for vulgar deception,
a woman who wouldn't bother to lie. Was I meant to understand that she might consciously mislead me about the depth
of her uncle's spiritual faith?

Dr. Soukoup's soft hands drummed lightly on the white
damask tablecloth, sending a wordless message. "I mean only
that the true Masaryk was misunderstood. I was a witness to his
religious faith. It wasn't like his father's or sisters', he just believed in God, but it went very deep. I was the one who looked
up those verses of St. Paul's when he asked me to, a few days
before he died; they weren't marked at the time. There couldn't
have been a question in my mind when I heard of his death.
The verses told us something, but his way of dying spoke volumes. People say he would never have chosen voluntarily to
jump out of the window, because he was so terrified of pain.
But that was the whole point, don't you see? Obviously he
might have slashed his wrists, or put a bullet through his head,
or taken sleeping pills. He deliberately chose not to: it would
have been too easy. He was offering his life on the altar of the
nation. It was self-immolation, the supreme sacrifice. *He
wanted his death to be harsh.*"

The delivery was biblical, the assertion strikingly at odds with
everything I'd heard, read, taken for granted about Jan Masaryk.
I studied the face of my dinner companion, the regular features
flushed and curiously indistinct, the virtuous mouth with its
petulant lines, the narrow eyes, shiny now. Was he a religious
crank? A disingenuous fraud? Could he be right?

I proposed that we try, together, to eliminate the litter of clues which didn't fit Dr. Soukoup's theory of ritual suicide. We might start with the disarray in Masaryk's apartment on the morning of March 10. Although Dr. Soukoup was not at the palace that day, he had doubtless heard about it from the other two secretaries? Yes. Would the description of the bedroom and, more important, the bathroom, conflict with his suicide theory? Not at all. Masaryk was a typical bachelor.

So I'd heard. But even typical bachelors wouldn't customarily leave their pillows in the bathtub, would they?

"Well, *he* did." Dr. Soukoup was serene. "Masaryk always had trouble getting to sleep, and his arm bothered him a lot, the one he dislocated on his trip to New York for that last UN session. He liked to rest in the dry bathtub, when the bedroom was stuffy, or too hot, or his shoulder was paining him. You'd be surprised how comfortable it can be, with a pillow tucked in behind your head. I saw him like that more than once."

Aside from the bodyguard, Vyšín, who had rarely entered Masaryk's rooms—and had probably picked this up from Soukoup himself—nobody at Czernin Palace knew a thing about the Minister's habit of resting in a dry tub: not the butler Příhoda, in the Masaryk family's service for twenty-eight years, or the household purser Topinka, in and out of the flat from morning to night, or the other two secretaries, Špaček and Šum. All were on the staff long before Soukoup came over from Scotland in December, 1947. Could he have learned more than everyone else about Masaryk's personal habits, in just three months?

Granting Masaryk's unconventional ways, I insisted, it wasn't so easy to dismiss the pillows. Several witnesses maintained that there were actually two in the bathroom, one in the tub, the other on the floor, and that they were dirty. . . .

"Oh, that would be his dog." The pale fingertips waved this aside as of no moment. "The Minister's dog was all over the place, mostly on the bed. It was obviously the dog who dirtied the pillows."

From a chance remark overheard in London (verified later by the senior secretary, Špaček, in Prague) I knew Masaryk had left his dog in England when he went back to Czechoslovakia in 1945. The conversation at our Glasgow dinner table was taking a fascinating turn.

And how would Dr. Soukoup explain the broken glass on the bathroom floor? He wasn't sure, imagined that the Minister might have looked through the medicine chest for sleeping pills or razor blades—a number of blades were reportedly found scattered about—and then changed his mind. But when I inquired about the excrement on Masaryk's body, pajamas, the bathroom window sill, he was on firmer ground.

"To be perfectly candid, I strongly disapprove of all this public talk about such matters. Things of that kind oughtn't to be discussed openly, out of piety towards the deceased; they should be kept for the court record, where they belong. Inasmuch as it *is* being discussed, though, you might as well hear the truth. The Minister suffered from chronic constipation. He was always trying quack remedies. I was the one who gave him the suppositories that finally worked. That's why his bowels were loose —since you insist."

It occurred to me that Dr. Soukoup might be pulling my leg. Reconstructing his theory of ritual suicide on the basis of these answers along with the proven evidence, it would come out something like this:

Masaryk, having completed a routine afternoon's work with his secretaries, settled down comfortably in bed in his pajamas, ate a good dinner, left orders to be waked in the morning, wrote the draft of a speech to be delivered the next day, took two sleeping pills and a laxative suppository, leafed through the Bible to find St. Paul's views on circumcision, trailed a dog's dirty pillows into the bathroom and rested up for a bit in the waterless tub, emptied the contents of the medicine chest in search of the means to destroy himself, realized that sleeping pills and razor blades weren't sacrificial enough, ground the medicine bottles under his bare heel and, to use Dr. Soukoup's closing words in the *Scotsman,* "opened the window and . . ."

But it was apparent, from another careful glance, that Dr. Soukoup was not given to levity. He was positive that these suppositories explained the excrement? Quite: he would advise me to ask the State Prosecutor about it; the secret police had cut out a piece of the window sill with some of the excrement on it, and laboratory tests should establish the point. I told him that the State Prosecutor had rather leaned toward the laxative effects of Krandorf mineral water when last I'd seen him, and Dr. Soukoup frowned slightly. What did he make of the fingerprints on the window frame and surrounding wall, I went on. They were the final proof, he said.

"As a matter of fact, there were no prints on the wall. They were only on the inside of the top hinge of the right half of the window frame. It happened that there were also indentations on the fingers of Masaryk's right hand, as if they'd been caught in the swinging hinge. I noticed this when I was putting the nosegay behind Masaryk's ear in the coffin, to hide the autopsy scar. It came to me at once that he must have hoisted himself into a standing position, after he got the window open, by grabbing onto this hinge . . ."

Though rocked by the nosegay—Masaryk's second secretary, Šum, having told me that *he* put it behind Masaryk's ear—I let that pass. As for the window-hinge theory, however, I objected that Masaryk was six feet tall, whereas the bathroom window was only three feet high, and the excrement on the sill indicated a sitting rather than an upright position. Furthermore, the former head of the Czech CID, Dr. Gorner, thought the fingerprints were all around the window casing, while the senior secretary, Špaček, remembered them as being on the dusty wall and the *outside* of the window frame.

Dr. Soukoup leaned confidentially closer over the table. "I've already told this to the State Prosecutor, so I might as well tell you. There wasn't the slightest doubt about whose fingerprints

they were, or what they meant. I was so certain of this myself
that I felt they must be preserved in case the investigation
should be reopened some day. What I did was to cover the
prints with a coat of clear varnish, and top that with another
coat of white paint. They must still be there, if anybody cares
to look."

Did State Prosecutor Kotlar take much interest in this item?
I asked cautiously. Not too much. But then, they'd had a lot to
talk about in the eight-hour interview. And Dr. Kotlar was
sympathetic, by and large? Oh, yes. Of course, he'd brought an
interpreter along, which seemed peculiar to Dr. Soukoup, a born
Czechoslovak. Otherwise, though, the interview was relaxed and
informal. On the whole, he'd felt they saw eye to eye.

It was getting late, and I had to catch the night train back
to London. There was hardly the time and I was scarcely inclined to ask him an apparently useless question, but I did.
So much material appeared to have come his way, I said, that
I wondered if Dr. Soukoup knew anything about a case which
several witnesses insisted on connecting with Masaryk's: the
police doctor Teplý's. The State Prosecutor assured me that the
two deaths were altogether unrelated. No doubt Dr. Soukoup
felt the same. Nevertheless, I'd been advised in Prague to ask
him about this when I got to Glasgow. Did he by chance have
information in regard to a document purporting to be Dr.
Teplý's secret testament?

And suddenly, in the rush to summon the waiter, pay the
bill, collect luggage and coat, check timetables with the hotel
porter, and sprint for the station, I discovered the other side of
Dr. Soukoup.

"Funny you should ask me that. No, I haven't a thing on
Teplý's secret testament. But something seems to be fishy there.
You know that burial certificate I gave to the British press, the
Ohledacti List? Well, I got it from the other secretary, Špaček,
who brought it to Switzerland and gave it to me to pass on to
Masaryk's sister Alice. I didn't realize then that it was supposed

to have Teplý's signature on the first page: the document I was given didn't even *have* a first page. And I had no idea that the back page, the summary of the autopsy report, had to be signed by the doctor who did the post-mortem, Hájek. It wasn't. The signature was Tesař's, the fellow who used to be Hájek's aide. The funny thing is that State Prosecutor Kotlar asked me about this Ohledacti List, and can you guess why? Because Tesař told him he'd never signed it!"

Dr. Soukoup, enjoying his effect, was plainly preparing to spring something bigger. Tightening his grip on my elbow as he steered me toward the sleeping cars, he bent closer to my ear. "All those people you met in Prague: did they go into the question of what was supposed to come next?"

I didn't understand.

"After the coup," he explained with an impatient shake. "What were Beneš and Masaryk going to do after the Communist coup? You didn't imagine they were going to stick with Gottwald forever?"

No, certainly not. Both secretaries in Prague told me that President Beneš and Masaryk had agreed shortly after the coup to resign together fairly soon—at any rate, before the election in May.

"Right!" His pause was dramatic, and conspiratorial. "And how do you think the Russians would have felt about that?" he asked, punctuating each word. Not overjoyed, evidently. Right again. The fact was, said Dr. Soukoup, that the Russians didn't believe for a moment in Masaryk's lasting allegiance to the Communist cause, nor did they want him even if they could have him, once the Communists were safely in control of the country. Czechoslovak Communist leaders, not yet fully initiated into the Stalinist rites of power, might assume that they could live with a Western-oriented bourgeois democrat like Jan Masaryk for some time; the Russians knew better. They were not going to run the risk of letting Tomáš Masaryk's son resign, however, let alone leave the country to use his name and enormous popularity against them. Neither could they risk the usual, more or less public methods to dispose of him: imprisonment, execution, deportation. Therefore, he would have to be murdered.

I had boarded the sleeping car, was leaning from the window looking down at him in the murky light. The whistle had blown, we'd be gone in a minute.

"They were planning to kill him within two or three months." His voice came up muffled through the mist. "I'm not guessing. Masaryk had the documented proof. Somebody we both know has the proof right this minute."

"Who?" I yelled, as the train pulled out of the station into a choking yellow fog.

"Somebody you saw in Prague," he yelled back, waving.

Chapter 18

I'm not going to quote Benno Weigl verbatim because he had
a tape recorder in his office. The smallest slip and he'd be on
the phone to his lawyer, or so they said in Fleet Street. He was
a controversial figure, a source of endless irritation to the Kremlin, a drain on State Prosecutor Kotlar's time and the state's
money, the man who forced open the Masaryk case practically
singlehanded. Naturally he was being slandered right and left.
Personally, though, I had no reason to slander Mr. Weigl. Compared to most published material on Masaryk's death, his article
in *Der Spiegel* seemed to me to stand up rather well. Besides, he
didn't tell me anything.

Mr. Weigl was plump, a snappy dresser, expansive, voluble,
wary. His office in Cheshire Court was snug once you got up
the rickety firetrap of a staircase, his secretary friendly, his desk
large and orderly as a Swiss banker's. He had set up as a free
lance in London in the early sixties, soon after his release from
prison in Czechoslovakia, where he'd gotten to know Masaryk's
second secretary, Antonín Šum, from whom I brought greetings.
He must have gotten to know a lot of other political convicts
during his ten years in jail, but he didn't go into that. Wherever
he'd found his information for the *Spiegel* article, he clearly had
no intention of sharing his sources.

Otherwise, he was anxious to be helpful. Once, he told me, he'd spent an afternoon in Rome with Josef Cardinal Beran, former Primate of Prague; and the Cardinal told him that the wife of a high American diplomat in Prague had told *him* (the Cardinal) that Masaryk was undoubtedly murdered. Then there was the story about Ján Papánek, head of the Czechoslovak UN delegation in 1948, and a close friend of Jan Masaryk's. When Dr. Papánek demanded a Security Council debate on the sinister circumstances surrounding Masaryk's death, his desk drawers at UN headquarters were mysteriously rifled, said Mr. Weigl. (So they were, Dr. Papánek later informed me.) This, too, was a clue of sorts, he suggested. But none of it had anything to do with details in the *Spiegel,* which, according to Mr. Weigl, were taken in good part from the secret files of the Czechoslovak Interior Ministry.

When State Prosecutor Kotlar went to see him in London, Mr. Weigl said the documents in question weren't his, nor could he produce them without permission from the owner, who kept them in a bank vault. I didn't even get that far with Mr. Weigl, who, when the conversation got around to Dr. Kotlar, took the interview in hand himself. What was the State Prosecutor saying about him? Was he abusive? Did I know that Dr. Kotlar brought an interpreter along to interview him— *Weigl,* a born Czechoslovak? Furthermore, did I know who the interpreter *was?* A fellow named Samuele, an old-timer in the Czechoslovak security police, who happened to have been Weigl's interrogator in prison. I might draw my own conclusions.

Of course Mr. Weigl was expecting bumpy weather when Dr. Kotlar came, and indeed all along, after *Der Spiegel* published his article in 1965. That was why he'd used an assumed name: Michael Rand. But such secrets couldn't last long in Fleet Street. Some of the boys had pried his right name out of a United Press deskman in no time. Once his identity became known, he'd had the book thrown at him by certain interested parties, who accused him of everything from posing as a Spanish grandee to spying for the British secret service. His lawyer had already hauled the London *Times* into court, and would do the same to anybody else making reckless charges. Was there anything else he could do for me? Alas, I doubted it.

Unlike the State Prosecutor in Prague, I didn't mind wasting time on Mr. Weigl. Whatever the errors in his *Spiegel* article, he couldn't have written it without access to inside information. I would have settled for a small hint. But after an hour's amiable talk and several cups of tea, I gave up. The one thing I'd learned, when he showed me to the door, was the name of the agency holding the copyright to his article.

It wasn't until the day before I left London that I found what I believe to be Mr. Weigl's main source. By then, I had more or less run out of people to see. Masaryk's close friend, Sir Robert Bruce Lockhart, was too old and ill. None of the surviving Czech émigrés appeared to have known Masaryk half as well. Here and there, somebody would fit in a small piece of the background: Masaryk's gaiety before Munich, gallantry during the war, growing skepticism about Russian intentions, heavy gloom on his last visit to London, coming back from the UN session in New York. Several spoke of his love for London, for the charladies who scrubbed the floor with their hats on, the plumber who would offer him, or the King, a Player, the English in general: "I just can't help myself. I like them." His old friend Dr. Papírnek told me about the flat at 137 Marsham Court, which he'd kept an eye on in Masaryk's absence, complete with morning suits, dinner jackets, riding clothes, linen, silver, china, books, and pictures, even an office with typewriters and mimeograph machine. But as Dr. Soukoup had observed so tartly in Glasgow, not many of the London émigrés had firsthand knowledge of Masaryk's death. I would have left almost empty-handed if three or four, sorry to disappoint me, hadn't suggested almost casually: "Why don't you go to see Madame Smutný?"

Chancellor Jaromír Smutný's widow was reluctant to receive me. Since the death of her husband in July, 1964, she'd been living in semiretirement. She was not a politician, had nothing to say that could conceivably be of interest, would rather not be upset by reviving sad memories of Jan Masaryk, she said when I telephoned. Yes, he'd been an intimate and beloved friend: all the more reason to spare her the pain of recollection. Yes, her late husband had left sixteen volumes of unedited memoirs—she believed there was a chapter on Masaryk's death—but she herself had not reread the manuscript for a long time and would rather not let anybody else read it for some years to come. The manuscript was in a vault at Barclay's Bank, and she preferred to keep it there. Some day, when old political vendettas were forgotten and historians could be perfectly detached, the sixteen volumes might be brought out, edited, published. Not now.

In the end she let me come. Her fairly large but unpretentious red-brick house in Putney was the one President Beneš had bought during the war, taken over by his Chancellor when the Smutnýs fled Czechoslovakia at last in July, 1949. I approached the door with misgivings, expecting, from her reception on the telephone, to be met by a dragon. She turned out to be small, delicate, elegant, pretty even in her seventies, with eyes of cornflower blue, short straight nose and beautifully coifed gray hair. She was sharp-witted too and, with me at least, extremely generous.

The sitting room was conventionally middle-class: Persian throw rugs, velvet upholstery, silver cigarette boxes, and framed family photographs. Our opening conversation was stilted. She didn't know me, had no reason to trust me, had learned in this still alien Anglo-Saxon land to trust nobody except a few fellow Czechs, by no means all. She didn't warm to me until, going through the list of all the people I'd seen in Prague, I came to the former National Socialist Minister of Justice, Prokop Drtina. They were old friends, and she asked me eagerly for news: she hadn't seen Drtina since the night he jumped out of his window, twenty-four hours after the Communist coup.

I repeated to her what I remembered offhand of my long talk with that upright, admirable man. He told me that when he'd jumped from the window, people were sure he was pushed, just as they were about Jan Masaryk eleven days afterward. Hospitalized under heavy guard for five months and imprisoned for the next twelve years, Drtina had no chance to set this straight. He did so as soon as he could, in April, 1968, feeling it was his duty to declare publicly that nobody had pushed him, that he'd tried to commit suicide. He explained the reasons to me with touching simplicity. From the day the twelve democratic ministers resigned in February, 1948, the secret police had followed his every step. He was certain they meant to arrest him and afraid it would happen at night, when he would have no chance to get away. With all else lost, he was determined, at least, not to give them the pleasure of arresting him. He could have fled the country, but lacked the will to go, his resolution drained away because he was heartbroken and disillusioned. It wasn't the democrats' defeat that broke his spirit—he'd seen that coming for months—but the nature of their defeat, the fact that they were abandoned by the people who had their deepest confidence, President Beneš up to a point but above all Jan Masaryk. He had never dreamed that Masaryk would stay on with Gottwald after the democrats left, still less join the Communist cabinet afterward. He would never understand it. Physically, he was all right now, seemed well, had retired on an old-age pension and was expecting, when I saw him, to be formally rehabilitated in a few weeks. That was in late September, soon after the Red Army's arrival. I didn't know how things had gone for him since.

Madame Smutný listened carefully, her frail figure—smartly dressed, jeweled, and shod—erect in the overstuffed armchair. She sighed when I finished, for the past, her old friends, her tormented country. Poor Masaryk, she said at last, so many people counting on him, pulling at him from every side. Who could tell why he'd acted as he did? Of course she was no politician, it was her husband who had a better understanding of Jan's behavior in the crisis. Her knowledge of Jan was just personal, though it went back so many years . . . he'd been a witness at her wedding. Their paths didn't cross much in the prewar years, but after the war, in Prague, they practically lived in each other's pockets. Her husband would see Jan every day, sometimes more than once, and he would dine with the Smutnýs at least once a week. It was always a joy to have him, he brought a breath of fresh air into the house, right up to the end. Even that Tuesday, his last day alive, he'd been enchanting at Sezimovo Usti, full of jokes . . .

"You were at Sezimovo Usti that Tuesday?" Not once, in all the published testimony, had this been mentioned.

"Yes, of course, I was there with my husband, for the ceremony with the new Polish Ambassador. We stayed to lunch, and Jan was supposed to stay too. Hana Beneš invited him first thing, before the ceremony began, and he accepted. But then, when the ceremony was over and he'd spent some time alone with the President, Jan changed his mind. He told Hana he had to get back to Prague to see somebody—the American Ambassador Laurence Steinhardt. He had us all laughing about something, though, before he left."

Did she tell this to State Prosecutor Kotlar? No, he didn't try to get in touch with her when he was in London; under the circumstances, it wouldn't have occurred to her to make the first move about seeing him. Had she any idea of what Masaryk talked about with President Beneš when they were alone together before lunch that Tuesday? None. The two were closeted in the President's study. Beneš, who tired easily after his two strokes, wasn't well enough to have walked in the garden with Masaryk, as some newspapers had reported. In fact, the President was inclined to rest on a divan for much of the time. Masaryk, emerging from the study, betrayed no particular emotion. No, he certainly didn't hint that he might be planning to leave the country. But then, if he had actually been making secret preparations, he would never have mentioned it, least of all to them. It was already understood by then that the last people you would inform of such plans were your best friends, obviously the first to be approached by the secret police when you were gone. The less your friends knew of your preparations, the easier time they would have in facing police interrogation. When the Smutnýs themselves left Prague in 1949, for instance, they didn't tell Hana Beneš they were going. It was sad not to say goodbye, but necessary, for her sake.

And did Madame Smutný notice anything to suggest that Masaryk wasn't his usual self when he left Sezimovo Usti? Did he seem feverish, distracted, inordinately tired, depressed?

"Nothing unusual. He always looked tired in those days, and I suppose all of us were pretty depressed. Who wasn't? I remember Hana Beneš remarking that they weren't seeing enough of Jan lately, and I said something of the sort, too. He promised to come and dine with us later that week."

She wasn't prepared, then, for the news of his death? No. Somebody from the palace had telephoned around seven on Wednesday morning—at least that was when her husband finally answered the phone. By a stupid oversight, they'd forgotten to bring the telephone into the bedroom the previous night, and so did not hear it ring earlier that morning. They were both stunned. Her husband had dressed hurriedly and rushed to Czernin, but stayed only a few minutes once there. He was anxious to break the news to President Beneš, who was in such fragile health, before Premier Gottwald paid an official call. After telephoning to the President's physician, Oskar Klinger, and arranging to meet him at the President's country seat, the Chancellor had left at once for Sezimovo Usti.

In months of pursuit, numberless interviews, more than a million printed words, I'd heard and read nothing to indicate Chancellor Smutný's presence in Masaryk's apartment early in

the morning on March 10. However long he stayed, he was
there; and he was President Beneš's most trusted aide, surely a
more believable witness than most. What, I asked Madame
Smutný, did her husband see? She looked a little flurried:
plainly she hadn't meant to get into this.

"I don't know that he saw very much," she answered slowly.
"His first impression was that Masaryk must have committed
suicide, and then he wasn't so sure. The situation in the flat
was confusing, a good many things about the death were confusing. He went back to the flat a second time, I remember, and
noticed things. . . . I'd really rather not discuss it, I didn't
see it myself. My husband wrote it all down, you know, he
always made notes of whatever happened, every day—he'd
keep a pencil and paper at the side of his bed, in case he forgot
to make a note of anything, he was extremely exact about this.
But of course, that material hasn't been published. He didn't
write about this in his published works, you see, he kept it all
for this manuscript."

Nobody outside had been allowed to read the manuscript,
she explained. Chancellor Smutný himself had used some of the
material dealing with Masaryk's death for a lecture he gave,
shortly before he died, at the Beneš Institute in London. People
said that Benno Weigl might have picked up some of his material from this lecture—she herself had no idea if this was so—
and there was probably a copy of the text around somewhere.
Would that help me? Well, yes. But it might hardly be more
helpful than a dozen fragments of evidence I'd discovered,
each breaking off just where it might have led to something
meaningful. Without seeing what Chancellor Smutný wrote, I
naturally couldn't say how important his testimony was. But
he couldn't be thought of as just another witness, after all. Considering his authoritative position at Hradcany Castle, his
habits of precise observation, his methodical note-taking and
reputation as the President's most responsible aide, the Chancellor's information was bound to be more valuable—at any rate

more reliable—than most. Probably there would never be another chance to clarify the circumstances of Jan Masaryk's death: the Russian occupation looked as though it would last indefinitely, the State Prosecutor's inquiry appeared to be leading purposefully nowhere, sources inside Czechoslovakia were already drying up. Wasn't it a pity to withhold her husband's knowledge, not to publish what he'd written in full?

She surrendered with grace but not all at once. She really didn't think so, would have to reread the manuscript to refresh her memory of the contents, wasn't even sure where, among all those sixteen volumes of typed pages, the material on Masaryk's death might be buried. And of course, it was all written in Czech. Who could be trusted to go through this mass of material, selecting the useful portions for translation? She couldn't think of a soul in London whom she'd willingly leave alone in a room with those volumes. She half-rose, half-regretfully, from her armchair. How about Daniela, I asked, and she sat down again. Daniela Kottnauer, the late Chancellor's secretary at the Beneš Institute, was one of the younger Czech émigrés, engaging, bright, and if outward signs counted for anything, loyal. Madame Smutný yielded. "Daniela would be much, much too busy. But if she's willing, all right."

Daniela was willing. I couldn't reach her on the telephone until theater time, the bell already ringing for the first-act curtain. Though my explanation was ragged, she understood. She would try to get a look at the material before I left London the next night, she promised, and send the translations on to Rome later. I had a hard time keeping my mind on the stage.

There was one more visit I had to make, on my last day in England, to the expert recommended by Scotland Yard. Getting to him was a disappointingly prosaic affair: I just walked into the resolutely impersonal glass-and-marble lobby of Scotland Yard's new office building near Parliament and asked the receptionist to put me on to somebody who could put me on to the best criminologist in Britain. He rang upstairs, wrote the name on a slip of paper, and handed it over. When I phoned for an appointment, a wonderfully homey secretary cut short my explanation, saying simply: "Certainly, dearie! He'd love to see you! Why not?"

Professor Francis Camps, Director of the Forensic Medicine Institute of London Hospital and consultant to the Home Office, operated out of a cubbyhole just big enough for him, a desk, an extra chair, a shelf of books, and a row of evil-looking skeletal objects, atop one of the smaller buildings in the London Hospital compound. A large and cheery man, he was unpompous, unhurried, and judging from the state of his desk, regrettably unconscientious about his correspondence. He let me stay for hours, and I had a grand time.

He made it clear right off that I hadn't enough exact information for him to go on. Did the Czech authorities make a reconstruction of the body's fall? Not that I knew of. A laboratory analysis of the broken glass on the bathroom floor, the pillows in the tub, the fingerprints on the window and wall? I doubted it. Could I give him the exact height and weight of the corpse, and precise measurements of the window, its height from the floor and distance to the courtyard below? Not precise. The State Prosecutor in Prague had promised to give me all this information, but not until later. Well, then, my dear lady . . .

Still, Professor Camps was curious about Masaryk's death, and ready to talk it over without a professional commitment. We talked until the secretary, obviously the Professor's sword and shield, drove us both out so that she could lock up and go home. Much of what he said was speculative, therefore not publishable; and most of the rest was, in effect, a suspended judgment, depending on information that I was supposed to get from State Prosecutor Kotlar before the year was out. I'll come to it, after my next meeting with Dr. Kotlar.

From the London airport that night, I called Daniela. She had gone to Putney, talked with Madame Smutný, taken a first look at the sixteen volumes of memoirs. There were several passages that she thought would be of interest and something more that I might like to know about. Attached to the chapter in Chancellor Smutný's memoirs dealing with Jan Masaryk's death were copies of the testimony given to the secret police on the morning of March 10, 1948, by sixteen witnesses interrogated at Czernin Palace. Madame Smutný had told Daniela that these documents were shown to the Chancellor under conditions of the tightest secrecy, by a functionary of the Czechloslovak Interior Ministry. The functionary had smuggled them out one or two at a time, the Chancellor had copied them hurriedly in his own hand, and they were then slipped back into the archives. She could probably have these documents translated in full by the time I got back to Rome, after stopping off in Prague for a week or so. Did I want them? Yes, dear Daniela, I did.

Chapter 19

The Czechs hadn't yet gotten used to their cage again—the phrase was theirs—when I returned to Prague in December. But they'd lost the buoyancy of those early weeks after the August invasion. Before leaving in October, I'd spent my last Sunday picking mushrooms in the Bohemian forest with a Communist very high on the Russians' wanted list. Nobody would have guessed, watching him crash through the wet bracken in floppy galoshes and sodden canvas hat, hearing his victorious "Ahaaaa!" as he spied a fungoid beauty and raced shamelessly to beat his eight-year-old daughter to it, that Soviet tanks were bivouacked in the woods not ten miles away, or that Soviet KGB agents had already been around to pick him up at the Prague flat he hadn't set foot in since the Red Army came. You wouldn't have thought either that, refusing even to consider flight in October, he'd be an exile in Paris by Christmas.

The end came surprisingly soon. Two months were enough for the Russians to get a signed treaty, legalizing their occupation of a country so united against them that not a single citizen could be found to form a puppet government: a unique case in history. Time and again, my Czech friends would go back over the sad, familiar ground. Was it best for them to go under like this, little by little, hoping against hope, forced at last to sign away their independence without firing a shot? Would they be better off if they had "bared their breasts to the bayonets" as National Assembly Chairman Josef Smrkovský asked in despair, and defied the Kremlin to do its damnedest? Could they be much worse off, either way, whatever they did?

There were moments in those first weeks when we Western reporters would have said yes to all three questions. We were sure the Czechs were doomed, half-certain of their resurrection, unable to believe they could get away with things they were in fact getting away with day after day. What struck us wasn't so much their nerve or ingenuity or sheer mulishness as their fault-less, intuitive solidarity. It was their one frail chance to get out from under the crushing weight of half a million occupation troops, and they were making the most of it.

Unable to reach Prague until a week after the Red Army did, I'd missed the dramatic phase of resistance: desperate unarmed assaults on troop carriers and armored cars, human chains barring the road to Soviet tanks, a clandestine press, radio, and television operating with breath-taking courage and precision. All that remained of this, when I got there, were the young students standing vigil at the feet of King Wenceslas, little shrines of fresh flowers on the cobbled streets where others had been shot dead by Russian soldiers, the defaced street names, signs, numbers, painted over in black, or torn down, or twisted and rewritten to point toward Warsaw, East Berlin, Moscow.

It was a curious sensation to walk through this lifeless city, caught like a fly in amber, streets empty, shops closed, windows shuttered over doorways guarded by silent Russian sentinels. The sensation of moving in a dream grew stronger as I drove blindly through a countryside stripped of signposts, searching for friends who had vanished from the capital within hours of the Russians' arrival. Every now and then a convoy of Russian trucks would loom up at me, quickly pulling to the side to let me pass. At intervals, I could see the blunt noses of Soviet tanks poking from a coppice, the glitter of artillery caught by a ray of sunlight in a clump of trees. There were no other cars on the road and no people; the villages I passed were draped in black flags, the letters on their walls six feet high: "Russians Go Home."

It took the better part of a day to track down the first of my friends, hiding out in his village only sixty miles from Prague. Relieved that he wasn't yet in jail, I offered the help he must surely need to cross the border: hard currency, a place to stay, introductions for a decent job. He declined politely. He would be miserable as an émigré, he said, and preferred to face what was coming with his countrymen at home. He was expecting arrest momentarily, not to mention dismissal from the university, and though hating the idea of imprisonment, didn't at all mind working in a factory again, as he'd done under the Stalinist Novotný regime. He had given up any thought of a better life for himself and his children. He didn't share his leaders' innocent belief that they had merely failed to explain their planned reforms properly to Moscow, that all this was just a misunderstanding which could somehow be ironed out. Still, whatever happened, he meant to give the Russians a run for their money.

Most of the Czechs I knew agreed. Of course there were some who wanted no further part of it: since the revolution was done for, why wait around? "As a good Marxist, I do not believe in the Second Coming," one remarked, taking off for London. But they were barely a handful. A good many others were severely critical of their leaders for treating with the Kremlin instead of fighting it head on. The lives spared now were bound to be lost or hopelessly blighted later, they argued, and since the Kremlin was going to run things anyway, it should be made to bear the shameful responsibility alone. All the same, they had no intention of leaving, and those hiding out in country cottages were already drifting back to the capital, if only to move from house to house. Nearly all had been warned by Party leaders or the

Czech police that they were wanted by the Russians; the list had been prepared in Moscow and brought to the scene of the crime by KGB agents. Several were so dangerously exposed that a white-faced Party functionary appeared in person at the Alcron to beg Western journalists not to get in touch with them. So far, however, no more than three or four Czechs had actually been arrested, within hours of the invasion, to be quickly released. For all the three thousand KGB agents fanning out on the hunt, with special Soviet military tribunals waiting in Prague to handle summary trials (and in some cases, executions), not one arrest had been made since.

That first arrest was what everybody was waiting for, as one waits for the second shoe to drop. We could imagine the Russians making do without a puppet government, though the fact that not a soul in the country would touch the job must have been a stunning shock. We could even see them turning this to advantage, by forcing the very men who had the Czechs' deepest trust to do the dirty work. But we could not see them letting the dirty work go undone. An occupation army must travel with its guillotine, an occupied nation must understand that it is occupied, the price of defiance must be high enough to destroy any lingering romantic illusions. Besides, the Russians would have to prove how right they were to come in the first place, by bringing to justice the seditious counterrevolutionaries—forty thousand, by *Pravda*'s count—whom an irresponsible Communist leadership had left at large.

Nevertheless the days passed and my friends were still turning up to meet me at street corners, uneasy about sitting in a restaurant but more than ready to walk. As we paced the streets for hours on end under an everlasting, dreary rain, I began to see why all those KGB agents were getting nowhere. From the President, Premier, and entire Communist leadership to the national army, Workers' Militia and security police, to the humblest janitor and street cleaner, the Czechs had formed a human wall around the KGB's intended victims.

Twenty-four hours after the troops came, with high Party
leaders in handcuffs and an iron ring of tanks encircling his
headquarters, Interior Minister Josef Pavel informed Soviet
commanders that he would neither make arrests nor permit his
staff to help the Russians do so. No sooner had he shown them
the door than he ordered criminal proceedings against suspected
collaborators on his staff and fired his evidently guilty Deputy
Minister, Colonel Salgovič, who thoughtfully took refuge in the
Soviet Embassy. Obliged then to resign under imperious Soviet
pressure, Pavel promptly moved into the safety of Hradcany
Castle on President Ludvík Svoboda's invitation.

Among the President's other guests were Premier Oldřich
Černík, Party Secretary Alexander Dubček, and National Assembly Chairman Josef Smrkovský, just back from the first
Moscow talks. Little was known then about their brutal treatment at Russian hands. We knew only that President Svoboda,
a Hero of the Soviet Union for his wartime services, had saved
their lives in Moscow by pulling out a gun and threatening to
take his own, before the Russians' eyes: the world would never
believe it was suicide, he had warned. Upon coming back, they
had been forbidden to leave the Castle until they proved their
cooperative inclinations. That was where they named their
new Interior Minister, with whom the Russians fared no better.

The KGB was thus thrown on its own resources, in a city that
had turned into a trackless jungle overnight. Occasionally Soviet
agents might get their bearings, by locating one of the Tuzex
(hard-currency) chain stores and working out from there. But
wherever human inquiry was needed, they were right up
against the wall. When people spoke to a Russian at all, it was
only to abuse him or shame him into tears. It became their
favorite sport. I myself, one unforgettable evening, was dragged
by a Czech writer friend—far along on vodka by then—to a small
park between the railroad station and Esplanade Hotel, clogged
with Soviet tanks backed up end to end. My friend, who had
learned colloquial Russian at the Moscow Partisan School, was

tired of wasting his most offensive Russian phrases merely on one or two Soviet soldiers at a time; he wanted a good-sized crowd. Even when I succeeded in pulling him away, he continued to shout profanities over his shoulder until the soldiers were out of earshot.

The effect on Soviet troops, on the officers in particular, was pitiable. The same Czech writer told me of his conversation with a Soviet colonel four days after the invasion, in a Western Bohemian village whose inhabitants still refused to supply the invaders even with bread and water. My friend called the colonel over to explain the situation in Russian: "You must understand that our people think of your army as they did of the Nazi Wehrmacht. Tell your men to stop asking for water; they won't get it." The colonel drew his gun, walked back to his men, and announced that the first among them to ask for water would be shot.

Here and there, inevitably, the Russians would find some poor wretch to help them. But the few offering to guide KGB agents had no time to regret it: a movie camera caught one as he was beaten to death by an outraged mob near Old Town Square. Never shown to the public, the film was run off privately for educational purposes, by an underground group in the Interior Ministry—the group including Karel, the security police officer I interviewed later. Those on the Ministry staff who failed to get the point were quietly taken care of.

The group's existence rarely came up in my talks with Czech friends. Its work was ugly, hardly a score of lumpenproletariat collaborators had materialized, and there were worse things to worry about. "Optimism equals lack of information," I had read somewhere, scrawled on a Prague wall. My friends had no lack of information.

They were reasonably safe for the moment. "I couldn't answer for my own head three weeks from now," a high Communist official told one, "but until then I can vouch for yours." From top to bottom, indeed, the grapevine was in perfect working order. Twice in as many days, a journalist I knew was tipped off in time to slip away from home before KGB agents came to get him in a military ambulance. Everybody carried a valid passport, ready for instant flight if the word came and sure of willing hands to help him across the border. There was, too, a memorable Sunday when the signal went out—premature by six months—that Soviet agents were going to provoke an incident as an excuse to crack down. Some Praguers took off for the country with their mushroom baskets, others dropped in on a military band concert at the Castle, the rest stayed indoors. That afternoon, local police picked up a number of KGB agents for circulating with false identity papers and handed them over to the Soviet Embassy. They had betrayed themselves by the carefully pressed crease in their blue jeans.

Anybody knowing no better might have thought this exhilarating game could go on forever. With troops and tanks withdrawn to the outskirts of town by mid-September, Prague looked normal again, even gay. On Vaclavske Namesti, the young honor guard had gone, leaving behind a neatly planted flower bed at the Good King's feet. Crowds of shoppers strolled casually down Narodny and Prikope, *horké párky* venders were back at their old stands, lovers posed for snapshots and kissed in doorways, restaurants were open after dark and doing a roaring trade. But this kind of normalcy, if pleasant, was irrelevant.

Whatever the Russians meant by "normalization," it was a distinctly dirty word which the Czechs were trying studiously not to hear. At best, it implied going back to the gray mid-sixties, at worst to the Stalinist dark ages, and the worst appeared to be what a hysterical press in Moscow, Warsaw, East Berlin, and Sofia had in mind. Apart from publishing the drollest samples of this prehistoric thought, however, the Czechs were going about their business almost as if none of those capitals had ever sent an army to Prague. Measures taken by the Dubček regime—"temporary" censorship, "exceptional" restrictions on free assembly, a ban on new political parties, replacement of three cabinet ministers and two directors of the mass media (one a Soviet sympathizer) —were indeed concessions to the armies' presence. But there was no recantation of heresy, no fraternization with the invader, no sign of a quisling, no purge. As a Polish newspaper aptly observed, this version of normalization was "not sincere." In fact, it was so patently halfhearted that the Russians couldn't conceivably put up with it.

I was often told in Prague that Dubček, an honest but not brilliant man, was genuinely puzzled by the discrepancies between what he thought he had heard in Moscow and what the Russians had really said. Two or three of his more sophisticated colleagues in the Presidium were trying gently to set him and the public straight. It was plain to them that the Kremlin expected more from this operation than withering criticism from practically every existing Communist party and most of the civilized world. Half a million troops had not come here only to turn around and march home again. Neither could they have come with paternal blessings for an ideological revolution threatening to undermine every orthodox Communist regime in Eastern Europe. Yet Czech leaders had confidently assured the public since August that the troops would leave at any moment, while they themselves went right ahead with their post-January policies, recognizing the rights of man and humanizing Communism in general. The Kremlin agreed, they said, but those with sharper ears knew it didn't. "You may as well get out while you can," a member of the Presidium told students coming for advice. "Your generation has no future."

And still most of my friends were determined to stay. They would tell me so jauntily at times, or with a shrug of resignation, depending on the news and the weather. A sunny morning, a spirited quip in *Rudé Právo,* and they would give way, as we all did, to an unreasonable belief in miracles. With the inevitable evening drizzle, however, would come the realization that miracles do not happen. They were simply staying because they could not bear to go. They believed, first of all, that short of consigning the lot of them to a dank dungeon, Moscow would like nothing better than to see the departing backs of this country's intellectuals, the scourge of Stalinist nonthinkers like Antonín Novotný and the cause of so much torment since his fall. Furthermore, they thought it unpardonable to leave the working class in the lurch. The conversion of Czech workers in barely seven months had been altogether remarkable. Suspicious or actively hostile when the January revolution got going, they were a worse plague to the Kremlin by the following September than even the incorrigible intellectuals. "After all, we got them into this," I was reminded by a writer I knew, who did. "I could never forgive myself if I ran out on them now."

He probably wouldn't be forgiven too easily either. Drawn together by adversity, workers and intellectuals had formed a singularly intimate friendship, warmly affectionate and mutually protective. So far, the workers had shown nothing but compassion for men who, with a price on their heads, had chosen exile. The Russians, though, were doing their best to stir up rancor in the factories against rats leaving the sinking ship; and anguished appeals from Czech party leaders showed how desperately they wanted to keep the front unbroken. "We understand the complexity of your situation," they said in a joint proclamation to the émigrés. "But staying abroad multiplies distrust and confusion. Your place is here. The Republic needs your abilities, knowledge, education, creative work. Our greatest strength is reason and honor, our best property tenacity. Let us prove it now."

We could hardly believe it, but they came back. One had only to drop in at the Writers' or Journalists' Union to come across yet another Czech colleague just returned from Paris, London, Vienna, apparently unconcerned by the likelihood that the KGB would catch up with him sooner or later. Within hours, they were back at their desks, writing the same old scurrilous stuff. "What more can the Russians do, besides putting some of us in prison?" one asked with a shrug. "After all, they can't invade *twice*."

I had rarely seen such a brave people, and never any so lonely. Though grateful for a thousand proofs of sympathy from all over the globe, they didn't think for a moment that world sympathy was going to save them. Nor had they ever believed salvation might come from the West. Popular sentiment, they knew, had nothing to do with the great strategic decisions made in Moscow and Washington. No force on earth could change the Yalta-Teheran line unless Moscow and Washington drew another one—worse, more likely than not.

The Czechs took it for granted, then, that the White House wouldn't lift a finger to interfere with the Russians in Prague. Some suspected, what's more, that American strategists might be privately relieved to see the end of an unsettling experiment in humanized Communism. The experiment could be dangerously contagious, if successful, on both sides of the line. It was in any case demonstrably disruptive on the Soviet side, and thus an impediment to smooth intercourse between the two superpowers.

The last point particularly intrigued them. Why was the White House so unaccountably calm when Warsaw Pact troops were in movement on NATO's doorstep, not just in the hundreds of thousands but in millions, not just pressing on Czechoslovakia but on Rumania, Yugoslavia, Albania, the entire southern tier of Soviet Russia's Eastern European empire? Could Czechoslovakia have been no more than an initial pawn's move in a vastly bigger game, with the United States as a silent partner? The highest Czech military officers thought so. The Kremlin's ultimate move, they said, would be an attack on Red China to knock out Mao Tse-tung's nuclear installations while there was still time. Prior to such an immense undertaking, the Russians would understandably want total military security in their unstable European backyard. No doubt they failed to anticipate the mess they would get into with the Czechs. Even so, they could count on compliance from the White House, surely advised in advance.

True or not, the theory fascinated the Czechs, underlining as it did their sense of being eternally trapped by their geographical contours. Three times in this century their tiny but valuable patch of real estate had invited inescapable tragedy: and the last one looked final. "We were always sure Hitler would go to pieces someday," a writer told me, "and even in the black Stalinist fifties we dreamed of making Communism better eventually. The Russians have taught us at last that nothing of the kind is going to come from here or anywhere except Moscow. My grandchildren may live to see it, by the grace of the Kremlin."

I was not in Prague when Dubček returned from his second Moscow visit in mid-October, but the effects were plain enough when I came six weeks later. He did not at once reveal the full text of the treaty he brought back with him, reducing his country to the status of a Soviet protectorate; he didn't dare. Under its terms, Soviet troops would be stationed in Czechoslovakia in unspecified numbers, for an unlimited period, concentrated around Prague and Bratislava, the Slovak capital. Soviet "coordinators" would open offices in both cities. Soviet civilians, naturally including KGB agents, could enter Czech territory at will without checking in at the frontier. Doubtless they would find house numbers and street names clearly marked for their convenience.

Toward the end, nearly everybody knew it was coming. There were only two ways to get rid of the Russians, ran the popular joke: the natural way, wherein the Angel Gabriel would descend from heaven with his flaming sword to drive them out; and the supernatural way, wherein they would just go. Now, said those of my friends who had realized this all along, the Dubček regime must do what improbable optimism had kept it from doing since August 21: say no and be damned to the Kremlin.

To sign the infamous treaty, they declared, would be to give

Soviet Russia legal title not only to Czechoslovakia but to every country in its captive "socialist commonwealth"—a surrender bound to leave its mark on many more than fourteen million Czechs, perhaps for several generations. The treaty must never be signed; the Russians must be obliged to govern Prague with a Soviet Gauleiter, by naked military force, taking full responsibility for their criminal act before the world.

It was too late. The world was already forgetting a criminal act which, according to the French Premier, was merely one of history's traffic accidents; and the Czechs' magnificent unity, built on taut nerves and impossible hopes, was cracking.

Even so, they might have responded to a militant call from their leaders. Sentiment ran so strong against capitulation that workers threatened a general strike, and nearly a third of the deputies in Parliament refused to endorse the treaty. Nevertheless the government signed and Parliament ratified. When the press published a heavily abridged text of the treaty, without comment, the Czechs, for the first time since the January revolution began, didn't bother to buy their morning papers. Defiant Czech editors, who had accepted censorship again only on condition that they could "look directly into their readers' eyes," couldn't do that any more; *Rudé Právo* could have little more to say that the Czechs cared to read.

The same leaders were still in office when I came back to Prague in December and again late in January, a keepsake of their country's grand illusion. They'd been through too much with their people to be reviled as traitors; and if they failed to save the revolution, they at least won a precious reprieve for the helplessly vulnerable intellectuals who were still, incredibly, at liberty. For a number of my friends, though, the question of how much more the Dubček regime could do, for how much longer, was almost a matter of indifference. It could not be very much, for very long, they said, and they'd been after something grander than merely saving their own skins.

They were right, of course. Schweik, all very well for the

Hapsburgs, was not up to the Russians; one presumed they had
read the book too. The arrests begin in April, 1969. Smrkovský
was already gone. Dubček went next. The press was effectively
hobbled soon after. In protest, the progressive-minded censor
appointed after the August invasion resigned; he was replaced
by a former functionary of the Interior Ministry who had personally directed police operations for Novotný's government
in October, 1967, when the student demonstrations were so
brutally suppressed. Marxist self-criticism came back into
fashion, the counterrevolutionaries were unmasked, the sins
of revisionism repented and renounced. The Interior Ministry,
its patriotic underground disbanded, was becoming its old self.
The late Major Pokorný, consummate artist though he was,
could hardly have improved on the Ministry's performance in
those critical months. When the Charles University student
Jan Palach set himself afire in January to protest the Soviet
occupation, the rumor campaign synchronized by the secret
police would have done them credit in the Stalinist fifties:
Palach was a calculating anti-Communist who didn't really
mean to die; his fellow students were supposed to save him with
a fire-extinguishing chemical but ran away instead; behind their
betrayal were agents of Western imperialism. And when a girl
student followed suit, the Interior Ministry produced a suicide
note—indignantly disclaimed by her parents, who threatened
to bring suit for libel—saying she'd been forced to do it by
Western agents parked below her flat in a big Mercedes.

When the final excuse for a crackdown came, the Czech police
were no longer bothering to look for carefully creased blue
jeans, or to ask KGB agents for identity cards. Nobody doubted
the spontaneity of nationwide demonstrations, involving half
a million Czechoslovaks, after their team beat the Russians in
an international ice-hockey match. But they weren't the ones
who wrecked the Soviet Aeroflot office in downtown Prague—
the ultimate provocation for Moscow, the end of Dubček, the
squalid epilogue to the January revolution. The KGB did it.
Czechoslovakia was normalized at last.

Chapter 20

"I'm afraid you've caught me at a bad moment." State Prosecutor Kotlar seemed sincerely sorry. "I wasn't expecting you until Christmas."

Christmas might be too late, I explained. Events were moving quickly in Prague: there was no telling how much longer the Czechoslovak government might take an official interest in the Masaryk investigation. I needn't have worried, said Dr. Kotlar, at once kindling a comfortable understanding between us. Naturally he'd lost a little time because of the August events and their aftermath. He doubted now that he could complete the investigation by next spring, still less by the year's end, as he'd hoped. It ought to be finished by the following autumn, though. If I came back to Prague late in January, say, he might have something more for me.

In any event, Dr. Kotlar had nothing for me at present. He was engaging and friendly as always, and attentive, too. The frank blue eyes didn't wander, the tranquil balding forehead had that small absorbed pucker, the notebook was out on his knee, as I told him about witnesses I'd seen in Prague, Paris, London, Rome, Glasgow. He found it all very interesting. I went into detail about my meeting with Lumír Soukoup in Scotland: his admission that he did not, after all, go to the Lany

cemetery with Masaryk on March 7; his claim to have preserved
the fingerprints on Masaryk's bathroom window with a coat of
varnish and another of white paint; his laxative suppositories,
supposedly explaining the excrement on Masaryk's body, pajamas, window sill; the Minister's eccentric liking for dry bath-
tubs; the dog Soukoup must have known could not be there;
his last-minute assertion about documented proof of the Russians' intention to kill Masaryk within a month or two.

"You don't say?" Dr. Kotlar looked mildly surprised, but did
not press the point.

I'd also tried to look into the case of the alleged NKVD agent
Major Schramm and his possible connection with Masaryk's
death, I went on. Evidently, it wasn't just Benno Weigl who
maintained that there *was* a connection. The young Miloslav
Choc, supposedly Schramm's assassin, had said in court that
Schramm murdered Masaryk. Choc's leader in the anti-Communist underground, Vávra-Stařík, had said the same in prison;
and a Czech émigré who knew Vávra-Stařík well had told me
more about it. Did the State Prosecutor know that Vávra-Stařík
vigorously denied, to his own close political colleagues, that
he'd ever given orders to assassinate Schramm—insisted that
Schramm was wanted alive in Regensburg to confess his responsibility for Masaryk's murder?

Dr. Kotlar brushed this aside with an amused quirk of the
eyebrow. Nothing attributed to the shifty Vávra-Stařík would be
too tall a yarn, he said.

Yet an old-timer in the Czech secret police had more or less
confirmed it, I continued. In fact, this secret police officer assured me that Schramm was not murdered by Choc but by a
Czech operative working for Beria's gorillas in the Soviet
Centrum: Jarin Hosek. Did Dr. Kotlar know about this fellow,
still alive, residing not far from Prague? No. Would he perhaps
like to have a word with the man? The address, having been
offered to me, would surely be available for the State Prosecutor. Dr. Kotlar showed not a flicker of interest.

I'd heard, furthermore, that the Stalinist leader who or-

ganized the plot to assassinate Masaryk in September, 1947, with
a bomb in a perfume box, was also alive: Gottwald's son-in-law
Alexej Čepička. Had Dr. Kotlar interrogated Čepička?

Apparently not.

There was another surviving witness who ought to be useful:
Richard Spurný, Interior Minister Nosek's private secretary,
intimate collaborator, and confidante. According to the household purser Topinka, Spurný was in the room with Teplý, the
police doctor, when Masaryk's household staff were brought in
to see his body. The self-styled Western intelligence agent,
Major Chlumský, also claimed that it was Spurný who received
Dr. Teplý's medical report on the corpse. Spurný now directed
the Institute for Compatriots Living Abroad, obviously an
intelligence device for keeping tabs on Czechoslovak émigrés.
He wasn't talking to the press but could hardly turn down the
State Prosecutor. Had *he* been questioned?

Apparently not.

And by the way, whatever happened to Major Chlumský?

The State Prosecutor glanced heavenward, in the wordless
hope that nothing had happened to Major Chlumský which
might remotely concern him, the State Prosecutor.

I went on to describe my visit to London, the fruitless conversation with Benno Weigl, my call on Madame Smutný. Why,
incidentally, didn't Dr. Kotlar see her while he was in England?

"There wouldn't have been much point," he answered. "I'd
read through Chancellor Smutný's published reports, among
the Beneš Institute papers in London. One had a detailed description of the 1948 period, and there was only a short para-
graph on Masaryk's death. Smutný's work was very objectively
written. If he'd known more about the Masaryk business, he
would have given it more space."

Then Dr. Kotlar had never heard about the sixteen volumes
of unpublished Smutný memoirs in a London bank vault?

For the first time, there was something disingenuous in his
reflective glance. What about the memoirs, he asked.

I couldn't say with certainty, not having yet seen them in

translation. But I imagined that this was where Benno Weigl had somehow mined a good part of his material. At least, the attached codicils of testimony given to the secret police on the morning of March 10 sounded very much like it. Naturally Dr. Kotlar would have seen this testimony long ago, in the material passed on to him from the Interior Ministry archives. I myself, however, looked forward impatiently to reading it.

The pause was brief, his hesitation scarcely noticeable. "You ought to be careful," he said at last. "We've found certain inexactitudes in Smutný's published papers. I wouldn't take everything he says for granted, if I were you."

President Beneš's Chancellor having thus been disposed of as at once objective and inexact, we went on to more technical questions. Before leaving London, I said, I'd consulted the Director of the Forensic Medicine Institute there, Professor Francis Camps. He'd been fascinated by the little I could tell him about the circumstances of Masaryk's death, but had needed more information to form a professional opinion: precise weights and measurements, the exact position of the body, photographs of the bedroom and bathroom and results of laboratory tests, and the contents of the autopsy report, as well as the police doctor's preliminary findings. The State Prosecutor had mentioned his plans for a reconstruction of the body's fall. Had this been done? Unfortunately, not yet. Could I at least have the precise weights, measurements, distances? Not until the reconstruction was done. How about the psychiatric conclusions about Masaryk's behavior, the condition of his flat, the excrement? Unhappily, there'd been no time to complete that either. Could he tell me the exact date of Teplý's death? He'd give me all that when I returned in January. How about the date and circumstances of Constable Staněk's death—the police guard on duty in the residence wing of Czernin Palace on the night of March 9? He'd try to give me that in January, too. And did he have any precise information on Benno Weigl's background, which he'd mentioned on my last visit? He'd have to look that up as well.

We left it about there. I would come back on January 20, and he would give me what he could. Again he strolled amiably at my side through the twisting corridors of Pankrac, relaxed, unofficious, looking as if he belonged anywhere but there. Did he honestly think there was no hurry, that we could talk about the Masaryk case freely, in Prague, by January 20? He honestly did.

I didn't go back on January 20. The student Jan Palach's funeral, more massive than Jan Masaryk's twenty years earlier and still more charged with tension, had taken place just the weekend before. I'd cabled Dr. Kotlar asking if I should come but understood, from press reports of the anguished atmosphere, why he didn't answer. When he hadn't answered by the end of January, I went to Prague anyway, hoping for the best. He would not see me, his secretary made clear: then, in a week or a month, ever.

In effect, neither would anybody else. Some did see me, so distressingly torn between conscience and caution that I couldn't bear to make them more miserable. Others simply didn't come to the telephone, or didn't ring back when I left my name. A few made no bones about it, bluntly saying no. Several, having sworn they'd never leave the country, had left. Western reporters were gone, too, the larger hotels crammed with Russians and East Germans, the dreary Alcron lounge openly taken over now by KGB agents. As far as human communication went, Prague, for me, might have been Sofia or Warsaw.

I took a last look at the star-crossed city—the Tyn Church where kings of ancient Bohemia were crowned, the pink and ocher Renaissance façades of Old Town Square, Mala Strana's vaulted colonnades, the Castle's spires soaring over Charles Bridge and the river—and left.

It was almost a month later, reading the morning papers at home, that I noticed a short news item on the inside pages of the Rome *Daily American*. The dateline was Prague. Unknown assailants had fired at a car on its way to the Czechoslovak capital, driven by a man who said he had information showing that Jan Masaryk was murdered. The man's briefcase, reportedly containing the documentary proof, had been stolen from the car. Bullets sprayed from a passing sedan had pierced the car door and windshield, as well as the man's hat, coat, and scarf. His car had overturned and crashed into a tree. He had been taken to the hospital in Louny, fifty kilometers northwest of Prague. He was identified by his initials only: V.K.

Recognition was intuitive. I knew who V.K. was without looking through my notes: the man I'd been so warmly advised to forget, the deranged Vítězslav Kadlcák, alias Major Chlumský.

It happened on February 19, when Czechoslovakia's free press was going down but still fighting. Despite strong harassment from the Interior Ministry, Prague's gallant newspapermen continued to investigate and report on this episode for some weeks: their valedictory service. Here is what they said:

Vítězslav Kadlcák-Chlumský was arrested September 8, barely a fortnight after the Soviet invasion, on the formal request of State Prosecutor Kotlar. He was charged with falsely alleging that Masaryk was murdered, thus libeling and defaming the Republic and its representatives. Among those he was said to have defamed and libeled were the late Communist Premier Klement Gottwald and his still living son-in-law—Jan Masaryk's would-be assassin, Alexej Čepička. It was Čepička who brought suit for libel.

The trial opened on February 11. Several witnesses testified that the defendant had manufactured evidence to prove that Masaryk was murdered. The two television writers who had prepared the documentaries on Masaryk's death were ordered to produce in court not only the footage actually shown of Kadlcák-Chlumský's testimony but the unused footage as well. They were also threatened with arrest and prosecution for libel and calumny, unless they could produce proof to back up this and other testimony presented in their four documentary films on the Masaryk case. In addition, the state put psychiatrists on the stand who testified that Kadlcák-Chlumský was a "psychopathic criminal."

After the second day of testimony, the trial was adjourned for two weeks: the psychopathic criminal was released *without police guard* so that he could go to his home in Radnice to find additional documentary proof of his claims. The shooting occurred as he was returning to Prague with the documents in his briefcase. The Interior Ministry at once announced that he had done the shooting himself. It was certainly the most convenient explanation, if not necessarily the most plausible.

Whether or not Kadlcák-Chlumský was psychopathic, he did appear to be an inveterate liar. That, at least, was the impression gained from State Prosecutor Kotlar's account of his dealings with this slippery gentleman. From the time those banner headlines appeared on April 11, 1968—"WHERE'S CHLUMSKÝ?"—he had rarely told the same story twice. The public didn't know the half of it. Newspapers had carried his report of the leather-coated man in a black Tatra who warned Masaryk to leave Prague at once; his version of the police doctor Teplý's secret testament; his assertions that the NKVD, through Major Schramm, was responsible for Masaryk's death. But even at the apogee of their liberty, Czech editors had judiciously expunged a few lurid paragraphs in the anonymous letter about Chlumský, which turned out to have been sent by Chlumský himself. Those were the paragraphs, included in his letter to the State Prosecutor, that landed Kadlcák-Chlumský in Pankrac.

He had claimed to have the minutes of a secret meeting held in the home of Premier Klement Gottwald directly after Masaryk died, attended among others by Alexej Čepička, Stalin's emissary Valerian Zorin, and Gottwald himself. Reportedly, Gottwald opened the meeting by saying: "At last we've gotten rid of this cripple, and it's suicide. We needn't worry about popular unrest: people believe in this suicide version because of the Western telegrams. Now we'll have to see to it that Clementis [Deputy Foreign Minister] keeps his mouth shut. He's saying queer things, he's crying like a baby. He must be prevented from babbling at the funeral. . . ."

Summoned to the State Prosecutor's office to explain where
he got these secret minutes, Kadlcák-Chlumský offered a number of explanations. His first was that he was approached in
May, 1948, by an attaché of the American Embassy named Jack
Novak and a Czech agent of Western intelligence named Benno
Weigl (!) to bring certain papers from a Mr. S. of Z. to Prague;
he would be paid five thousand crowns. On the way to the capital with these documents, he looked at them, finding the minutes of Gottwald's secret meetings, photographic material on
Masaryk's death, decoding clues to secret signatures, and so
forth. He made notes of this, passed the material on to Novak,
and received his five thousand crowns.

The notes he submitted to Dr. Kotlar having been typed,
Kadlcák-Chlumský was asked to bring the original notes in his
handwriting. He agreed, but instead of bringing them in person,
he sent them in an envelope which, on arriving at Dr. Kotlar's
office, was empty. He insisted that he'd mailed the notes in the
envelope, adding that he himself was getting letters threatening
that he would be liquidated if he persisted in providing information on Masaryk's death. He hinted that Alexej Čepička was
involved in this. He was most frightened, he said, by a letter
using a code he himself had used as a resistance fighter during
the German occupation:

"Mr. V.K.-Chlumský! We warn you by using your own last
code: 079566430. Mountains are always black. 7874616540711.
The ice does not break up. 48919612. The child weeps at the
window. Is it still ill?"

All of this, according to State Prosecutor Kotlar, was patiently
processed by his staff at Pankrac: the empty envelope, the
anonymous letters, the code. Fingerprint tests were made, the
typeface used for the letters was examined, the blood group was
determined on the basis of the envelope's dry glue and postage
stamp. Everything, down to the staples on the empty envelope,
was traced directly to Kadlcák-Chlumský. The code, said the
experts, was nonsense.

Confronted with such damning evidence, Kadlcák-Chlumský

changed his story several times, ending up on the fifth try with his most convincing version: he had picked up all his information in prison. Alas, he was in prison for anything but noble reasons. Indeed, said the State Prosecutor, Mr. Kadlcák-Chlumský had a record a mile long. He had never been in the resistance movement. He had been caught pillaging after the war as administrator of a spinning mill, a flour mill, and a sawmill. He had fraudulently obtained a journeyman's certificate as a miller. He had passed himself off as a resistance hero condemned to death by the Germans four times. He had printed official forms and thank-you letters with false seals and stamps. He had claimed that his wife and four children were tortured to death by the Gestapo, whereas his wife had merely divorced him: the smartest thing she ever did. He now lived with a concubine and worked as a job dispenser on a collective farm. He was fifty-four, and had been in jail seven times before the war and four times after, never for political reasons. In short, Vítězslav Kadlcák-Chlumský was a crackpot.

If he was dangerous, though, why let him loose without a police guard? If he wasn't dangerous, why shoot him?

The Interior Ministry insisted that nobody tried to shoot him. In their first version, the security police maintained that he shot himself, from inside his moving car, lowering the back of the driver's seat and flattening himself out to avoid his own bullets, managing somehow to perforate the outside of his car door as well as his hat, coat and scarf, disposing of the weapon so cleverly that it was never found, thereupon going into a guided skid so well calculated that the car would hurtle against a tree and come to a stop upside down, emerging from all this without a scratch.

This version generating a certain skepticism, the Interior Ministry tried again. Kadlcák-Chlumský had paid somebody to shoot at him—and miss, naturally—in a final and desperate effort to clear himself. It was either this or curtains for Chlumský.

None of the Czech reporters on the scene turned up anything to bear out either theory. The first to arrive discovered the name of an eyewitness, living in the nearby village of Postoloprty, and tried to phone the man. The operator told him that Postoloprty had no telephone connections; a random call to some other inhabitant there proved that it did. Later, reporters got to the eyewitness. He told them he had been driving by around six in the morning and noticed the disabled car, an old red Volha. The road was flat, crossing a long plain, and deserted, the nearest habitation being a state farm about half a mile away. He himself was stopped by two men whose truck was pulled up already, and they asked him to call an ambulance. The two were pulling an unconscious man out of the car. The car itself lay with its wheels in the air, its roof caved in. There were heavy marks of skidding on the highway.

The two witnesses previously on the scene worked for an auto repair shop in Louny. They saw the bullet holes in the car door —three, they said; and they agreed that the driver was unconscious.

Later, the head surgeon of Louny hospital told reporters: "Kadlcák was brought here at 6:45 A.M. He was in a grave state of shock and unable to move. It was absolutely impossible for him to simulate this condition—above all, the uncontrollable trembling: I would not even have excluded a cerebral disturbance. The first thing he said when he regained consciousness was that he'd heard glass breaking, and applied his brakes hard, releasing the mechanism on the driver's seat, which fell backward. Then he immediately asked us where his briefcase was; we told him none was found in his car. Personally, I think what saved Kadlcák was that seat falling back: the first bullet passed through his beret and grazed his scalp, while the others only pierced his coat and scarf. The police surgeon from Usti nad Labem was called in, and thought that another injury, on the left ear, was caused by a bullet also. I couldn't conceive of anybody knowingly taking the risk of faking such an accident, or being shot at in this way. . . ."

None of the reporters got to see Kadlcák-Chlumský's car, impounded by the security police. One who got close was thrown out of police headquarters rather brusquely. The police did issue a communiqué, though, with the findings of ballistic experts. Trajectory studies demonstrated, said the experts, that two of the five known shots were fired from within the car, while the other three could not have been fired from a moving vehicle. The experts did not say why this was so. Neither did they mention powder marks or other indications of firing at close range. Nor did they say that a firearm of any sort had been found in the car or anywhere around it.

Eventually, the correspondent for *Svet Prace* got to see Kadlcák-Chlumský in Louny hospital. He was under the protection of the security police, who feared, he said, that another attempt might be made on his life. He was all right from the waist up, but still shaky on his legs. The documents in his stolen briefcase were hardly worth such an uproar. One was a copy of the police doctor Teplý's findings after examining Jan Masaryk's corpse, expressing Teplý's doubts about the cause of death. The other was a letter written by Masaryk on March 9, after he'd tried to see Deputy Foreign Minister Clementis, who was not at home. Kadlcák-Chlumský had kept the documents hidden in the false bottom of a wardrobe. He had no idea who shot at him. He simply saw a car tailing him and finally realized what was coming. "Believe me, I'm no Catholic, but at that moment I prayed."

Could that be all? Would a man under heavy police guard, six months after the invasion of Czechoslovakia by half a million Warsaw Pact troops, tell a reporter everything a reporter might like to know? Was this man, with nothing more than these documents, twenty years old and in themselves surely not decisive, worth killing? What could this crackpot, mentally disturbed if not positively deranged, possibly know that made him a candidate for murder? By whom was he to be silenced? The Czechoslovak secret service? The Soviet Centrum? The Soviet Interior Ministry's swiftest, most secretive, most lethal arm—the Rote Kappella?

Chapter 21

The excerpts from the late Chancellor Jaromír Smutný's papers were in Rome when I got back. They weren't sensational. But here for the first time was evidence recorded while memories were fresh—firsthand observations by the President's Chancellor, depositions given to the police on March 10, 1948—preserved by a responsible Czechoslovak who, far from trying to use the material for personal or political purposes, had kept it in a vault at Barclay's Bank for twenty years.

This is what Chancellor Smutný wrote about Masaryk's death:

"On the 9th of March, Jan Masaryk had to be present for the first audience of the new Polish Ambassador at Sezimovo Usti. He arrived half an hour before the Ambassador, accompanied by General Hasal, and spent some time alone with Dr. Beneš in the President's study. Then we all waited for the Ambassador's arrival. Masaryk drank several glasses of sherry. The President was in good form, mentally and physically. (He had made his political decision and knew why he made it; now he was just watching the new government's behavior carefully, from the wings, so to speak.)

"Ambassador Olszewski arrived in the company of the For-

eign Affairs Protocol officer, Dr. Skalicky. Dr. Clementis of the
Foreign Ministry came too. Olszewski was a young man, attractive, with a good presence, but he was obviously very much a
new man, trusted by his Communist regime. He was not note-
worthy one way or another.

"The visit was short; and after brief speeches on both sides
and a little conversation with the President, the new Ambassador and his entourage left the presidential villa. While I accompanied the Ambassador to his car, Masaryk went with the
President into the study, where Dr. Beneš retired to a sofa. Outside the study, Madame Beneš and my wife were watching the
Ambassador's departure through the village toward Prague. Masaryk joined them and was charming as ever. Madame Beneš
had invited Masaryk earlier that morning to stay for lunch and
he had seemed to accept. But now, when asked again, he said he
should really return to Prague. (General Hasal previously had
asked Masaryk whether they should return to Prague together,
and Masaryk had declined, saying he would stay for lunch and
return later in the day.) Now Masaryk excused himself, saying
he had to see someone (an Ambassador?) in the afternoon at
the Ministry and—much more important—that he had to prepare a speech for tomorrow's Polish-Czechoslovak celebrations.
'No doubt we shall see each other once again!' he added. He
said goodbye to Dr. Beneš and promised my wife that he would
dine with us at our place one evening of the same week.

"Masaryk looked tired that day, but no more so than he
usually did in those days. We talked about him after his departure, but we were not troubled by anything strange in his
behavior, except for his parting words: 'No doubt we shall see
each other once again.' This was the last time any of us saw Jan
Masaryk alive.

"The next morning, my telephone rang at around seven. The
chief of protocol, Dr. Skalicky, was calling from Czernin Palace
to inform me that Jan Masaryk had committed suicide. He
asked me to come immediately, adding that he'd been unable

to reach me on the phone for a long time. This was true, as I had unluckily forgotten to bring the telephone into my bedroom the night before. Therefore, when I arrived at Czernin Palace, some time before eight A.M., Jan Masaryk's body had already been removed from the courtyard.

"In the flat I found Interior Minister Nosek and Dr. Clementis of the Foreign Ministry. There were also several plainclothes policemen and detectives. The Ministers told me briefly what had happened. They asked me to go to Sezimovo Usti to inform the President, so that he would be prepared for the bad news before they, Nosek and Clementis, would come to inform him officially about Masaryk's death.

"From what Nosek told me, and as far as I could ascertain myself in so short a time, I had no doubts at that moment about the way Masaryk died. I believed it to be suicide. I looked into the bedroom where the body lay. There were several people there, presumably policemen. I asked about letters. Did they find any? None, I was told. I did not find it strange at that time, because I thought letters would probably be hidden somewhere else. I was extremely moved. We had parted with Jan less than twenty-four hours before, and nothing in his manner then pointed to the idea that he might be planning to commit suicide. . . .

"Madame Beneš left Sezimovo Usti with my wife at about eleven in the morning, to visit Jan's sister Alice in Prague. I stayed with Dr. Klinger at Sezimovo Usti. We had lunch with the President, and during the meal, we naturally talked only about Jan and the possible reasons that could have led to his suicide. Dr. Beneš accepted the suicide theory as the only explanation for Masaryk's death.

"At that time there was no reason to think otherwise. But even then a few circumstances seemed somewhat strange to me. Masaryk had refused to stay for lunch at the President's country house, because he had to prepare a speech for the following day —on which he meant to commit suicide? And when Madame

Beneš asked him to visit them more often, he said, 'No doubt we shall see each other once again.' Also, when Masaryk left Sezimovo Usti for the last time, I gave him a folder with some of the President's personal papers. Masaryk was supposed to dispose of them in a certain way. *These documents were never found in Masaryk's apartment.* [All italics in documents added. C.S.] At least, the police never reported finding any. Interior Minister Nosek personally assured the President that no papers were found in the flat.

"Two days after Masaryk's death, I visited his apartment again. The bedroom was relatively tidy, but the adjacent bathroom with the fatal window giving onto the courtyard was, oddly, left just as it had been on the morning of his death. On the floor next to the washbasin lay the soiled pillow from his bed, the same pillow mentioned by the butler Příhoda in his deposition to the police. Příhoda was the only one present when I was there. He drew my attention to the two things which could have had special significance: on the doorknob between the bathroom and hall there hung a rope which looked like a thick pajama cord. I was led to a cupboard in the bedroom and shown a pair of pajama trousers without a cord. Then Příhoda showed me a pile of razor blades in red wrappings thrown on the glass shelf above the washbasin. He told me that normally all the spare blades were kept in a cupboard in the hall next to the bathroom. Masaryk apparently never selected his blades; each morning the butler laid out a new blade for him.

"Presumably, during the night between March 9 and 10, Masaryk brought the blades from the hall into the bathroom himself, and left them there. Both things, the cord and blades, were to point to the fact that Masaryk was thinking of different ways to end his life. The whole thing was naïvely prepared by someone whose interest it was to persuade me, or anybody entering the bathroom, that Masaryk really did think about ending his life, and really did kill himself.

"Neither the Interior Minister nor the police ever mentioned this to me. Here I must add that Masaryk had a large supply of sleeping pills, and also a revolver in his bedside table. The things in the bathroom were prepared so naïvely that I refused to believe they were done by people really concerned with the circumstances leading to his death. Nevertheless, it all showed that, in fact, not everything was as plain as the Interior Minister made it out to be, before Parliament and the people.

"The behavior of the butler Příhoda seemed bizarre from the start, and I could not find a satisfactory answer. I do not doubt that Příhoda showed the articles in Masaryk's flat to other people, not just to me; perhaps others have found out more than I could. These things he showed me in the flat: *were they there on the day of Masaryk's death, and seen by the police? If so, why is there no mention of them in the depositions? If not, who prepared them later, and why?* I think there is only one answer: the Communists knew there were strong doubts about Masaryk's death and needed to reinforce the suicide theory. The first person to be convinced was Dr. Beneš. I had to be absolutely convinced before that; through me, Dr. Beneš was to be informed about Masaryk's preparations for suicide.

"If Příhoda was a tool in the Communists' hands, the question arises of what role he really played in the tragedy itself. I can testify that he showed me the bedroom and the rest with an air of spontaneity and sincerity. There were no signs that he was being forced to do anything, and we were alone. . . ."

Chancellor Smutný goes on to describe his mounting suspicions, the popular assumption that the police doctor Teplý was murdered for knowing too much, and that Major Schramm was murdered because of his responsibility for Masaryk's death. But this was all the Chancellor had seen at first hand—too little for a dazzling solution, too much for State Prosecutor Kotlar to talk around. Apart from private speculation, his evidence contradicted Dr. Kotlar's assertions on two significant points:

1. *The visit to Sezimovo Usti on March 9:* Masaryk did not lunch alone with President and Madame Beneš, or indeed lunch

there at all. Nor did he walk in the garden with the President, where the two probably could not have been overheard. Closeted *twice* with Beneš that morning, both times in the President's study, Masaryk's words might easily have been picked up either by microphones or by whoever it was on the presidential staff collecting information for Stalin's agents.

2. *The correctness of police procedure:* Obviously the secret police tampered with evidence. For one thing, the confidential papers given to Masaryk in a folder by President Beneš the previous noon were already missing by eight in the morning, when Chancellor Smutný reached Czernin Palace. More important were those suggestive razor blades and pajama cords in the bathroom. Chancellor Smutný did not see them on the morning of March 10. Neither did such trained professional observers as Dr. Borkovec and Dr. Gorner of the CID. Nor did any other eyewitness I'd met except the butler Příhoda, who, nearing eighty, might understandably overlook a lapse of two days, so long ago. Nor did any of the witnesses questioned by police on March 10, as I learned from the depositions. There was hardly a doubt, then, that the razor blades and pajama rope were planted in Masaryk's bathroom after his body was found.

That wasn't the only thing wrong with the police investigation—if investigation is the right word for it. Here, for instance, are the sworn statements about the discovery of Masaryk's body, copied out by Chancellor Smutný from the Interior Ministry's archives:

Jan Pomezný, one of the palace stokers: "When I reported for duty this morning in the Ministry boiler room, I went with my brother-in-law Jan Merxbauer to take the flag down on the Ministry roof, as we'd been told to do by the building management. As I went through the corridor with its two glass archways, leading into the first and second courtyards, I did not notice anything, nor did my brother-in-law. It was already quite light outside, one could see well, but we were in a hurry to take the flag down. We picked up the key to the roof from the butler Příhoda's wife; and coming down from the roof again, I saw a man in pajamas lying in the courtyard. . . . We didn't even open the courtyard door, just hurried to the porter's lodge, where we informed the porter Liman and the sergeant major of the SNB. The sergeant at once called the ambulance station. I asked my brother-in-law to fetch a blanket and cover the body. When he returned, we both went back to work. I don't know what happened next. I must add that at this time of morning all the servants are usually still asleep—that is, they stay in their flats—so it's very likely we were the first to discover the body. I cannot say how long the body lay there. I can assert that it was *exactly 7:25* A.M. when I was telling the porter and SNB sergeant the news, because I looked at the clock on the wall."

Jan Merxbauer, palace stoker: "I started work at *five* A.M. with my brother-in-law Jan Pomezný . . . *soon after five* we went through the passage and main corridor of the Ministry toward the roof. We went rather fast, without looking through the glass-paneled archways into the first and second courtyards: I did not notice anything there at all, though the second courtyard was quite bright. We went by lift to the top floor and rang the butler Příhoda's bell. His wife opened the door—she was still in her dressing gown—and gave us the key to the roof. Coming back down, my brother-in-law drew my attention to a figure lying in the second courtyard. . . . I looked through the glass panel and saw a human body *perhaps five meters away from the glass.* I ran to the porter's lodge. Present was the SNB sergeant Josef Klapka and the porter Liman. My brother-in-law told them about the dead person in the courtyard. As the sergeant rang for the ambulance, I ran for some blankets. . . . I do not remember the time precisely but *it could have been six-thirty* A.M. when I saw the body.

"I took the blankets and called the head porter, Emmanuel Jindříček, on duty in the second porter's lodge. We both opened the second courtyard door and approached the dead Minister. I knelt and touched the knees, then I caressed his hand. I learned by this that he was already stiffened. . . . The lower parts of his feet were crushed but I could not see any injuries on the top part of his body. . . ."

Jaroslav Filipovský, police guard in office wing: "I began my duty at 1 P.M. yesterday, three hours on, three off, sharing my duty with Sergeant Major Klapka. During my three hours off I stayed in the SNB guard room in Prague IV (local police station). In the evening, I stood duty from seven to ten, after that the main entrance is closed. The porters leave around eight in the evening, and after that only SNB members stay in the porter's lodge. During my duty I did not notice anything suspicious—absolutely nothing, and no stranger entered or left the building."

Josef Klapka, second police guard in office wing: "I was on duty in the first porter's lodge in three-hour turns, from 4:00 P.M. During my duty I did not notice anything strange, especially no strangers entering the building. On my turn starting at 4:00 A.M., it was *perhaps around* 6:25 A.M., I was told by porter Liman that Mr. Minister jumped out of the window and would I call an ambulance. I phoned Dr. Hora (State Security Chief) and asked him to come to Czernin Palace at once. . . . Before he got there, I went to have a look at Mr. Minister. I took him by his right hand, it was already cold, his face was pale and bloody on the left side. Mr. Minister was in pajamas, and both of his heels were crushed, the pieces of bone scattered nearby. Five minutes after my call the ambulance came, and Dr. Hora, too, and he examined the body on the spot. He asked me when it happened, I said perhaps twenty-five minutes past six, but Dr. Hora told me it must certainly be earlier."

Václav Staněk, police guard in residence wing (whose widow later claimed he'd seen government cars arrive but was told to keep his mouth shut) : "I was on duty in the second porter's lodge; my duty turn started at 1:00 A.M. for three hours. I did not notice anything extraordinary, no stranger passed by. At

1:00 A.M. I made an inspection of the premises. I also went into the courtyard where the body was later found. At the time I did not notice anything strange. Certainly Mr. Minister was NOT lying in the courtyard then, and I remember positively that everything was in darkness and there was no light in Mr. Minister's windows."

Emmanuel Jindřiček, second police guard in residence wing (who, Klapka told me, had slept soundly through it all) : "I was on duty in the second porter's lodge starting at 4:00 A.M. Nobody except the porters walked through. The porter Liman passed by around 5:30. When the two palace stokers, Pomezný and Merxbauer, went to the roof to lower the flag, *around 6:15,* the body was not in the courtyard. The yard was already well lit by then, the glass panels are large, it's quite out of the question that they wouldn't have noticed the body there. From the porter's lodge one can see the courtyard quite well. After the two men went up to the roof, I went outside and walked up and down in front of the gates. I did not hear any thump or thud. I couldn't have heard it, as the gate is some distance away, separated by two doors. I walked up and down about a quarter of an hour, and then the palace stoker Merxbauer came carrying some blankets. He took me to the glass archway and we entered the courtyard together. The body was already cold, not quite stiff because I could effortlessly lift his hand. Merxbauer and I covered him in blankets and I went to report it. At 6:35 the ambulance got there. I want to mention my continuous presence in the corridor until the ambulance arrived, and I saw into the yard. I can therefore state that nobody approached the body prior to the ambulance men. After mature deliberation, I am sure that Minister Masaryk could only have fallen or jumped into the courtyard between the departure of the two stokers for the roof and the time Merxbauer discovered the body—that is, *between 6:15 and 6:30* A.M. I wish to add that I have excellent eyesight and see especially well at long distance."

Václav Liman, porter: "All the keys are in the porter's lodge, and I lock this room myself and keep the key. The night guard has no access to the keys. This morning, *around perhaps 6:25* A.M., I gave the two stokers the key to Mr. Minister's private lift, so they could go up to the roof to lower the flag. I found the lift key where I'd left it. *Some fifteen minutes later,* when the two stokers were coming down, I saw them look into the courtyard and then run toward me. They were shouting that it was Mr. Minister lying there. I at once informed the Minister Plenipotentiary Skalicky, Mr. State Secretary Clementis, and Ambassador Heydrich (Ministry Secretary-General). Mr. State Secretary ordered me to inform Interior Minister Nosek. I did not notice anything suspicious today or yesterday."

From this testimony, which the police apparently took down without batting an eye, we are given to understand the following: the two palace stokers started out for the roof either shortly after 5:00 A.M. or at 6:25 A.M., spent anywhere from one and a half to two and a half hours on the roof to lower a ceremonial flag, found the body on descending sometime between 6:25 and 7:25 A.M., disregarded the second porter's lodge ten yards away, sprinted a hundred and thirty-five yards to the first porter's lodge in the office wing, and there reported the news to Sergeant Klapka and the porter Liman—who, at one and the same moment, was in that first porter's lodge with Klapka and at the other end of the palace in the second porter's lodge, where, by his own testimony, he dispensed the key to Masaryk's lift and *personally saw* the two stokers discover the body. (We aren't told why Liman was wandering around in the first place since, as State Prosecutor Kotlar told me, he wasn't supposed to report for work until nine that morning.)

Next we have the household purser Topinka, singularly untalkative for Topinka, but volunteering one piece of exceptionally interesting information, which, apparently, was ignored:

"I have been Mr. Minister Masaryk's housekeeper-manager

since 1945. My duty was to look after the household, the apartment, shopping, and so forth. Mr. Minister mostly used the bedroom, and he lived alone in the flat. Following his return from Sezimovo Usti yesterday, at around 2:30 P.M., he came to the apartment, had his lunch, and went to bed, having asked Příhoda to wake him two hours later. I spoke to Mr. Minister for the last time last night, before 8:00 P.M., while he was dining; again he was alone. After dinner he said the meal was very good. That was the last time I spoke to him. Butler Příhoda was the last one to be with him. As far as I know, Mr. Minister had a visitor from our London Embassy around 5:00 P.M. I did not notice anything special about Mr. Minister. On the contrary, I would say he was joking. . . . I cannot add anything that would help to explain what has happened. . . ."

But Topinka did add something that might have helped, if police had explored it: he provided a list of those who had keys to Masaryk's private lift: "Mr. Minister had two, one of which was damaged; I myself have two; Storkan, the building manager, has two; there is one in the porter's lodge; the cook Nezerka has one; the cleaner Pečírková has one; the chauffeur Dohnálek has one; the butler Příhoda has two; Mr. and Mrs. Lipa, the Minister's cousins, who lived here for a while some time ago, have one; Dr. Oskar Klinger, Mr. Minister's physician, has one; Mr. Minister's secretary Jiří Špaček has one; the electrician Klan has one; the porter Kozlík has one; the bodyguard Vyšín has two; Dr. Alice Masarykova has one; the handyman Prchal has one; the laundrywoman Krbková has one; and Mr. Minister's sister Olga Revilliod, who lives in Geneva, has two. Now I remember that when Trygve Lie, the Secretary General of the United Nations, stayed here with Mr. Minister, a key was lent to Mr. Lie's secretary. That key was never returned."

Twenty-five keys in all.

Yet not a single witness possessing a key was asked whether he still had it, or had lost it, lent it, given it away. What, for instance, had happened to the key that must have been in the possession of that second bodyguard working with Vyšín, the one who was relieved of his duties less than two weeks before Masaryk died? Was that one of the two keys Vyšín had? Or did the key pass into the hands of those two leather-jacketed thugs taking the former bodyguard's place?

Another item of considerable interest, though evidently not to the police, appeared in the testimony of Bohumil Příhoda, the butler:

"I was employed by the family of the first President Masaryk starting in 1920, and when Jan Masaryk became Foreign Minister I came to him as butler. I noticed that Mr. Minister was somewhat ill in the last few weeks, and quite frequently would stay in bed the whole day.

"When he returned from Sezimovo Usti on March 9, around 2:00 P.M., he lunched and went to bed, asking me to wake him after four. I woke him at the appointed time, but he did not get up. He received Dr. Kavan of our London Embassy while still in bed. Dr. Kavan was brought to see Mr. Minister by the secretary, Dr. Špaček. That was at 5:00 P.M., and Dr. Kavan stayed twenty minutes or a little longer. As far as I know there should have been another visitor, but the person did not arrive. I served dinner just before 8:00 P.M. He ate it with appetite, saying how much he enjoyed it. In the evenings, I usually put two bottles of mineral water and one of beer next to his bed. I put the bottles there and left—perhaps just before 8:30 P.M.—*after having opened the window in the bedroom, as was customary.* As I was leaving, he said, again as usual: 'And Příhoda, tomorrow morning at half-past eight! Thank you and good night!' Then I left and the Minister stayed in the flat alone as usual. As far as I know, nobody came to see him.

"What happened there this morning is not known to me. Sometime after 7:00 A.M. I was called downstairs, and there in the lift I met Mr. State Secretary Clementis, who told me the news. I cannot throw any light on the case. Especially I cannot say that Mr. Minister was in any special state of excitement yesterday. He was not. I assume from the fact that both the bottles of water and the one of beer were empty, that Mr. Minister stayed up late.

"How the pillows from the bedroom came to be in the bathroom I cannot explain, because *nothing like this ever happened*. Also *the objects in the bathroom were never so upside down as I saw them this morning.* I entered the bedroom perhaps ten minutes past seven with Mr. State Secretary Clementis. We were the first in the flat. *The window in the bedroom was still open as I left it last night,* but the window in the bathroom, which was closed last night, was now wide open. I cannot add anything more."

So Masaryk's bedroom window was open all night long: easily accessible, radiator built into the wall and thus affording no obstruction, no screen or window seat in front of it, no bother about forcing it open despite a tendency to stick, no trouble even about standing erect on the sill, since *its aperture was twice the height of the window in the bathroom.*

Apart from revealing several errors in his statements to me—particularly Masaryk's lunch and walk in the garden at Sezimovo Usti—there was nothing new in the short statement of the bodyguard, Vilém Vyšín:

"I was appointed as personal security officer to Mr. Minister in June, 1945. My duty was to accompany the Minister everywhere from the moment he left his flat until he returned to it and told me he did not require my services any more. My duty was not regular. He was not well in the last weeks and complained especially about an inability to sleep. I accompanied him to Sezimovo Usti on March 9. He seemed tired, but I did not notice any deterioration in comparison to the previous days of the past week. We returned about 2:15 P.M. The Minister just passed through the office, saying he still had to prepare his speech for tonight at the Lucerna, on Czechoslovak-Polish friendship. I accompanied him to his bedroom door, where he dismissed me from duty, around 2:30.

"The suicide of Mr. Minister was a surprise for me."

At the time, indeed, the suicide appeared to have surprised everyone who was questioned—which is more than several would admit to twenty years later. Here is the testimony of Masaryk's last caller, Dr. Pavel Kavan of the London Embassy (who died soon after his release from prison in 1960) :

"I spoke to Minister Masaryk yesterday morning for about five minutes, and started to give him the usual civil servant's report on coming home from abroad. But this was interrupted because the Minister was going to Sezimovo Usti. . . . He postponed my visit to the afternoon, adding that he wished to speak to me.

"I reported again in the afternoon through the offices of Dr. Špaček, who took me to the Minister's apartment. He sat up in bed, dressed in pajamas. I sat in a chair facing him. I gave him the usual report about the situation in London, the echo that our state crisis produced in the British press, Parliament, in general. . . . He was pleased when I told him that the name Zenkl (National Socialist Chairman) was an empty word for the Americans, but when they heard about Masaryk staying in the cabinet, their comments were: 'There must still be some democracy left.' He added to this that it was obvious for him to accept the post of Foreign Minister when it was offered by Gottwald: he did not hesitate, and accepted.

"Then we discussed the situation in our London Embassy. . . . Our discussion turned to Ambassador Slavik in Washington. The Minister remarked that he had the impression Dr. Slavik was the victim of a forged telegram from Prague.

"Mr. Minister then mentioned his intention to prepare a speech for March 10 on Czech-Polish cooperation. *He also said he was going to write a letter for Ambassador Kratochvíl in London, and that I should collect it from Dr. Špaček in the morning.*

"During my stay he phoned State Secretary Clementis and asked if there was any news. He mentioned my visit, and also that he was expecting Dr. Klvana next, and that he must write

a speech for the next day. I left him after an hour. The butler
Příhoda escorted me from the flat. I did not notice any signs of
excitement about the Minister—not in the least. He only complained about the state of his health, especially the pain in his
shoulder. But most of all he was troubled by bronchitis, he said.
He should have stayed in bed when he first got it. During our
talk he smoked. I cannot add anything more."

The letter which Dr. Kavan was supposed to take to London
from Masaryk was never found. But there was no doubt that
Masaryk had indeed spoken of it to Dr. Kavan. This was confirmed by the second secretary, Antonín Šum:

"I have been a private secretary to Minister Masaryk since
September, 1947. Concerning the last few weeks I cannot say
anything further, as I was ill with measles from February 19
until March 4: I was at home in bed for all that time. I cannot
say anything further as regards the reasons for Mr. Minister's
death. He was rather unwell lately, and often had a raised temperature. I saw him for the last time yesterday, around two in
the afternoon, on his arrival from Sezimovo Usti. He was in a
good mood, a little tired, and he asked me about some official
business I'd been dealing with the same morning. Then he went
into his flat. I would only like to stress that in the afternoon,
yesterday, Dr. Kavan told me and Dr. Špaček both that the
Minister would have a letter ready for him this morning, which
he wished to have passed on to Ambassador Kratochvíl."

Apart from the news of his measles—I'd have liked to know
about that, when he was making all those oracular statements
to me—Dr. Šum's testimony was not much use. Jiří Špaček's
was, though. Here is what the senior secretary had to say:

"I have been private secretary to Minister Masaryk since
October, 1945, and was in daily contact with him not only in the
office but often in his flat here. Perhaps two days prior to the
resignation of some cabinet ministers, maybe on February 18,
Mr. Minister caught a chill. His temperature rose, and from
that day on he stayed mainly in his flat. Despite this constant

temperature, he went out to several functions where he thought his presence was imperative. So, for instance, he visited the President of the Republic for discussions on the new cabinet, then he went to the review of SNB troops in Old Town Square on February 28. On March 7 he went to the Sokols' jubilee parade in Old Town Square; on the same day, toward evening, he visited his father's grave in Lany. On March 8, he attended a commemorative evening of the Theater of May Fifth, and on March 9 he was present at the audience for the new Polish Ambassador in Sezimovo Usti.

"He returned from the audience at 2:15 P.M. He just walked through the office and went into his flat. I visited him there several times during the afternoon, the last time around six-thirty or a little later. Mr. Minister was in bed and signed some photographs for me. I talked to him mainly about the speech he was preparing for tonight. I brought some material with me, some papers, and he worked on it and elaborated on it himself. From his behavior I had the impression that he was preparing the speech very seriously.

"As I was taking my leave, I reminded him of his program for the 10th. Mr. Minister acknowledged it and we parted in the usual manner. I did not notice any special excitement in him, but for the last couple of weeks his nerves were not in good shape. I noticed that myself, and he commented upon it. The events of the past weeks had impressed him very much, especially the changes in the office. He also complained of sleeping badly—not sleeping at all in the last week. His doctor was Dr. Klinger, who used to come to see him daily in the last weeks; *and it was decided that today, the 10th, after the introduction of the cabinet to Parliament, he would leave Prague for a fourteen-day rest cure.*

"I cannot add anything more to explain the case. The suicide came as an absolute surprise to me."

Why had Masaryk's senior secretary not mentioned to anybody else for twenty years that Masaryk was in fact planning to leave Prague on the very day his body was found? And why hadn't State Prosecutor Kotlar, who must have seen this testimony, mentioned it either? There could not have been any question about Dr. Špaček's statement, because it was confirmed explicitly to the police by Dr. Klinger himself:

"I treated Jan Masaryk for the last ten years. In the last four weeks he had a lingering inflammation of the mucous membrane of the top bronchial tubes, and his aorta was enlarged too—which, luckily, never showed itself in any critical way. Otherwise he was healthy. In the last fortnight he had somewhat lost his usual appetite—he was well known as an epicure.

"He was bothered by heartburn, and used to take oreamalin for stomach upsets. When his blood pressure went over 150 he would take small doses of Luminal. For sleeplessness he had Seconal, one pill per night. He told me that after the pill he would fall asleep at once, but that he sometimes woke up around five or six in the morning and could not sleep any more.

"When in Prague, I visited Mr. Minister daily, between 8:00 and 10:00 A.M. in his flat, or in his office. I saw him for the last time on Tuesday, around 9:30 A.M., as he was leaving his apartment with General Hasal. He returned with me to his bedroom, where he let me take his blood pressure: it was 160. He thanked me for looking after him so well. He seemed calm, and he left for Sezimovo Usti.

"Minister Masaryk often used to have changeable moods. Sometimes he was very gay, sometimes rather depressed. I noticed this mainly in the last two or three months. *That is why I suggested he should go to Gräfenberg, where he would undergo a water cure,* and he only stipulated that it should be after March 10, as he had to go before Parliament."

Was this to have been the cover for Masaryk's departure with Dr. Klinger—on the very day named by Dr. Klinger in his subsequent story of the planned escape? Might the secret police have heard of this planned departure and assumed it meant escape? How was it possible that not a word of this was breathed by anyone, even during the spring of 1968?

There remained only two depositions of the sixteen copied down by Chancellor Smutný. One was police doctor Jaromír Teplý's:

"Today, at 8:00 A.M., I was ordered to examine the body of Minister Jan Masaryk, which was found at 6:30 A.M. in the courtyard of Czernin Palace, under the window of the bathroom which formed part of the Minister's second-floor flat.

"Findings: the body lies on its back in the yard. The rigidity of the masticatory organs is obvious. The limbs are still supple but cold, the back of the body is still warm, lukewarm, that is; light violet postmortal patches are visible on the back and on the head. Both legs are broken—in the area under the ankles there are open parts, and bits of bone and tissue were found on the paving stones near the body. On the belly there is a narrow vertical scratch, dirty with dust from the wall; the hands are also marked by the wall. The rectum is soiled with excrement. Otherwise there are no marks on the body that would point to violence. Marks of excrement were also found on the bathroom window.

"My opinion: The findings show death by suicide (a jump from the window). The fall was directly on the feet, which explains the broken heels. Death occurred at once, by internal injuries. As far as I can judge from my findings, death occurred perhaps two to three hours previously."

But there was evidently a question in Dr. Teplý's mind—at least about the time of death. To a friend, who reported it directly to Chancellor Smutný—"an absolutely trustworthy and very experienced person," the Chancellor noted in his memoirs —Dr. Teplý had said "that at first he had no doubts about suicide. As he had no time to look at the body carefully, he recommended an autopsy. He told my informant, however, that later some doubts crept into his thinking. He was now putting back the time of death, to *four or five hours before the body was discovered.*"

This was confirmed in the official report submitted to the security police by one of its own ranking officers, Vilibald Hofman, whose summary of the situation on the morning of March 10 is surely the most curious single document in the Masaryk case:

"On March 10, 1948, at 6:45 A.M. I was sent to the Ministry of Foreign Affairs with other executives of our force: V. Hora, B. Beneš, Novák, Baloun, Smrček, and Šulc. When we arrived at Czernin Palace, we saw in the courtyard, under the window of Mr. Minister's bedroom [sic], the body of the tragically deceased Minister of Foreign Affairs, Jan Masaryk. The body was already covered by two blankets.

"After members of the Interior Ministry arrived, the spot where Mr. Minister fell was secured, and other arrangements were also made so that nobody could approach this spot.

"According to information provided by Constable E. Jindříček of the SNB Station 11, and the narratives of Ministry employees J. Pomezný and J. Merxbauer, it is possible to accept the view that the deceased Mr. Minister of Foreign Affairs jumped out of the window with suicidal intentions. He jumped from the second floor of the *bedroom* into the courtyard, *between 6:25 and 6:30* A.M.

"The aforementioned employees passed the courtyard at 6:25 A.M. to take down the flags, and when they were returning at 6:30 A.M., again by the same courtyard, they saw Mr. Minister there. They did not see him lying there before, at 6:25 A.M. [sic].

"Constable Jindříček quickly called the ambulance and when it arrived, Dr. Horák, the medical practitioner, ascertained that Mr. Minister showed no sign of life.

"Shortly after our arrival, Dr. Hora of the Interior Ministry arrived, too, and after him Dr. Borkovec from the crime office; and State Secretary Clementis arrived last.

"On orders from Dr. Hora, we secured the place in such a way that no unauthorized persons had access to it. At 7:35 A.M. the chief of protocol, Ambassador Skalicky, arrived. At 7:38 A.M. the photographers from the crime squad came, and two minutes later Interior Minister Nosek arrived.

"The police doctor called to the palace was Dr. Teplý; and *he stated, at 7:52 A.M., that the death occurred four hours previously.*

"At 8:04 A.M. the body of the tragically deceased Mr. Minister was laid on a stretcher and carried to his bedroom, where the bed was still undone.

"At 8:10 A.M. Mr. Chancellor Smutný arrived at the bedside of the deceased. Then at 8:17 A.M. he and Ambassador Skalicky, State Secretary Clementis, and Interior Minister Nosek left the building of the Foreign Affairs Ministry.

"On orders from Chief Counselor Dr. Hora, guards were posted in the anteroom of the deceased's bedroom: Smrcka, Novák, and Šulc. They had orders not to allow anybody to enter the bedroom. Also on orders from Dr. Hora, I occupied Mr. Minister's study. It was done as follows: at the middle door leading to the passage, stood B. Beneš; on the left side stood Baloun; and at the door leading out of the study I stood myself. Inspector Houra was to prevent all persons, especially reporters, from entering.

"On orders from Dr. Hora nobody was to be allowed to enter the study except members of the cabinet and eventually Ambassadors Jína (of the President's staff), Skalicky, Smutný, and Heydrich.

"At 9:16 A.M. Ambassador Jína of the President's office entered the study and stayed there in quiet recollection for about three minutes, that is, from 9:16 to 9:19 A.M.

"At 9:35 A.M. Dr. Hora issued a stronger order, that nobody, not even the above-mentioned persons, were to be allowed into the study without the supervision and direct presence of Dr. Říha of the Interior Ministry.

"Dr. Riha was issued with a written order from Dr. Hora, and Dr. Hora personally assured me it was to be so. At 9:41 the study was visited in the presence of Dr. Říha by Ambassador Heydrich.

"Later, persons arriving at Czernin Palace were: the chairman of the STB (security police) in Prague; Chief Counselor

Staněk; Chief Counselor Zámiš; Dr. Smolek of the Interior
Ministry; the chairman of the central state security, Dr. Wajs;
and Colonel Janda.

"At eleven A.M. I undertook—on orders from Dr. Hora, and
in the presence of Dr. Říha of the Interior Ministry and Mr.
Minister's private secretary Dr. Špaček, an inspection of the
study of the deceased. The purpose of the inspection was to
find some papers that would somehow explain more clearly the
motive for his death. After a detailed inspection, nothing of
the sort was found. A proper entry of the proceedings was
given to Chief Counselor, Dr. Hora.

"At eleven forty A.M., on orders from Dr. Hora, we were
dismissed from duty. Smrcka, Novák, and Chief Inspector Šulc
were in charge of sealing the death chamber."

Having copied out this *official police report*, Chancellor
Smutný put a large exclamation point at the end of it. Reading it, one did have the impression that Inspector Hofman of
the security police must have been romping through his work
that morning—and, in fact, that none of the security officers
present would have made the grade in a Hollywood B-movie.
Inspector Hofman, for instance, had Masaryk falling from the
bedroom window. He accepted the view that Masaryk's intentions were suicidal solely on the basis of testimony offered by
two workmen from the palace boiler room, who couldn't even
agree about what time they went up to the roof and came down
again. He stated flatly that the time of death was "between 6:25
and 6:30 A.M.," and five paragraphs later said death occurred
"four hours previous [to] 7:52 A.M." He had the Interior
Minister arriving unhurriedly on the scene about an hour and
a quarter after being informed of Masaryk's death, and leaving
hurriedly just a half hour later. He had the wrong constable
calling the ambulance (it was Klapka, not Jindříček). His entire description of the state of Masaryk's apartment was confined to the observation that the bed was unmade. He himself—
demonstrably among the least observant security officers pres-

ent—was assigned to search Masaryk's study for evidence of suicidal motives—this at 11:00 A.M., four and a half hours after the body was supposedly found. Searching for such evidence, he forgot to turn up that Bible lying open to St. Paul's Epistles. He even forgot to discover the hostile Western telegrams which, so Interior Minister Nosek told Parliament that very day, were found neatly piled under a paperweight in Masaryk's study.

It was on the basis of this testimony, and this official police report, that the Masaryk case was closed at noon on March 10, 1948.

Chapter 22

State Prosecutor Kotlar said that Jan Masaryk was neither shot, nor strangled, nor poisoned, which is probably true. The editors of the Czech television documentary concluded that, whether he jumped or was pushed, it was political murder. That is certainly true. Beyond this, nothing can be proved conclusively even now; the revolution didn't last long enough. But quite a lot came to light between January and August, 1968, known before then only to the innermost Communist circle. This much can be taken as reasonably sure:

The immediate sequence of events leading to Jan Masaryk's death began on Saturday, March 6, when he lunched with President Beneš at Sezimovo Usti. Both were accustomed to speak freely before Dr. Oskar Klinger, who was present at the lunch and reported the conversation to Marcia Davenport. From Dr. Klinger's statements to the press later, and Masaryk's to Mrs. Davenport that same evening, we know Masaryk was distraught when he left Sezimovo Usti that day. We're told that he asked to be released from his bond to the President, who, in an arteriosclerotic rage, gave him no coherent answer. We may fairly assume that Masaryk felt himself free from then on, to leave the country or take his life. Either way, he would be running out on President Beneš; but the President, a burned-out shell, was past caring.

Inasmuch as Stalin had boasted of knowing what Beneš and Masaryk said to each other in the utmost secrecy as early as July, 1947, his agents presumably had ways of knowing whatever was said within the four walls of the presidential villa some two weeks after the Communist coup.

On Sunday, March 7, Masaryk was outraged by the Communists' proprietary references to his father, and realized that he must break cleanly and quickly with the Communists somehow: escape, resignation from the cabinet, suicide. There is strong evidence that he opted for escape. Two of his few intimate friends believed his secret message to this effect: Sir Robert Bruce Lockhart, to whom he sent the message, and Marcia Davenport, who brought it to London. He may even have planned to escape with Dr. Klinger, an often maligned witness whose testimony was nonetheless borne out in several other respects. At any rate, he was unquestionably planning to leave Prague on March 10, ostensibly for a two-week rest cure. Whether or not he meant to use this as a cover for escape, the secret police might plausibly have thought so. Again, they were in a position to know practically everything he said or did about it.

All the same, he had spoken to others of suicide, and was under appalling strain. Even intending to leave, he may have lacked the will at the last. Too old and despairing to face exile, too much his father's son to live in a police state, he might have seen suicide as the only way out. To break with the Communists and stay on in Prague would have been one form of suicide. He didn't need documented proof—even if he had it, as his third secretary Soukoup assured me—that "they" were bound to kill him eventually: he had told Mrs. Davenport so over and over again, and put it bluntly to the Papáneks in New York the last time he saw them. He might have preferred his own way of dying to whatever "they" would think up for him.

On Monday, March 8, he went through his papers and burned baskets full, along with wads of dollar bills, if we are to believe the butler Příhoda. This suggests *a* decision, but not *which*. If it was suicide, one would think he'd have taken the occasion to give Příhoda a letter to keep, or deliver somewhere for safekeeping. Then again, if he was planning to escape, he might still have changed his mind.

On Tuesday, March 9, he was alone twice with President Beneš at Sezimovo Usti. This time there was no indication whatever of a stormy talk. On the contrary, Chancellor Smutný and his wife both recalled that Masaryk was charming and amusing when he came out of the President's study; and his secretaries found him in a good mood when he got back to the palace. On the other hand, President Beneš seemed depressed after Masaryk left for Prague. Madame Smutný, who was there, told me so; Dr. Klinger claimed to have heard as much from the President's wife on the telephone that afternoon. This suggests that Beneš and Masaryk reached an agreement, more agreeable to the latter than the former. We know, because all three of Masaryk's secretaries confirmed it, that some time in those very last days the two men agreed in principle to break jointly with the Communists soon. They scarcely appeared to have settled the issue at their turbulent lunch the previous Saturday. They did not see each other on Sunday or Monday. We might logically gather, then, that they settled it in their last encounter on Tuesday. Once more, their decision would almost certainly have been transmitted to the secret police in a matter of hours.

That Tuesday afternoon, Masaryk stayed in bed after his nap, still bothered by bronchitis. Nevertheless he got through his routine work, with the senior secretary and Dr. Kavan of the London Embassy. As far as we know, nothing happened to upset him. If anything, he was probably cheered up by Dr. Kavan's assurance that Western commentators took his presence in the Communist cabinet as a sign that some democracy was still left in Czechoslovakia.

He told Dr. Kavan to pick up a letter in the morning for the Czechoslovak Ambassador in London. He told his butler to wake him at 8:30 A.M. He went over the next day's schedule with his senior secretary, Dr. Špaček, and said he was going to finish writing a speech, which he did. He dined heartily, joking with his household purser. He drank two bottles of mineral water and one of beer after dinner. He took two sleeping pills which, according to his physician, would ordinarily put him to sleep at once until five or six in the morning.

Since traces of the sleeping pills turned up in the autopsy, and three hours were needed to digest them fully, he died less than three hours after taking them. Privately, the police doctor Teplý estimated the time of death as between three and four in the morning. This suggests that Masaryk was not contemplating immediate suicide until at least well past midnight: he would scarcely have taken two sleeping pills if he were.

He must still have been in a drowsy state at three or four in the morning. Before he died, either he or somebody else upset his night table, the bottles and glass on it, the bedclothes, and perhaps other articles of furniture in the bedroom, and created a kind of disorder in the bathroom which the butler, in the family's service for twenty-eight years, had never seen before. There was a soiled pillow in the tub and another under the sink; "everything else was topsy-turvy"; the contents of the medicine chest were tumbled to the floor and crushed, seemingly ground underfoot; the window seat was overturned; there were fingerprints on the dusty wall and window frame; and there was a smear of excrement on the window sill, sawed out and taken away by the secret police in the morning.

The bathroom window was the same size and height as all the others on the second floor of the palace, but its aperture was cut in half by a glass partition creating storage space in the ceiling. It was also inclined to stick, hard to open, and awkward to get at because of a protruding and sizable radiator, a screen in front of that, and a window seat before the screen. The bedroom window, with none of these inconveniences, was found open in the morning, as the butler had left it the previous night.

He was in pajamas and barefoot when his body was discovered, lying on his back with his head toward the wall, about four yards away from the wall and well over a yard to the side of the window. The only external injuries were the shattered bones of his heels, light violet postmortal patches on the back and head, both legs broken at the ankles, a "narrow vertical scratch on the belly, dirty with dust from the wall," and hands also marked by the wall, according to Dr. Teplý.

This description, taken from Dr. Teplý's formal report to the secret police, was curiously phrased: ". . . The rectum is soiled with excrement. *Otherwise* there are no marks on the body that would point to violence." (Italics added. C.S.) There were also substantial discrepancies in Dr. Teplý's estimates of the time of death. In his formal report, he wrote "perhaps two or three hours" previous to his examination; Inspector Vilibald Hofman's report says Teplý put this back to "four hours"; a reliable confidante of Teplý's told Chancellor Smutný it was "four to five hours." The difference would be significant. The palace guards were changed at 4:00 A.M. Dawn and the first light, furthermore, would have come soon after. It's interesting that the Communist government's communiqué put the time at 6:30 A.M., the least likely of Inspector Hofman's many improbable statements.

Apart from the question of time, Dr. Teplý's report to the police seems accurate. No other eyewitness said anything much different. Whether or not the autopsy report was just as accurate will probably never be known. Dr. Hájek, who performed the autopsy, was peculiarly vulnerable to Communist pressure; his assistant, Dr. Tesař, appears to have played an ambiguous role; and his report is still unpublished.

No farewell message was found; the evidence of an opened Bible was too slender to be credited. There was no scene of solemn leavetaking at Tomáš Masaryk's grave in Lany. There were no hostile Western telegrams in Masaryk's flat which might have caused his nerves to snap.

I wasn't yet entirely sure of all this when I talked with Professor Francis Camps, consultant to the British Home Office and Director of the Forensic Medicine Institute in London. Even if I'd read the sixteen depositions to the police before seeing him, I couldn't have provided all the precise information he needed for a professional judgment. I'd heard merely that Masaryk was about six feet tall, weighed roughly two hundred pounds, had fallen more or less thirty feet. Professor Camps couldn't get far on that, without a scientific reconstruction of the fall, and a study of both the autopsy findings and Dr. Teplý's.

Informally, though, Professor Camps was puzzled by what I could tell him about the position and condition of the body when found. In itself, there was nothing unusual about jumping feet first, or backward either. He had seen dozens of such cases. But Masaryk would have had to jump with appreciable force to have propelled himself so far out and to the side. To do this, he would theoretically have had to stand erect. He couldn't, within the window frame, whose opening was barely half his own height. He might have sat on the sill and hunched himself around and out to the ledge running about two feet below all the windows on the courtyard side, and then stood upright. If he did this facing toward the room, and let himself go, he might well have grazed his stomach while falling; but it would be a near certainty that he would land either on his back, head *away* from the wall, or on his *face*, head *toward* the wall. If he jumped from the ledge facing outward, he might more logically have landed as he did—but wouldn't have grazed his stomach while falling. Finally, if he did that backward somersault people spoke of in Prague—and Professor Camps was unfamiliar with suicide jumps of this sort—the chances were ninety-nine in a hundred, because of weight distribution, that he would have fallen on his head.

Freak falls do happen, of course. Without a reconstruction

and the autopsy findings, Professor Camps couldn't exclude that. Nor was he prepared entirely to rule out the proposition that Masaryk's mind went at the last minute, explaining the insane disorder he left behind and, for Masaryk in particular, the singularly uncharacteristic way he chose to die. A complete mental breakdown, coming on in a matter of one or two hours, without warning, when drowsy with barbiturates, was improbable but not impossible. Naturally, one couldn't have it both ways. The theory of sudden insanity wouldn't fit, for instance, with the calm and inspirational courage of Masaryk's last hours —despite an odd impulse to rest in the bathtub—as described by his third secretary, Lumír Soukoup. It would also demolish State Prosecutor Kotlar's explanation for the excrement on Masaryk's body, pajamas, and bathroom window sill: a symptom of rational fear, he'd assured me, in a man whose decision to take his own life was rationally arrived at. But Dr. Kotlar's explanation didn't stand up to inspection anyway.

I spent several hours going over the evidence with Professor Camps. He was curious about the case but detached, precise in evaluating details and seeing both sides of every question, unwilling to express an opinion on anything without reservations. In all our lengthy conversation, he made just one categorical statement: *people who commit suicide do not lose control of their bowels*. Not once, in his long professional experience, had Professor Camps seen it happen.

To be altogether certain of this, I put the question some weeks later to the Director of the Forensic Medicine Institute in Rome, Professor Gerin. His reply was no less categorical. During his forty years in the business, Professor Gerin had never known of such a case. Neither had any of his assistants.

Fear would have little to do with it, Professor Camps went on to explain. Some suicides are indeed afraid of pain, often jumping backward without looking down because of this, as Masaryk was said to have done. Not only do they never lose control of their bowels, however, but the phenomenon is almost unheard of for anybody facing death, even if not of his choosing. Sometimes, a man going into battle might urinate involuntarily. But this occurs much less frequently than a layman might suppose, and rarely if ever is there loss of control of the bowels. Personally, Professor Camps hadn't come across a single instance.

It was here, in a two-by-four cubicle in the London Hospital compound, feet propped up comfortably on a drawerful of unanswered letters, desk chair tilted restfully back, that Britain's foremost criminological expert then tossed me, in a few offhand words, what I believe to be the key to the Masaryk case. Professor Camps did know about a form of violent death—the only one, he believed, and Professor Gerin in Rome agreed—which causes a physiological reaction of this kind: *a man loses control of his bowels in the last stages of suffocation.*

Would that explain the pillows in Masaryk's bathroom?

Would the police doctor Teplý have taken that in at a glance?

There was a marvelous simplicity about it, as far as Dr. Teplý was concerned. His close friends said he'd been nervous and depressed after examining Masaryk's corpse. Inspector Borkovec of the Czech CID believed he had died because he knew something about Masaryk's death which he couldn't stand to live with, or which persuaded somebody that he, too, had to die. People had been hunting all over the Continent for his secret testament, convinced of finding lurid secrets there. Supposing there was nothing secret about what he knew? What if he saw nothing that wasn't seen by a dozen other people on the morning Masaryk's body was found? What if he'd merely seen the most obvious of clues with an expert medical eye? ". . . The rectum is soiled with excrement. *Otherwise* there are no marks on the body that would point to violence." What other marks would Dr. Teplý need?

I don't know how you feel after getting this far in the book. For me, this *physiological fact* was the hardest and most damning piece of evidence in the Masaryk case.

There was no tangible proof that Masaryk committed suicide.

The supposition at the time was that he must have done so because he was thinking of doing so, and because nobody had a motive for murder. But he might have thought of suicide—even decided on it—and still have been murdered. There were clear and compelling motives.

It seems obvious, looking back, that from the moment Czechoslovakia was consigned to the Soviet orbit during the war, Jan Masaryk's liquidation was merely a matter of time. He knew, when he went to Moscow with Beneš in 1945, that Stalin distrusted him utterly because he was incurably Western, and because he bore his father's name. The Kremlin was no more disposed to tolerate Masarykism in those days than it proved to be twenty years later. For Tomáš Masaryk's son, the period of grace lasted only so long as Stalin cared to keep up a mock friendship with Russia's wartime Western allies. No sooner did Stalin cut that short than an attempt was made to murder Jan Masaryk. The plot was carried out by Czech Communists, but directed by the Soviet NKVD.

Perhaps it's true that Czech Communist leaders would have preferred to have him alive rather than dead at the time he actually died, two weeks after they seized power. They needed him in that early stage when they were already the government, but not yet the Establishment. They may even have been fond of him personally. We're told that Gottwald was shaken and Interior Minister Nosek had tears in his eyes on learning of Masaryk's death. Yet their final plans for him were evident at the very first meeting of the all-Communist cabinet, where the Communist Information Minister made coarse jokes at his expense, and the others jeered at him as if he were a creature in a cage.

For all we know, Gottwald might have liked to keep him around for some time. There was always a taint of social democratic sentimentality in his party, repeatedly and sharply rebuked by the Comintern. From the day of the Communist coup in Prague, however, Stalin set out to abolish every trace of this within and outside the Czech party: Plan TB, he called it. Even if Masaryk were on his best behavior, then, the Russians would have been less inclined than Gottwald to dally.

He was no longer on his best behavior when he died. He hadn't been since at least March 6, when he told President Beneš that he wanted out. At the very least, this would mean open repudiation of the new Communist regime by the most popular man in Czechoslovakia, a folk hero larger than life size. If he still had the strength left in him, it would mean that his beguiling voice would be coming over the air from London, the voice detested by the Nazis, second only to Winston Churchill's during the war. Probably he wouldn't have had the strength for such resistance, at his age, against his own countrymen. But the Czech Communists couldn't have been sure of that, and the Russians probably wouldn't have cared much, even if not. Any number of émigrés from Soviet Russia and Eastern Europe have been murdered for less.

Marcia Davenport didn't know if there were hidden microphones in her Loretanska flat, where Masaryk spoke most freely. There was no question about it at Czernin Palace, though, and none, really, at Sezimovo Usti either. Masaryk must have made his position plain to the secret police on at least two occasions: on March 6, when he asked President Beneš for his freedom; on March 9, when both men evidently decided to break with the Communist regime. We don't know if they set a date for the break, or if Masaryk also discussed plans for leaving the country. It would hardly have mattered. What counted was the certainty that the Communists could not make use of him any more. Stalin's rule of thumb was that anybody who was not with him was against him. He was the last man to let a man like Masaryk get away with it.

Not everybody agrees about the precise security arrangements at Sezimovo Usti. Either the Interior Ministry's secret police or the Army's Second Bureau might have been in charge. That, too, would hardly have mattered. Directing the first group was Major Bedřich Pokorný, an operative of the Soviet Centrum.

Directing the second group was General Bedřich Reicin, the security officer Masaryk feared most, also a Centrum operative. General Reicin's liaison with the Centrum was Major Augustin Schramm. Major Pokorný's liaison was Schramm's alleged assassin, Jarin Hosek. Whether through the one or the other, proceedings at President Beneš's villa would have become known to the Centrum in a matter of hours. As we know from my informant in the secret police, the Centrum's radio communications were very good. A message transmitted to Moscow, say, in the early afternoon hours of March 9, 1948, would surely have brought a reply to Prague by evening.

Chapter 23

I believe Jan Masaryk was murdered. It wasn't a perfect crime. They should never have left the Foreign Minister's bedroom and bathroom in that state, or that barefoot body in pajamas lying in the wrong place. But they were likely to have been in a hurry, and the new Communist government could be counted on to take care of loose ends. We know of at least twenty-five Czechs with some information about Masaryk's death who went to prison afterward, of whom ten were executed, one died in prison, one died of physical attrition shortly after release, one committed suicide, one was murdered. Some of these deaths, if not all, were directly connected to Masaryk's. Two others may have been: Dr. Jaromír Teplý's and Major Augustin Schramm's. Still another we can be sure of, the murderer having testified in court that Engineer Konečný was murdered for knowing who murdered Masaryk's alleged murderer. We can also be sure that an attempt was made nearly twenty-one years later to murder yet another witness, who claimed to have proof that Masaryk was murdered: deranged or not, Vítězslav Kadlcák, alias Major Chlumský, was unmistakably ambushed and shot at.

For all the missing pieces, it is no longer impossible to discern the essential design. Relying on responsible testimony, I think Masaryk died like this:

Shortly after noon on March 9, 1948, a message was relayed to the Soviet Centrum in Prague, either from Major Pokorný's secret police or General Reicin's Second Army Department. It reported Masaryk's private conversation with President Beneš at Sezimovo Usti that morning: their joint decision to break with the Communist government soon, and Masaryk's immediate plans. If nothing else, Masaryk told the President that he was leaving for a two-week rest cure the next day. He might very well have said something more immediately alarming to the Communists, perhaps that he did not intend to show up for the Parliamentary session in the morning, or even that he was making preparations for escape to London.

The message was transmitted to Moscow at once with that superlative equipment made originally for the German Navy, and the response came back in a few hours. Masaryk must be prevented from leaving Prague, or doing anything else he might have told Beneš he meant to do.

The Soviet Centrum had all the necessary information to move quickly. Its liaison men would long since have picked up whatever the Czech secret services knew about Masaryk's habits, resources for self-defense, living quarters. The two leather-jacketed thugs assigned to tail him since March 2 might also have picked up a key to his lift, along with any details over-looked previously. Doubtless there was at least one palace guard either in their employ or weak enough to be bullied or bribed into keeping his mouth shut if necessary.

Probably two men were assigned to the job. Two was the number mentioned on the convict's international grapevine—when it got as far as Budapest anyway—and it appeared to fit. One alone couldn't have managed Masaryk, and more than two would have managed better.

In the sense that Masaryk was expecting "them" to kill him momentarily, he was expecting them. He'd sensed a confrontation coming since Ambassador Slavik's resignation on March 2. What an imbecile thing for Slavik to do. He'd begged Slavik and Papánek both, in New York last December, not to make a move until hearing from him when the crisis came. Slavik wouldn't wait, and see what happened. The Communists jumped on this, just the excuse they needed to "prove" a Western conspiracy. They didn't lose a minute to tighten their security measures, take his bodyguards away, put those two almost comic toughs on him. Obviously they were closing in.

He'd been a fool to speak of anything important with Beneš inside the presidential villa. A child could tell you that somebody on the President's staff was leaking like a sieve. But what could he do? The old man wasn't up to walking in the garden. In fact, let's face it, the old man wasn't up to anything any more. Not that walking in the garden would have helped much. The Communists had him under such close watch now that he could hardly go to the bathroom without their knowing it. He was unlikely to keep any secret from them for long.

He could fool them, of course, feed this, that, and the other thing into those mikes in the walls, until they couldn't be sure —how did the old joke go?—if he was actually traveling to Minsk or Pinsk. Suicide, London, Gräfenberg for the water cure, suicide, London . . . And whom did he think he was kidding? They must have a dozen men on his tail, or twice that for all he knew. He might as well be a monkey trying to make a getaway from the zoo.

Amusing that he'd once imagined he could outwit them. All these months, even years, he'd tried to jolly them along, make them believe he was with them, say what they instructed him to say. And he hadn't deceived them for a moment. They were on to him all right: a Westerner, a democrat, a Masaryk: a little Jewish blood and he'd be a really ideal target. Still, it had seemed like a good idea at the time, staying on in Gottwald's cabinet until he could perfect plans for escape. He hadn't had much choice anyway. How the hell else could he have gotten out? But that was all over. The time for Schweikism was past. What was the time supposed to be for, nowadays? He was too tired to think. Maybe while going through the motions of taking the cure at Gräfenberg, he could figure something out, or his friends could for him—assuming "they" would let him leave for Gräfenberg. You never knew. It would be a help if they did. He could use the rest, if only to clear his mind.

At least he'd gotten Marcia off safely: one big worry less. He must make arrangements for his sister Alice, too, see to it that somebody would get her out of the country when and if he wasn't around to take care of her. The women in his life. Whatever would Frances Leatherbee ex-Masaryk have thought of all this? No, you couldn't even picture her in the situation. Poor Marcia. How she'd adored that house on the Loretanska. She was right, too; she understood about Prague. But she didn't appear to realize how dangerous it got to be for her, especially after Slavik quit. Naturally the Russians thought she was an American spy—Masaryk's personal spy. Would she have the brains to stay out of trouble in London? He'd promised to join her in a few days, but that was Saturday. This was Tuesday. Another day, another inch of ground gone. He'd heard they were picking people up like stray sheep at the frontier now, with those concentration-camp floodlights of theirs. Wouldn't it be perfect if the floodlights had been left behind by the Nazis? Just that afternoon, the palace *fournisseur* told somebody on the staff that military roadblocks were going up on the road to Ruzyne airport. Supposing somebody did fly a light plane in for him. Was he ass enough to suppose the bastards would allow him to board it?

Whatever happened, it was a relief to have gotten things settled with Beneš. At least the nightmare farce with Gottwald's cabinet would be over. His British friends would never have *believed* that first cabinet meeting. Kopecký, the Information Minister, certainly made the situation clear: an uncommonly objectionable pig of a man. It had been a mistake, of course, staying on with the Communists even for a short while. Looking back—was it just two weeks ago?—he could see that now. But

Beneš had insisted. Besides, who would have thought that even Gottwald would have been so appallingly crude, so utterly without compunction? Would Tomáš Masaryk have seen that in time? Would he have felt that his son had failed him? When hadn't his son failed him, come to think of it? Was there any conceivable use in asking such questions now?

The palace was quiet. There wasn't a sound upstairs: Příhoda, soaked in booze, was sleeping it off, as usual. Topinka, that domestic pearl, was still awake: his light was burning across the courtyard. Was there another soul awake in this godforsaken pile of stone? Maybe the night clerk, what's-his-name, over there in the office wing: he might as well be in Patagonia, or on the moon. The constables must be snoozing; they seemed to think that was what they were paid for. Fat lot of good they'd do anyway, considering what they *were* paid for.

Supposing General Unspeakable Reicin got wind of what was said at Sezimovo Usti that morning? Supposing? Let's start from the premise. The arrangements for his so-called safety at Czernin Palace were laughable. He and Marcia had counted eleven ways they could get into his flat without using the main entrance or corridors. They could come through a service passage straight into his bedroom; or they could come through another directly into his bathroom without so much as crossing his bedroom; or they could do it in style, just come up in his private lift. Any of those twenty-five keys would do. The glass in the porter's lodge was frosted, opaque. That lump of solid oak on duty, no doubt snoring away, would never even have a clue.

How would they go about it? They would assuredly have orders to be careful. He mustn't be killed in any way that couldn't be made to look like suicide. For instance, he couldn't be shot, or poisoned, or strangled. If possible, he shouldn't show signs of having been mauled either. He would swear that they'd try first to talk him into killing himself. A Westerner would never think of that. But Stalin and Beria were Communist and Byzantine. What a combination! He'd had an earful about those

Moscow purge trials in the thirties. All you had to do, apparently, was torture *and* frighten somebody half to death to make him confess to crimes he'd never dream of committing, recite his confession like Sarah Bernhardt in an open court, accept a death sentence without even appealing. It must be pretty simple when you got down to it: threaten to arrest wife, children, parents, relatives; break down resistance by physical pain or hunger or sheer misery; guarantee death on the gallows unless the prisoner cooperates; slyly promise salvation at a price; come out with it bluntly at last. The Party needs your confession (or execution). You're going to die anyway; sooner or later they'll kill you. Isn't it better to die for the Party, instead of just dying?

Of course, Masaryk was no Communist. There would have to be a small change in the script. The Communists controlled Czechoslovakia now, and Soviet Russia was behind them. No power on earth could unseat them. They'd never let Masaryk leave the country. Eventually, they'd have to kill him. Meanwhile, his break with the Communist regime would disrupt the country, provoke the Communists to otherwise unnecessary acts of repression, maybe even incite some reckless Czechs to open opposition and civil war: there was no limit to the sanguine optimism of the bourgeoisie. Naturally, these bourgeois cretins couldn't win. But they might be too far gone to care. Would Masaryk prefer to avoid this possibly bloody clash by remaining loyal to the Communist regime? Frankly, it didn't appear likely. Well, then, his continuing presence in the country, during the time left to him, could only be a divisive force, pitting Czech pointlessly against Czech, arousing false bourgeois hopes, preventing the Communist regime from getting on with its business, obliging it to commit excesses it would much rather avoid. He was standing in the way of internal peace. His discreet departure from the world would be the last service he could perform for his countrymen. Czechoslovakia would be better off if he were dead.

It was a diabolic argument. He could *hear* them running

through it, was half-tempted to agree. But his father would never have given up without any sort of fight, even when the odds were hopeless. Curiously, neither would he. He was no physical giant, God knows, or moral giant either. He was terrified of pain, uncombative by nature, born for a less challenging life, frozen with fear at the thought of dying. He was a rotten folk hero, if only his people knew it. They thought he was his father; how sadly mistaken they were. But they did think so, and he was damned if he'd let them down without a whimper. If he had to die, he was going first to give the Communists a run for their money.

It was too quiet. You could have heard a pebble drop in the courtyard. The Loreta Church carillon, ringing the hour, might be coming from the next room: midnight. Such incredibly beautiful bells: he'd always loved them.

The speech for that blasted Polish-Czechoslovak Friendship Society was finished. Short and sweet. Bad cess to them. The beer was finished. The *Good Soldier Schweik* was finished. Czechoslovakia was finished. Jan Masaryk was finished. Was he? Oh yes, he was. Why think about it? They knew his address. If they wanted him they'd get him. He might as well get some sleep.

He took the two sleeping pills his butler had left on the night table, and turned out the light.

I don't know precisely what happened after that. The best I can do, with so many gaps in the evidence, is to reconstruct the scene to fit the largest number of facts.

I think they came over the rear garden wall, long after midnight but well before dawn. Except for a lonely light burning on the mezzanine floor of the office wing, the palace was dark. They slipped in through the unguarded back door, up the servants' staircase, through the little-used servants' passage into his bathroom. Or else they came up in his private lift using, say, the key (or a copy) taken from the second bodyguard who'd been relieved of his assignment after the Communist coup.

Constable Staněk would have been out at the palace gate, getting a breath of air, or asleep in the porter's frosted-glass cubicle. If not, they could still have taken care of him. But the passageway to the bathroom seems more plausible. It was safer from observation; and the partition creating storage space in the ceiling made it more soundproof than any other room in Masaryk's flat. Masaryk would be sleeping only a few feet away, through the bathroom door into the adjoining bedroom.

They were going to talk to him first. They entered the bedroom quietly, and woke him almost gently: it wouldn't do for him to cry out. Or else, he sensed danger even in his drugged sleep, woke with a cry that nobody heard, was silenced with a firm hand over his mouth while his nocturnal visitors tried to make him see reason. They sat on his bed like the civilized people they were and he was, talking and smoking—his bedside ashtray was soon overflowing with cigarette stubs of different brands—explaining why he ought to jump out of that open bedroom window. He was frightened stiff, but he wouldn't jump.

It was getting on for 4:00 A.M. The police guard would be changed any minute now, one waking from a doze in the porter's lodge to go off duty, another coming in wide-awake for the four-to-seven shift. There would be some movement below, and before long, the first light. Talking was all very well, but only up to a point.

They moved in on him. Overweight, flabby, ungainly, he resisted with surprising force. They hadn't expected it, and were only two. They were obliged to improvise. I imagine they would have tried first to force him through the open and accessible bedroom window, and failed. The three men struggled from bedroom to bathroom, leaving a trail of violence behind: bed awry, night table tilting over, bottles and glass flung to the floor, closet doors lurching open from the impact of heavy bodies.

He never doubted that they'd get him, and he wouldn't give

in: his last act of tribute to his father, or indestructible love of life. He was still resisting when they forced him to the bathroom window, overturning the window seat, tugging at the stubborn sash. He clutched at the wall, the sash, the frame, getting paint under his fingernails, ripping the front of his pajamas, grazing his abdomen, managing somehow *not to fall out*. It isn't so easy to throw a man six feet tall, weighing two hundred pounds, out of a window four feet from the ground, with an opening only half his height and no wider. Defenestration was a method familiar to them and preferable, too, as a national tradition. But they gave it up, for the moment. Somebody's elbow, or head, struck the medicine chest. The contents tumbled to the floor, to be at once trampled underfoot. They finally got him into the bathtub, where two men alone could more easily pin him down, arms immobilized. They held the pillow over his mouth and nose until he was half-gone, resistance drained away. They hauled him to the window, got his legs up—lighter than his torso —and rested him on the sill to get purchase. Then they pushed him out, with a vigorous shove.

Nobody heard him fall. They left as quietly as they had come, a bit winded. Who would have thought the old boy had so much fight in him?

Bibliography

Bartosek, Karel. *The Prague Uprising*. Prague: Artia Press, 1965.

Betts, Reginald R. (ed.). *Central and Southeast Europe, 1945–1948*. London, Royal Institute of International Affairs, 1950.

Bolton, Glorney. *Czech Tragedy*. London: Watts, 1955.

Borsody, Stephen. *The Triumph of Tyranny*. New York: Macmillan, 1965.

Brown, J. F. *The New Eastern Europe*. New York: Frederick A. Praeger, 1966.

Brown, John (pseud.). *Who's Next? The Lesson of Czechoslovakia*. London: Hutchinson, 1951.

Brzezinski, Zbigniew. *The Soviet Bloc: Unity and Conflict*. Cambridge, Mass.: Harvard University Press, 1960.

Burks, R. V. *The Dynamics of Communism in Eastern Europe*. Princeton, N.J.: Princeton University Press, 1961.

Busek, Vratislav, and Nicolas Spulber. *Czechoslovakia*. London: Stevens, 1956.

Calvocoressi, Peter. *Survey of International Affairs, 1947–1948*. New York: Oxford University Press.

Communist Party of Czechoslovakia. *Action Program*. April, 1968.

Dallin, David. *The New Soviet Empire*. London: Hollis & Carter, 1951.

Davenport, Marcia. *Too Strong for Fantasy*. New York: Scribner's, 1967.

Friedman, Otto. *The Break-up of Czech Democracy*. London: Gollancz, 1950.

Gunther, John. *Behind the Curtain*. New York: Harper & Row, 1949.

Hašek, Jaroslav. *The Good Soldier Schweik*. New York: Doubleday, 1930.

Healey, Denis (ed.). *The Curtain Falls.* New York: Frederick A. Praeger, 1951.

Kennan, George F. *From Prague After Munich.* Princeton, N.J.: Princeton University Press, 1968.

Kertesz, Stephen D. *The Fate of East Central Europe.* Notre Dame, Ind.: University of Notre Dame Press, 1956.

Kolarz, Walter. *Books on Communism.* Princeton, N.J.: Ampersand Press, 1963.

Korbel, Josef. *The Communist Subversion of Czechoslovakia, 1938–1948.* Princeton, N.J.: Princeton University Press, 1959.

Kozak, Jan. *How Parliament Can Play a Revolutionary Part in Transition to Socialism.* London: Independent Information Centre, 1961.

Lettrich, Jozef. *History of Modern Slovakia.* London: Thames & Hudson, 1955.

Lockhart, Sir Robert Bruce. *Jan Masaryk: A Personal Memoir.* New York: Putnam, 1956.

London, Artur. *L'Aveu: Dans L'Engrenage du Proces de Prague.* Paris: Gallimard, 1968.

Macartney, Carlile A., and A. W. Palmer. *Independent Eastern Europe: A History.* New York: St. Martin's Press, 1962.

Macek, Josef. *The Hussite Movement in Bohemia.* London: Lawrence & Wishart. 1965.

Masaryk, Jan. *Speaking to My Country.* London: Lincolns-Prager, 1944.
————. *Speeches in America.* New York: Czechoslovak Information Service, 1942.

Masaryk, Thomas G. *The Spirit of Russia,* rev. ed. New York: Barnes & Noble, 1961.

Mousset, Albert. *The World of the Slavs.* London: Stevens, 1950.

Neumann, William L. *After Victory: Churchill, Roosevelt, Stalin.* New York: Harper & Row, 1967.

Paloczi-Horvath, George. *The Undefeated.* London: Secker & Warburg, 1959.

Perrault, Gilles. *L'Orchestre Rouge.* Paris: Librairie Artheme Fayard, 1967.

Pragopress Features. *The Road to Democratic Socialism.* July 1968.

Reisky de Dubnic, Vladimir. *Communist Propaganda Methods.* New York: Frederick A. Praeger, 1961.

Ripka, Hubert. *Czechoslovakia Enslaved.* London: Gollancz, 1950.

Schmidt, Dana Adams. *Anatomy of a Satellite.* Boston: Little, Brown, 1952.

Selver, Paul. *Masaryk: A Biography.* London: Michael Joseph, 1940.

Seth, Ronald. *The Executioners.* New York: Hawthorn Press, 1967.

Seton-Watson, Hugh. *Eastern Europe Between the Wars,* 3d ed. Hamden, Conn.: Shoe String Press, 1963.

————. *The Eastern European Revolution,* 3d ed. New York: Frederick A. Praeger, 1956.

Shepherd, Gordon. *Russia's Danubian Empire.* London: Heinemann, 1954.

Smutný, Chancellor Jaromír. Unpublished papers.

Starr, Richard F. *The Communist Regimes in Eastern Europe: An Introduction.* Stanford: Stanford University Press, 1967.

Student of Affairs, A. *How Did the Satellites Happen?* London: Batchworth Press, 1952.

Sulzberger, Cyrus. *A Long Row of Candles.* New York: Macmillan, 1969.

Taborsky, Edward. *Communism in Czechoslovakia, 1948–1960.* Princeton, N.J.: Princeton University Press, 1961.

Thomson, S. Harrison. *Czechoslovakia in European History.* Princeton: Princeton University Press, 1943.

Tigrid, Pavel. *Le Printemps de Prague.* Paris: Seuil, 1968.

Western, J. R. *The End of European Primacy, 1871–1945.* New York: Harper & Row, 1965.

Zinner, Paul E. *Communist Strategy and Tactics in Czechoslovakia, 1919–1948.* New York: Frederick A. Praeger, 1963.

Index

The word *photo* refers to a section of photographs following page 110.

Action Program, 16, 26, 27
Albania, 293
Ashton Abbots, Buckinghamshire, 177
Auschwitz, 111
Austria, 22, 101, 110, 159
  Constitution of 1867, 23

Bacílek, Karel, 19
Baloun, police officer, 326, 327
BBC, 4, 93
Belsen, 111
Beneš, B., police officer, 326, 327
Beneš, Eduard, 6, 39, 71, 79, 88, 89, 99, 178
  Churchill describes, 118
  in Communist *Putsch*, 10, 97–98, 189–191
  Communists demand his submission, 97–98, 103–104
  death of, 109–110
  in England, 176, 177, 276
  in German occupation of Czechoslovakia, 111
  Gottwald's list of deputies signed, 104, 164
  illness, 10, 109, 183, 186, 189
  Klinger's account of, 163–164, 167
  leaves Prague for Sezimovo Usti, 190
  Lloyd George describes, 116
  Masaryk asks for release, 330–332
  Masaryk's attitude toward, 9–10, 81, 177

Beneš, Eduard (*Cont.*)
  Masaryk's death reported to, 167, 193, 310, 312
  in Masaryk's diplomatic career, 122–123
  Masaryk's last meeting with, 10–11, 107, 140–141, 157, 166, 191–192, 278–279, 308–309, 311–312, 332
  memorandum on Marshall Plan, 78, 193
  in Moscow, 92–93; Friendship Treaty negotiated, 114–115
  papers given to Masaryk, 311, 313
  policies analyzed, 110–117
  resignation considered, 81, 271
  resignations of cabinet members accepted, 106–110
  Russia, attitude toward, 110, 112, 114–116
  Stalin, attitude toward, 116–117
  Stalin deceives, 7, 114
  Tomáš Masaryk compared with, 116
  Tomáš Masaryk writes to, 122
  violence opposed, 128
  warned of danger in 1947, 162
  photo
Beneš, Mme. Eduard (Hana), 166, 180, 192, 194, 278, 279, 309–311, 332
  last meeting of Beneš and Masaryk described, 140–141
  Masaryk's attitude toward, 10
Beran, Josef, Cardinal, 274

Beria, Lavrenti:
  accused of killing Masaryk, 18, 58, 263
  in Czechoslovakian police operations, 218, 221, 222
Bielkin, General, 229
B.J., taxi driver, evidence on Masaryk, 38–39, 255–256
B.L., friend of Vávra-Stařík, 238–239
Blanik, mountain, legend of, 28
Bohemia, kingdom of, 210–211, 214–215
Bohemicus, pseudonym of Lumír Soukoup, 170–171
Bomb plot, 8–9, 51–54, 95–96, 181
Borkovec, František, 33, 46, 231
Borkovec, Zdeněk, 56, 66, 231, 243, 252, 313, 326, 337
  evidence on Masaryk, 33–35, 37–38
  interview with, 45–50; on Teplý, 256–259
Bouda, Jaroslav, 235
Brandon, O. Henry, Saturday Evening Post article on Klinger, 163, 168–169
Bratislava, 38, 294
Břestanský, Josef, 32
Brezany, 166
Brno, 52, 69
Buchenwald, 108

Camps, Francis, 282, 300, 335–337
Čapek, Karel, 37
Catholic Populists, 27, 91, 95, 102
Čepička, Alexej, 299, 303
  in bomb plot, 8, 53
  as Minister of Justice, 8–9, 54
  in Putsch of 1948, 102
  as spy, 39
Černík, Oldřich, 288
Černoušek, M., 232, 237
Ceteka, news agency, 33
Chamberlain, Neville, 110–111
Charles IV, Emperor, 210
China, Communist, 293
Chlumský, Major, alias of Vítezslav Kadlcák, 72, 146–147, 157, 231, 252, 299
  investigation of, 302–307
  Masaryk warned by, 39–40

Chlumský, Major (Cont.)
  minutes of meeting at Gottwald's home, 303–304
  in prison, 305
  shooting of, 301–302, 305–307, 341
  on Teplý's secret testament, 251, 303
  trial, 302–303
Choc, Miloslav, 231, 298
  associates of, 232, 237
  Eva Duškova's account of, 240–242
  execution of, 240–241
  Schramm killed by, 234–236
  trial, 236–237
  Vávra-Stařík's connection with, 238–239
Churchill, Sir Winston, 5, 94, 123, 176
  on Beneš, 118
  Masaryk on, 180
CIC (U.S. Counter-Intelligence Corps), 161–162, 228, 234, 236, 238, 239
CID (Czechoslovak police department), 48, 56
Clementis, Vladimír, 18, 39, 72, 146, 188, 195, 231, 251, 303, 309
  at Czernin Palace after Masaryk's death, 47, 50, 65, 247, 310, 317, 319, 326, 327
  death of, 54, 227
  Soukoup's emigration arranged, 261 photo
Comenius, John Amos, 215
Communist Party:
  Central Committee, 24, 27
  Cominform, 99–100, 221
  Comintern, 113, 221
  Politbu^ro, 101
Communist Party in Czechoslovakia, 16–21, 28, 88–97, 100, 178
  Action Program, 16, 26, 27
  Beneš doubts danger of, 97–98, 117
  Central Committee, 104
  Communization of police, 96, 99
  criticized in press, 16–17
  criticized by Cominform, 100
  economic policies, 92
  government controlled by, 88–97
  handbook, 88–90
  Masaryk's attitude toward, 180
  Moscow conference on, 90–91, 178
  1968 purge of, 17
  percentage of vote, 91, 100

Communist Party in Czechoslovakia, postwar aim, attachment to Russia, 105, 107
workers and students in, 103
in World War II, collaboration with Germany, 94
youth organization, 103–104
Cookridge, E. H., 250, 256
Crane, Charles, 126
Czechoslovakia:
cabinet members resign, 79, 98–99; Beneš accepts resignations, 106–110
Communist cabinet, 6, 79–81, 98–99; Masaryk in, 79–81, 99, 106–107, 164, 189
Communist Party, see Communist Party in Czechoslovakia
Communist Putsch, 1948, 8–11, 18–19, 29, 79–81, 96–98, 100–104
economic conditions, 21–22
elections planned, 106, 165, 186
escapes from, in 1948, 159–162
Friendship Treaty with Russia, 114–115
German occupation of, 4, 90, 110–112
investigation of Masaryk's death, 2, 31–40, 133
Ministry of Agriculture, 6, 92
Ministry of Defense, 6, 25, 92
Ministry of Education, 6
Ministry of Finance, 92
Ministry of Foreign Affairs, 80
Ministry of Industry, 6, 92
Ministry of Information, 6, 92, 102
Ministry of the Interior, 6, 92, 93, 101, 117, 216, 274, 296, 302, 305; in police operations, 218, 220, 221
Ministry of Social Welfare, 6
National Front, 27, 90, 98, 107, 115
National Historical Archives, 54
police forces, 93, 96, 99, 101; Karel's information on, 217–228; secret operations in 1968, 216–217; see also CID; OZB; SNB; STB; ZOB
political parties, strength of, 91, 94–95, 100
resistance, possibilities of, 118–119
Russia as friend and ally of, 105, 107, 110, 112, 113

Czechoslovakia (Cont.)
Russian occupation, 1945, 2, 5–6, 17–18, 90, 117–118
Russian occupation, 1968, 3, 11, 13–15, 28, 101, 102, 119, 133, 216–217, 284–296, photo
Russian purge (Plan TB), 218–220, 338
Workers' Militia, 25, 79, 93, 101, 218
Czechoslovak National Council, 17–18
Czernin Palace, 13, 60
entrances to, 195
keys to Masaryk's private lift, 318–319
Masaryk's apartment described, 33–34, 47, 56–57, 60, 63, 65, 67–68, 73, 86, 139, 195, 311–312
plan of, 144–145
photos

Dachau, 111
Davenport, Marcia, 73–74, 85, 179, 182, 186, 187, 198, 222, 264, 330, 331, 339, 344
account of Masaryk, 189–192, 195–196, 198
flight to London, 70, 127, 190–191
Masaryk's relationship with, 70–71, 126–127
sends detectives to watch Soukoup, 262
Dohnálek, chauffeur, 61, 71, 128, 263, 318
Doležal, Jindřich, 232, 237
Drtina, Prokop, 87, 108, 117, 276–277
bomb plot exposed by, 95–96
bomb sent to, 8, 51
Pokorny's work exposed by, 95
in prison, 9
report on Communization of police, 96
suicide attempted, 9, 129, 164, 167, 168, 277
Dubček, Alexander, 16, 17, 27, 31, 133, 288, 290–291
arrested, 296
attitude of Czechs toward, 20, 26
treaty with Russia, 294–295
Dušek, husband of Eva Duškova, 240
Duškova, Eva, 232
interview with, 239–242

Eisenhower, Dwight D., 17–18
Engels, Friedrich, 88
England, see Great Britain
Ennals, John, 141

Fiala, friend of Choc, 241
Field, Noel, 229
Fierlinger, Zdeněk, 91, 93, 98–100, 102, 117
    photo
Le Figaro, article signed Bohemicus, 170–171
Filipovský, Jaroslav, 143, 148, 150
    interview with, 150–151
    testimony, 315
Fischer, Jan, 237
Fišerová, Růžena, 234–235
Forensic Medicine Institute, 245
France:
    in Munich Agreement, 112
    Secret Service report on Teplý, 249–250, 257
Frederick, King of Bohemia, 214–215
Friedman, Otto, 178
Friendship Treaty, Russia and Czechoslovakia, 114–115

Geminder, Bedřich, 219, 221–222, 231, 233
George VI, King of Great Britain, 6
Gerin, Professor, 336, 337
Germany:
    Communist collaboration with, 94
    Czechoslovakia occupied by, 4, 90, 110–112
    Russia invaded by, 113
    Russian pact with, 94, 112–113
Germany, West, Czechoslovaks escape to, 159–160
Gestapo, 39, 93–94, 111–112, 117–118, 153, 245
Gluck, Alma, 127
Gorner, Josef, 227, 252, 253, 269, 313
    in bomb-plot investigation, 51–52
    interview with, 54–59
    theory on Masaryk's death, 48–49, 56–57
Gottwald, Klement, 6, 29–30, 42, 71, 75, 90, 91, 113, 146, 160, 186, 187, 188, 189, 190, 279, 338
    Beneš meets, 114

Gottwald, Klement (Cont.)
    Beneš signs his list of deputies, 104, 164, 189–190
    in bomb plot, 8–9
    cabinet of, see Czechoslovakia, Communist cabinet
    Chlumský's report of meeting after Masaryk's death, 303–304
    in Communist Putsch, 29, 96, 98, 100–101, 103–104, 189, 190
    at Czernin Palace after Masaryk's death, 47, 50, 54
    Fierlinger's pact with, 98
    letter to Nosek, 115
    Masaryk warned by, 165
    Masaryk's death reported to Beneš, 193
    Masaryk's first interview with, 7, 179
    Masaryk's last visit to, 251
    in police operations, 218, 223–224
    Russia, attachment to, 107
    Stalin's choice of, 29–30, 100, 183
    photo
Gottwald, Mme. Klement, photo
Great Britain:
    destruction planned by Molotov, 112
    Masaryk in, 4, 68, 123, 126, 175–177, 184–185, 275
    Masaryk hopes for aid from, 113–114
    Masaryk plans escape to, 70–71, 82, 127
    Munich Agreement, 110–112
Greece, 184
Gunther, John, 196

Hájek, František, 36, 334
    autopsy on Masaryk, 83, 136, 153, 155–156, 254–255
    burial certificate not signed by, 245, 254, 271
    evidence on Masaryk, 34
    Kacl's testimony on, 153–155
    Masaryk's suicide doubted, 154–155
Halifax, Lord, 188
Hapsburg dynasty, 3, 60, 110, 209, 215
Hasal, General, 62, 71, 308, 309, 324
Hašek, Jaroslav, The Good Soldier Schweik, 47, 65, 119
    Masaryk influenced by, 200–201
    Schweikism, 199–209, 295–296
Havlíček, Karel, 209
Heidrick, Arnost, 317, 327

Heydrich, Reinhard, 112, 166, 238
Hitler, Adolf, 90, 294
  in Czechoslovakia, 111
  invasion of Russia, 113
  Munich Agreement, 110–111
  Stalin's pact with, 94, 112–113
  see also Germany
Hofmann, Vilibald:
  evidence on Masaryk, 34
  police report by, 325–329, 334
Hora, Jan, 161, 227
  in bomb-plot investigation, 51
  at Czernin Palace after Masaryk's
    death, 48, 51, 54, 149, 315, 326–
    328
Hora (Houra), V., police officer, 326–
    328
Horák, Dr., 326
Horáková, Milada, 239
Hosek, Jarin, 222, 227–228, 298, 340
Houdek, Vlado, 197
Hungary, 26, 218
Hus, Jan, 209–213, 261
  martyrdom, 198, 212–213
  statue of, 13
Hušák, Gustav, 19
Hussites, 213–215

Italy, Communism in, 89

Janáček, Leos, Kát'a Kabanová, 180
Janda, Colonel, 328
Jína, Jan, 106, 327
Jindříček, Emmanuel, 143, 149, 151,
    314, 326
  testimony, 316
Juri-Sosnar, J., in bomb plot, 53

Kacl, Karel, 136, 156, 255
  testimony, 153–155
Kadlcák, Vítezslav, see Chlumský, Ma-
    jor
Kadlec, Josef, 35
KAN clubs, 27, 35
Kaplan, Vlastimil, 232, 236
Karel, Communist security officer, 289
  interview with, 216–228
Katyn forest massacre, 153, 245
Katz, Otto (André Simon), 231, 248,
    250, 256
Kavan, Pavel, 62, 231, 319, 322, 332–
    333
  testimony, 321–322

Kazil, Josef, interview with, 244–245
KGB, 14, 216, 284, 287–290, 294, 296
Klan, electrician, 318
Klapka, Josef, 143, 314, 316, 317
  interview with, 148–150
  testimony, 315
Klima, Masaryk's servant, 195
Klíma, Ivan, 23
Klimek, Adolf, photo
Klinger, Oskar, 34–36, 82, 169–170, 186,
    195, 279, 318, 323, 330–332
  conclusions on Masaryk's death, 167–
    168
  story told in Saturday Evening Post,
    163–170; doubted, 169–171
  testimony, 324
Klvana, Dr., 321
Konečný, P., 224–226, 341
Kopecký, Václav, 80, 344
Kopka, Jan, 52–53
Korbel, Josef, 52, 97
  on Beneš's meeting with cabinet
    ministers, 108
Kotlar, Jiří, 39, 40, 43, 49, 169, 243,
    249, 252, 254, 257, 258, 263, 265,
    270, 278, 282, 330, 336
  Chlumský's dealings with, 303, 304
  falsehoods told by, 148, 150, 153, 156–
    158, 171
  interviews with, 132–147, 297–301
  investigation conducted by, 31–32,
    133–134
  Smutný's evidence contradicts, 312–
    313, 317, 324
  Weigl interviewed by, 275
  photo
Kottnauer, Daniela, 281–283
Kozlík, porter, 318
Krajina, Viktor, 94, 95
  in bomb plot, 53–54
  photo
Kratochvíl, Ambassador, Masaryk's let-
    ter for, 321, 322
Krbková, laundrywoman, 318

Land, Herberta Masaryk, Jan Masaryk's
    niece, 43, 44, 71, 121, 136, 200,
    263, 265, 266
  interview with, 120–131
Land, Jaromír, 76
Lany cemetery, 11, 29

Lany cemetery (Cont.)
Masaryk visits, 41–42, 44, 71, 128–129, 263, 323
Lausman, Social Democratic Minister, 236
Lenin, Nikolai, 6, 58, 116, 178
Leopoldov prison, 19, 230
Liberec, Czechoslovakia, photo
Lidice, destruction of, 111–112
Lidová Demokracie 165, 231, 245, 246, 264
Lidove Noviny, 108
Lie, Trygve, 196, 318
Liehm, Antonín, 25, 208
writings quoted, 23–24
Liman, Václav, 36, 314–316
testimony, 317
Lipa, Mr. and Mrs., 318
Literární Noviny, 23, 24
Lloyd George, David, 116
Lockhart, Sir Robert Bruce, 198, 275, 331
memoir of Masaryk, 172–195
Loebl, Eugen, 19
London, Arthur, 219
London:
Czechoslovak leaders in, 98
see also Great Britain
London Times, 138, 163, 275

Majer, Václav, 189
Mao Tse-tung, 293
Mařenka, washerwoman, 66
Marshall, George Catlett, 184
Marshall Plan, 7–8, 99, 100
Beneš's memorandum on, 78, 193
Masaryk forced to veto, 7–8, 77–78, 182–183
Stalin's veto of, 8, 77–78, 99
Martin of Volyn, 213
Masaryk, Alice, Jan Masaryk's sister, 44, 67, 70, 71, 85, 121, 127–129, 131, 164, 191, 265, 270, 310, 318, 344
Masaryk's relationship with, 61, 125
in prison, 122
photos
Masaryk, Anna, Jan Masaryk's niece, 5, 43, 121, 136, 200, 265, 266
interview with, 120–131
photo

Masaryk, Herbert, Jan Masaryk's brother, 125, 266
Masaryk, Herberta, see Land, Herberta Masaryk
Masaryk, Jan:
apartment of, see Czernin Palace
in Austrian army, 122, 126
Beneš's last meeting with, 10–11, 107, 140–141, 157, 166, 192–193, 278–279, 308–309, 311–312, 332
Beneš's papers given to, 311, 313
bomb sent to, 8–9, 51, 95, 181
character of, 3–4, 68–69, 122–124, 172–174, 181
Chlumský's warning, 39–40
in Communist cabinet under Gottwald, 79–81, 99, 106–107, 190–191
death of, 1–3, 333–338, 341–349
autopsy, 82–83, 134, 153, 155–156, 254–255
body found, 1, 36–38, 46–47, 65, 67–68, 73, 135, 149–150, 248, 334–335; testimony on, 314–317, 325–326
burial certificate, 245, 254, 270–271
Communist version of, 11, 18, 58, 188
Communists responsible for, 271–272, 338–339, 342
conclusions on, 341–349
Czechoslovak investigation of, 2, 31–40, 133–134
interviews on, see Borkovec, Zdeněk; Gorner, Josef; Kotlar, Jiří; Příhoda, Bohumil; Soukoup, Lumír; Špaček, Jiří; Šum, Antonín; Topinka, Václav; Vyšin, Vilém
Klinger's interpretation of, 167–168
Marcia Davenport's opinion of, 195–196, 198
official communiqué on, 11
opinions of his nieces, 127–131
police report on, 325–328
Schramm connected with, see Schramm, Augustin
secret investigations, 227
Smutný's account of, 308–329
Soukoup's account of, 40–44

Masaryk, Jan (*Cont.*)
  death of (*Cont.*)
    Student article on, 31, 33–35, 46;
      evidence summarized, 33–35
    Teplý's secret testament on, 246–
      249, 251–253
    testimony of witnesses at Czernin
      Palace, 283, 300, 313–329
  as diplomat, 122–123
  education of, 69, 124
  in England, 4, 68, 123, 126, 175–177,
    184–185, 275; radio talks, 4, 123,
    176
  escape planned, 70–71, 82, 124, 162–
    166, 170, 190, 191–192, 193, 194–
    196, 197, 331
  events leading to death, summary of,
    330–333
  family of, 122–126
  funeral of, 11
  Gottwald warns, 165
  Gottwald's first interview with, 7,
    179
  grave of, 11
  honored after death, 11–12
  at Lany cemetery, 41–42, 44, 71, 128–
    129, 263, 323
  letter for Kratochvil, 321, 322
  letter of March 9 in Chlumský's
    possession, 307
  letter to Dorothy Thompson, 185–186
  Lockhart's memoir of, 172–195
  Marcia Davenport's account of, 189–
    192, 195–196, 198
  Marcia Davenport's relationship
    with, 70–71, 126–127
  marriage, 126
  Marshall Plan, action on, 7–8, 77–78,
    182–183
  money burned before his death, 63,
    67, 332
  in Moscow, interview with Stalin, 7–
    8, 77–78, 178, 188
  mourning for, 132
  musical talent, 68, 122, 173
  papers burned before his death, 196
  plans for flight to London, 70–71, 82,
    127, 166, 190
  plans to leave Prague for cure, 323–
    324, 331, 344
  plot to kill, 271–272, 298

Masaryk, Jan (*Cont.*)
  resignation considered, 81, 271–272,
    330–332
  Russia, attitude toward, 113–114,
    177–178
  speech at Communist rally, 181–182
  speech at Zofin Island, 165
  at UN General Assembly in New
    York, 61, 78, 164, 184–186
  in United States, 61, 69–70, 114, 124,
    126, 164, 176, 179–180, 183–185
  warned of danger in 1947, 162
  photos
Masaryk, Mme. Jan (Frances Crane
    Leatherbee) , 126
Masaryk, Olga, *see* Revilliod, Olga
    Masaryk
Masaryk, Tomáš Garrigue, 3–4, 28, 69,
    110, 111
  Alice Masaryk's relationship with, 125
  Beneš compared with, 116
  Bible of, 41, 85, 264
  birthday rally for, 71, 81, 165
  character of, 122
  Communist view of, 58, 71, 81, 165–
    166
  Constitution of, 88, 105
  in exile in World War I, 122, 125
  grave of, 11; *see also* Lany cemetery
  honored after death, 11–12
  Jan Masaryk's attitude toward, 9–10,
    174–175
  letters to Beneš, 122
  Russia, understanding of, 116
  on suicide, 130
  on violence, 128
  photos
Masaryk, Mme. Tomáš Garrigue
    (Charlotte) , 122, 124, 125, 175,
    photo
Mathias, Emperor, 214
Merxbauer, Jan, 65, 149, 313, 316, 326
  testimony, 314–315
Mikoyan, Anastas, 19
Mlada Fronta, 102
Molotov, Vyacheslav, 112, 178, 179–180,
    188
Morovec, General František, 197
Moscow, Stalin's conference with Czech
    leaders, 7–8, 77–78, 178–179

Munich Agreement, 110–112, 175–176
MVD (Russian Interior Ministry),
229, 230

Nationalist Democrats, 91
National Socialist Party, 27, 91, 95, 102,
106–108
Nazis, see Germany
Népszabadság, 234
New York Times, 136–137, 163, 243
account of Masaryk's death, 246, 250,
252, 255–259
Nezerka, cook, 66, 318
NKVD (Russian secret police), 53–54,
60, 137, 138, 146, 189, 193, 237,
239, 261
in Masaryk's death, 34–35, 303, 338
organization in Czechoslovakia, 101,
218, 220–221, 223
Nosek, Václav, 98, 189, 193–194, 329,
338
at Czernin Palace after Masaryk's
death, 38, 48, 50–51, 54, 63, 65–
66, 149, 247, 256, 310, 317, 326,
327
Gottwald's letter to, 115
Masaryk's death reported to Beneš,
193
personnel policies, 96
police units organized, 93
in Putsch of 1948, 101–102
statement on Masaryk's death, 86–87
Workers' Militia organized, 93
photo
Novak, police officer, 326–328
Novak, Jack, 304
Novotný, Antonín, 16, 20, 21, 23–25, 30,
292
Novotný, František, 224, 225

Obrana Lidu, 25
Ohledacti List (burial certificate),
245, 254, 270–271
Olomuc, 8, 52–53
Olszewski, Jozef, Ambassador, 308–309,
photo
Opletal, Choc's associate, 241
Opluštil, witness in bomb plot, 53
OZB, 93, 162

Palach, Jan, 198, 296, 301
Palacký, František, 209

Paloczi-Horvath, George, on security
police, 229–230
Pankrac prison, 19, 32, 93, 133, 227,
230, 240, 303
Pan-Slavism, 110, 113, 114, 182
Papánek, Ján, 179–180, 185, 189, 192–
193, 196–198, 218, 331, 343
office at UN headquarters searched,
274
Papírnek, Dr., 275
Patton, General George S., 5, 17, 116,
118
Pavel, Josef, 231, 288
in investigation of Masaryk's death,
32
in prison, 19
Pečírková, cleaner, 318
Perfume-box plot, 8–9, 51–54, 95–96,
183
Petrarch, 210
Pich-Tůma, Captain M., 222–226
Pietor, Minister of Transportation, 189
Pilař, Stanislav, 52
Pilsen, 5, 116
Plan TB, 218–220, 338
Počepický, Jiří, 32
Podivín, ex-convict, 95
Pokorný, Bedřich, 98, 183, 222, 226, 227,
232, 296, 339, 342
career of, 93–95
death of, 32–33, 226
Poland, 7
Polish-Czechoslovak Friendship Day,
72, 84
Pomezný, Jan, 65, 316, 326
testimony, 313–314
Pope John XXIII, 15th-century anti-
pope, 211
Portugal, 22
Práce, 20
Prague:
Alcron Hotel, 14, 68
Café Slavia, 58
Charles University, 35, 124, 153, 210,
212
Czernin Palace, see Czernin Palace
Hradcany Castle, 288; Beneš's offices,
6, 104, 163, 190; Defenestration
of 1618, 214; student demonstra-
tion, 79–80, 117; Tomáš Ma-
saryk's apartment, 111, 125

Prague (Cont.)
  Hus statue, 13
  Mala Strana, 13, 24
  Nazi occupation of, 4
  Old Town Square, 41, 43–45, 81, 103,
    165, 323, photo
  in Putsch of 1948, 102–103
  Russian capture of, 1945, 5
  Russian occupation of, 1968, 13–14,
    16, 285–286, 290, 294, 301
  Strahov dormitory, 24
  student riots, 24, 79–80, 117
  uprising in 1945, 5, 17
  Wenceslas Square, 14, 75, 103, 104,
    109, 290
Pravda, 287
Pravo Lidu, 99
Prchal, handyman, 318
Press:
  Communist control of, 102
  freedom of, 16–17, 25
Příhoda, Bohumil, 60, 67, 68, 71, 72,
    86, 141, 190, 267, 311–313, 318,
    322, 332
  evidence on Masaryk, 34, 36
  interview with, 62–64
  testimony, 319–320
  wife of, 63, 65, 314
Procházka, Jan, 23, photo
Provazník, Václav, 232, 237

Quaroni, Pietro, 179

Rajk, Lazslo, trial, 218, 219, 229
Rand, Michael, pseudonym, see Weigl,
    Benno
Regensburg, U.S. counterintelligence
    operations, 161–162, 234, 236, 238
Reichel, ex-convict, 95
Reicin, Bedřich, 189, 222–223, 225, 231,
    233, 340, 342, 345
Reston, James, 196
Revilliod, Herbert, Jan Masaryk's
    nephew, 125–126, 265
Revilliod, Leonard, Jan Masaryk's
    nephew, 125–126
Revilliod, Olga Masaryk, Jan Masaryk's
    sister, 125, 164, 265, 318
    photo
Říha, Dr., 327–328
Řípa, Zdeněk, 226

Ripka, Hubert, 108–109, 183
  bomb plot described by, 51–52
  escape from Czechoslovakia, 160–161
Ročvara, Štefan, photo
Rome Daily American, 301
Roosevelt, Franklin D., 5, 114, 118, 186
Rote Kappella, 220–221, 307
Rudé Právo, 11, 58, 250, 291, 295
Rumania, 7, 230, 293
Russia:
  Beneš's attitude toward, 110, 112,
    114–116
  Czechoslovak attitude toward, 104,
    105, 107, 110, 112, 113
  Czechoslovakia occupied, 1945, 2,
    5–6, 17–18, 90, 117–118
  Czechoslovakia occupied, 1968, 3, 11,
    13–15, 28, 101, 102, 119, 133, 216–
    217, 284–296, photo
  Czechoslovakia purged (Plan TB),
    218–220, 338
  Friendship Treaty with Czechoslo-
    vakia, 114–115
  German invasion of, 113
  German pact with, 94, 112–113
  Masaryk's attitude toward, 113–114,
    177–178
  Ministry of the Interior (MVD),
    229, 230
  postwar policies, 99–100
  security police, 229–230, 339–340; see
    also KBG; NKVD
  troops on Czechoslovak border in
    1948, 101
  Truman's attitude toward, 118–119
Ruzyne prison, 19, 32, 93, 227, 230, 233

Sabinus, Friar, 209–210
Sadek, Slavoj, 232, 234, 241
  trial, 236–237
Salgovič, Colonel, 288
Samuele, interpreter, 274
Sargent, Sir Orme, 187, 191
Saturday Evening Post, Brandon's
    article on Klinger, 163, 168–169
Scheinpflugová, Olga, 37, 70, 142–143
Schramm, Augustin, 34, 35, 40, 138, 146,
    152, 157, 222–225, 340
  career of, 232–233
  death of, 34, 46, 222, 226–228, 234–
    235, 298; Choc as killer, see Choc,

Schramm, Augustin *(Cont.)*
  death of *(Cont.)*
    Miloslav; Masaryk's death connected with, 234, 236, 241, 298, 312, 341
  suspected of killing Masaryk, 227, 236, 237, 241, 298, 303, 312
  Vávra-Stařík's connection with, 238–239
Schramm, Mme. Augustin, 35, 233
  description of her husband's death, 234
Schweik, Good Soldier, see Hašek, Jaroslav
Scotland, Soukoup in, 76, 81, 261–262
Scotsman, Soukoup's article in, 40–44
Sedm, Václav, 34, 137–138, 152–153, 157
Šejna, Jan, 25
Sezimovo Usti, Beneš's country house, 10, 62, 71, 140, 141, 164, 166, 167, 169, 190, 191, 278, 279, 309, 310, 323, 331, 339, *photo*
Sigismund, Holy Roman Emperor, 212, 214
Simon, André (Otto Katz), 231, 248, 250, 256
Sis, Vladimír, 231, 245–246
Sis, Mme. Vladimír, 246
Skalicky, Dr., 309, 317, 326, 327
Slánský, Richard, 18–19
Slánský, Rudolf, 189, 231, 233
  bomb plot denounced by, 51
  family of, 18–19
  trial and execution, 18–19, 219–220, 227
Slavik, Václav, Ambassador to Washington, 190–191, 321, 342–343
Slovak Democratic Party, 94–95
Smolek, Dr., 328
Smrček (Smrcka), police officer, 326–328
Smrkovský, Josef, 101–102, 189, 285, 288, 296
  on Russian occupation of Czechoslovakia, 1945, 17–18
Smutný, Jaromír, 106, 167, 169, 222, 332, 334
  at Czernin Palace after Masaryk's death, 279–280, 309–312, 327
  manuscript on Masaryk, 276, 280–281, 283, 299–300; text, 308–329
  published reports, 299

Smutný, Mme. Jaromír, 283, 299, 309, 310, 332
  interview with, 276–281
SNB, 93, 102, 323
Social Democratic Party, 91, 96, 98–100, 102
Sokols, 111, 323
Sommer, Josef, 32
Soukoup, Lumír, 55, 61, 71, 76, 81, 85, 128, 129, 146, 195, 254, 336
  article in *Scotsman,* 40–44
  Bohemicus article in *Le Figaro,* 170–171
  emigration to Scotland, 261–262
  interview with, 260–272, 297–298
  Kotlar interviews, 142
  on Teplý, 270–271
  photo
Soukoup, Mme. Lumír, 261–262
Špaček, Jiří, 61, 62, 76–77, 243, 252, 253, 264, 267–270, 318, 319, 321, 328, 332–333
  information withheld by, 169–170
  interview with, 76–87
  testimony, 322–324
Spain, 22
Der Spiegel, Weigl's article on Masaryk, 152–153, 231, 273–275
Spurný, Richard, 66, 251, 299
Stalin, Josef, 5, 6, 15, 17, 50, 79, 89, 94, 178, 331
  Beneš deceived by, 7, 114
  Beneš fears to offend, 116–117
  Czechoslovakian purge (Plan TB), 218–220, 338
  Gottwald chosen by, 29–30, 100
  Marshall Plan vetoed, 8, 77–78, 99
  Masaryk distrusted by, 338
  Masaryk's interview with, 8, 77–78, 178–179, 193
  Moscow conference with Czech leaders, 7, 77–78, 178–179
  pact with Hitler, 94, 112–113
  postwar policies, 99–100
  in *Putsch* in Czechoslovakia, 18–19
Staněk, Chief Counselor, 327–328
Staněk, Václav, 143, 149, 151, 152, 300, 348
  testimony, 315–316
  widow of, testimony, 150–151
STB (Czech security police), 34, 38, 40, 60, 61, 70, 93, 163, 235

Steinhardt, Laurence, 162, 278
Stolte, Istvan, 229
Storkan, building manager, 318
Straka, Pavel, 72, 150, 231
  evidence on Masaryk, 36–38, 142–146
  imprisoned, 37, 142
  photo
Stránský, Jaroslav, 108–109
Student, article on Masaryk's death, 31, 33–35, 46, 137, 231
Šulc, police officer, 326–328
Sulzberger, C. L., 246, 249–250, 252, 253, 256
Šum, Antonín, 61, 76, 231, 252, 253, 267, 269, 273
  information withheld by, 169–170
  interview with, 76–87
  testimony, 322
  photo
Šváb, Karel, 231
Svet Prace, 307
Sviták, Ivan, article in *Student*, 35, 231; *see also Student*
Svoboda, Ludvík, 92, 97–98, 162, 234, 236, 288

Talich, orchestra conductor, 180
Tass, 58
Teheran conference, 5, 116, 118
Tellini, Father, 241
Teplý, Jaromír, 40, 46–47, 56, 66, 135–137, 146, 149, 155, 157, 243–259, 299, 333, 337
  Borkovec's account of, 256–259
  death of, 36, 49, 137, 243–244, 300, 312, 341
  evidence on Masaryk, 33–34, 38, 136, 325
  Kazil's account of, 244–245
  report on examination of Masaryk's body, 303, 325, 327, 334
  secret testament on Masaryk, 246–249, 251–253, 257–258, 303
  Soukoup's information on, 270–271
  photo
Teplý, Mme. Jaromír, 36, 137, 243, 244, 257–258
  account of her husband's death, 244, 246
  suicide, 246, 258
  photo
Terezin, 111

Tesař, František, 83, 134, 245, 252, 254–255, 271, 334
  interview with, 155–156
Teschen, 116
Thompson, Dorothy, Masaryk's letter to, 185–186
Togliatti, Palmiro, 89
Tomíček, Professor, 134
Topinka, Václav, 60, 71, 72, 86, 141, 252, 253, 255, 267, 299
  interview with, 64–68
  testimony, 317–318
  wife of, 60, 66
Trade Union Congress, 101, 103, 107
Truman, Harry S., 118–119, 184
Truman Doctrine, 119, 184
Turkey, 184

United Nations:
  General Assembly, Masaryk in, 61, 78, 164, 184–186
  Masaryk's faith in, 179
  Security Council, debate on Masaryk's death demanded, 274
United States:
  Counter-Intelligence Corps (CIC), 161–162, 228, 234, 236, 238, 239
  Marshall Plan offered, 7
  Masaryk in, 61, 69–70, 114, 124, 126, 164, 176, 179–180, 183–185
  Masaryk's attitude toward, 114, 184
  Prague occupied by troops in 1945, 17–18
  productivity, 21
  reaction to Masaryk's death, 188
  and Russian occupation of Czechoslovakia, 1968, 293
URO, 103

Vaculík, Ludvík:
  Manifesto of Two Thousand Words, 22, 27–28
  writings quoted, 22–23, 27–28
Vávra-Stařík, 232, 237–239, 241–242, 298
Veselý, Jindřich, 93, 96
  on Beneš, 6
  at Czernin Palace after Masaryk's death, 48, 50–51
  death of, 6, 54, 227
Vilím, Blazy, *photo*

Vyšín, Vilém, 61, 67, 83, 86, 141, 252, 264, 267, 318, 319
interview with, 69–74
testimony, 320–321

Wajs, Dr., 328
Waldensians, 210, 212
Weigl, Benno (Michael Rand, pseudonym), 280, 291, 299, 300, 304
article in Der Spiegel, 35, 137–139, 152–153, 231, 273–275
interview with, 273–275
Wenceslas IV, 211
Workers' Congress, see Trade Union Congress
Workers' Militia, 25, 79, 93, 101, 218
Writers' Congress, 23–24

Writers' Union, 23–24
Wyclif, John, 210, 211

Yalta conference, 5, 89, 110, 116, 118–119
Yugoslavia, 7, 293

Zámiš, Chief Counselor, 328
Zápotocký, Antonín, photo
Zenkl, Peter, 95, 108, 321
bomb sent to, 8, 51, 95
Žižka, Jan, 214
ZOB, 93
Zorin, Valerian, 51, 89, 303
interview with Masaryk, 78–79
in Putsch in Czechoslovakia, 18, 101, 189
photo